WHERE WE LIVE

WHERE WE LIVE
A GUIDE TO ST. LOUIS COMMUNITIES

EDITED BY TIM FOX
INTRODUCTION BY ERIC SANDWEISS

MISSOURI HISTORICAL SOCIETY PRESS
ST. LOUIS

©1995 by the Missouri Historical Society Press
Published in the United States of America by the
Missouri Historical Society Press, P.O. Box 11940,
St. Louis, Missouri 63112-0040
5 4 3 2   99 98 97 96

Library of Congress Cataloging-in-Publication Data

Where we live : a guide to St. Louis communities /
    edited by Tim Fox ; introduction by Eric Sandweiss.
        p.   cm.
    Includes bibliographical references and index.
    ISBN 1-883982-12-X (alk. paper)
    1. Saint Louis (Mo.)—Guidebooks.
    2. Neighborhood—Missouri—Saint Louis—
    Guidebooks. 3. Saint Louis (Mo.)—History.   I. Fox,
    Tim, 1966–   .   II. Missouri Historical Society.
    F474.S23W48   1995
    917.78′660443—dc20   95-45700
                                                      CIP

∞ This paper meets the requirements of the American
National Standard for Permanence of Paper for Printed
Library Materials, Z39.48, 1984.

Designed by: Tracy Ritter
Design Assistants: Robyn Morgan and Paula Kapfer
Map Production: Lanny Chambers Creative Services
Printed by: Fiedler Printing Company

CONTENTS

PREFACE

An essential part of the Missouri Historical Society's mission is helping communities engage in discussions of identity. Underlying this goal is the assumption that "identity" is not something we are born with, but rather something that is created through the stories we share about our families, communities, states, and nations. "History"—the process of recording and interpreting the stories we share—is thus wrapped up in identity, in who we are, where we have been, and where we are going.

In June 1991 we at the Missouri Historical Society launched a new program to encourage St. Louis communities to study one fundamental aspect of identity: Where We Live. Selecting twelve neighborhoods to serve as the initial centerpieces of our discussions, we created a variety of accessible studies that were featured through various media—brochures, newspaper pictorial essays, and radio and TV spots. But the brochures were the heart of the program. Each one outlined the history of a certain area and included a map to help readers locate landmarks and historic sites. The response to these brochures, and to the other aspects of the Where We Live program, was overwhelming.

To expand the program, in 1993 we collaborated with The New Theater on a play called *St. Louis Stories: Scenes From Where We Live.* We also worked with city and county schools on programs like Time Trackers, which helped engage students in their neighborhoods' histories and the ways in which those histories are made. As the scope of Where We Live grew, so did the public's interest; by the end of 1994, thirty-one brochures had been produced by seven different writers, covering many of the St. Louis metropolitan area's communities. Those thirty-one brochures were the genesis of this book.

Where We Live: A Guide to St. Louis Communities thus represents the capstone of one phase of the Where We Live program. But it is not only that. By organizing the book the way we have, and by including short interpretive essays that discuss some of the larger themes that emerge from the individual sections, the book sets the stage for the next phase of Where We Live.

In 1995 the focus of the brochures changed to emphasize persistent issues in the larger St. Louis area rather than individual communities within that area. Our current Where We Live studies of St. Louis are defined by issues that transcend geographical boundaries, issues such as education, conservation, immigration, and housing. Working with other organizations, the Missouri Historical Society will utilize these studies so that we may continue to emphasize the many political, economic, and social forces that have been fundamental in shaping St. Louis and that must be dealt with in the course of change.

The lesson of all of this work is that history is forever present. All around are representations of other ways of life, symbols of progress, expressions of sacredness, signs of blight and struggle. Every community must share certain beliefs, accept certain narratives, to remain a community. Without agreement about what is important in each community's narrative, sense of place disintegrates. To encourage such agreement, this book provides accounts of the places that make St. Louis. Whether you're from here or other parts of the country and world, we hope that *Where We Live: A Guide to St. Louis Communities* will deepen both your experience of St. Louis and your perception of the ways in which history manifests itself in our daily lives.

ROBERT R. ARCHIBALD
PRESIDENT
MISSOURI HISTORICAL SOCIETY

When you meet someone from here someplace else—say, in a bar in Minneapolis—and ask, "Where're you from?" usually he or she will say, "St. Louis."

But as Eric Sandweiss points out in his introduction to this book, the answer to such a question depends a lot on circumstance. If you pitch it to the same person while waiting in line for tickets to the ball game downtown, for example, likely as not the person will get more specific.

"Lemay," he'll say.

"Clayton," she'll say.

"St. Louis Hills."

"Ferguson."

"East St. Louis."

"Chesterfield."

"Eureka!"

And so it goes, geographically, on and on and on.

That's a quirk, amusing sometimes, sort of like our penchant for further delineating ourselves by where we went to high school.

But this means of self-identification is a symptom of one of the most destructive problems confronting those of us who live in St. Louis and love it: our persistent civic inability to behave regionally.

It might seem to you that the Where We Live series, by taking sections of the community and poking around in their scrapbooks and trunks and summoning up memories of them and hopes for them, reinforces this devotion we have to the fragmented metropolis. But that was neither the intention, nor, I think, has it been the result, of this endeavor.

Fragmentation doesn't just happen. As cities developed in the United States, they became chopped up by boundaries based on class and race, by customs and choices and economics and laws, by natural and artificial barriers.

In this century in the United States, men and women of good will have worked diligently to remove some of the legal and traditional walls that separated various segments of the community.

But in many cases, the barriers aren't based on anything more complicated than simple lack of knowledge.

For example, there are people who live in Florissant who have traveled the Silk Road but would not know how to get to Carondelet on a bet. Similarly, there are those whose worlds end or begin at Skinker Boulevard who are surprised to find that Illinois is *only* a bridge-crossing away.

There is no question that celebration is an element of the Where We Live program and this book, prideful gestures in words and pictures to our communities, municipalities, and neighborhoods.

But that is only an element. The purpose of Where We Live is to introduce ourselves to one another. Our hope has been that by knowing and better understanding our similarities and differences we can grow closer, and to begin to solve the big problems that face us: racism, decaying infrastructure, waste of resources, duplication of services, and inadequacies in education, housing, public health services, and public transportation.

In 1991, the *St. Louis Post-Dispatch* signed on to this project enthusiastically and continues to support it. It has enjoyed the interest of our readers, and reporters who have contributed to the series have found it stimulating and rewarding.

All of us—readers, writers, editors, designers, photographers, historians, researchers—have learned a thing or two, not only about the places where we live, but also about who we are. Toward our goal of bringing the people of this region together for the common good, the Where We Live program is an eloquent and purposeful beginning, and *Where We Live: A Guide to St. Louis Communities* is a permanent document of it.

ROBERT W. DUFFY
CULTURAL NEWS EDITOR
ST. LOUIS POST-DISPATCH

ACKNOWLEDGMENTS

Although each chapter of this book has its own acknowledgments, there are several people and institutions who deserve special thanks.

The *St. Louis Post-Dispatch* has been a valuable supporter of the Where We Live Program since its inception. The articles that the paper published in conjunction with the original Where We Live brochures increased the brochures' popularity immensely and brought countless new friends and supporters to the Missouri Historical Society. For that reason, it seemed only natural that the *Post* be involved with the publication of *Where We Live: A Guide to St. Louis Communities,* and we are most grateful for their contribution. Nicholas G. Penniman IV, publisher of the *St. Louis Post-Dispatch,* was instrumental in working out the details of the partnership, and the staff of the *Post* has been helpful at every stage of the process.

Thanks are also due to several staff people of the Missouri Historical Society and the Missouri Historical Society Press, especially the authors of the original Where We Live brochures. Elizabeth Metzger Armstrong and Dina Young wrote the majority of them, with Katharine Corbett, Karen Goering, Candace O'Connor, Eric Sandweiss, Lee Schreiner, and Kris Runberg Smith all contributing. Their research, diligence, and ability to fit the writing of the brochures into their already busy schedules at the Missouri Historical Society made this book possible. The brochures—which were not written with a book in mind—hold together well under the structure that has been imposed upon them here, and that is due in no small part to the talents of the many people who had a hand in the making of the brochures.

Finally, several people not affiliated with either the *Post-Dispatch* or the Missouri Historical Society helped by supplying maps on computer disk for the project at no cost. Mike Webb of the St. Louis Community Development Agency and Les Aubuchon and Esley Hamilton of the St. Louis County Department of Parks and Recreation all contributed in this way, and all were forthcoming with advice for manipulating maps on disk. Lanny Chambers did an excellent job of standardizing and producing the maps for publication. The Society is most grateful for these experts' generous commitment of time, resources, and know-how.

Where We Live: A Guide to St. Louis Communities has been put together with the traveler in mind. The sites in each section are organized to allow readers to move as effortlessly as traffic will allow from one to another. For example, a reader wishing to explore "St. Louis' 'Original' Urban Landscape" could start in Cahokia, Illinois, follow Interstate 55 to the Carondelet neighborhood across the river, take Interstates 70, 170, and 270 to Florissant, and return to Interstate 70 to enter St. Charles.

The first site in each section has written directions for getting to it from St. Louis, with the distinction between St. Louis City and County being made when necessary. Within each section, chapters have simple written directions for finding the first site of the new chapter from the last site of the preceding chapter. However, it is still advisable to study the individual chapter maps and a larger map of the area before venturing out.

Of course, you will not be able to visit all of these sites in a day. In fact, if you took the time to visit all of the points of interest in each site, it is doubtful you could visit all of the sites in a single *section* in a day, especially the large "Spreading Metropolis" section. But we hope that this book will become a well-worn friend, and that it will accompany you whenever you want to explore some part of Where We Live.

WHERE WE LIVE

By Eric Sandweiss

"Where do you live?"

Most of us could think of a dozen quick answers to that simple question. We might describe the precise location of our apartment or home; we could name a neighborhood or a nearby street intersection; perhaps we would begin with the name of a city or a county, a state or even a nation.

How we respond depends on who asks us, and where we are at the time. And while we may not think much of it, our answer will reflect a great deal of deliberation and care. In fact, defining where we live is not much simpler than defining who we are. It is a question that masks many other questions, and it cannot be answered without raising still more. The pizza delivery man and the woman sitting next to us on the plane might seem to be asking the same thing—but the answers they expect are likely to be quite different.

It happens that this book is only partly about where we live. It is also about who we are. For just as it is hard to describe our surroundings apart from what they mean to us, it is impossible to think about our own lives without anchoring them to a place. The history of a street means little if it's not tied to the story of the farmer who sold the land, the developer who bought it from him, the families who campaigned to have it paved, the men who laid the asphalt, or the children who rode their bikes on it. The history of a family, on the other hand, is also inevitably the story of the apartments they rented, the stores in which they shopped, and the parks where they played. These places are more than scenic backdrops; they also give shape to our lives.

So it may not mean much to describe the subject of this book as a patch of ground. Yet what better way to begin? The place is St. Louis—or more accurately, a metropolitan region of approximately 2.4 million people that extends into two states, comprises seven counties, and includes a municipality of that name. That should be a start. But locating this place is one thing; understanding it is another matter.

The problem is that there are as many stories about this shared ground as there are people to tell them. Even more than most big cities, St. Louis defies easy characterization. There are any number of reasons why this is so. To begin with, the place we rather generically call "St. Louis" is just so spread out. This is not simply a phenomenon of our postwar, suburban era: St. Louisans have been moving out from the center of the city since 1818, when Auguste Chouteau and J. B. C. Lucas opened their addition at the top of the bluff that rose beside the Mississippi River, extending the tiny city as far west as what would become Seventh Street. Their speculation ensured that St. Louis would forever maintain two faces: one jammed up against the river, the other looking west, across miles of rolling prairie and flat bottomland. Since then, the race away from the center has continued in earnest.

With the city's tendency to spread came a tangle of political boundaries that splinter the region's identity still further. A recent study showed nearly seven hundred units of government operating in the metropolitan area. This again is not a new phenomenon, but a logical continuation of trends set long ago. The separation of the city from its surrounding county, in 1875, has ensured a legacy of fragmentation in the west, while the Mississippi River has forever marked a line of distinction to the east—first between empires, eventually between two states of the union.

Still more identities are generated by St. Louis' placement directly in the murky, overlapping zone between at least three of America's cultural regions: the South, the Midwest, and the West. St. Louis transforms itself from an aging rust-belt city to a southern hamlet to a sprawling Sun Belt megalopolis (and back again) in the course of a twenty-minute drive. Once more, history proves that our current plight is nothing new. Depending on whether you are studying the Lewis and Clark expedition, the Dred Scott case, or the founding of Washington University, St. Louis will seem to have been located in entirely different parts of the country throughout its history. This is due in part to the city's melting pot character, its forced interaction of people and cultures from wildly varied backgrounds and origins. They have come together here in a way that has never been duplicated elsewhere.

So it is not surprising that this common ground has meant so many different things to so many people through the years. Writers have delighted in pronouncing the last word on the city's character, only to be refuted by someone else down the line. Antebellum visitors like Charles Dickens, who stepped onto the levee in 1841, were likely to see St. Louis as the crumbling, quaint outpost of a dead empire. To Fannie Hurst and others living in the prosperous years of the early twentieth century, the city's "stability and conservatism" seemed key to its character. Closer to our own time, however, the same setting has offered a metaphor for urban decay: "What becomes of a city no living person can remember," the novelist Jonathan Franzen recently asked, "of an age whose passing no one survives to regret? Only St. Louis knew."

Whatever St. Louis "knows," you're not likely to find out by asking St. Louisans themselves. Their stories are more diverse than anything that the most imaginative essayist or novelist could contrive. While citizens of the region periodically rally around symbols of their common heritage, they never fail to return their loyalties to *their* neighborhood, *their* town. Thus, the 1904 Louisiana Purchase Exposition fueled a rash of civic-mindedness; but ten years later a leading city planner could complain that "the city remains no more than a group of segregated villages." Thus, in the mid-1960s, area residents celebrated the city's bicentennial and the topping of the Gateway Arch; yet ten years later the city had earned the reputation of being America's chief exporter of used bricks. At the time of this writing, a new professional football team, based downtown, is being heralded as the civic symbol that will once again tie together the region's disparate communities. But symbols are one thing, facts are another: the East-West Gateway Coordinating Council reports that the population of once-rural St. Charles County, for example, grew by more than 25 percent in the 1980s—while the City of St. Louis, which will host the new team, lost nearly one in six of its residents. In fact, census figures show us that the city surrounding the new stadium—the city whose name the new team will bear—has bid farewell to more than four hundred thousand people over the last forty years.

The point of this is not that St. Louis' time has "passed," as some critics have proclaimed. It is simply that it is harder and harder to speak of the place called St. Louis and assume a common point of reference. Now more than ever before, that place is in fact many places, and their relation to one another continues to change.

Yesterday's farm community is today's office center; today's residential neighborhood is tomorrow's shopping strip. The pattern can be seen over and over in the pages that follow.

Is there a way to understand or anticipate this change? History offers a key, and that's where this book comes in. The past is, of course, our only gauge for anticipating the future of this and other cities. But history misunderstood is worse than no help at all. For that reason, we should be careful of how we use the past—and books like this one—to understand the present. When people complain about what has become of St. Louis (and they have been doing just that for nearly two hundred years) they usually begin with an image of the past. They recall different ways of moving about, shopping, or working, and they look to history to suggest a path of return to the city of their recollections. But, to borrow a phrase from one-time St. Louisan Thomas Wolfe, we can't go home again; history only proves that no such path exists. If the past teaches us anything about urban America, it is that we should expect such things to change, and to keep changing. Our challenge is not to reverse time, but to make it work to our collective benefit.

Where We Live, then, is not *The Way We Were*. Rather than revive an ideal time now past, this book reveals the ever-changing character of the common ground in which St. Louisans' stories of themselves have taken root. To do so, we survey this unique region both as it once was and as it is today. We tell not only the story of the single place, "St. Louis"—however defined—but also the stories of the many places that it comprises.

In order to organize this survey of past and present, part and whole, we have chosen to focus on a selection of representative communities located across the metropolitan area. The book is by no means comprehensive; it leaves out some places that you might expect, and includes others that may surprise you. The chapters are organized within five discrete sections: The "Original" Urban Landscape (communities founded in the colonial period, before the Louisiana Purchase of 1803); Central St. Louis (the older neighborhoods closely clustered around downtown); The Spreading Metropolis (more distant urban neighborhoods, built up in the late-nineteenth and early-twentieth century); The Suburbs (newer towns outside the city limits); and Communities Beyond (smaller communities that have remained outside of the urban region). Read individually, you can take each chapter as an introduction to a single place: its architecture, its people, and its historic sites. Looking at the sections as a whole, you may gain a broader sense of the way the region has grown since the time of the first Euro-American settlement here over two centuries ago. You will see that, for all the variety of this sprawling region, there are only a handful of basic historic patterns that have repeated themselves again and again. The more we understand these patterns, the better able we will be to make sense of the issues that today seem to divide us from one another—and from our past.

We begin with the "original" urban landscape, a term we use advisedly to refer to St. Louis' colonial roots in the French and Spanish empires. Although this region was in fact home to one of the greatest urban concentrations on the continent in the first half of this millennium—the mound builders' settlement of Cahokia—it is with the more recent, and more familiar, Euro-American period that we concern ourselves here. Today, the traces of this early period are hard to find; at first glance, the differences between such places as Carondelet (an older, urban neighborhood in the southern part of the city) and Florissant (a big, postwar suburb) seem vast indeed. But these places, with a handful of other communities scattered about our metropolitan region, share common roots in the colonial period. And in their rough outlines (still visible to the careful visitor today), they reflect traditions of settlement that date as far back as the Roman Empire.

From 1764 to 1803, St. Louis was an outpost of European culture at the edge of unexplored wilderness. To make sense of this place, the traders, soldiers, and administrators sent north from New Orleans relied upon time-honored instructions for laying out towns, doling out land, and sustaining local economies. Like other colonizers throughout the New World, they brought with them specific ideas of what a town should look like and how it should function. They viewed the town not just as a collection of streets and buildings but as an integrated settlement pattern, linking public and private space, rural and urban functions. Settlers received house lots and outlying field lots from their overseers; these properties were granted in proportion to existing social status. If you started out wealthy, you received additional wealth in the form of property; if your means were modest, so were your entitlements. In exchange for property, settlers would do their part to improve the landscape. They agreed to build on their house lots within a year and a day; to till their fields; to keep the fence around the town common in good repair. In its basic outlines, this carefully conceived system of social and spatial functions wasn't much different from the system by which colonial towns were conceived from Peru to California, from Boston to Charleston, or across the world from Northern Ireland to South Africa.

Of course, St. Louis doesn't look much like any of those places now. The fact is that every city's history depends as much on the peculiarities of local geography and politics as it does on the timeless ideals of the people who founded it. Yet those ideals stay with us, if only as subtle fragments in the world we know today. To walk the streets of Carondelet today is to follow the lines of the long, narrow common field lots first surveyed two centuries ago. To visit the Old St. Ferdinand's Shrine in Florissant is to return to a time when cities were conceived as centers of faith, as well as commerce. In these and other ways, the original urban landscape casts its shadow on the brick and asphalt of the contemporary city.

In this book's second section, "Central St. Louis: The Nineteenth-Century City," you will find the neighborhoods that best correspond to our time-honored images of the big American city. Here are the corner butcher shop and the high-rise housing project; the stark factory and the elegant row house. If our picture of what cities look like corresponds to these kinds of features, it is no accident: it is here, within a circle extending roughly two miles from the center, that the greatest numbers of people have lived, the greatest amounts of money been invested, and the greatest numbers of memories been formed.

The story of the nineteenth-century city is in many ways the story of where people worked and how they got there. The workplace—whether factory, shop, or office building—did as much to shape and preserve neighborhoods as the church or the fraternal hall. The vast majority of Americans of the last century followed economic opportunity—something that remained for most of them a limited commodity. In cities like St. Louis, opportunity came in the form of a handful of basic functions, commonly centering on natural resources like grain, fur, cotton, and wood: these included warehousing and storage, processing and manufacture, and finance and marketing. Each of those functions left its mark on the nineteenth-century landscape; today, we find their legacy in the warehouses, factories, shops, and office buildings that still line the streets of the central city.

For the wealthy, private carriages did a wonderful job of supplying transport from home to these workplaces. If you were a clerk or a factory hand, however, your options were more limited. So most people chose homes within easy walking distance of employment. In this way, densely built residential neighborhoods soon surrounded logical work sites along the river or the railroad tracks; in turn, the presence of these developed residential quarters encouraged other business enterprises—stores, restaurants, and the like—to move to the area. Their presence promoted a cycle of growth: retail services attracted home builders, the presence of new residents encouraged more commercial development, which itself brought more residents, and so on.

Postwar urban renewal has destroyed much of what

once stood in these areas—especially along the waterfront and in the Mill Creek Valley, just north of today's Interstate 64. But in neighborhoods like Hyde Park or Soulard, or along streets like Cherokee, the nineteenth-century city lives on. The surprising fact is not that so little of this world remains in St. Louis, but that we can still find so *much* of it. It is still easy to find the *Turnverein,* the carriage factory, the cramped apartment buildings crowded two to a lot. Beside them, however, you are likely to confront messengers from another world: the interstate off-ramp, the supermarket parking lot, the grass-covered land where once a row of houses stood. History is not absent in these abrupt intrusions on the landscape; it has simply moved along, in ways that we are not always prepared to recognize. It is our purpose in these pages not to favor one period over another, but to look at the continuities that tie together the varied faces of the central city.

The third section focuses on a different type of community: the neighborhoods that experienced their biggest growth in the boom years of the early twentieth century. These are urban neighborhoods, and they generally lie within the city limits. Yet their landscapes reveal a way of life that is different from that of the neighborhoods developed in previous generations. The first thing that strikes you about these newer areas is their location: they are further from downtown, the city's historic heart. This fact is due in part to the streetcar, and eventually to the automobile, which by the 1900s allowed working- and middle-class St. Louisans a greater number of residential choices. Yet new forms of transportation only sped up the existing process of outward migration; they didn't initiate it. The rise of outlying urban areas simply continued patterns evident for over a century, as city residents continually sought cheaper land, quieter neighborhoods, and, in a more general sense, more predictable lives. In some cases, an existing recreational attraction—like Forest Park, Tower Grove Park, or the Fairgrounds—served as the anchor that drew new tenants and homeowners out from their old neighborhoods. In others, developers simply leapfrogged over one another to promote new neighborhoods along established lines of outward movement.

A second major difference is that most of these neighborhoods look more uniform, more comprehensible in their architecture and their land uses, than the older blocks of the central city. While some, like Oak Hill or Granite City, grew up beside the industrial sites that bolstered the region's economy, most were exclusively residential. Whether they housed the well-to-do—like the private streets of the Central West End—or the widening ranks of the middle class—like the Shaw or Penrose areas—these neighborhoods reflected conscious efforts to push business and industry away from residential streets, and into their own limited areas. Homes and apartments, often built a block or more at a time, reflected the work of builders and developers who sought to supply their clients with a tidy, quiet environment, free from the noise and soot of downtown. At the edges of such developments, busy streets like Grand Avenue provided new sources of shopping and employment, making city residents ever less dependent on downtown.

In section four, we look at a few examples of what has become the most prevalent settlement form in America: the suburb. The word itself has become so common that we may have lost sight of its origins. "Suburbs," in one form or another, have been sprouting up around the edges of European and North American cities for hundreds of years. They have included squalid workers' settlements, aristocratic estates, and everything in between. But it is only in the last century that a coherent, popular image of suburban living has developed in this country. According to that image, the suburb is the province of the middle class; a refuge from urban grime where respectable professionals and their families look out upon a little piece of nature from under the protective eaves of their modest homes.

But this hazy picture of broad front lawns and spreading trees, of carpools and backyard barbecues, no longer suffices to explain the ubiquitous suburb. Consider St. Louis: Kinloch and Wellston are suburbs; so are Huntleigh Village and Frontenac. All of them share a common identity as separately incorporated municipalities outside of the city, and all of them are predominantly residential in their land use patterns. But their demographic makeup, their architecture, and their tax bases are as different as they can be. In like manner, you will see the variety of the suburban experience from the communities included in this book. While all of them have deep historic roots (for instance, as train or stage stops on the way out of the city), each has grown differently through time. Today's University City, to cite one example, is a very different place from Manchester. The reasons for those differences, which we explore in these chapters, require from us a deeper understanding of the influence of many different things: location, public policy, cultural institutions, and sometimes sheer accident. Today, the suburbs of St. Louis, as of all American cities, are as diverse as Americans themselves.

The final section of this book takes you further out still: to the perimeter of the metropolitan region. Here, the residents of smaller towns measure their own sense of historic separateness against an increasing interdependence with the city and its suburbs. In some senses, places like Augusta or Kimmswick—which we cherish today as picturesque reminders of small-town America—

are in the same position as Florissant in 1910, or Carondelet in 1860: they stand a good chance of being overtaken by the metropolis that continues to spread in their direction. Metropolitan St. Louis has been swallowing up surrounding communities for centuries.

Is this a bad thing? Certainly there are aspects of their proximity to the city (television stations, professional sports teams, and shopping centers, to name a handful) that few residents of such towns would offer to live without. At the same time, however, the citizens of even a larger town like Alton take pride in moving at a different pace; at living in a place where neighbors still know one another and where even strangers say hello in the street. To these people, the advantages of living *apart from* the city and its suburbs—even if that separation is slipping away—are sufficient to keep them where they are. The residents of Elsah, Kimmswick, or countless other small towns might be recently relocated from the city, or they might be fourth-generation locals. Their journey to work might require an hour's drive to the Ford plant in Hazelwood, or it might consist of a walk to the restaurant down the street. More and more, the decision to live in a small town is a decision of choice, not necessity. That choice is made possible, ironically, by the increasing availability of "urban" amenities to all Americans, regardless of their residence. The viability of the towns that remain at the fringe of metropolitan areas like St. Louis, then, depends on the very things (the city, its jobs, its attractions) that most threaten their continued existence.

That paradoxical note seems about as good a place as any to leave the urban wanderer of the late twentieth century. The American city—and St. Louis is no exception—has always sown the seeds of it own endangerment. Limited resources and space, polluted air and water, poverty and crime—these familiar ills are not new; in fact, they are all, in a way, the consequences of our success at what we do. The innovations that occur in response to these consequences, in turn, are what keep cities moving forward: adapting, transforming, surviving.

If this book were just about the past, we could leave the matter at that. But as the next century approaches, the residents of St. Louis and other cities have begun to question whether we can continue to escape our self-made problems with the same ease we have enjoyed in the past. Whether we seek to avoid them or to make them better, our urban crises have an annoying way of persisting after we've rolled up the welcome mat. (Just ask the residents of St. Charles County if they ever think about the radioactive waste buried at Weldon Spring.) If the last fifty years have shown us anything, it is that the problems of city living are metropolitan—perhaps even national—in scope. To solve those problems, we

have, naturally enough, tended to look "up": to the government, to policy-makers and professional experts, to the academic authorities who claimed to understand the larger context in which our local issues are shaped. All of them have taken us a long way toward finding solutions. Yet their expertise can never fully replace the value of looking "down": of coming to an understanding of who we are by examining the web of places, associations, and memories that is Where We Live.

Fifth & Missouri

001

1005

Bi-State Development Agency

MetroLink: An Overview of the Metropolitan Area

METROLINK: AN OVERVIEW OF THE METROPOLITAN AREA

There is no better way to get a quick introduction to the St. Louis metropolitan area than to climb on board MetroLink, the city's new light-rail system. Stretching eighteen miles from East St. Louis, Illinois, to Lambert–St. Louis International Airport, MetroLink passes by or through many of the neighborhoods and points of interest discussed in this book.

However, MetroLink provides more than an inexpensive and convenient way to see St. Louis; it also dramatically illustrates two underlying themes of this volume: the city's growth from a series of trading outposts to a unique urban landscape, and the important role transportation has played in that growth.

This tour of MetroLink begins at the Fifth and Missouri station in East St. Louis—not too far from Cahokia, Illinois, the site of the oldest European-American settlement in the Mississippi Valley. Continuing west, it crosses over the Mississippi River on the Eads Bridge before traveling through and under downtown, through the Mill Creek Valley to the Central West End, and along the northern edge of Forest Park. It then turns northward through a series of suburban communities that would have been unimaginable to the city's founders over two centuries ago. The fact that the tour ends at an international airport further emphasizes the distinction between St. Louis past and St. Louis present and the dependence on rapid transportation that most modern-day cities share.

In the nineteenth century, of course, transportation in the city was limited to ground travel, and for over one hundred years—from 1859, when St. Louis' first horse-drawn streetcars began carrying passengers, to 1966, when the last electric streetcar stopped running on the Hodiamont line—St. Louisans enjoyed a vast transportation network. Wealthy patrons, for the most part, led the way, taking private carriages or commuter trains to their homes on what were then the edges of town, while the arrival of electric streetcars in the 1890s allowed middle- and working-class residents to follow. By the early twentieth century, business and residential districts stretched in a radial pattern far into St. Louis County and across the river to Illinois. Large portions of this network exist today; in fact, much of MetroLink's route follows that of the old St. Louis, Kansas City & Northern Railway, later the Wabash Railroad, which was laid down in 1876.

Automobiles and, after World War II, federally subsidized interstate highways accelerated the decentralization of St. Louis. Buses continued this trend, but increasingly St. Louisans chose the convenience of their cars over public transportation. The costs of that convenience soon became clear in the form of traffic congestion and air pollution.

MetroLink was made possible by some of the same federal funding and popular support that once built highways throughout the area. The first phase, which comprises the route in this tour, debuted in 1993. On August 2, 1994, voters in St. Louis City and County approved a sales tax increase to expand the system more extensively throughout the region.

Thanks to MetroLink, St. Louisans are once again discovering the ease of taking public transportation to get to jobs, shopping districts, and recreational facilities. They are taking advantage of a mass transit system that has been carefully designed to complement bus routes, highway access, and other elements of the area's transportation infrastructure.

This tour takes approximately forty-five minutes if you stay on the train the entire way, but at many of the stops you will probably want to get off the train and look about. There is much to explore, particularly at Laclede's Landing, the downtown stops, Union Station, and Forest Park. A ride on MetroLink offers a chance to explore the historical patterns that contributed to the growth of the region. So with this book in hand, climb on board, take a seat, and relax. Enjoy a moving picture of St. Louis history.

MetroLink is operated by the Bi-State Development Agency. The fleet of thirty-one light-rail vehicles is powered by overhead electrical wire. Trains run continuously from approximately 5:00 A.M. to 1:00 A.M. daily. During morning and afternoon peak hours they run every five to seven minutes; during off-peak hours and weekends, every ten to fifteen minutes. For fare, schedule, and parking information, call the Bi-State Customer Information Center, 231-2345.

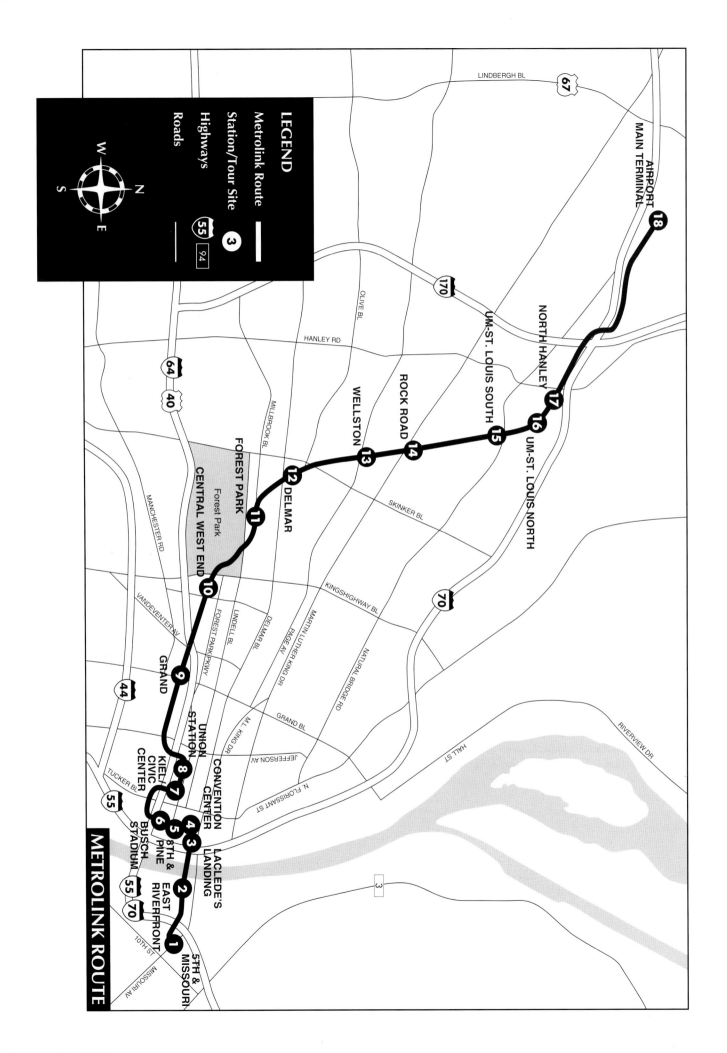

Passengers on MetroLink enjoy a view of both the St. Louis and East St. Louis riverfronts from the Eads Bridge, which first opened in 1874. Photograph by Jerry Naunheim, Jr. Courtesy of the *St. Louis Post-Dispatch.*

❶ FIFTH AND MISSOURI
On Fifth Street at Missouri Avenue, two blocks east of Collinsville Avenue, East St. Louis

Transportation has always been important to East St. Louis. In the 1790s, the town's founder, James Piggot, built a landing for ferryboats to transport people across the river to Missouri. Long before St. Louis gained prominence as a railroad hub, Illinoistown (East St. Louis) was the second-largest railroad center in the country. Before the Eads Bridge opened to rail traffic in 1874, all railroads connecting St. Louis with the East terminated here. The MetroLink station itself is a major hub for Metro East bus connections and will continue to function as such after MetroLink's planned extension from East St. Louis to Scott Air Force Base.

The downtown station was built on the former site of First Federal Savings and Loan. The tall, empty 1920s-era Spivey Building dominating the skyline once housed offices, a newsstand, and bowling alley. Directly across from the station is Southern Illinois University at Edwardsville's East St. Louis Campus, formerly the Broadview Hotel. Nearby St. Mary's Hospital, located on Missouri between 11th and 13th, is among the city's major employers.

As the train pulls out of the station, you can see the old Southern Illinois Bank Building immediately to the north. Heading west toward the East Riverfront Station, the train passes through what was the original Illinoistown, laid out in the flood plain along the river.

❷ EAST RIVERFRONT
On the riverfront at the eastern edge of the Eads Bridge, on Broadway and Front Street, East St. Louis

When the Eads Bridge was completed in 1874, it was the first railroad bridge to span the Mississippi at St. Louis. Named for its chief engineer, James B. Eads, the bridge linked St. Louis to a national rail network and helped turn the city into one of the busiest train centers in the U.S. The two-deck, three-span bridge carried both vehicular traffic and trains. Its stone piers, sunk into bedrock one hundred feet beneath the sandy river bottom, hold fast against the turbulent Mississippi River currents. At normal water stage, more than 1.5 million gallons of water surge underneath the bridge every minute. Innovative for its time, the bridge was the first to add steel to traditional cast iron in its tubular arches. The last train crossed the Eads Bridge in 1974, and the lower deck was closed until 1993, when the first MetroLink train rumbled across it.

From the elevated MetroLink station, you can see the Illinois riverfront, levee, and Casino Queen below. Railroads once filled this now-empty land. Plans are in the works for the National Park Service to extend the Jefferson National Expansion Memorial to the east riverfront, beginning with a one-hundred-acre park.

As the train crosses the Eads Bridge on the lower deck, you can see the St. Louis riverfront and skyline ahead to the south and Laclede's Landing to the north. The bridge directly to the north of the Eads Bridge is the Martin Luther King, Jr., Memorial Bridge (formerly Veterans Bridge), opened in 1950. The Poplar Street Bridge to the south opened to interstate highway traffic in the 1960s.

❸ LACLEDE'S LANDING
On the Eads Bridge between First and Second Streets

With its granite-block streets sloping down to the river, Laclede's Landing is the last survivor of St. Louis' original eighteenth-century grid street pattern and nineteenth-century riverfront. Located just north of the actual landing of Pierre Laclede, the city's founder, this warehouse district was renovated in the 1970s under the auspices of the Laclede's Landing Redevelopment Corporation, which continues today as the major umbrella organization for coordinating and managing the restored buildings.

"Laclede's Village," as eighteenth-century inhabitants called St. Louis, extended west from the bluff above the river to Fourth Street at what is now the site of the Arch. A bucolic stream, *La Petite Riviere* (Mill Creek), flowed through rolling prairies and a wooded valley west of the village. After 1817, steamboats lined the levee, and as downtown took on a commercial character, the townspeople moved west.

Most of the restored buildings, now housing restaurants, shops, and businesses, were built after the Civil War. From the MetroLink station, you can see or easily walk to the Witte Hardware building, Raeder Place Building (built on the original site of the first Missouri legislature), and the Switzer Candy building, whose sweet aroma was a riverfront area trademark for many years.

Looking through the new brick arches at the station, you get a breathtaking view of the 630-foot stainless-steel Gateway Arch, designed by the late Finnish architect Eero Saarinen and completed in 1965. The Arch is part of the Jefferson National Expansion Memorial, which is administered by the National Park Service and also includes the Museum of Westward Expansion and the Old Courthouse, where the Dred Scott slavery case was heard.

④ CONVENTION CENTER

Underground station in the tunnel at the intersection of Washington Boulevard and Sixth Street, one block southeast of the new America's Center

The first addition to St. Louis extended west to 7th Street, well beyond the limits of urban settlement at the time. After the opening of the Eads Bridge pushed commercial growth west along Washington Avenue, the area around 6th Street and Washington enjoyed its first major building boom.

By the turn of the twentieth century, this intersection and its environs had grown into St. Louis' major retail district. To go downtown meant shopping; Famous Barr, with roots going back to the 1880s, moved to the new Railway Exchange Building in 1912; and Stix, Baer and Fuller—now Dillard's—moved to its present site in 1905. These buildings are now part of St. Louis Centre, completed in 1985.

Further west, Washington Avenue became the center of St. Louis' garment and shoe industry, whose factories and warehouses are being renovated as a residential loft

district. "America's Center," as the expanded Convention Center is now called, was expanded and redesigned in 1991 by Hellmuth, Obata & Kassabaum (St. Louis), who used trademark brick, limestone, and copper to harmonize the building with the historic garment district.

Leaving the Laclede's Landing station, MetroLink begins its underground passage down a mile-long tunnel, extending from the Eads Bridge to the Busch Stadium station. The tunnel was created at the same time as the bridge to allow trains to bypass the busy downtown streets and take their freight directly into the Mill Creek rail yards. Made from Missouri limestone, the historic tunnel was cleaned and lit for MetroLink.

⑤ EIGHTH AND PINE

Underground station in the tunnel at the intersection of Eighth and Pine Streets, one block southeast of the Old Post Office

Before the Civil War, this area was filled with single-family townhouses; as the neighborhood changed from a residential to a business and government district, wealthy St. Louisans moved west of Twelfth Street to Lucas Place (now Locust Street west to Eighteenth Street), Lafayette Park, Compton Hill, and Vandeventer Place near Grand Avenue.

The neighborhood around the Eighth and Pine station is a legacy of that late-nineteenth-century business and government district. Many of St. Louis' most important landmarks are within a short distance from the station.

The Old Post Office, designed in 1872 by Isaac Taylor (St. Louis) and finally built in 1884 as the United States Custom House and Post Office, was the first building in Missouri to be entered on the National Register of Historic Places; the Wainwright Building, designed by Adler & Sullivan (Chicago) and often cited as America's first skyscraper, was renovated in 1979; and the nearby Chemical Building, designed in 1896 by Henry Ives

Washington Avenue from Sixth Street looking west, 1891. The old Lindell Hotel (formerly Stix, Baer and Fuller and now Dillard's) is on the right. This intersection is just outside MetroLink's Convention Center station. Missouri Historical Society Photograph and Print Collection.

Cobbs (Chicago), is noteworthy for its bay windows and Italian Renaissance ironwork.

❻ BUSCH STADIUM
South of Market Street, between Spruce Street and Clark Avenue at Eighth Street

By the 1890s, St. Louis had two important commercial districts: an older, river-linked downtown and a rail-linked manufacturing and warehouse district to the west in the area around Market Street. Busch Memorial Stadium, officially opened on May 8, 1966, was built on one portion of the latter district, which by the 1960s had also become home to rooming houses and transient hotels. To the west of the stadium, where parking lots now lie, was a small Chinatown that was torn down in the 1960s as part of the area's urban renewal project.

The new Busch Stadium was one piece of the Civic Center Redevelopment project that spurred the revitalization of downtown. Promoters of the new stadium promised easy parking and access to stores, hotels, shops, and the new Gateway Arch.

St. Louis' Chinatown, razed in the mid-1960s for urban renewal, was near the site of Busch Stadium and its MetroLink station. This building is on the east side of Eighth Street, between Market and Walnut. Missouri Historical Society Photograph and Print Collection.

The MetroLink station at Busch Stadium is the western terminus of the old train tunnel. Immediately to the north of the station is the Cupples Station complex, a reminder of the neighborhood's warehouse and railroad history. Cupples Station, an ensemble of eighteen buildings constructed between 1894 and 1917, was a thirty-acre freight depot that connected directly to the major railroad lines through an intricate system of tunnels. Most of St. Louis' heavy wholesale trade was handled here. The future of the ten remaining buildings, currently owned by Blue Cross & Blue Shield, remains in limbo.

❼ KIEL CIVIC CENTER
South of Market Street, west of Fourteenth Street at Spruce behind the Kiel Center

In the early nineteenth century, the area around the Kiel Civic Center station was a one-hundred-acre pond named for the man who assisted Pierre Laclede in establishing St. Louis. Surrounded by trees and fed from a freshwater spring, Chouteau's Pond was a popular place for picnicking and boating until it was drained in the 1850s. Between 1890 and 1940, the Market Street area west of Twelfth Street (Tucker Boulevard) was the focus of an extended campaign of public building. Today it is one of America's most extensive civic centers.

Kiel Auditorium opened in 1932. The nine-thousand-seat Convention Hall and the smaller adjoining Opera House served as venues for the St. Louis Symphony Orchestra, the St. Louis Philharmonic Orchestra, Dance St. Louis, and the annual Veiled Prophet Ball, as well as the home court for the St. Louis Hawks and the St. Louis University Billikens. They also hosted everything from rock concerts, roller derby competitions, and wrestling matches to Broadway productions of *Annie* and *A Chorus Line*.

In 1992, the Convention Hall was torn down to make way for the new, multipurpose Kiel Center. This new addition adjoins the renovated Opera House, a link to the structure's past.

Directly northeast of the station is the Edison Brothers warehouse. The exterior painting, designed by Richard Haas in 1984, consists of different design elements from the 1904 World's Fair, which was held in St. Louis.

❽ UNION STATION
South of Market Street at Eighteenth and Clark Streets near the southeast section of the Union Station parking lot

The city's largest preservation project, the renovated St. Louis Union Station, which opened in 1985, is a multilevel complex that houses shops, restaurants, food courts, and the Hyatt Regency St. Louis. Though no longer operating as a train station, Union Station was the largest single-level passenger train terminal in the world when it first opened in 1894.

At one time more than 93,000 trains a year moved in and out of the Union Station train shed. In addition, 269 trains operated daily, including 35 commuter trains carrying passengers between the station and suburban depots. Before the last train pulled out of Union Station on Halloween, 1978, only six trains a day were operating from the station.

As the MetroLink train pulls into the station, you can see the old mail handling facility to the south. As the train heads toward Grand Avenue, it passes through the old baggage tunnel, which was extended west of Twentieth Street for MetroLink.

 GRAND
Grand Avenue at Scott Avenue, beneath the Grand Avenue Viaduct

Soon after Chouteau's Pond was drained in the 1850s, the wide, flat floor of the Mill Creek Valley became the route for most of the major railroad lines, and rail-related industries and warehouses soon filled the landscape. Nearby neighborhoods were occupied by African Americans from the South, who were both pulled there by the lure of jobs and pushed there by discriminatory housing practices elsewhere in the city. In the early twentieth century, Chestnut Valley, along Chestnut and Market Streets near twentieth Street, was a famous honky-tonk district where Scott Joplin and other musicians played ragtime and jazz. After a federally funded urban renewal program leveled much of the valley in the 1960s, its displaced residents moved west and north.

The rail yards of Mill Creek Valley are still very much alive, and as MetroLink passes through the valley toward the Grand station, you might see trains from the Union Pacific and Burlington lines pass by alongside the track. Heading toward the Grand station, you'll also pass the site of the future St. Louis Regional Transportation Center and the new MetroLink yard and shops.

South of the Grand station are Pevely Dairy, in operation for over one hundred years, and the St. Louis University Medical Center. The fifteen-story building with the green roof is Fermin Desloge Hospital, built in 1933 and currently part of SLU's medical complex. The St. Louis University Medical School is directly across Grand Avenue from Fermin Desloge.

CENTRAL WEST END
At Washington University/Barnes Hospital Medical Complex, near Euclid and Audubon Avenues

From the end of the nineteenth century into the 1940s, affluent St. Louisans settled in the Central West End,

especially on the private streets between Taylor Avenue and Union Boulevard.

St. Louis' major medical institutions followed the westward movement. Washington University Medical School, formed in 1899 after a merger of the St. Louis and Missouri Medical Colleges, moved from its Locust and 18th Street location to its present site in 1914. Barnes Hospital opened the same year. After the additions of St. Louis Children's Hospital and Jewish Hospital, which moved from its Delmar and Union Boulevard home in 1927, the Central West End's hospital complex continued to expand and helped turn St. Louis into a major medical research center.

MetroLink's route into the station goes by the Ray Carroll County Grain Elevator, the last major landmark along this industrial corridor. This grain storage and transit center is still in operation. After switching to the old Wabash Railroad right of way, the train enters the station directly under the hospital complex. Washington University Medical School's power plant sits on the south side of the track. A five-minute walk north on Euclid Avenue will take you to the Central West End's shops and restaurants.

Leaving the station through the Washington University Medical Center tunnel, look for the fields of recycled multicolored stained-glass fragments on the slopes of the tunnel. This project, titled *Light Passage,* was designed by San Francisco artist Anna Valentina Murch as part of Bi-State Development's unique Arts in Transit program.

 FOREST PARK
DeBaliviere Boulevard, between Forest Park Parkway and Pershing Avenue

By 1876, St. Louis' western city limits had reached Skinker Boulevard. Streetcars, along with the Wabash Railroad trains that ran through the neighborhood, helped bring middle-class families into the area north of Forest Park, known today as the Skinker-DeBaliviere neighborhood. Public transportation also helped make Forest Park and the 1904 World's Fair accessible to residents from throughout the city.

Since the turn of the twentieth century, DeBaliviere Boulevard has undergone several transformations. From the 1920s to World War II, the strip was a major restaurant and shopping district. By the 1960s, DeBaliviere was known mostly for its bars and nightlife. Beginning in 1976, the neighborhood underwent yet another transformation, a major redevelopment project called DeBaliviere Place.

Heading west from the Central West End station, the train passes Forest Park, on the south side of the train, and the DeBaliviere neighborhood, on the north. Most of the homes and apartment buildings here were built in the early decades of the twentieth century. The site of the

This double-decker bus, shown outside of the Jefferson Memorial Building near MetroLink's Forest Park Station, took visitors through the park. Modern-day visitors to Forest Park can take Bi-State's Shuttle Bug from either the Forest Park or Central West End MetroLink Stations to all of the park's major attractions. Call 982-1400 for information. Missouri Historical Society Photograph and Print Collection.

main entrance to the World's Fair is just one block south of the station at Lindell and DeBaliviere boulevards, where the Missouri Historical Society's Missouri History Museum is located.

⑫ DELMAR
North of Delmar Boulevard, east of Skinker Boulevard at Des Peres Avenue

The western edge of St. Louis and nearby University City were mostly farm country until the early decades of the twentieth century. The Delmar station was an important link in the growth of the area. Originally built by the Wabash Railroad as a transfer point for St. Louis passengers heading to Chicago and Kansas City, the station also became a major stop on "The Comm," a popular commuter train that ran from St. Charles to the elevated tracks at the Eads Bridge until 1933. The nearby Hodiamont streetcar line, running from downtown St. Louis to Florissant, also aided the growth of this region.

The MetroLink train goes underneath the old Wabash Delmar train station, a limestone structure with a marble interior that opened in 1929 and closed in 1970. A few blocks to the west is the University City Loop; to the east is the St. Louis Regional Medical Center.

⑬ WELLSTON
Plymouth and Kingsland Avenues, south of Page Avenue

Wellston has played a special role in the St. Louis region's transportation history. The town was named for one of its early residents, Erastus Wells, who not only launched the first horse-drawn streetcar line in St. Louis, but also helped start a successful commuter railroad, the West End

Narrow Gauge Railroad Company, which ran from Olive and Grand to Normandy and Florissant. The Wellston Loop, today a hub for bus lines, was once one of the busiest streetcar transfer points in the country. The loop helped develop Wellston's shopping strips along Easton (Dr. Martin Luther King, Jr., Drive) and Page Avenues.

By the early twentieth century, Wellston grew into an industrial district and blue-collar town. The Wagner Electric Plant, a major manufacturer of electrical transformers, motors, and brake linings, which opened in 1906 and closed in 1982, employed more than two thousand workers in its heyday.

The now-empty Wagner Electric complex on the north side of the station dominates the landscape here. The complex is currently owned by the St. Louis County Land Clearance for Redevelopment Authority, and plans are in the works to convert the main plant to a manufacturing-technology training center.

Leaving Wellston station, the train continues through an industrial area, passing by the Page Avenue electrical substation and transmission towers on the north.

⑭ ROCK ROAD
St. Charles Rock Road and Kingsland Avenue in Pagedale

In the early nineteenth century, St. Charles Rock Road was one of the main highways that fanned out of St. Louis into St. Louis County. It was the first east-west highway through the county, and it connected with a ferry at the Missouri River, across from St. Charles. Country roads were made of dirt until about 1840, and when St. Charles Road was paved with rocks in 1865, "Rock" became part of its name. Today, St. Charles Rock Road is an extension of Dr. Martin Luther King, Jr., Drive, formerly Easton Avenue.

The station is located in Pagedale, a major destination for blue-collar workers after World War II. As office parks and manufacturing plants opened or relocated in St. Louis County, many working-class families followed, moving out of the city in search of jobs and a house in the suburbs. St. Louis enjoyed a postwar manufacturing boom, and pockets of the county quickly filled up with blocks of modest brick homes whose owners worked at large firms such as McDonnell Douglas, Monsanto, and Wagner Electric. Originally called Hazel Hills, Pagedale was incorporated in 1950.

As MetroLink travels toward the Rock Road station, you'll see a huge automobile cemetery to the south; to the north is Bethany Cemetery (1870). The new parking lot at the station has a flea market on weekends.

⑮ UNIVERSITY OF MISSOURI–ST. LOUIS, SOUTH
South of Natural Bridge Road on the east edge of University of Missouri–St. Louis' South Campus (the old Marillac Campus), Normandy

Normandy's history goes back to the early nineteenth century, when it was the country estate of Jean Baptiste Charles Lucas, who named his land Normandy because it reminded him of his native province in France. Well into the early twentieth century, Normandy was still a bucolic rural settlement, known for its Catholic institutions, which included St. Vincent's ("The Castle"), a sanitarium "for nervous and mental ailments" that moved from its Soulard neighborhood site to Normandy in 1895, and Marillac College, the administrative center for the West Central Province of the Daughters of Charity.

One of the first steam railroads in Missouri rolled through Normandy, stopping at a station located at the intersection of Natural Bridge and Florissant Roads. After 1920, Normandy rapidly grew into a St. Louis suburb and eventually split into fourteen separate municipalities.

Before reaching the University of Missouri–St. Louis South station, MetroLink passes St. Peters Cemetery, established in 1855, and the Glen Echo Country Club, which opened in 1901. St. Vincent's is visible through the trees. Marillac College, where the MetroLink station is located, became part of University of Missouri–St. Louis in 1976.

⑯ UNIVERSITY OF MISSOURI–ST. LOUIS, NORTH
On the North Campus near the Florissant Road entrance, East Campus and Bellerive Drives, Normandy

The University of Missouri–St. Louis' original campus was built on the former grounds of the Bellerive Country Club, which opened its doors in 1910 on land once owned by Normandy's founding family, the Lucases. After the country club decided to move from its site on

Natural Bridge Road to Mason and Ladue Roads in the late 1950s, the Normandy Board of Education bought the 128-acre site, along with a spacious clubhouse.

The University of Missouri–St. Louis began as a two-year college in 1960 with 205 first-year students; they attended classes in the remodeled clubhouse. A second-year course was added the following year. In 1963, the campus became part of the University of Missouri system. By 1968, the University of Missouri–St. Louis had more than 8,000 students. More than 15,000 from around the St. Louis region were enrolled at the campus in 1993-94.

Leaving the University of Missouri–St. Louis South station, MetroLink travels underneath Natural Bridge Road, then winds along the edge of the campus until it emerges on the northern edge of the campus at the University of Missouri–St. Louis North station across from the campus police building. Heading west toward the North Hanley station, the train goes underneath the campus via a tunnel that was built for MetroLink.

⑰ NORTH HANLEY
North Hanley Road between Geiger Avenue and Interstate 70 at the North Hanley south interchange

After World War II, St. Louis continued its role as a transportation hub as it became a major junction for several new interstate highways funded by the 1956 Federal Aid Highway Act. Like many other cities around the country, St. Louis found itself losing business and population to its suburbs, as residents moved in droves into the now accessible St. Louis County.

The new suburban shopping centers were a direct result of this exodus. Moreover, unlike the older commercial strips that boomed because of their accessibility to streetcars and trains, the suburban malls met the needs of the growing automobile-driving public. About the time that Northland Shopping Center (1953) and Crestwood Plaza Shopping Center (1957) opened up for business, Famous Barr and Stix, Baer and Fuller opened up branch stores in the suburbs.

The North Hanley station is dominated by Interstate 70 (1961) directly to the north, which created a direct corridor between St. Charles, McDonnell Douglas Corporation, the airport, and downtown. It's hard to imagine that these surroundings were once empty tall-grass prairies and that North Hanley Road was a two-lane country road. The greenhouses on Geiger Road are a reminder of its rural past.

18 AIRPORT MAIN TERMINAL
Outside station, east of the airline ticket counters on the main level

Lambert–St. Louis International Airport had its origins on a 170-acre hayfield, which Major Albert Bond Lambert turned into an airfield in 1920. Dubbed "the new Union Station of St. Louis," Lambert's airfield was originally known as the "St. Louis Flying Field." In the late 1920s, the City of St. Louis bought the airfield from Lambert and renamed it Lambert–St. Louis Municipal Airport, one of the first municipally owned airports in the U.S.

The terminal, built in 1956, was designed by Minoru Yamasaki; its concrete-shell design was a forerunner in contemporary airport architecture.

The airport station, the final link in MetroLink's first phase, opened in June 1994. From the North Hanley station, the track crosses a bridge over Interstate 70 and then travels through a nine-acre portion of the 1920s-era Washington Park Cemetery. After a year's delay and much public controversy, twenty-five hundred graves were relocated from the cemetery to make room for MetroLink. A single-track, half-mile elevated section takes passengers over the airport roads before stopping at the outside station.

True to the St. Louis region's tradition as a major transportation hub, Lambert–St. Louis International Airport is one of the busiest and fastest growing airports in the country.

FOR MORE INFORMATION

Corbett, Katharine T., and Howard S. Miller. *Saint Louis in the Gilded Age.* St. Louis: Missouri Historical Society Press, 1993.

Grant, H. Roger, Don L. Hofsommer, and Osmund Overby. *St. Louis Union Station: A Place for People, A Place for Trains.* St. Louis: The St. Louis Mercantile Library, 1994.

Landmarks Association of St. Louis, Inc. *What Are Buildings Made of? A One-Hour Walking Tour of Downtown Architecture.* St. Louis: Landmarks Association of St. Louis, Inc., 1993.

Miller, Howard S., and Quinta Scott. *The Eads Bridge.* Columbia: University of Missouri Press, 1979.

Primm, James Neal. *Lion of the Valley: St. Louis, Missouri.* Boulder, Co.: Pruett Publishing Company, 1981.

Toft, Carolyn Hewes. *St. Louis: Landmarks and Historic Districts.* St. Louis: Landmarks Association of St. Louis, Inc., 1988.

Young, Andrew D. *The St. Louis Streetcar Story.* Glendale, Ca.: Interurban Press, 1988.

Special thanks to Thomas R. Shrout, Jr., John H.M. McCarthy, Carolyn Hewes Toft, Carolyn Tuft, Willis Goldschmidt, Jim Ballard, Ann Ruwitch, Emily Blumenfeld, Charles Brown, Debbie Brown, Duane Sneddeker, Les Sterman, Darin Allan, Kenneth M. Benson, Claude Louishomme, Norman Ross, Larry Thomas, Doris Cason, Laurie Sperling, Esley Hamilton, Kathy Corbett, Eric Sandweiss, Kris Runberg Smith, and other MetroLink riders and residents of St. Louis.

AN OVERVIEW OF THE METROPOLITAN AREA

St. Louis' "Original" Urban Landscape: Colonial Settlements and How They've Changed

ST. LOUIS' "ORIGINAL" URBAN LANDSCAPE: COLONIAL SETTLEMENTS AND HOW THEY'VE CHANGED

Priests, hunters, explorers, fur traders—these are just a few of the groups that played a role in shaping the St. Louis metropolitan area we encounter today. Though they came to the Upper Louisiana Territory in the seventeenth and eighteenth centuries with motives ranging from mercantile to missionary, they all had one thing in common: a perceived obligation to explore uncharted country, to go into wilderness and establish order.

Of course, there were people in the area before the Europeans founded the communities of Cahokia, Carondelet, Florissant, and St. Charles. For centuries the Missouri, Osage, Kansas, Otoe, Iowa, and Omaha Indian tribes had inhabited the area, and before them were the "mound builders," the Mississippian peoples who migrated to the region over twenty thousand years ago and left their mark in the form of temple and burial mounds that gave St. Louis, in its formative years, the nickname "the Mound City." But much of that legacy is gone now, the stuff of museum collections and memory.

Progress has taken its toll on the European legacy as well. Walking down the streets of Cahokia, for example, you can still see the Old Courthouse and the Jarrot Mansion, but you can also see the post–World War II subdivisions and the Parks Air College, sites that not only make it impossible to experience the region as the Europeans did but also indicate the radical changes this urban landscape and this urban society have undergone in the past two hundred years. And as you read in this book about the tortured history of some elements of that European past—the Cahokia Courthouse's dismantling, moving, and reassembling *twice* before its final return to its hometown is but one example—you will realize how committed these communities are to preserving those elements that remain.

In spite of the best intentions of preservationists and historians, however, urban landscapes do change. An interstate highway is built and a town is cut in half; a court case is decided and the ethnic makeup of a neighborhood shifts; a shopping mall is built and a small downtown business district falters. But history is never one-sided. At the other end of the highway is a community that is rejuvenated; on the other side of a court case is a community enjoying access to better and more equitable housing; down the street from shopping mall is a group of citizens who decide to rebuild the business district too, with their own time, money, and effort.

The neighborhoods you explore today with the help of this guidebook will not look exactly the same tomorrow, but they will not look completely different either. As you move about the streets of these communities that make up St. Louis' original urban landscape, ask yourself, "Two hundred years from now, how much of what I see today will remain? How much of what I see will be used in the same way? How much will not be used at all?" Though many of the buildings and monuments you see now will shift and change with time, they will more than likely remain part of an urban landscape—a landscape constructed by people and subject to the choices that people make.

CAHOKIA, ILLINOIS

From St. Louis: Interstate 64 (Highway 40) east, over the Mississippi River. State Highway 3 south to Cahokia. Right (west) at Second Street.

The Old Courthouse is an important symbol for residents of Cahokia. It was restored to its original size and location in 1938 and currently houses a museum with exhibits on the history of the courthouse, the fur trade, and French Colonial Cahokia. Photograph by David Schultz.

Priests from the Holy Family Missions in Quebec established the Village of Cahokia as a mission among the Tamaroa and Cahokia Indians in 1699, some sixty-five years before the founding of St. Louis. But it was the rich alluvial soil of the area and its position on the Mississippi River that attracted even more French settlers to this remote outpost; by 1752 the population, mostly farmers and fur traders, totaled 136, including both black and Indian slaves. Since these early years, Cahokia has struggled to hold on to its identity as a French settlement, in spite of changes in rulers and the influence of the burgeoning city to the west.

In fact, even after Cahokia came under British rule in 1763, the villagers remained loyal to France. Then, in 1778, George Rogers Clark peacefully took Cahokia for the Americans during the Revolutionary War. Fort Bowman, established within the village boundaries, became the westernmost American fort during the Revolution. Cahokia gained prominence on the frontier when, in 1790, the village became the seat of St. Clair County, the first county established in the Illinois country.

However, frequent devastating floods in the early 1800s, along with the occasional earthquake and the growth of nearby St. Louis and "Illinoistown," as East St. Louis was originally called, hampered the village's development. After the county seat moved to Belleville in 1814, Cahokia saw only modest population gains for the remainder of the nineteenth century.

But the village would not remain dormant for long. In 1927 Cahokia entered a new era when Curtiss-Steinberg Airport began operation on a one-thousand-acre prairie on the northern edge of the village. The following year aviator Oliver L. Parks opened nearby Parks Air College. This venture proved so successful that in 1940 the federal government commissioned Parks to triple the capacity of the school to train pilots for the military. Parks Air College rose to the challenge and instructed one of every ten U.S. Army Air Corps pilots from 1940 to 1945.

The postwar years were a period of tremendous growth for Cahokia. At a time when there was little affordable housing on the Missouri side of the river, subdivisions of three-bedroom prefabricated homes quickly sprang up in Cahokia. Oliver Parks presided over the sales agency that developed subdivisions such as St. Joseph Gardens, located across from Parks Air College. The prospect of buying a home for as little as forty-nine dollars a month proved enticing to many young couples who were renters in St. Louis. As a result, Cahokia grew from a village of 794 in 1950 to 15,829 in 1960. Today the village is best described as a bedroom community, as many residents commute to work at such St. Louis industries as Anheuser-Busch, Southwestern Bell, McDonnell-Douglas, and Monsanto.

Cahokia's village motto, "Pride in the Past, Faith in the Future," is clearly evidenced in the community today. Annual events such as La Guiannée Ball and the Rendezvous of the Milice de Ste. Famille re-create the atmosphere of French-colonial Cahokia. An increasingly popular event, the *Fête du Bon Vieux Temps* (Festival of the Good Old Days) is a moveable feast held on the Saturday before Ash Wednesday. The *fête*, featuring eighteenth-century music, entertainment, and fashions, culminates in *La danse de la fête,* a colonial Mardi Gras ball.

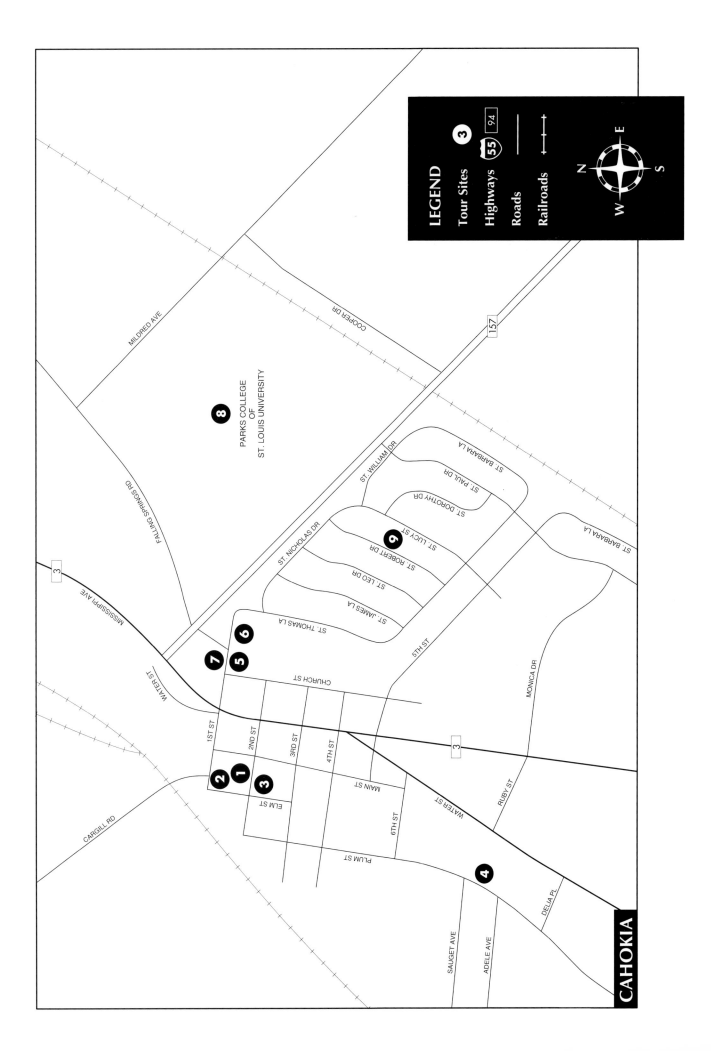

CAHOKIA

LEGEND

Tour Sites

Highways

Roads

Railroads

Cahokia has ambitious plans for its future. In 1986 an extensive archaeological excavation of the original settlement of Cahokia yielded artifacts and evidence of several structures, including what is believed to have been Fort Bowman. As a result of these findings the Village of Cahokia has created a plan for developing this area, known as "the wedge," as a historic landmark park. In this way, and in many others, this small French settlement continues to cherish its important role as one of the first European settlements in the St. Louis area.

❶ VISITORS' CENTER
Second and Elm Streets

The Visitors' Center nearby the Old Courthouse serves tourists visiting the historic sites in Cahokia. The center provides guides, pamphlets, artifacts, and exhibits on the Jarrot Mansion and Old Courthouse.

On the front porch of the log building rest two millstones taken from the site of a nearby eighteenth-century mill built by the Franciscan Seminarians of Foreign Missions.

❷ CAHOKIA COURTHOUSE STATE HISTORIC SITE
First and Elm Streets

The Cahokia Courthouse was constructed in 1737 as a dwelling for the Saucier family. Constructed in a French style known as poteaux-sur-solle, the house features upright logs, chinked with stone and mortar, resting on a foundation almost two feet thick. In 1793 the Village of Cahokia purchased the building and adapted it for use as the first courthouse of St. Clair County. After the county seat moved to Belleville in 1814, the building served a variety of purposes before finally falling into disrepair. In 1901 ownership of the property passed to Alexander Cella, who dismantled the building and placed it in storage until the 1904 World's Fair. The courthouse was then reassembled, at reduced size, as a fairground exhibit. When the fair ended, the Chicago Historical Society gained ownership, and the building, in its smaller size, became an attraction at Chicago's Jackson Park.

MOUNDS VS. VILLAGE

A shared name is the only common characteristic of Cahokia Mounds and the Village of Cahokia. The mounds, named for the Cahokia tribe of the Illini Confederation, are located outside the nearby town of Collinsville. The Indians of the once-thriving Mississippian civilization (probably not the ancestors of the Cahokian tribe) built the mounds between the eighth and thirteenth centuries for ceremonial, burial, and residential purposes.

In 1938 the dismantled courthouse returned at last to its original site in Cahokia. In planning its reconstruction, architects studied old photographs of the building and employed general information on French Colonial architecture. To guide the work, they used the original foundation, fragments of porch columns, and archaeological evidence of fireplace footings. The Cahokia Courthouse is now home to a museum featuring artifact reproductions displayed in open cases for hands-on interpretation. The Courthouse and Visitors' Center are open from 9:00-5:00 p.m. Tuesday through Saturday. For further information call (618) 332-1782.

❸ CHIEF PONTIAC SITE
Second and Elm Streets

Chief Pontiac, the renowned Ottawa Indian, met his end in 1769 across the street from the Old Cahokia Courthouse. As legend holds, a British officer bribed an Illini Indian with a barrel of whiskey to assassinate Pontiac, who had collaborated with the French in fighting the British across the Northeast. His murder sparked one of the greatest of the Indian wars. It also led to a still-unsolved mystery concerning the whereabouts of his remains. One story has it that Pontiac lies buried near present day Walnut and Fourth Streets in St. Louis.

❹ SAUGET CENTENNIAL FARM
Plum Street and Sauget Avenue

The Sauget farm was one of the first in Illinois to be designated a Centennial Farm by the Illinois State Historical Society, a distinction reserved for farms that have remained in the same family for one hundred years. Armond Sauget purchased the farm in 1870. The land had been a section of the Cahokia common fields. Wheat and soybeans are still grown on the fifty-acre tract.

The Mission of the Holy Family Parish used the Jarrot Mansion as a schoolhouse from 1904 to 1948. This photograph is from 1905. Missouri Historical Society Photograph and Print Collection.

5 CHURCH OF THE HOLY FAMILY
First and Church Streets

Built in 1799, the Church of the Holy Family is the last surviving example of French Colonial church architecture in the United States. The present building replaced the original chapel of the Holy Family mission, dating from 1699, which was destroyed by fire in 1784. The early history of Cahokia is intertwined with that of the church, for the town began as a mission settlement under the Seminary of Quebec. Even after the settlement expanded into a thriving colonial village, the church, following French custom, served as its focal point.

In 1978 parishioners constructed, alongside the historic building, a modern facility to house daily activities. The historic building is open to the public.

6 THE JARROT MANSION
First Street

Completed in 1806, the home of French émigré and Cahokia entrepreneur Nicholas Jarrot is the oldest brick building in Illinois. Except for the twelve-pane glass windows imported from France, all building materials, such as walnut for timbers and clay for bricks, came from Jarrot's own estate.

The house has endured multiple natural disasters, including earthquakes in 1811 and 1812, which account for the jagged shifting of bricks in the back wall. In the 1844 flood, the first floor remained underwater for several weeks.

After serving as home to the Jarrots, the mansion housed a school for the parish of the Church of the Holy Family, which is located next door. The house is open to the public by appointment and for special events.

7 FORT BOWMAN
First Street

When George Rogers Clark and his American troops occupied the area in 1778, his subordinate, Capt. Joseph Bowman, set up Cahokia's local government in a stone building on Holy Family parish property. The building would later become known as Fort Bowman, the westernmost fort of the Revolutionary War. Although the fort no longer exists, 1986 archaeological investigations indicate that the fort faced south from the southern edge of the wedge. Plans have been considered to reconstruct Fort Bowman's entrance as part of a historic landmark park.

Falling Springs, located south of the Village of Cahokia, was for generations a popular picnic site. Visitors came from near and far to enjoy the picturesque setting. Missouri Historical Society Photograph and Print Collection.

❽ PARKS AIR COLLEGE
Falling Springs Road

Oliver Parks founded Parks College, the nation's first federally approved flying school, in 1927 with a fleet of only two planes. The college now trains more than eleven hundred men and women in mechanical, engineering, and piloting skills. Parks bought the nearby Curtiss-Steinberg Airport at the beginning of World War II, when the U.S. Government commissioned him to train pilots. He and his staff trained one-tenth of all Army Air Corps pilots.

In 1946 Parks donated the 113-acre campus to St. Louis University. Parks College of St. Louis University offered bachelor's degrees in twelve areas including Aerospace Engineering, Aviation Science, and Meteorology. In the summer of 1996, the academic portion of the program will move to St. Louis University's Frost Campus in St. Louis, but the Flight Training program will remain at the Cahokia campus.

The first weekend in October, Parks College holds its annual Open House for aviation enthusiasts and prospective students. The Open House is free and open to the public, featuring an air show as well as a display of aircraft. For further information call Parks College at (314) 241-0280 (Missouri) or (618) 337-7500 (Illinois).

❾ ST. JOSEPH GARDENS
5th Street and St. Lucy Street

Oliver Parks responded to the need for low-cost housing for young couples after World War II by developing subdivisions of prefabricated homes. St. Joseph Gardens was the first of these subdivisions. Rushed into construction with only minimal planning, it sprang up less than one thousand feet away from the Cahokia Courthouse Historic Site. The hurried development led to a boom in Cahokia's population, which rose from a mere five hundred in 1946 to nearly fifteen thousand only twelve years later.

Oliver Parks planned the homes in his new subdivisions for young families with three children. The one-story modified-Colonial homes came equipped with three bedrooms and "amenities." Today 95 percent of homes in Cahokia are prefabricated dwellings for one of Parks' subdivisions.

Baldwin, Carl R. *Echoes of Their Voices: A Saga of the Pioneers Who Pushed the Frontier Westward to the Mississippi.* St. Louis: Hawthorn Publishing Company, 1978.

Faherty, William Barnaby, S.J. *Parks College: Legacy of an Aviation Pioneer.* Ocean Park, Wash.: Harris and Friedrich, 1990.

Gums, Bonnie L. *Archeology at French Colonial Cahokia.* Springfield: Illinois Historic Preservation Agency, 1988.

Hannon, Robert E., ed. *St. Louis: Its Neighborhoods and Neighbors, Landmarks and Milestones.* St. Louis: St. Louis Regional Planning and Growth Association, 1986.

St. Clair County Bicentennial Commission Book Project Committee. *Tapestry of Time: A Bicentennial History of St. Clair County, Illinois, in Pictures.* Belleville, Ill.: St. Clair County Bicentennial Commission, 1991.

Special thanks to Paul McNamara, Molly McKenzie, Jeffrey Peyton, Nita S. Browning, Mayor Michael King, and the residents of the Village of Cahokia.

Oliver Parks (1900-1985) played a major role in the look of present-day Cahokia. After founding Parks College, the nation's first federally approved flight school, he developed several housing subdivisions in Cahokia, including St. Joseph Gardens. Missouri Historical Society Photograph and Print Collection.

CARONDELET

CARONDELET

Clement DeLore DeTreget could stand up here looking over the gentle sweep of this great River bend, and could see the homes of his village nestled in the sylvan vale below.
In 1767, four years after Spain acquired all west of the River, DeLore, a Frenchman of worthy ancestry, came across the sea with his wife and children. With followers, they came up the Mississippi and chose the site below, at the foot of what became Elwood Street, for their new home. Parcels of land including a long Common Fields strip, were allotted. DeLore called it Louisbourg, but the nickname "Vide Poche" was often used.
1794-DeLore changed the name to Carondelet in honor of the Spanish Governor General, and in 1795 Carondelet was given 6000 acres extending some ten miles along the River.
1803-The United States purchased Louisiana from France who had regained it from Spain three years before. American influence grew in Upper Louisiana. By now Carondelet was a hamlet of some 50 homes with 250 people.
1825-On his triumphal return visit to our Country, LaFayette stopped here.
1826-Carondelet "sold" the United States 1700 acres for Jefferson Barracks, for $5.00.
1832-Carondelet became a Town - a survey defined the Town, the Common Fields, the Commons and the Towpath along the River.

From Cahokia: State Highway 3 north to Interstate 55. Interstate 55 west across the Mississippi. Continue on Interstate 55 south to the Broadway exit. The first site in this chapter, Sugar Loaf Mound, is visible from the highway.

Bellerive Park, founded in 1908, offers an impressive view south onto Broadway and the Mississippi, Carondelet's major avenues of commerce. Photograph by David Schultz.

For much of its history, Carondelet was separate from St. Louis. Although St. Louis annexed the working-class community in 1870, it has, like Cahokia, retained its small-town character, with a population today of just over 22,300. Its area stretches roughly from the Mississippi River on the east to the River Des Peres on the south, with Morganford Road on the west and Meramec Street on the north.

Clement Delor de Treget, a Frenchman, founded Carondelet in 1767, naming the village in honor of Baron François Louis Hector de Carondelet, the Spanish governor general of the Louisiana Territory. The settlement soon acquired the French nickname *Vide Poche,* which translates as "empty pocket," a disparaging comment on the gambling skills of the village's Creole inhabitants.

The community's location at the confluence of the River Des Peres and the Mississippi made it a prime site for the development of industry. The Carondelet Marine Railway, with tracks sloping down to the edge of the Mississippi, provided a necessary resource for shipbuilding and repairing. In 1861, James B. Eads, a successful St. Louis businessman, used the marine railway to launch ironclad gunboats built for the Union at his Carondelet shipyard (the first one launched was named the *Carondelet*). The Iron Mountain Railroad, completed in 1858, brought iron ore from southern Missouri and linked the village to St. Louis. Several local companies, including Vulcan Iron Works and Jupiter Iron Works—by the 1870s the largest such concern in the world—produced pig iron to be converted into steel.

From its earliest days Carondelet was a diverse community where racial lines were often blurred. Creoles of combined French and Spanish parenthood coexisted peacefully with Native Americans and free African Americans. The broad range of business and industry ensured that all of these groups found opportunities as craftsmen, entrepreneurs, or industrial laborers.

With the influx of laborers came a need for relief agencies. Before the enactment of government insurance programs, mutual benefit societies provided their members with both financial and moral support. The *Arbeiter Kranken Unterstuetzungs Verein* (Workmen's Sick Benevolent Society), founded in 1870 and still in existence, offered help in cases of sickness, death, or unemployment. In addition to offering tangible benefits, such organizations helped foster a sense of community.

The twentieth century brought a decline in heavy industries and, consequently, economic hardship to the area. Then, in the 1960s, the opening of Interstate 55 rerouted traffic around Carondelet, taking with it many of the customers who had shopped on South Broadway. Residents of Carondelet, however, responded to these challenges with a strong sense of community. Today they are working to revitalize the neighborhood.

The Carondelet Community Betterment Federation, established in 1971, with sponsorship from the Monsanto Corporation, created a house-repair program for the elderly. Other federation activities include the rehabilitation of older properties in the neighborhood and the possible development of an industrial park on the river-

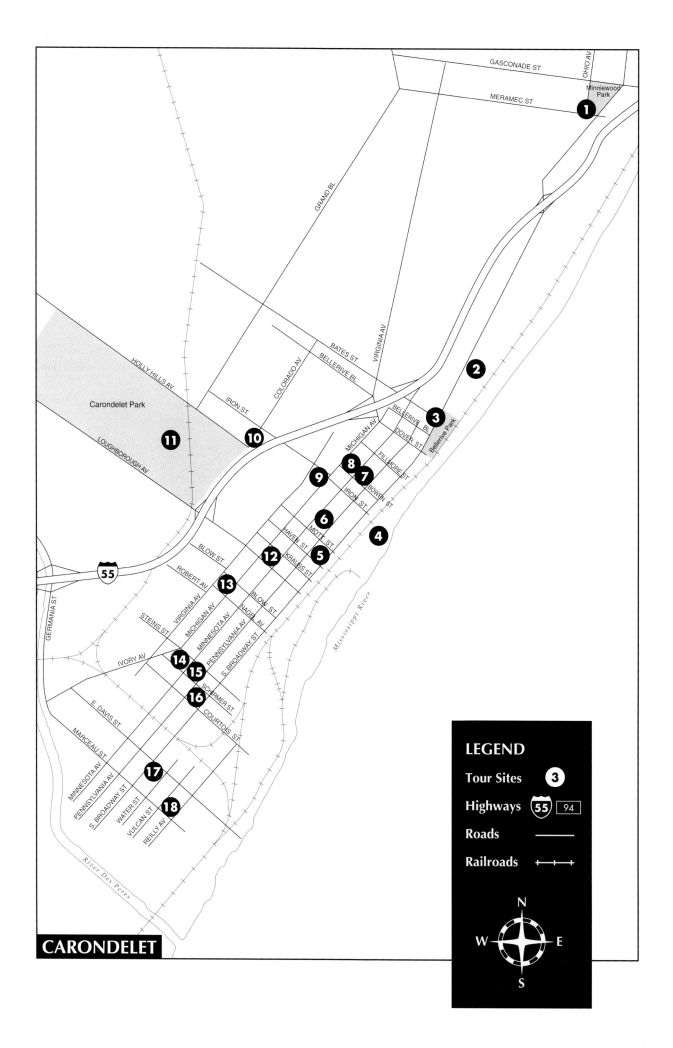

front. With help from a city grant, the South Broadway Merchants' Association is making improvements to the storefronts and surrounding shopping areas.

In 1967 the Carondelet Historical Society was organized to increase appreciation of the community's history by researching and documenting historic buildings, among which are some of the oldest in the city. The Carondelet Family Care Center handles fifty thousand cases a year, providing a vast array of health services that range from prenatal care and nutrition education to an emergency triage system and a food pantry.

The people of Carondelet are shaping their future with farsighted and committed leadership. In 1991 the Borden Pasta Group opened the largest pasta plant in North America on the Carondelet riverfront. Plans for expansion are already in motion, promising to make the plant the largest in the world. Efforts are also underway to develop the Ivory Triangle, the area in the vicinity of St. Boniface Church, as a bed-and-breakfast district. Such development would showcase and enhance Carondelet's character as a proud, historic neighborhood.

❶ SUGAR LOAF MOUND
Ohio Avenue, near South Broadway

Motorists driving south along Interstate 55 near the 4500 South Broadway exit can see Sugar Loaf Mound, one of the few surviving Native American mounds in metropolitan St. Louis. The mound dates from A.D. 800-1200 and was built by the Mississippian people. Over two dozen such mounds once dotted the area, giving St. Louis its nickname, Mound City. French settlers of Carondelet named Sugar Loaf for its resemblance to a cake of brown sugar. It forms a platform about 141 feet long and 109 feet wide. The mound has never been excavated, but archaeologists believe the Mississippians constructed one or two houses atop it, perhaps for a village leader and his family. A nearby billboard makes Sugar Loaf easy to spot from the highway.

❷ ST. LOUIS ALTENHEIM
5408 South Broadway

In 1899, before there were public provisions for the care of the aged, many prominent members of the German community came together to form the Altenheim Society for the care of the elderly. Almost immediately some four hundred members of the ladies' division set to work raising money for a building. Fundraisers included steamboat excursions, card parties, and a week-long Christmas bazaar. In 1901, the Altenheim purchased the fifteen-room Charles P. Chouteau mansion, positioned on the bluffs overlooking the Mississippi River. The mansion saw many modifications and additions until 1972, when it was razed to make way for

a six-story residential building. Furniture and fixtures original to the Chouteau estate, including chandeliers and a marble fireplace, are still in use in the Altenheim's Victorian parlor. Today nearly 140 people live at the St. Louis Altenheim, a private, not-for-profit life-care retirement home.

❸ BELLERIVE PARK
5600 South Broadway

Bellerive Park, founded in 1908 as Riverview Park, gained its new name in 1918, in honor of St. Ange de Bellerive, the area's last French commandant. A marker placed by the Carondelet Historical Society overlooks the site where Clement Delor de Treget founded the village in 1767. The 5.6-acre park, a narrow strip atop a bluff on the east side of Broadway, offers a scenic panorama of life on the Carondelet riverfront, including the hundreds of barges that pass by daily, towing cargoes of petroleum, chemicals, grain, coal, and steel.

❹ UNITED STATES COAST GUARD BASE ST. LOUIS
South Broadway at the foot of Iron Street

Base St. Louis, located on 4.43 acres of land purchased in the early 1940s, is responsible for the operational and logistical support of the Second Coast Guard District. The Second District is a twenty-two-state area encompassing over sixty-four hundred miles of navigable waters. The forty Coast Guardsmen and nine civilian employees of Base St. Louis direct the overall operation of service to navigation, boating, and marine safety. They also manufacture navigational dayboards, distribute buoys, and conduct search and rescue activities for the Second District. Public tours are offered on Saturdays and Sundays between 9:00 A.M. and 4:00 P.M. Reservations are required. To schedule a tour contact the base administration office at 832-5941.

❺ FRANZ SHEET METAL
6725 South Broadway

Franz Sheet Metal Works, one of the oldest continuous businesses in Carondelet, was founded by Lorenz Franz around 1887. Franz had come to Carondelet after obtaining a contract for munitions work at Jefferson Barracks. The business moved to the present building in 1892. Franz himself fashioned the elaborate frieze below the building's cornice. Cast in zinc, it is a lasting tribute to his craftsmanship. Today the shop is run by Eugene Franz, the founder's grandson.

The *Sumac,* the flagship for the Second Coast Guard District, is the largest river buoy tender in the United States. Photograph by David Schultz.

6 SISTERS OF ST. JOSEPH OF CARONDELET
6400 Minnesota Avenue

In the spring of 1836, at the request of Bishop Rosati of St. Louis, six Catholic nuns of the Sisters of St. Joseph arrived in St. Louis from France. A few months later, they established a convent in Carondelet. As the first foundation of the Sisters of St. Joseph outside Europe, it would be the cradle of the American congregation. The nuns soon opened the first school in Carondelet, housed in a log cabin and open to all. They then began to take in orphans and teach deaf children, finally establishing the St. Joseph Institute for the Deaf. St. Joseph's Academy and Fontbonne College also began in this motherhouse.

The two-block complex went up in stages from 1840 through the early 1900s. Architectural adaptations have updated the convent for its modern-day role. The Holy Family Chapel, a Romanesque structure designed by Aloysius F. Gillick and completed in 1899, features marble sculptures, paintings, and a hand-carved altar. In 1980 the convent was listed on the National Register of Historic Places. Tours are offered by appointment only. For more information call 481-8800.

7 QUINN CHAPEL AFRICAN METHODIST EPISCOPAL (AME) CHURCH
225 Bowen Street

The City of Carondelet began construction of this building for use as the North Public Market in 1869. The structure remained unoccupied for a decade, however, until it was sold to the African Methodist Episcopal Church of Carondelet in 1880. The chapel's name honors William Paul Quinn, the first African American Methodist bishop, who preached to slaves in Illinois and Missouri and established St. Paul AME Church in St. Louis in 1841. The early Quinn Chapel congregation included seamstresses, rivermen, teamsters, teachers, fishermen, and laborers. Various fraternal organizations met here, and congregants often gathered on the lawn for fish fries, lectures, and songfests. The church's belfry and bell, originally used on a steamboat, are 1899 additions. Quinn Chapel, dedicated in 1882, is in its 110th year of continuous use and has been on the National Register of Historic Places since 1974.

8 CARONDELET-MARKHAM MEMORIAL PRESBYTERIAN CHURCH
6116 Michigan Avenue

The Carondelet Presbyterian Church, organized in 1850, is the oldest Protestant congregation in the community. The small brick church, built on the site in the 1860s, is still in use. Next to it is the larger stone church, dating from 1896, which houses most of the church services. In 1958 Markham Memorial Presbyterian Church from the Soulard area merged with the Carondelet church to become Carondelet-Markham Memorial Presbyterian Church.

Des Peres School, built in 1873, is now the Carondelet Historic Center. Photograph by Emil Boehl. Missouri Historical Society Photograph and Print Collection.

9 CARONDELET HISTORIC CENTER, FORMERLY DES PERES SCHOOL
6303 Michigan Avenue

Completed in 1873, Des Peres School achieved distinction for housing the first successful continuously operating kindergarten program in the United States. Carondelet native Susan E. Blow began the kindergarten in 1873 after observing German kindergartens developed by educator Friedrich Froebel. Froebel's methods focused on creativity and understanding. Instead of grim, institu-

tional classrooms, kindergartners learned in plant- and flower-filled environments; they sang songs and worked with blocks and balls covered with colored yarn. Blow declined a salary for her eleven years of work guiding the development of the St. Louis kindergarten system. She trained many teachers who went on to establish kindergarten programs in cities across the nation.

The building, designed in a simplified Italianate style by Frederick W. Raeder, served as a school until 1935. During the following decades it served as a restaurant, veterans' post, and supermarket warehouse. The Carondelet Historical Society, through a joint fundraising effort with the Susan E. Blow Foundation, purchased the building in 1981. In its present incarnation as the Carondelet Historic Center, it features a museum with exhibits of kindergarten and education artifacts. Also housed here are CHS archives and pictorial collections. The National Register of Historic Places listed the building in 1982. The center is open to the public Tuesday, Wednesday, and Friday, 9:30 A.M. to noon, and Saturday from 10:30 A.M. until 2:00 P.M. For more information call 481-6303.

10 CORINTHIAN BAPTIST CHURCH
6326 Colorado Avenue

Corinthian Baptist Church, like Quinn Chapel, has served African Americans in Carondelet for over one hundred years. The congregation, organized in the 1870s, met at several locations through the years before building this structure on Colorado Avenue in 1950. Today church members come from throughout the metropolitan area to attend services.

Boating is a traditional pastime in Carondelet Park. The park's Horseshoe and Boathouse Lakes were formed through the enlargement of a series of sinkholes. Photograph by W. C. Persons. Missouri Historical Society Photograph and Print Collection.

11 CARONDELET PARK
Bounded by Interstate 55, Holly Hills Boulevard,
Loughborough Avenue, and Leona Street

Carondelet Park, the third largest park in the city park
system, encompasses land that was once part of the
Carondelet common fields. It was established in 1876
when local residents complained of the inconvenience
of Forest Park, then hours away by horse and buggy.
The 180-acre park has undulating topography marked
by sinkholes, which were formed by the collapse of
underground limestone chambers. The park's Horseshoe
and Boathouse Lakes came about through the enlargement of a series of these sinkholes.

The Alexander Lacy Lyle home, at Grand and
Loughborough, dates from the 1840s, making it one
of the oldest frame houses in Carondelet. During the
Civil War, ownership of the Colonial-style house passed
to a cousin of poet Eugene Field. The city eventually
purchased the house and turned it into a residence for
the keeper of Carondelet Park. It now serves as a recreation center for senior citizens.

12 CARONDELET BRANCH LIBRARY
6800 Michigan Avenue

Funds for the construction of the Carondelet Branch
Library came from industrialist Andrew Carnegie.
Opened in 1908, it was the third Carnegie library in
the St. Louis system. The building, made of Bedford
limestone in the Classical Revival style, is the work of
Vienna-trained architect Ernst Preisler. The library has
always played an important role in the community; early
in the century, for example, it offered citizenship classes
to Spanish immigrants who had settled in Carondelet.
Today the library contains over thirty thousand books,
prints, records, CDs, and periodicals, along with an
extensive collection on the history of Carondelet.

13 SPANISH SOCIETY
7107 Michigan Avenue

Carondelet's Spanish community began forming in
the early 1900s, when immigrants from the Asturias
region of northwestern Spain came here to work at the
Edgar Zinc Company. As they settled in, more of their
countrymen came to join them. In 1927 community
members organized *La Sociedad Española* (the Spanish
Society) to preserve the traditions of Spain, including the
national game of soccer. The Spanish Society moved to
its present location in 1937. Today, membership in the
Spanish Society is open to anyone regardless of ancestry.

14 ST. BONIFACE CATHOLIC CHURCH
7600 Michigan Avenue

The establishment of St. Boniface Parish in 1860 gave
Carondelet's growing German Catholic community the
first church of its own. Designed by Thomas Brady, the
church was constructed in stages, not seeing final completion until 1890. The Romanesque building is notable for
the two one-hundred-foot towers flanking its entrance.

15 STONE ROW HOUSES
200-204 Steins Street at Pennsylvania Avenue

Ignatz Uhrig, proprietor of a local cave and brewery,
built this four-house row in about 1851. The one-and-a-
half story houses are of limestone, with their irregularly
shaped stones joined together like puzzle pieces. These
houses, set flush with the street, are among the best
examples of the stone architecture produced by German
immigrants in the mid-nineteenth century. On the
National Register of Historic Places since 1980, the
Steins Street row houses are remarkable for their clean
lines and fine craftsmanship.

16 SOUTH PUBLIC MARKET AND ST. LOUIS
SQUARE PARK
7701 South Broadway

The South Public Market is one of the oldest continuously
existing public markets in South St. Louis. Built in 1869-
70, it was one of three public markets erected by the
City of Carondelet in the year prior to its annexation by
St. Louis. It shares structural features with Quinn Chapel,
also built then as a market. The market is part of South
St. Louis Square Park, public land that is part of the
original Spanish grant of Carondelet. The historic Anton
Schmitt house now occupies a site in the southeastern
corner of the park. The house, built of local limestone in
1859, achieved listing on the National Register of Historic
Places in April 1992. Originally at 8000 Alaska Street,
the Schmitt house sat isolated on the grounds of the
Monsanto Carondelet plant until the company, with
the help of Union Pacific Railroad, Union Electric,
Southwestern Bell, and TCI Cable, relocated the structure.

17 CARLIN-RATHGEBER HOME
122 East Davis Street, southeast corner of
South Broadway

This house, dating from 1848, was originally a Greek
Revival villa. It was the summer home of Delphy Carlin,
a wealthy merchant from New York. In 1882 John
Krauss, the German-born manager of Klausmann's
Brewery, and his wife, Maria, bought the home for their

daughter, Julia Rathgeber. She and her family added a new roof, porch, and subordinate wing, thereby transforming the villa into a Victorian-style home. Members of the Rathgeber family still occupy the home today.

⓲ THE PATCH
Southeast Carondelet

Irish immigrants first settled in Carondelet in the late 1840s. After 1870 many of them found employment at Vulcan Iron Works in southeast Carondelet and took up residence nearby. In time, this Irish enclave came to be known as "the Patch." It covered an area roughly bordered by the Mississippi on the east and South Broadway on the west, with Davis and Catalan on the north and south. The large Irish population led to the founding of St. Columbkille's Church in 1872. The church, which closed in 1952, served as the neighborhood social center and as the meeting place for many organizations, ranging from altar societies to benevolent orders and dramatic clubs. When Vulcan Iron Works closed at the turn of the century, the Patch experienced a slow decline as an Irish neighborhood. Today the name lives on at the Patch Neighborhood Center, 7925 Minnesota Avenue, which offers services for youth and senior citizens as well as a variety of self-help programs.

FOR MORE INFORMATION

Carondelet Historical Society. "Carondelet Landmarks, Volume 1." St. Louis: Carondelet Historical Society, 1987.

Harris, NiNi. *A History of Carondelet.* St. Louis: The Patrice Press, 1991.

Southern Commercial and Savings Bank. *Reflections of Carondelet, 1891-1966.* St. Louis: Southern Commercial and Savings Bank, 1966.

Toft, Carolyn Hewes, ed. *Carondelet: The Ethnic Heritage of an Urban Neighborhood.* Washington University, St. Louis: Social Science Institute Ethnic Heritage Studies, 1975.

Special thanks to Lois Waninger, Ron Bolte, Mary Ann Simon, the Carondelet Historical Society, Sister Marie Charles Buford, Kathy Clark, Mary Ann Gatewood, Alderman Dan Gruen, Mary Lopinot, Sister Charline Sullivan, and the residents of Carondelet.

Florissant

From the Patch (Carondelet): South Broadway north to Interstate 55. Interstate 55 north to Interstate 70. Interstate 70 west to Interstate 170. Interstate 170 north to Interstate 270. (The first site in this chapter, the John B. Myers House and Barn, is visible from the I-170 and I-270 interchange.) Interstate 270 east to the New Florissant Road exit. Turn left (north) to enter Florissant.

This aerial view, taken in 1949 looking north from Dunn Road near New Florissant Road, shows early construction in the Duchesne subdivision. The area marked by the X is now the site of Our Lady of Fatima Catholic Church. Courtesy of Our Lady of Fatima Parish.

When Ed Arkes returned from overseas at the end of World War II, he scarcely recognized his Florissant home. Arkes, who grew up on his family's eighty-acre farm, came back to find that most of it had been sold to developers. Where a scattered handful of houses had stood before the war, one subdivision after another now stretched into the distance, with neat rows of new homes lining freshly paved streets.

Ed Arkes was not the only St. Louisan to marvel at the postwar explosion of Florissant. But better than most, he understood that this growth was but one more chapter in a story that began over a century earlier. Florissant, a symbol of twentieth-century suburbanization, is also one of the oldest communities in the St. Louis region.

As in Cahokia, both soil and religion lured the first homesteaders to the area. French settlers had been attracted

to this fertile valley south of the Missouri River since the 1760s. The Spanish, who organized the first civil government there in 1786, named the community St. Ferdinand. They laid out a grid of streets (today's Old Town District), each named for a different saint. The landmark Old St. Ferdinand Shrine, the oldest Catholic church building between the Mississippi River and the Rocky Mountains, is just one part of the legacy of Florissant's early role as a Catholic mission. While St. Louis and other communities developed industries in the mid-nineteenth century, Florissant's main product was Jesuit missionaries, who received their training at St. Stanislaus Seminary and went out into the world to do their work.

For generations Florissant remained an agricultural village, its only link to St. Louis being a narrow-gauge rail line constructed between the two cities in the 1870s.

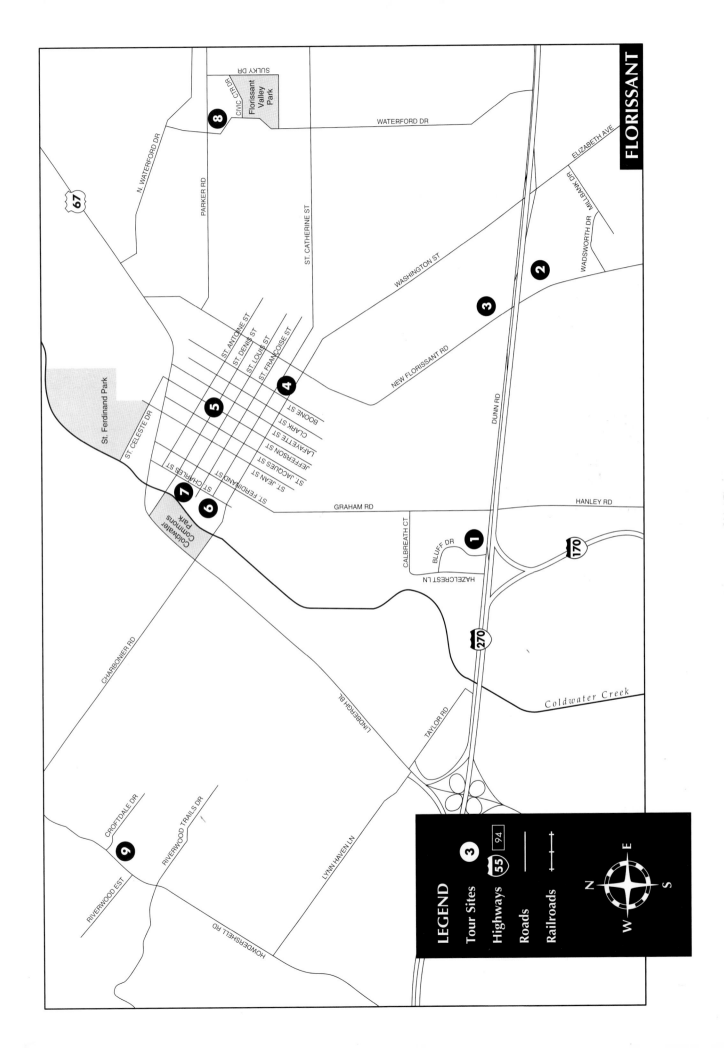

Rural Florissant, at the end of the line, became a popular place for St. Louisans to visit during the summer months in their search for relief from the heat and congestion of the city. Incorporation in 1857 did little to change Florissant's small-town character.

With the growth of St. Louis County in the 1920s, this character began to change. New water and sewer systems were installed in 1939, and through annexation, Florissant grew to ten square miles. When World War II brought new industrial plants like McDonnell-Douglas and Ford Motor Company to the area near Lambert Airport, Florissant was ready to meet the challenge of providing housing for the growing number of families moving to North County.

In the late 1940s, developers like Joseph Vatterott and Alfred Mayer bought up farmland in and around Florissant. The ideal home buyers in their new subdivisions were returning veterans who qualified for guaranteed mortgages under the Veterans Administration housing program, which required only a small down payment. The availability of such easy financing in many ways made home ownership more affordable than renting, and thousands of young families left the aging row houses and apartments of their city neighborhoods for the lawns and ranch houses of Florissant.

Between 1950 and 1970, nearly sixteen thousand homes were built in Florissant and the city's population mushroomed from 3,737 to 65,908. Scores of schools, churches, and commercial centers were built to serve the needs of the new neighborhoods. Residents began to identify themselves by their subdivisions instead of their city.

Still, Florissant's long-established municipal government was able to lend some order to the city's growth. The city planning firm of Harland Bartholomew and Associates developed a master plan for the city in 1960. This plan set the course for the annexation of undeveloped land and the adoption of density control zoning, which permitted houses to be grouped in flexible patterns rather than the rigid rows of a typical subdivision.

As commercial development burgeoned, Florissant developed excellent facilities and services for its residents. The city's outstanding park system and two civic centers provided public sites for recreation and community activities. In the 1980s, an FBI report declared Florissant to have the second-lowest crime rate in the nation for a city its size.

Florissant today continues to build on its two-hundred-year past. Historic Florissant, Inc., a local preservation group, works to restore buildings in the Old Town District, while the city's building regulations and commercial guidelines ensure the district's historic integrity. Meanwhile, in the fields where Ed Arkes played as a boy, the houses and yards of postwar suburbia have begun to acquire their own place in the city's history.

❶ JOHN B. MYERS HOUSE AND BARN
180 West Dunn Road

Motorists passing through the interchange where Interstate 170 meets Interstate 270 may see a building on the north side of the highway which looks strangely out of place. The John B. Myers House, built in the late 1860s, barely escaped demolition when the U.S. Department of Transportation decided to extend the Inner Belt (I-170) in 1974. The highway was rerouted and Historic Florissant, Inc., took ownership of the Victorian-era house and barn and subsequently restored both buildings. Today Historic Florissant leases commercial space in the buildings. Present occupants include antique, art, and craft shops and a deli. The complex is open Tuesday through Saturday from 10:00 A.M. until 4:00 P.M. and Sundays from 1:00 P.M. until 5:00 P.M. Call 921-4606 for information.

❷ TAILLE DE NOYER
1 Rue Taille de Noyer (on the campus of McCluer High School)

Around 1800 a log cabin was built on the Spanish land grant of Hyacinthe Deshetres. The cabin took its name, Taille de Noyer, from the grove of walnut trees in which it stood. John Mullanphy, a prominent St. Louis philanthropist, purchased the cabin in 1805 and for several years used it as a hunting lodge and trading post. Mullanphy gave the cabin to his daughter Jane and her husband, Charles Chambers, as a wedding gift in 1817. The house and property remained in the family for nearly 140 years, during which time various additions to the house enlarged it from three rooms to twenty-three. In 1954 the R-2 School District purchased twenty acres of the estate, and six years later, when the school district needed more land to build a new high school, the house was threatened with demolition. The Florissant Valley Historical Society worked out a plan with the school district whereby money was raised to move Taille de Noyer two hundred yards to the west to save it from destruction. The Florissant Valley Historical Society has restored the house, which now serves as a museum. Taille de Noyer is open to the public Wednesday through Sunday from 1:00 P.M. until 4:00 P.M. There is an admission charge. Call 524-1100 for more information.

❸ DUCHESNE SUBDIVISION AND OUR LADY OF FATIMA CATHOLIC CHURCH
Dunn Road and New Florissant Road

Construction in Duchesne, one of Florissant's earliest subdivisions, began in the late 1940s. Joseph H. Vatterott bought a parcel of farmland, owned for over 150 years by the Arkes family, and developed a series of circular, self-contained tracts. A devout Catholic, Vatterott named the subdivision in honor of Mother Rose Philippine Duchesne (see tour site #6), whose work in Florissant led to her beatification in 1940. All the streets in the subdivision bear the names of saints. Many of the curving roads are cul-de-sacs, lined with the three-bedroom, brick ranch houses that were popular with young families in the postwar years.

The community's growth led to the founding of a new Catholic church, the first in Florissant since 1866. Our Lady of Fatima Parish was established in 1950, and the congregation celebrated its first mass in a temporary frame church built by Vatterott on land that the developer donated. In 1953 a permanent church and school building was erected at 4550 Washington, on the eastern edge of the subdivision. Our Lady of Fatima Church testifies to the growth of Duchesne—during the late 1950s, five new parishes evolved from the church. At its peak, the parish school enrollment exceeded eleven hundred students. The later addition of the Duchesne Hills Shopping Center and the Duchesne Elementary School helped make the subdivision a self-contained neighborhood.

4 NARROW GAUGE RAILROAD STATION
1060 Rue Ste. Catherine

Built in 1878, the West End Narrow Gauge Railroad Station stood at the end of a sixteen-mile route which ran north and west from the corner of Grand and Olive in St. Louis. Erastus Wells, who had financed St. Louis' first streetcar company some twenty years earlier, formed the railroad company to provide transportation to the summer homes of the elite in St. Louis County, including his own in Wellston. The steam train made four round

trips daily. The journey from Grand and Olive to Florissant took slightly more than an hour, with a fare of three cents per mile. In 1892 the railroad converted to electricity, and trolley service on the Hodiamont line to Florissant continued until 1931. In 1969, through the efforts of Historic Florissant, Inc., and the City of Florissant, the station building was relocated to its present site in Tower Court Park, where it serves as a visitors' center operated by the Florissant Chamber of Commerce. The center is open Monday through Friday from 9:00 A.M. until 5:00 P.M.

5 SACRED HEART CHURCH
751 Jefferson Street

German Catholic families began moving to Florissant in the mid-nineteenth century, but they had to travel sixteen miles to St. Louis to make confession in German. In 1866 the village's German Catholic community received permission from Archbishop Peter Richard Kenrick to erect a church and school of their own, and Sacred Heart thus became Florissant's second church. The church site, at the approximate center and highest elevation of the town, had long been a coveted parcel of land. The original building, blessed by Father Pierre DeSmet at its dedication in 1867, was razed and replaced by the present church in 1892. Flanking the church are the former *Herz Jesu Schule*, constructed in 1889 and now a preschool and kindergarten, and the Sacred Heart Convent, built in 1904. Today Sacred Heart Parish serves nearly 1,430 families. About five hundred students from grades one through eight attend the Sacred Heart Elementary School.

For years the West End Narrow Gauge Railroad Station in Florissant marked the end of the sixteen-mile line. Now the building is home to the Florissant Chamber of Commerce. Courtesy of Historic Florissant, Inc.

The convent wing at Old St. Ferdinand's Shrine was expanded when the Sisters of Loretto came in 1847. When they left forty years later, the eastern half (right side of photograph) was taken down to restore the building to the size it was when Mother Philippine Duchesne lived there. Missouri Historical Society Photograph and Print Collection.

❻ OLD ST. FERDINAND'S SHRINE
1 Rue Ste. François

Old St. Ferdinand's Shrine is the oldest Catholic church building between the Mississippi River and the Rocky Mountains. The Federal-style church, built in 1820, replaced an earlier log structure, which was erected upon the founding of St. Ferdinand Parish in 1789. The convent wing, to the right of the church, was built in 1819 for Sister Rose Philippine Duchesne and became the Mother House of the Sisters of the Sacred Heart, the first of that order to be established outside France. Duchesne and the sisters ran a school for Native American girls in the convent, as well as the first novitiate for women in Upper Louisiana. The Sisters of the Sacred Heart moved from their convent in 1846. The following year the Sisters of Loretto took up residence in the convent and constructed several large buildings in the area, all of which were razed when the order moved in 1887.

In the 1880s the church was enlarged and its Victorian Gothic steeple was built. A new altar was installed with relics of St. Valentine enshrined in a waxen figure in a glass crypt below. When Archbishop Joseph E. Ritter changed the parish boundaries, a new St. Ferdinand Church and Convent were built about a mile west of the old church. The Friends of Old St. Ferdinand undertook the restoration of the buildings, which are now maintained as a museum. Tours may be arranged by calling 837-2110.

❼ COLDWATER COMMONS PARK
Coldwater and Fountain Creeks

This ten-acre park with walkways and a gazebo was once part of the Florissant Commons, a seven-square-mile area extending south to present-day Kinloch, where eighteenth-century villagers pastured their livestock, collected firewood, and cut timber. West of Coldwater Creek, extending almost from New Halls Ferry on the north, to Bridgeton on the south, and westward to the Missouri River, were the Common Fields of St. Ferdinand. In contrast to the undivided commons, the common fields were long, narrow strips allotted to individual residents for agricultural use. Standing on the bank of Coldwater Creek today, facing west, one sees only the brick and asphalt of the Florissant Meadows Shopping Center.

❽ FLORISSANT CIVIC CENTER
Parker Road and Waterford Drive

Since its opening in 1972, the Florissant Civic Center has served as a symbol for the community, offering residents of all ages a wide variety of recreational activities. The two-level facility, built at a cost of $2.3 million, includes an indoor swimming pool; a gymnasium/multipurpose room; a six-hundred-seat theater equipped to handle stage productions, concerts, films and recitals; a youth lounge; meeting rooms; an exercise room; and a two-hundred-foot ice rink. Adjoining the civic center is the thirty-acre Florissant Valley Park, known for its rose garden. Florissant's extensive park system includes six recreational parks, eleven neighborhood parks, and two civic centers, the second being the John F. Kennedy Community Center on Howdershell Road.

This log structure served as the St. Stanislaus Seminary and mission school for Native American children from 1823 until 1849. Missouri Historical Society Photograph and Print Collection.

9 MUSEUM OF WESTERN JESUIT MISSIONS, FORMERLY THE ST. STANISLAUS SEMINARY

700 Howdershell Road

Established in 1823 as a mission school for Native American children, St. Stanislaus Seminary was the first Jesuit novitiate west of the Mississippi. Bishop Louis W. V. DuBourg donated the farmland on which the seminary was built, and several log structures erected in the 1820s housed the school. By 1830 usage of the school had declined and the seminary began to concentrate entirely on preparing missionaries. Missionary priest Pierre DeSmet, called "Black Robe" by tribes of the upper Missouri River, received his seminary training at St. Stanislaus and is buried in the cemetery there.

The seminary's first permanent structure, the Rock Building, dates to 1849. It was built by the Jesuits in residence there, who fired bricks and hauled limestone blocks from the bluffs of the Missouri River. The seminarians also cultivated grapes on part of the seminary's farmland. From the 1820s until the 1950s, St. Stanislaus operated a winery that produced DeSmet Wine, a pure white wine for sacramental use, along with several other varieties for commercial consumption.

St. Stanislaus Seminary, which trained thousands of priests and served as a school of Saint Louis University, closed in 1971. While most of the seminary buildings were sold to the Gateway College of Evangelism, the Jesuits retain ownership of the Rock Building, which is now a museum housing relics and displays of Jesuit instruction. Many of its furnishings and artifacts were made by novices and used in the seminary since the 1850s. Tours of the Museum of Western Jesuit Missions are available. Call the museum at 837-3525 for information.

FOR MORE INFORMATION

Florissant Valley Historical Society. *Florissant Valley Historical Society Quarterly.* Vol. 1 (1959) to present.

Hannon, Robert E., ed. *St. Louis: Its Neighborhoods and Neighbors, Landmarks and Milestones.* St. Louis: St. Louis Regional Planning and Growth Association, 1986.

Schmitz, Antoinette Douglas. "Our Florissant." *Missouri Historical Society Bulletin* 24 (July 1968), pp. 153-59.

Starbird, Adele Chomeau. "Stories My Father Told Me." *Missouri Historical Society Bulletin* 7 (July 1951), pp. 473-81.

Special thanks to Rosemary Davison, Historic Florissant, Inc., Ed Arkes, Elizabeth Moore, Our Lady of Fatima Parish, Catherine Vatterott, and the residents of Florissant.

ST. LOUIS' "ORIGINAL" URBAN LANDSCAPE: COLONIAL SETTLEMENTS AND HOW THEY'VE CHANGED

ST. CHARLES

**From Florissant: Interstate 270 west to Interstate 70.
Interstate 70 west across the Missouri River on the
Blanchette Bridge (the first site in this chapter). Exit at
State Highway 94 (First State Capitol/Weldon Spring)
to enter St. Charles.**

This view of St. Charles in the 1850s shows a self-sufficient river town known as a jumping-off point for settlers
and traders heading west. Today St. Charles is a growing
commuter suburb closely tied to the bistate region.
Engraving from *Meyer's Universum*. Missouri Historical
Society Photograph and Print Collection.

A symbol of both separation and connection, the
Blanchette Bridge stretches across the Missouri River
to link the town of St. Charles to St. Louis County.
Once a small, self-sufficient community, St. Charles
today is a vital part of the expanding bistate region.

The city's roots, like the other sites in this section
of *Where We Live,* lie deep in the eighteenth century.
In 1769 Louis Blanchette, a French hunter, founded
the settlement that became St. Charles. He called the
village *Les Petites Côtes,* or "the little hills," for a range of
foothills rising along the northern bank of the Missouri
River above its confluence with the Mississippi. After
Spain gained control of the Upper Louisiana Territory
from France, the Spanish founded the San Carlos
Borromeo Church in the settlement; the name was later
anglicized to St. Charles.

Following the formal transfer of Upper Louisiana
to the United States in 1804, St. Charles became an
outfitting point for explorers, settlers, and traders heading west. Meriwether Lewis rendezvoused with William
Clark in St. Charles, and from there they began their
famed expedition up the Missouri River by keelboat
with forty-five men. Lewis and Clark took with them
supplies purchased in St. Charles, including castor oil
made from beans grown and pressed at a factory on
South Main Street.

Although St. Charles boosters called the city the
"castor oil capital of the world," brewing and tobacco
industries also flourished in the nineteenth century.
Workers dried, cured, and rolled tobacco shipped from
Kentucky and North Carolina into cigars at several factories in the city. One of these factories was the St. Charles

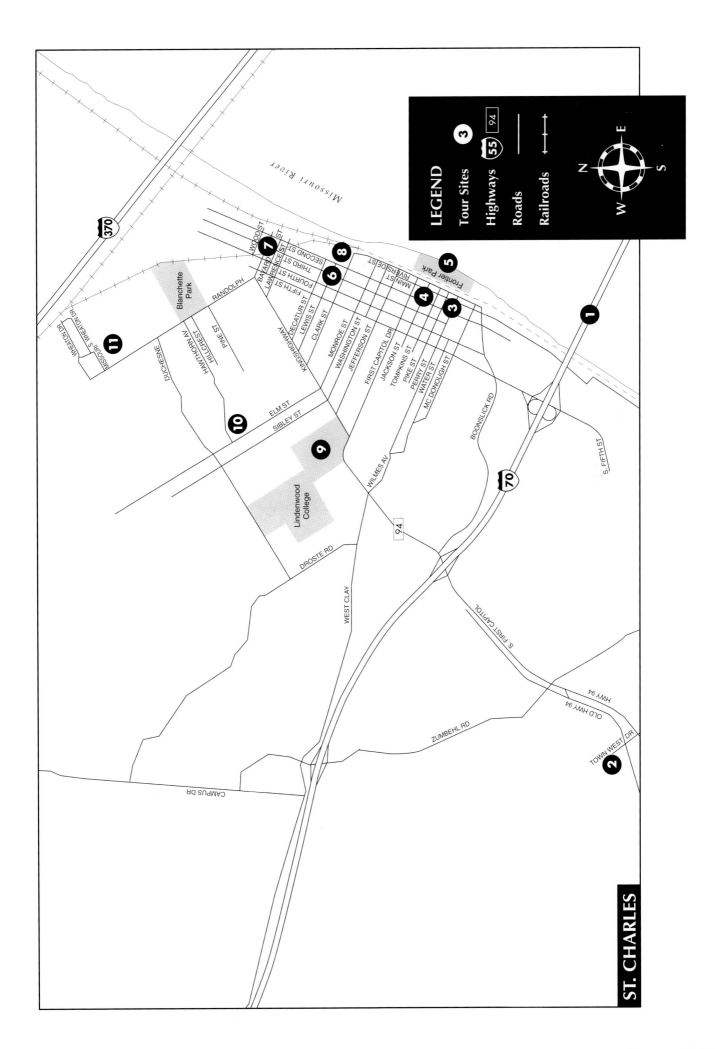

ST. CHARLES

Tobacco Company, located on Adams Street near the river. The city's most significant and longest-lasting industry, however, was the St. Charles Car Company (later the American Car and Foundry Company), which produced luxury rail passenger cars at its massive plant on the riverfront at North Main Street.

St. Charles grew slowly but steadily. The city's original boundaries encompassed the area from the Missouri River west to Fifth Street, and from Barbour Street on the south to Tecumseh on the north. In 1869 the boundaries were extended westward to Tenth Street between Barbour and Kingshighway. Subsequent expansions accompanied growth and development. From 1850 to 1950, the city's population rose from 1,498 to 14,314.

In 1958 the five-lane Blanchette Bridge opened and St. Charles entered a period of rapid change. St. Charles annexed vast amounts of farmland, doubling the size of the city in 1960. The self-sufficient city began to take on a new identity as a commuter suburb. Developers bought up large parcels of land and built subdivisions for workers employed by new industries located on both sides of the Missouri River. New houses in St. Charles cost considerably less than comparable housing in St. Louis County, and by 1990 the city's population had swelled to 54,555. St. Charles County has become the fastest growing county in Missouri and one of the fastest growing regions in the country.

While looking ahead to a promising future, St. Charles is vigorously preserving its past. The South Main Preservation Society, organized in 1972, saved the city's historic riverfront district from demolition and created the largest historic district in Missouri. South Main is now an active commercial neighborhood featuring restaurants and craft and antique shops in storefronts dating to the early nineteenth century. The Frenchtown Community Corporation organizes preservation work in its neighborhood along North Second Street and has developed a low-interest loan program to help people renovate homes. Frenchtown's successful nomination to the National Register of Historic Places in 1991 has encouraged efforts to stabilize and revitalize the district. The Midtown community, located near the Lindenwood College campus, is also active in preserving the historic integrity of its neighborhood.

Efforts to preserve historic St. Charles have created conflict between residents and developers, and disputes over land use have become political issues. Zoning ordinances now protect historic parts of the city from demolition, and preservationists continue their work in finding adaptive uses for historic structures. Through dialogue and debate, people have come to see that the seemingly opposite sections of "old" and "new" St. Charles actually complement each other. St. Charles civic leaders promote the city as a good place to live in and visit: St. Charles is both a suburban residential community and a tourist center featuring costumed festivals and reenactments in the historic district. Like that of

Cahokia, Illinois, St. Charles' motto—"Preserving the Past for Progress in the Future"—is a plan of action as well as a promotional slogan.

❶ BLANCHETTE MEMORIAL BRIDGE
Interstate 70 crossing the Missouri River

This pair of thirty-nine-hundred-foot bridges that span the Missouri River play a vital role in the life of St. Charles and St. Charles County. The present five-lane westbound bridge was hailed as "a milestone in the progress of St. Charles and St. Charles County" when it opened in 1958. Historically, access to St. Charles from other parts of the St. Louis region had been difficult at best. One early historian recalled that when trying to cross the Missouri River in 1834, "waiting up to six hours for a ferry . . . was not uncommon." A string of bridge collapses and failures during the nineteenth and early twentieth centuries kept St. Charles from forging strong economic ties with St. Louis and helped shape the city's future as a largely self-sufficient community.

Within two years of its opening, the first Interstate 70 bridge was constantly congested with traffic. Construction began on a "companion" bridge in 1978, and one year later a new bridge for eastbound traffic opened just south of the first one. In 1979 the structures were dedicated as the Blanchette Memorial Bridge in honor of Louis Blanchette, the founder of St. Charles. The city's rapid growth as a suburban residential community can be directly tied to the opening of the Blanchette Bridge, which gives tens of thousands of commuters a viable route between their jobs and their homes. As the St. Charles area continues to expand, new multiple-lane bridges on Highway 40 and Highway 115 will help ease congestion. Plans are also under way to extend MetroLink from St. Louis County to St. Charles County; MetroLink could accommodate an estimated eleven thousand passengers per day.

❷ THE "GOLDEN TRIANGLE"
Corner of Pralle Road at Town West Drive

Motorists turning west on Pralle Road from Highway 94 will encounter a telling juxtaposition. Both farmland and auto-related commercial establishments line the highway. The farm on the hill is a reminder of the days when the area bounded by Interstate 70, Highway 94, and Highway 40 was filled with farmsteads. In recent years this area has come to be known as the "Golden Triangle" for the housing explosion that has occurred there. Development companies snatched up available, inexpensive land and built subdivisions for commuters who work at local industries such as McDonnell-Douglas and General Motors. Affordable new housing led to a 54 percent increase in the population of St. Charles County in the 1970s. Some of those new residents live in subdivisions in the Golden Triangle.

❸ SOUTH MAIN HISTORIC DISTRICT
Bounded by Madison, Second, Jefferson, and the alley behind South Main Street

Tourists and shoppers charmed by the historical ambiance of the South Main district's restaurants, craft stores, and specialty shops may not realize that the community has undergone a major transformation in the last thirty years. After a long past as the city's commercial center, South Main kept few businesses in the 1960s. Moreover, many of the street's nineteenth-century structures badly needed repair. The threat of urban renewal projects demolishing a number of historic buildings sparked the formation of a grassroots preservation movement that resulted in the establishment of the South Main Preservation Society in 1972. This organization helped get the South Main district declared the first national historic district in Missouri. Today guidelines and ordinances control the use of signs, colors, building materials, and plans for additions in order to preserve the historic integrity of the community. Largely comprised of district shopkeepers and residents, the South Main Preservation Society is very active in helping shape future development in the community. The society uses its newsletter, the *Star*, to educate the public about matters that affect the South Main district.

Shown here as a busy nineteenth-century thoroughfare, South Main Street is once again a thriving historic commercial avenue in St. Charles. Missouri Historical Society Photograph and Print Collection.

The First State Capitol Building, seen here in the late nineteenth century, underwent renovation in the 1960s when it became a registered national historic place. This helped spur the restoration of many more historic buildings on South Main. Missouri Historical Society Photograph and Print Collection.

❹ FIRST MISSOURI STATE CAPITOL
208-216 South Main Street

In 1820, as statehood became a certainty for the Missouri Territory, legislators chose an undeveloped tract of land in the center of the territory to develop as "the City of Jefferson," Missouri's permanent capital. In the meantime, however, nine cities vied for the honor of hosting a temporary seat of government. St. Charles, by then a growing trade center on the Missouri River, offered to furnish free meeting space for the legislators. From 1821 until 1826, the Missouri government functioned in the upper floors of this Federal-style brick building owned by local merchants Charles and Ruluff Peck and carpenter Chauncey Shepard. The Pecks and Shepard resided on the ground floor. In 1961 the state of Missouri bought the capitol complex and began a ten-year restoration project that spurred the revitalization of St. Charles' historic core. The First Missouri State Capitol State Historic Site is open to the public Monday through Saturday from 10:00 A.M. until 5:00 P.M. and Sunday from 12:00 P.M. until 6:00 P.M. (summer) and 12:00 P.M. until 5:00 P.M. (winter) for a small entrance fee. Call 946-9282 for more information.

❺ FRONTIER PARK

Frontier Park is the site of many of St. Charles' annual festivals. The sixteen-acre riverfront park takes in the area once developed by the Missouri-Kansas-Texas Railroad (better known as the MKT, or Katy, Railroad). The railroad right of way has been transformed into a hiking and bicycling trail that begins in Frontier Park and continues thirty-eight miles southwestward to Marthasville, Missouri. When completed, the trail, managed by the Missouri Department of Natural Resources, will stretch two hundred miles to Sedalia.

The MKT depot, built in 1892 at the foot of Tompkins Street, was moved a short distance to its present site in Frontier Park in 1978. Until 1986 the building housed the Greater St. Charles Convention and Tourism Bureau. Efforts are under way to lease the building to the National Museum of Transport, located in St. Louis County, for the creation of a train museum.

Considered the grandest of its kind when it was built in 1909, the *Goldenrod* showboat is docked at the south end of Frontier Park. The *Goldenrod* plied the Mississippi and Ohio Rivers in the early decades of this century, presenting theatrical entertainment in an opulent setting for those who lived in small river towns. The city of St. Charles owns the *Goldenrod*, which is now a national historic landmark. A Broadway production firm has restored the showboat and operates a dinner theater on board.

❻ ACADEMY OF THE SACRED HEART
619 North Second Street

In 1818 St. Philippine Duchesne brought the Order of the Sacred Heart, founded in Paris, to St. Charles, a place she described as "the most distant village in the United States." The order soon opened a convent and school. The school, begun in a French-style frame house that Duchesne rented from Marie Duquette, was the first free school for girls west of the Mississippi. Although the first school building was razed, the original convent, built in 1834, still stands. Tours of the Shrine of St. Philippine Duchesne are available by appointment. Call 946-6127 for more information.

❼ FRENCHTOWN HISTORIC DISTRICT
Roughly bounded by North Fifth, Clark, the Missouri River, and Tecumseh

Named for the early French settlers who first resided in the community, the Frenchtown area began to take on its present contours in the mid-nineteenth century, when many German immigrants came to the neighborhood. By the late 1850s North Second Street was dotted with two-story brick buildings that combined commercial space on the first floor with residential space on the second. Butchers, bakers, shoemakers, tinners, grocers, and dry-goods merchants operated shops in the 800 and 900 blocks of North Second. Frenchtown boasts a wide range of architectural styles, from the ornamental cast-iron front of the Simmerman Building at 804-806 North Second to the French Colonial design of the Alfermann House at 233 Montgomery. The district is listed on the National Register of Historic Places. Today Frenchtown is known for its numerous antique shops housed in historic storefronts. The Frenchtown Community Corporation, comprised of residents and store owners, works to stabilize and revitalize the community as a residential and commercial area.

❽ AMERICAN CAR AND FOUNDRY COMPANY
600-700 North Second Street

The American Car and Foundry Company, for over a century the mainstay of St. Charles' economy, began as a building and maintenance facility for the North Missouri Railroad, which connected St. Charles to Hannibal and St. Joseph. Tradition holds that in 1873, after the city refused to locate a railroad bridge near the center of town, the railroad company closed its shops and withdrew the labor force. This prompted a group of local citizens to organize their own company. They leased the former railroad shops and began to manufacture railroad freight cars. The St. Charles Car Company gained a

The massive American Car and Foundry Company plant on the riverfront was a vital part of St. Charles' economy. At its peak during the wartime years in the 1940s, ACF employed three thousand people, many of them residents of the Frenchtown neighborhood. Courtesy of the St. Charles County Historical Society.

national and international market for its cars, and by 1890 the company employed eighteen hundred men. In 1899 it became the American Car and Foundry Company (ACF). By 1910 at least one member of nearly every family in Frenchtown worked for ACF. During World War I, ACF manufactured military equipment and built more than fifty thousand Army escort wagons. In World War II the Frenchtown plant produced tanks, railroad hospital cars, and other military items. ACF opened its Aircraft Division in 1951 and began production of the U.S. Air Force B-47 bomber. The St. Charles plant phased out rail passenger car production in 1959, but it continues to research and test cars built in other ACF factories.

9 LINDENWOOD COLLEGE
209 South Kingshighway

Named for the grove of linden trees in which its campus is set, Lindenwood College was established by Mary Easton Sibley in 1827. Sibley, the daughter of prominent St. Louisan Rufus Easton, had taught Native Americans at Fort Osage in western Missouri, where her husband, Major George C. Sibley, was stationed. In 1826 the couple moved to St. Charles, where Mary soon began teaching a small group of girls in their home. A few years later the Sibleys erected a log building on their farm to serve as a boarding school for young women.

In 1853 the school was incorporated as Lindenwood Female College and turned over to the Presbyterian Church. In 1860 Sibley Hall, a three-story brick building, was completed. Sibley Hall is listed on the National Register of Historic Places. Today Lindenwood is a private, coeducational liberal arts college with graduate and undergraduate programs. About forty-five hundred students enrolled at the college in 1993-94.

10 HAWTHORN HILLS SUBDIVISION
Hawthorn Avenue at Elm

The opening of the Hawthorn Hills subdivision in early 1959 represented something new for St. Charles—development of a virtually self-sufficient neighborhood away from the historic heart of the town. Developed by the Charles F. Vatterott Company, Hawthorn Hills was laid out between Duchesne Catholic High School and a public elementary school. Its 120 three-bedroom homes, built by the R. W. Chamberlain Building Company, were advertised as "family-size houses in a working man's price range." Prices of the homes ranged from $13,690 to $17,590. Vatterott's design also called for a shopping plaza. The plaza, then as now, included a supermarket, drugstore, gas station, and several small shops, giving residents the option of shopping in their own neighborhood rather than in the city's old commercial district.

11 ST. CHARLES BORROMEO CEMETERY
West Randolph Street between South Wheaton Drive and Mission Court

The St. Charles Borromeo Cemetery is the final resting place for some of the city's most significant early figures. Among those buried here are Louis Blanchette, St. Charles' founder, who established the settlement as a military outpost in 1769. Adjacent to Blanchette's memorial, a large marble stone marks the grave of Jean Baptiste Pointe DuSable, a Haitian-born fur trader of French and African descent who, in the 1770s, became the first non–Native American settler of the Chicago area. DuSable and his family moved to St. Charles around 1800. They lived in a stone house at the corner of Second and Decatur streets in Frenchtown.

FOR MORE INFORMATION

Hannon, Robert E., ed. *St. Louis: Its Neighborhoods and Neighbors, Landmarks and Milestones.* St. Louis: St. Louis Regional Planning and Growth Association, 1986.
Schneider, Sue. *Old St. Charles.* Tucson, Ariz.: Patrice Press, 1993.

Special thanks to Stephen Powell, Christy Brodeur, Kathleen Eggers, Archie Scott, Carol Wilkins, Katharine T. Corbett, Eric Sandweiss, David Miles, Julie Harding, Kirsten Hammerstrom, David Schultz, and the residents of St. Charles.

FROM THE BREWERY OF
LEMP
ST·LOUIS·MO·

WESTERN CABLE
RAILWAY COMPANY.

4

CENTRAL ST. LOUIS:

THE NINETEENTH-CENTURY CITY

CENTRAL ST. LOUIS:
THE NINETEENTH-CENTURY CITY

On May 27, 1896, a tornado ripped through three of the neighborhoods discussed in this section of *Where We Live*. Soulard, Cherokee-Lemp, and the Near South Side were all profoundly affected by the storm, which destroyed homes, businesses, and parks alike. However, the residents of these neighborhoods, mostly first- and second-generation Euro-American immigrants, immediately set about repairing the $13 million worth of damages. The repair job was so complete that few scars of the storm can be seen today. In fact, the Lafayette Park area of the Near South Side—which was hit especially hard and took the longest time to recover—looks better than ever.

A few miles to the north, the Hyde Park neighborhood was out of the swath of the storm, but half a century later it too would face a destructive force: the construction of Interstate 70. Unlike the streets devastated by the tornado, most of the homes that were destroyed here by the construction of the highway were not rebuilt; it took a marathon effort by preservationists to save just one building, the Bissell Mansion. Worse yet, the interstate divided the neighborhood, putting up a barrier between the residential district and the industries that had helped build the neighborhood.

Of course, all four of these communities have faced crises since; for example, Hyde Park's highway trouble also affected the three communities to the south. But throughout they have persevered, even prospered.

The response of these communities to the crises they have faced partly explains why they can be considered "central" St. Louis; they are central not only in terms of geography and settlement patterns, but also in terms of spirit. Home to some of St. Louis' most prominent and longest lasting industries (Mallinckrodt Chemical, the Anheuser-Busch Brewery, and the Ralston Purina Corporation are only the most obvious examples), as well as to the many ethnic groups who followed the industries into the neighborhoods to work, live, and raise their families, these communities developed in the nineteenth

century as self-sufficient units. They had their own churches, shops, parks, and restaurants, all within walking distance of work and home. Their independence was their strength, and when trouble came each community pulled together to face it down.

Today, these neighborhoods represent the best aspects of "city living" for many St. Louisans. Weekly trips to Soulard Market, for example, continue to be a St. Louis tradition after over 150 years, while the antique shops along Cherokee Street and restored Victorian manses in the Lafayette Park neighborhood draw thousands of visitors year after year. St. Louisans continue to be fascinated by the parks, the architecture, the street names, the smell of brewer's yeast in the air.

But it is not simply the nostalgia of visitors that keeps these neighborhoods going; it is also the commitment of the longtime residents who have chosen to stay in the neighborhoods while their neighbors were heading for the county, combined with the courage of the new residents—the preservationists, the rehabbers, the entrepreneurs.

These four communities, like many others in the St. Louis area, have faced many problems in the past, but they have all persevered. Even their independent natures remain, in spite of their complex relationship with the larger city and metropolitan area. As other St. Louis communities struggle with the problems that confront them, they can look to the neighborhoods of Soulard, Cherokee-Lemp, the Near South Side, and Hyde Park for inspiration and guidance.

SOULARD

From St. Louis: Interstate 44 east
to Interstate 55 north. Exit at
Park Avenue. Turn left (north)
on Park to Park and South Ninth.

The new Soulard Market building
and Civic Center opened at
Lafayette and South Eighth Street
in May 1929. A weekly visit to
Soulard Market is still a ritual
for thousands of St. Louisans.
Missouri Historical Society
Photograph and Print Collection.

Soulard, which extends from Seventh Street westward to Interstate 55, retains much of the diversity and vibrancy that characterized the neighborhood in the nineteenth century. Festive celebrations mark Mardi Gras, Bastille Day, and St. Patrick's Day, commemorating the rich ethnic past of the community. The area, originally part of the city's common fields, was given to Antoine Soulard, Surveyor General of Upper Louisiana, by the Spanish governor in the 1790s as payment for his services. Soulard's widow, Julia, later donated two city blocks for use as a public market; this market is still a vital part of the neighborhood and still bears the family name.

By the mid-nineteenth century, some Irish and larger numbers of Germans had settled in Soulard. Later in the century, many Eastern European immigrant groups populated the area, including Czechs, Slovaks, Croatians, and Lebanese. Most predominant of these were the Czechs, whose settlement in Soulard gave rise to the name "Bohemian Hill," a reference to the elevation in the heart of the neighborhood.

Nineteenth-century Soulard was a walking neighborhood, self-contained in the physical sense, with public buildings, churches, businesses, shops, and residences all clustered together. Human feet, not wheels or hoofs, were the heaviest users of streets. Residents could walk from home to work (at one of the neighborhood's several breweries or factories), to church, to a meeting hall, and then to a tavern within half an hour; this is a characteristic of all the neighborhoods that make up Central St. Louis.

The density of the neighborhood is evident in the many blocks of red-brick row houses, although many buildings, including most of the alley houses, are gone. Still, the four-family dwellings that survive, placed flush with the street, are situated so closely together on some blocks as to give the appearance of being joined together in one building; they give the visitor a good idea of what life was like here a century ago.

Although always culturally diverse, Soulard was, and is, a close community in more than just the physical sense. The neighborhood has a long history of charitable and benevolent associations. Throughout their histories the area's many churches, including St. Vincent de Paul and Saints Peter and Paul, have established programs to aid the needy. Currently these two parishes, in partnership with Trinity Lutheran Church, sponsor a neighborhood meals program and an overnight shelter for homeless men.

Like much of the working class in the nineteenth century, most of Soulard's residents worked long hours for low pay. In 1880, for example, a cigar maker typically worked a sixty-hour week for which he earned seven dollars. Yearly expenses frequently exceeded annual earnings in those days before unemployment insurance or social security. To address their own needs the neighborhood's various ethnic groups founded fraternal associations that offered benefits such as insurance and aided newly arrived immigrants in locating relatives, jobs, and lodging. The German *Turnverein* and the

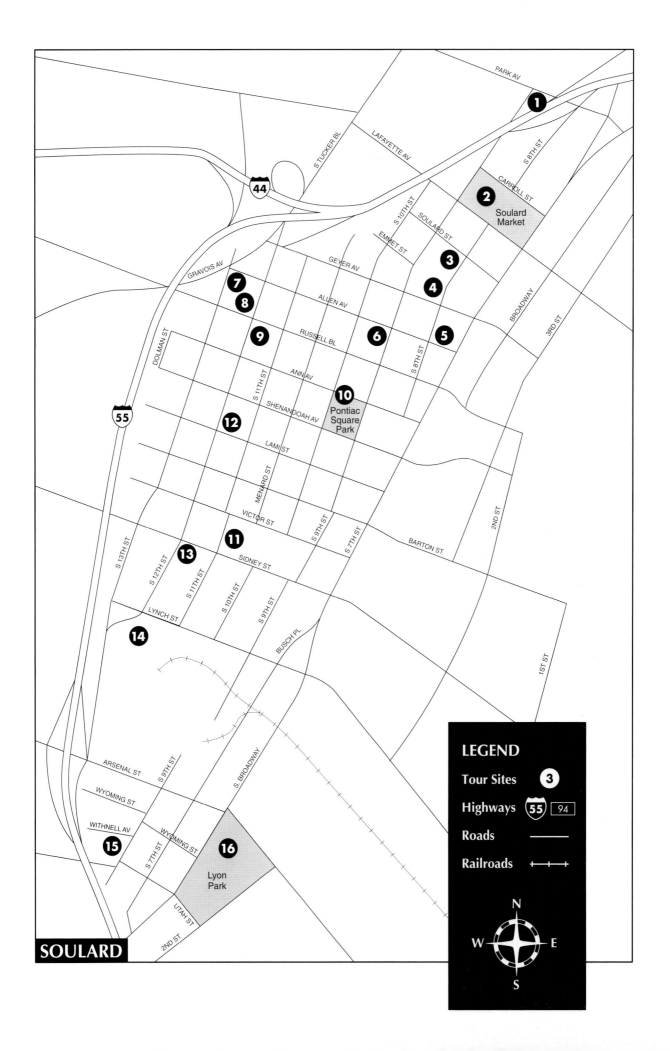

Czech *Sokol* fostered ethnic pride, preserving immigrant culture through programs centered on physical fitness, drama, music, and language.

Soulard has endured its share of difficult times. A devastating tornado in May 1896 wrought extensive damage on hundreds of churches, homes, and businesses in the neighborhood. When the city offered little financial help, residents rebuilt the area themselves. They restored some buildings, such as the Trinity Lutheran Church, in less than a year.

In this century, the construction of the Third Street Highway in the early '50s and urban renewal projects of the '60s and '70s destroyed many homes and businesses and threatened the integrity of the neighborhood. As immigrant groups prospered and moved out of Soulard, more rural whites from southern Missouri, Arkansas, Tennessee, and Kentucky moved in. These newcomers, along with the ethnic elderly, banded together to protect the neighborhood, parts of which were threatened with demolition. Simultaneously, historic preservationists and "urban homesteaders"—people who bought, moved into, and renovated historic structures—also became involved in redeveloping Soulard.

The efforts of these diverse groups have kept the neighborhood from being destroyed. The Soulard Neighborhood Improvement Association, founded in 1969, succeeded in placing Soulard on the National Register of Historic Places in 1972. The Soulard Restoration Group, established in 1974, has been active in preserving historic structures as well as developing neighborhood clean-up and crime prevention programs. The neighborhood groups, combined with institutions such as Youth Education and Health in Soulard, which teaches construction skills to out-of-work teens, ensure that the Soulard neighborhood will continue to thrive.

❶ ST. VINCENT DE PAUL CHURCH
South Ninth and Park Streets

Though Bishop Peter Richard Kenrick laid the cornerstone for St. Vincent de Paul Church on St. Patrick's Day, 1844, the church served German as well as Irish parishioners. The congregation was so mixed, in fact, that until 1932 two high masses were said on Sundays, one in English and the other in German. The parish was one of the first in the city to establish a conference of the St. Vincent de Paul Society, an international Catholic organization of lay persons dedicated to helping those in need. The society had its U.S. founding in St. Louis in November 1845, the same month St. Vincent de Paul Church was consecrated. The parish was physically severed from the Soulard neighborhood with the construction of the Third Street Highway in the early 1950s. Despite this, the church maintains an active role in community charitable works, sponsoring a daily meals-for-the-hungry program, aiding in a shelter for homeless men, and offering a Headstart program in what was formerly the parish school.

❷ SOULARD MARKET
Lafayette Avenue between South Seventh and Ninth Streets

In 1842 Julia Cerré Soulard, widow of Antoine Soulard, donated two blocks to the City of St. Louis with the stipulation that the land be used as a public marketplace. Buying and selling on the site had taken place since a much earlier time, perhaps as early as 1779, a date that would fix it as St. Louis' third public marketplace. Today, Soulard Market is the city's oldest existing public market, and it is the only one municipally operated.

For many years, sellers hawked their products from wagons or trucks, lined in rows under the sun. Then in the late 1920s, the city commissioned a market building, including a community center, taking the design of the south entrance from the Foundling Hospital in Florence, the work of Renaissance architect Filippo Brunelleschi. This allowed the present-day arrangement in which the city rents stalls to merchants selling a spectrum of wares, such as fresh fruit and vegetables, meat and fish, dairy products, flowers, handicrafts, and even shoes. The market's history lives on in a kind of sellers-and-buyers dynasty, with St. Louisans passing on to their children the lease on a merchant's stall or the tradition of a weekly visit.

❸ TRINITY LUTHERAN CHURCH
South Eighth and Soulard Streets

The parish of Trinity Lutheran Church was organized in the late 1830s by a group of immigrants from Saxony, a region in Germany. In 1842 they built their first church, on Lombard Street, but the congregation expanded quickly and outgrew the building in only twenty years. In the midst of the Civil War, parishioners donated and raised enough money to build a new church at Eighth and Soulard Streets, which celebrated its first service in 1865 unencumbered by debt. When the cyclone of 1896 destroyed that building, the church was quickly rebuilt on the same spot. Today, the congregation consists of over four hundred adults. Next door, the Trinity Lutheran School, which began operating in the 1830s on the ship from Saxony, serves approximately ninety-five children yearly in grades K-8.

④ ST. ELIZABETH DAY NURSERY
1833 South Eighth Street

St. Elizabeth Day Nursery first opened its doors in 1915 as a settlement house under the supervision of the Catholic Central *Verein*. Founded by internationally renowned Catholic sociologist and journalist Frederick P. Kenkel and operated by the Sisters of Notre Dame, the nursery served children aged six months to fourteen years, with supplementary services for adults. It offered clothes, medical care, a nursery, and kindergarten classes to children of working mothers. For adults, it provided classes in English, citizenship, and religion, along with free employment services and legal advice. By 1916, the nursery assisted an average of forty people a day. Members' donations and an allocation from United Charities helped fund nursery activities. St. Elizabeth Day Nursery served Soulard residents until its closing in 1987.

⑤ SAINTS PETER AND PAUL CATHOLIC CHURCH
1919 South Seventh Street

Saints Peter and Paul Catholic Church was founded in 1849, when the churches of St. Vincent de Paul and St. Mary of Victories (744 South Third Street) could not adapt fast enough to serve the area's rapidly expanding Catholic population. The first building, used for four years, was a temporary one-story structure with an entrance on Allen Avenue. A new brick church opened for services in 1853. The present building, completed in 1875, is built of Grafton limestone in the German Gothic Revival style after the design of Franz Georg Hempler. Stained glass windows from Innsbruck, and

The tornado of May 1896 completely destroyed many Soulard businesses like Louis Ottenad's Furniture Store, seen in the foreground, on Lafayette near South Broadway. Missouri Historical Society Photograph and Print Collection.

stations of the cross from Beuron, Germany, complement the majestic 214-foot spire. When the interior of the church was renovated in 1984, circular seating was installed; the building's present capacity of 350-400 people gives the church a more intimate atmosphere than did the original arrangement, which could accommodate 3,000.

Today, although only about one-third of the parishioners actually live in the neighborhood, SS. Peter and Paul maintains an active community role. The church's basement serves as a shelter for the homeless, and in 1992 the church reopened its convent as a hospitality house for families of patients in St. Louis hospitals. Tours of the church are conducted by appointment. For information call 231-9923.

⑥ TELOCVICNA JEDNOTA SOKOL HALL
("THE SMILE FACTORY")
2001 South Ninth Street

This building began its long and varied story in the early 1870s as a gymnasium and meeting place in a predominantly German neighborhood. In that same decade, with the increase of Czech immigration to St. Louis, the Bohemian community rented and eventually bought the hall to house their *Sokol* ("Falcon"). This secular organization had as its goal the fostering of national pride through social and cultural activities, including physical training. By 1890 the *Sokol* had a choir, a dramatic club, a readers' club, and a women's club, along with a gymnastics group. The building served the Bohemian community as a center of social activities until the 1920s, when it was sold to the Smile Soft Drink Company. Tile advertisements for Cheer-Up Soft Drink and Smile Orange Drink still adorn the lower portion of the building. In the early 1960s the building saw brief tenure as a roller rink before ownership transferred once again, this time to a mechanical-parts company. The next chapter in the story of the building is yet to be written; however, just above the door at the Allen Avenue entrance is a vestige of its past. There, close inspection reveals the words *Telocvicna Sokol*.

⑦ GRAVOIS AVENUE CHURCH OF GOD
2010 South Thirteenth Street

This church, built in the 1880s, originally housed St. Paul's Friedens Church, a German Evangelical congregation. St. Lucas Slovak Evangelical Lutheran Church bought the building in 1914 and held services there until 1958, when the Pentecostal Church of God purchased the site. Today the Church of God, through its Love in Action program, aids neighborhood residents in need of food and clothing, offers literacy programs for adults, and educates over five hundred children a year in Drugbusters, an anti–drug and alcohol program.

❽ BROWN SHOE COMPANY HOMES-TAKE FACTORY ("THE MEXICAN HAT FACTORY")
1201 Russell Boulevard, between South Twelfth and Thirteenth Streets

Built in 1904, the Homes-Take plant, designed by prominent St. Louis architects Weber and Groves, featured optimal safety, health, and sanitation conditions for employees in a time when state labor laws and factory inspection procedures were deficient. The plant specialized in women's dress shoes and offered neighborhood families convenient and desirable employment until the late 1930s, when the Homes-Take factory closed, relocating outside St. Louis. The International Hat Company used the building for warehouse and office space from 1954-76. In 1980 the building was converted into one hundred apartments for the elderly and disabled by the Allen Market Lane Apartment Associates. That same year the building won a listing with the National Register of Historic Places.

❾ ST. JOSEPH CROATIAN CHURCH
2112 South Twelfth Street

In 1904, the St. Joseph Croatian Roman Catholic Church Society purchased a former synagogue at Eleventh and Chouteau Streets to serve as a church for the St. Louis Croatian community, clustered mainly around Second Street, between Market and Arsenal Streets. In 1925, when a larger church and school were needed, the parish bought the old Ursuline Convent at Twelfth and Russell Streets and built a new church and hall on the site in 1927. Today it is the one ethnic parish remaining in the neighborhood. The American Croatian Relief Project meets at the church hall, as does the Croatian Junior Tamburitzans of St. Louis, a group of musicians and dancers, ranging in age from eight to twenty-one, who perform Croatian music. The group is highly regarded and has performed all over the country as well as in Yugoslavia.

❿ PONTIAC SQUARE PARK
South Ninth Street and Shenandoah Avenue

The city purchased this 1.91-acre square in 1908 for use as a park. The playground quickly became a popular spot for neighborhood youngsters; attendance in 1916 totaled nearly 300,000 children.

Since its founding in 1929 the Boys' Club of St. Louis has been an important recreational and educational center in the Soulard neighborhood. Photograph by David Schultz.

⓫ BOYS' CLUB OF ST. LOUIS
2524 South Eleventh Street

The Boys' Club of St. Louis, founded in 1929 by Father Charles Maxwell of Epiphany Parish, was the first Missouri chapter of the national organization. Its first home was at St. Vincent de Paul School, then came a tenure at Ninth and Lafayette Streets, and finally, in 1959, a move to the present location. Today the Boys' Club, which is funded through the United Way and private donations, serves boys ages six to eighteen from across the metropolitan area. It offers team sports such as baseball, softball, basketball, football, and soccer, as well as swimming and fitness training. Members can also learn skills in arts and crafts, receive tutoring, and make use of the Boys' Club library. The Boys' Club is truly a reflection of the neighborhood; most of the staff lived in Soulard and participated in the Boys' Club as youngsters. For more information call 772-5661.

⓬ DR. FRANZ ARZT HOME
2322 South Twelfth Street

When Franz Arzt, a prominent local physician, built his mansion in 1876, he incorporated several unusual and innovative features. The house owed its steel beam construction, the first for a St. Louis home, to Arzt's adaptive use of old railroad rails. It boasted the city's first residential hot-water heating system, as well as its first natural air-conditioning system, made possible by a series of flues with both floor and ceiling vents.

Although underground caves run through much of Soulard, none existed under Arzt's home until he created them himself, complete with stalagmites and stalactites imported from around the world. Aside from his professional and architectural accomplishments, Arzt won accolades in his avocational field of botany. His greenhouse was one of the first built at a private residence.

⓭ MAX J. FEUERBACHER HOME
South Twelfth and Sidney Streets

Called "the lion house" by neighborhood residents, this was the home of Max J. Feuerbacher, the proprietor of the Green Tree Brewery. It was the first private residence in St. Louis to feature a pair of sculpted stone lions as entryway guards. Other details include angular bay windows and a richly ornamented entrance hall.

⓮ ANHEUSER-BUSCH BREWERY
South Thirteenth and Lynch Streets

Eberhard Anheuser changed the name of Bavarian Brewery to Anheuser Brewing Co. when he acquired it in 1860. Adolphus Busch, Anheuser's enterprising son-in-law, became manager in 1864 and bought a partnership in 1869. In 1879 the company was renamed the Anheuser-Busch Brewing Association and quickly became one of St. Louis' leading breweries. Its position at the top solidified when the brewery survived Prohibition by diversifying its operations. By 1940, the brewery was the world's largest, and since then it has continued to grow. Currently Anheuser-Busch operates thirteen breweries nationwide and owns several sub-

sidiaries, including Eagle Snacks, the St. Louis Cardinals and Busch Stadium, and family entertainment grounds such as Grant's Farm, Busch Gardens, and Sea World.

In the one-hundred-acre brewery complex, three buildings have gained standing as National Historic Landmarks. Built in 1885, the Clydesdale Stables were originally the private stables of Adolphus Busch, whose home was on the brewery grounds. The Lyon School on Pestalozzi, built in 1868, remained a school until 1907, when Adolphus Busch bought the building from the city. It served as the brewery's central offices until the new corporate headquarters opened in 1982. August A. Busch, Sr.'s office occupied what had been his boyhood classroom. The Brew House at Ninth and Pestalozzi Streets (1891-92), with its distinctive clock tower, was built in Victorian Gothic style at the heart of the Anheuser-Busch complex. Its capacity has expanded from 1.25 million barrels annually to a 1991 high of 13.5 million. Anheuser-Busch offers tours of the brewery. For information call 577-2626.

⓯ ST. AGATHA ROMAN CATHOLIC CHURCH
South Ninth and Utah Streets

The end of the Civil War spurred growth in Soulard. Although construction on SS. Peter and Paul Church was just beginning in the neighborhood's northern corner, newly arrived German Catholics found the distance too great to travel for services. Their wish for a decidedly German church led to the formation of the new parish of St. Agatha in 1871. All of the parish school's classes were in German until 1906, when the church responded to the ethnic and cultural diversification of the neighborhood. The school closed in 1972.

A small building dating from 1871 provided education and services for the parish until 1885, when a new structure was built, complete with a bell and clock tower. That facility, including additions made in 1899,

The hearty workers of the Anheuser-Busch Brewing Association—many of them European immigrants—pose with their product in 1891. In pre-refrigeration days, many local breweries took advantage of the dozens of cool caves scattered throughout the Soulard and Cherokee-Lemp area. Photograph by D. C. Redington. Missouri Historical Society Photograph and Print Collection.

serves St. Agatha's parish today. St. Agatha's offers the St. Louis area's only Tridentine mass; Catholics from across Missouri and Illinois travel to hear the 10:00 A.M. Sunday services, which are said in Latin.

16 LYON PARK
Bounded by Broadway, Arsenal, South Second, and Utah Streets

In 1868 the federal government donated to the city a portion of the grounds of the old St. Louis Arsenal for use as a monument park. This was to honor Capt. Nathaniel Lyon, credited with saving the Arsenal from takeover by Confederate militiamen during the Camp Jackson Affair of 1861. A controversial statue of Lyon, unveiled in 1929 near the former site of Camp Jackson at Grand and West Pine Boulevards (now St. Louis University), found a new home in Lyon Park in 1960. At its original introduction, the statue, an awkward representation of Lyon astride a horse, prompted assessments from art critics ranging from "symbolical" to "artistic atrocity."

Hannon, Robert E., ed. *St. Louis: Its Neighborhoods and Neighbors, Landmarks and Milestones.* St. Louis: St. Louis Regional Planning and Growth Association, 1986.

Heritage/St. Louis. "Soulard Neighborhood Historic District: Preliminary Research Report." St. Louis, 1973.

Toft, Carolyn Hewes, ed. *Soulard: The Ethnic Heritage of an Urban Neighborhood.* Washington University, St. Louis: Social Science Institute Ethnic Heritage Studies, 1975.

Wayman, Norbury L. *History of St. Louis Neighborhoods: Soulard.* St. Louis: St. Louis Community Development Agency, 1980.

Special thanks to the Soulard Restoration Group, the Soulard Neighborhood Improvement Association, Charles M. Nash, Rev. Russell Dotson, Alderman Phyllis Young, and the residents of Soulard.

CHEROKEE-LEMP

From Lyon Park (Soulard): West on Arsenal Street to Benton Park, at the intersection of Arsenal and Jefferson Avenue.

Visitors to the Cherokee-Lemp neighborhood still flock to Antique Row. In the background is the old Lemp Brewery Complex. A victim of Prohibition, the brewery was closed in 1922, but the historic building is still in use. Photograph by David Schultz.

The streets of the Cherokee-Lemp neighborhood—bounded by Interstate 55 on the south and east, Jefferson Avenue on the west, and Gravois Avenue on the north—reflect the area's sporadic development. North of Arsenal, they are irregular and angled, retaining the boundaries of the eighteenth-century French common fields. South of Arsenal, however, the streets form a unified grid, since they were plotted according to surveys done by the city in 1836.

Early settlement of the neighborhood was scattered. Dotting the landscape were numerous sinkholes, quarries, brickyards, and cemeteries, the largest of which occupied the site of the present Benton Park. Though the topography made settlement difficult for some, local brewers were quick to see the value of the natural limestone caves that riddle sections of neighborhood. In the 1850s the ale firm of English and McHose took possession of a cave lying just east of Benton Park, using it for beer storage and operating an adjacent beer garden called Mammoth Cave and Park. German-born Adam Lemp,

St. Louis' first producer of lager beer, stored his brew in caverns at the northwest corner of Cherokee and De Menil Place, keeping it at the proper temperature with ice chopped from the Mississippi River.

Land usage in the neighborhood proved versatile; during the Civil War an earthen fortification not far from Benton Park strategically overlooked the arsenal to the east. The breweries lured numbers of German workers, as did Golden's Ropewalk, the Missouri Glass Works, and such brickyards as Hermann Stubenberg's near Arsenal Street. Never heavily industrialized, the area long retained rural pockets where families made their livings from small dairy operations.

The Benton Park district's ample supply of low-cost land attracted many immigrants. In some subdivisions, they could purchase a lot with twenty-five-foot frontage for two hundred to three hundred dollars with a small down payment and a three- to six-year mortgage. The area was soon home to a host of German bricklayers, brickmakers, carpenters, and masons.

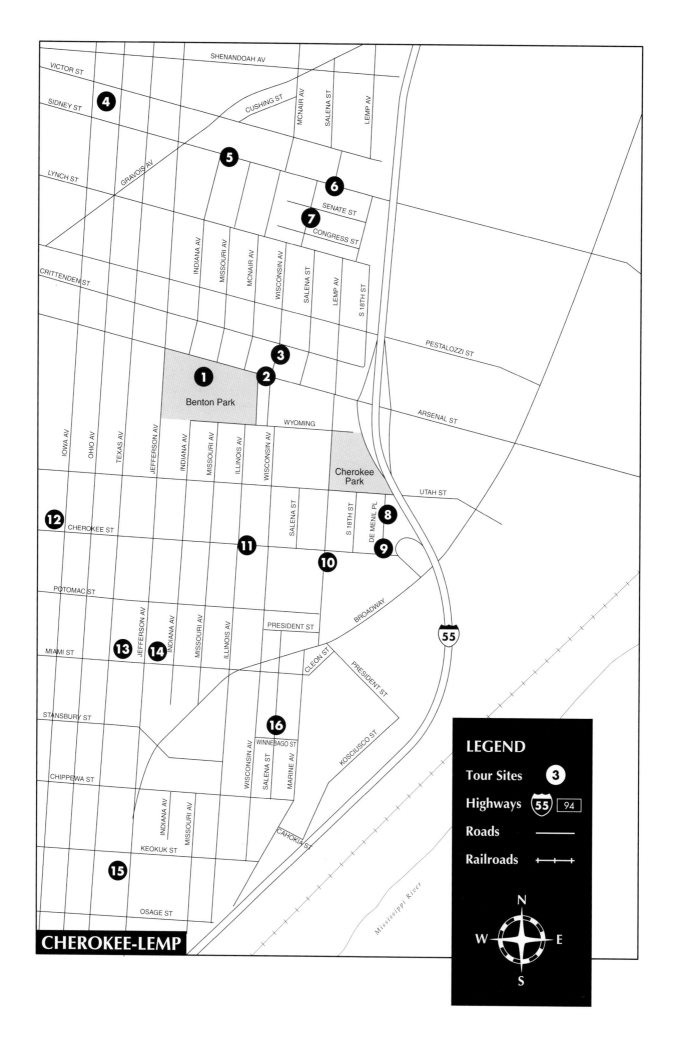

VICTOR ST

SIDNEY ST

④

SHENANDOAH AV

CUSHING ST

MCNAIR AV

SALENA ST

LEMP AV

LYNCH ST

GRAVOIS AV

⑤

⑥

SENATE ST

⑦

CONGRESS ST

CRITTENDEN ST

INDIANA AV

MISSOURI AV

MCNAIR AV

WISCONSIN AV

SALENA ST

LEMP AV

S 18TH ST

PESTALOZZI ST

③

② ①

Benton Park

WYOMING

ARSENAL ST

IOWA AV

OHIO AV

TEXAS AV

JEFFERSON AV

INDIANA AV

MISSOURI AV

ILLINOIS AV

WISCONSIN AV

Cherokee
Park

UTAH ST

⑫ CHEROKEE ST

⑪

SALENA ST

S 18TH ST

DE MENIL PL

⑧

⑩

⑨

POTOMAC ST

JEFFERSON AV

INDIANA AV

MISSOURI AV

ILLINOIS AV

PRESIDENT ST

BROADWAY

MIAMI ST

⑬ ⑭

CLEON ST

PRESIDENT ST

⑮⑤⑤

STANSBURY ST

⑯

WISCONSIN AV

WINNEBAGO ST

SALENA ST

MARINE AV

KOSCIUSCO ST

CHIPPEWA ST

INDIANA AV

MISSOURI AV

KEOKUK ST

CAHOKIA ST

⑮

OSAGE ST

Mississippi River

CHEROKEE-LEMP

LEGEND

Tour Sites ③

Highways ⑤⑤ 94

Roads ——

Railroads +—+—+

N
W E
S

Their handiwork survives in abundance, most notably in the ornamental detailing that adorns many buildings. Sidney Street in particular boasts an array of architectural features in terra cotta, pressed brick, stamped metal, and cast iron.

Major changes occurred in the area after World War II with the demolition of the neighborhood's eastern edge for the Ozark Expressway and the beginning of an influx of rural migrants. In the early 1970s over two hundred houses were razed and many more stood vacant. But the last years of the decade saw a spirited revitalization effort. Benton Park became the first St. Louis location for a Neighborhood Housing Service program, and by 1980, the number of vacant dwelling units had been drastically reduced. The Senate Square project reclaimed all buildings on Senate and Congress Streets owned by absentee landlords and successfully renovated them into 126 apartments.

Much has been accomplished over the past ten years in housing restoration, new construction, and street, sidewalk and park improvements. In 1985 the Benton Park area became the largest National Historic Register District in Missouri, a designation that insures the integrity of the neighborhood. Plans are underway to convert Fremont School on Wisconsin Avenue into a seventy-five-unit home for the elderly. Today artists, musicians, shopkeepers, and residents, old and new alike, are working together to preserve the Cherokee-Lemp neighborhood's rich heritage.

❶ BENTON PARK
Bounded by Jefferson Avenue, Arsenal Street,
Illinois Avenue, and Wyoming Street

Until 1865, a city cemetery occupied the site of the present Benton Park. As the neighborhood grew, the cemetery was removed and the site designated a public park, later named for Senator Thomas Hart Benton, an early Missouri statesman. The city improved the park with trees, a rustic stone bridge and tunnel, and an artificial lake, lined with cement to prevent water from draining into the caves below.

Standing on a hill in the park is a gray granite obelisk, a symbol of the neighborhood's German heritage and a monument to revolutionary politician Friedrich Hecker. Dedicated in 1882, at the peak of German immigration and ethnic consciousness in St. Louis, the monument is a tribute to Hecker's leadership in the public affairs of the city's German community. Hecker, who fled Germany during the 1848 revolution, served as a colonel in the Union Army during the Civil War and was known for his strong abolitionist stance. The monument is the work of St. Louis architect Ernst C. Janssen.

❷ SCHOLLMEYER BUILDING
1976-1982 Arsenal Street

Commission merchant Christian Schollmeyer built this structure at the northeast corner of Benton Park in 1889. It served as both a commercial building, with storefronts occupied by a shoe repair shop, a beauty shop, an upholsterer, and a grocer, and as a residence, which attracted some of the neighborhood's skilled laborers to its upstairs apartments. Architecturally, the building's mansard roof and dormers, along with its pattern of windows, exemplify features of the Queen Anne style and reveal a transition from the features of the older Italianate style commonly found in neighborhood commercial buildings of the day. Listed on the National Register of Historic Places in 1984, the Schollmeyer Building underwent renovation in 1985.

The site of a former cemetery, Benton Park has been a cornerstone for the neighborhood and its German residents since 1865. Here children enjoy the park around the turn of the century. Photograph by Emil Boehl. Missouri Historical Society Photograph and Print Collection.

③ ICARIAN COLONISTS' HOMES
3010 and 3016 Wisconsin Avenue

The Icarians, a group of French immigrants, came to this country in 1848 to establish a utopian colony. Led by Etienne Cabet, a social theorist and reformer, they settled first in Nauvoo, Illinois. When internal dissension split the group in 1856, some Icarians began a new colony in Cheltenham near Kingshighway, then outside the St. Louis city limits. Factionalism continued to plague the group, and by 1864 the colony had disbanded. At least a dozen Icarian families then took up residence in the Benton Park area. Joseph Loiseau, a perfumer, built the Creole cottage at 3010 Wisconsin in 1865. Next door to him, at 3016 Wisconsin, lived architect Charles Mesnier, formerly the secretary of the Icarian colony, who built his house in the 1870s.

④ ST. FRANCIS DE SALES CATHOLIC CHURCH
2653 Ohio Street

St. Francis de Sales' spire dominates the skyline on Gravois Avenue. At the time of its organization in 1867, the parish consisted mostly of German Catholics, many of whom worked in the neighborhood's small dairies. The parish grew out of the SS. Peter and Paul parish in Soulard. The present church was completed in 1908. The inspiration for its Gothic design came from St. Paul's in Berlin.

⑤ GIRLS INCORPORATED OF ST. LOUIS
2216 Sidney Street

In 1981 a group of concerned parents founded the Girls Club (later changed to Girls Incorporated) for the educational, recreational, and personal development of girls ages six to eighteen. Originally based in a small storefront, the group renovated the first floor of the St. Agnes School on Sidney Street in 1986. Later the second floor was renovated as membership grew. Today about 750 girls take part in programs ranging from education about nutrition and proper health care to Operation SMART, which focuses on science, math, and related technologies. Members of all racial, religious, and economic backgrounds receive tutoring, use the group's computer and science labs, and participate in dance as well as team sports such as volleyball, soccer, and softball. Girls Incorporated, a United Way agency, has two St. Louis centers directed by a full-time, professional staff that serves about two hundred girls a day during the school year. For more information call 771-0044.

⑥ ST. AGNES ROMAN CATHOLIC CHURCH
1933 Sidney Street

St. Agnes Church, dedicated in 1891, was founded by Father Constantine Smith, an Irish-born priest, to serve the neighborhood's Irish and Anglo-American families. The church resulted from a vow Smith made on a voyage from Rome to St. Louis. Midway across the ocean a terrible storm struck Smith's ship, and he cast a relic of St. Agnes into the water, praying to God to calm the tempest. He promised, upon his safe return to St. Louis, to devote himself to the erection of a church dedicated to and under the protection of St. Agnes. Designed by architect James McNamara in the Renaissance Revival style, the church's distinctive twin towers are a neighborhood landmark.

⑦ SENATE SQUARE
Congress and Senate Streets

With the development of the Benton Park area in the 1880s and 1890s came the enactment of deed restrictions that protected some blocks from mixed land use. Restrictions on lots fronting on Senate Street prohibited the use of buildings for schools, churches, beer saloons, meat shops, and groceries, as well as industry of any kind. Stipulations for houses specified brick construction, placement twenty feet from the curb, a height of at least two stories, and a minimum of five rooms. Many of the buildings were erected by German immigrants for use as rental property and private homes. In the late 1970s, Senate Square was redeveloped through the largest rehabilitation project in St. Louis undertaken without tax abatement. A private developer renovated vacant buildings, transforming Senate Square into a prime rental entity.

⑧ LEMP MANSION
3322 De Menil Place

In 1876 brewery head William J. Lemp and his wife, Julia, took up residence in this thirty-three-room Italianate home, built by Jacob Feickert in 1868. Today the restored home is operated by the Pointer family as the Lemp Mansion Restaurant. In the mid-1960s a substantial portion of the grounds and one of the two carriage houses were lost to the construction of the Ozark Expressway. Despite years of use as a boarding house, the home retains its original opulence. It features fireplace mantels of rare African mahogany, a hand-painted ceiling fresco, and several rare fixtures, including a glass-legged sink and a glass-enclosed marble shower stall. During the Lemp tenancy the mansion was the scene of multiple tragic events. Four members of the family—William, Sr., William, Jr., Elsa, and Charles—committed suicide, all but Elsa in the Lemp mansion.

The Lemp Brewery owned its own rail line, the Western Cable Railway Company, which connected all of the plant's main buildings with the shipping yards near the river and the major railroads. Photograph by W. C. Persons. Missouri Historical Society Photograph and Print Collection.

⑨ CHATILLON-DE MENIL HOUSE
3352 De Menil Place

Henry Chatillon, a guide and hunter with Francis Parkman on the Oregon Trail, and his wife, Odile Delor, the granddaughter of the founder of Carondelet, built the first portion of this home about 1849. In 1856 the Chatillons sold the house to Dr. Nicholas De Menil and banker Eugene Miltenberger. De Menil and his wife, Emile Sophie Chouteau, first used the house as a summer retreat, then expanded it for year-round habitation. Architect Henry Pitcher added a library, drawing room, reception room, three bedrooms, and a main hall to the home, transforming it into a Greek Revival mansion. The De Menil family resided here until 1929. In 1945 the property passed to Lou Hess, who opened to the public Cherokee Cave, located beneath the gardens. Hess used the mansion's first floor as a cave museum.

In the early 1960s, the house faced the threat of destruction when the proposed Ozark Expressway was routed directly across the property. After a campaign by preservationists forced the development of an alternate plan, the Landmarks Association took ownership and set about raising restoration funds. The Chatillon-De Menil House Foundation oversaw the final restoration work, with the doors opening to the public in 1965. In 1978 the house gained listing on the National Register of Historic Places. The house, which includes a restaurant, is open Tuesday through Saturday from 10:00 A.M. to 4:00 P.M.

⑩ LEMP BREWERY COMPLEX
Cherokee Street and Lemp Avenue

William J. Lemp moved the operations of the Western Brewery, founded by his father, Adam Lemp, to Cherokee Street in 1864. A limestone cave beneath the brewery, later known as Cherokee Cave, provided a natural cooling cellar for the brew. The brewery operated its own rail line, the Western Cable Railway Company, which connected all of the plant's main buildings with the shipping yards near the river and the major railroads. By the mid-1870s, the Western Brewery was St. Louis' largest producer of beer, with annual sales totaling over $1 million.

The complex, built in the Italian Renaissance style, features arched windows, pilaster strips, and corbelled brick cornices. The William J. Lemp Brewing Company—the brewery's name after 1892—underwent repeated expansion and eventually covered five city blocks. But the brewery did not survive Prohibition. In 1922 the complex was sold at auction to the International Shoe Company. An art center, the Cherokee-Lemp Studio, currently occupies one of the old brewery's main buildings.

Opened in 1870, the Alexian Brothers Hospital admitted only men until 1962. It continues to serve the Cherokee-Lemp neighborhood. This photograph of the surgical ward is from about 1922. Missouri Historical Society Photograph and Print Collection.

⑪ CHEROKEE STREET DISTRICT
Cherokee Street between Indiana and Lemp Avenues

In the early years of the twentieth century, the four-and-a-half block stretch of Cherokee from Lemp to Indiana bustled with the activity generated by its more than sixty stores. Shoppers hopped aboard the streetcar to reach the bakeries, butchers, hardware stores, drug stores, shoe stores, doctors, dentist, and midwife located in the district.

By the 1970s many shops stood vacant, and most of the basic services had disappeared. But by the decade's end, a new focus had begun to develop as several antique stores opened for business in the neighborhood. Since its organization in the early 1980s, the Antique Row Association has worked to revitalize the district by reclaiming many of the vacant buildings and improving the surroundings through sidewalk repair and tree-planting. Today the Cherokee district boasts fifty-five shops, all owned by the storekeepers, many of whom reside in their buildings.

⑫ ST. LOUIS CASA LOMA BALLROOM
3354 Iowa Avenue

A South St. Louis landmark since 1935, the Casa Loma Ballroom, the only remaining ballroom of its kind in the city, has featured such legendary performers as Tommy and Jimmy Dorsey, Frank Sinatra, Benny Goodman, the Mills Brothers, Tony Bennett, and Nat "King" Cole. At its peak two thousand people a night paid the thirty-five cent admission to waltz or foxtrot on the enormous five-thousand-square-foot wooden dance floor, which rested on a bed of rubber to prevent dancers from tiring.

One story holds that St. Louisan Tennessee Williams modeled the "Paradise Dance Hall" in his play *The Glass Menagerie* on the Casa Loma Ballroom. Having weathered a fire and changes in management, the Casa Loma continues to provide a cherished form of entertainment.

⑬ HOLY CROSS LUTHERAN CHURCH
2650 Miami Street

Concordia Seminary moved to Jefferson Avenue from Altenburg, Missouri, in 1850, bringing with it a number of Lutheran families to the area. This led to the formation in 1858 of the Holy Cross congregation, begun initially as a branch of Trinity Lutheran Church in Soulard. The Holy Cross congregation met in the chapel of the seminary until 1867, when the present Gothic-style church was built. The church has aged years well, its major restoration being the replacement of the 175-foot steeple, which fell victim to the tornado of 1896.

⑭ CONCORDIA PUBLISHING HOUSE
3558 South Jefferson Avenue

Founded in 1869, the Concordia Publishing House got its start in the Concordia Seminary, then located at Jefferson and Winnebago. Within a decade it had become known as one of the nation's leading religious publishers, a distinction retained today in its role as the official publication house of the Lutheran Missouri Synod. Concordia Seminary moved to Clayton in 1926, but the publishing house remained in the neighborhood and has expanded with the years.

15 ALEXIAN BROTHERS HOSPITAL
3933 South Broadway

Two members of the Alexian Brothers, a Roman
Catholic order devoted to the care of the sick and
insane, came to St. Louis from Chicago in 1869. After
a fund-raising campaign aided by banker and land developer James H. Lucas, the order purchased this South
Broadway site. The first building of the Alexian Brothers
Hospital opened in 1870 with 20 beds. By 1925 the
facility had 250 beds, a dispensary, a mental sanitarium,
and a clinic. The hospital began admitting women
patients in 1962. Substantial additions throughout the
years have allowed Alexian Brothers Hospital to respond
to the changing needs of the community.

16 FEDERAL RECORDS CENTER, FORMERLY
MARINE HOSPITAL
111 Winnebago Street

The U.S. Congress authorized the establishment of the
Marine Hospital for the treatment of sick and disabled
rivermen. Completed in 1855, the three-story building
served as a military hospital during the Civil War, at
which time temporary ward buildings sprang up adjacent
to the main structure. When the hospital moved to
Kirkwood during World War II, the ninety-year-old
buildings were demolished. A Federal Records Center,
housing civilian personnel records of former federal
employees, was built on the site in 1959.

FOR MORE INFORMATION

Hannon, Robert E., ed. *St. Louis: Its Neighborhoods and Neighbors, Landmarks and Milestones.* St. Louis: St. Louis Regional Planning and Growth Association, 1986.

Toft, Carolyn Hewes. *St. Louis Landmarks and Historic Districts.* St. Louis: Landmarks Association of St. Louis, Inc., 1988.

Wayman, Norbury L. *History of St. Louis Neighborhoods: Lafayette Square and Benton Park.* St. Louis: St. Louis Community Development Agency, 1980.

———. *History of St. Louis Neighborhoods: Marquette-Cherokee.* St. Louis: St. Louis Community Development Agency, 1981.

Special thanks to Mike Flood, Alderman Martie
Aboussie, Paul Faulkenberry, Esley Hamilton, the
Landmarks Association of St. Louis, Inc., and residents
of the Cherokee-Lemp neighborhood.

NEAR SOUTH SIDE

From the Federal Records Center (Cherokee-Lemp): North on Marine to Miami. Left (west) on Miami to Jefferson. Jefferson right (north) to Chouteau Avenue (northern boundary of Near South Side).

One of the oldest public parks west of the Mississippi, Lafayette Park displayed beautifully tended gardens in this 1872 scene. Though devastated by the 1896 tornado, the park and the surrounding neighborhood have now been restored to their former glory. Photograph by Emil Boehl. Missouri Historical Society Photograph and Collection.

Just to the south of St. Louis' central business district, the neighborhoods of the Near South Side were once places to escape the congestion and turmoil of a rapidly growing city. Bounded today by Chouteau Avenue on the north, Seventh Street on the east, Interstate 55 and Interstate 44 on the south, and Jefferson Avenue on the west, the area saw rapid urbanization after the 1840s, followed by a slow decline after World War I. St. Louisans responded to the resulting urban blight in a variety of ways in the years that followed. The resulting patchwork of beautifully restored streets,

new town-houses, and formidable blocks of public housing has created an area far different from the thinly settled countryside that once gently sloped up from the banks of Chouteau's Pond.

The blocks around Lafayette Park were among the earliest to be developed, and they remain the most similar to their original appearance. In March 1836, this thirty-acre parcel of land was set aside as the city's first public park. A part of the old St. Louis common fields, the area offered a sweeping view of Mill Creek Valley and the city to the north, but it was far enough

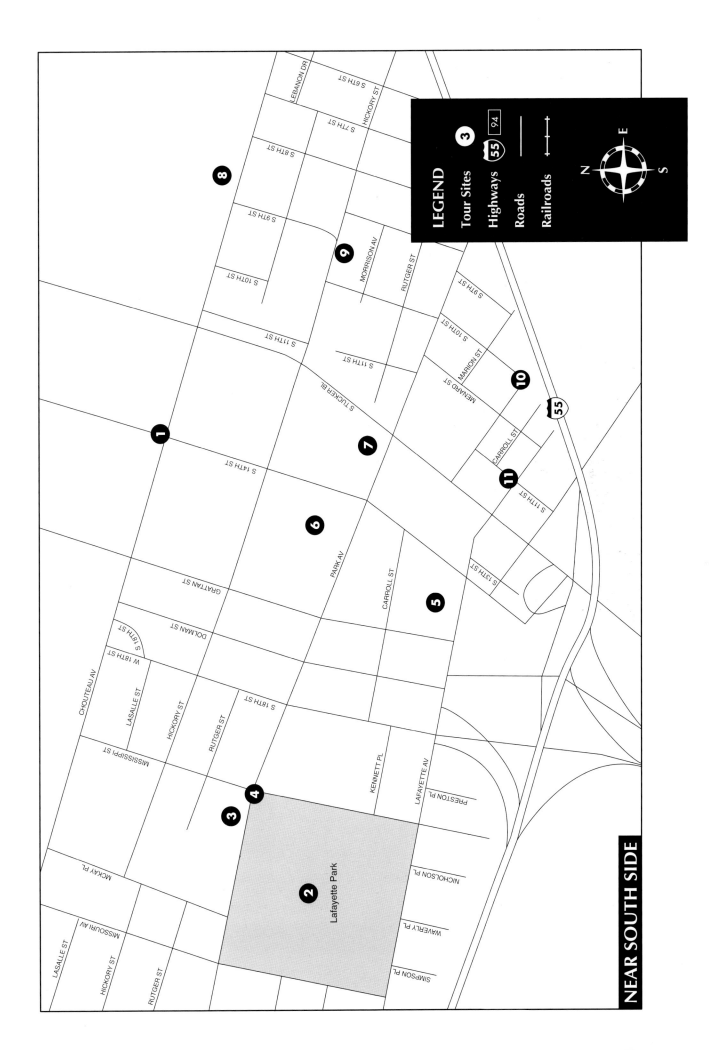

NEAR SOUTH SIDE

removed to create a fashionable suburban enclave for some of the city's wealthiest families.

After the area overcame the lingering impact of the Panic of 1837, a flurry of building activity took place around the park from the 1850s to the 1870s. Architectural features reflected the fashions of the period: mansard roofs with dormered windows, arched doorways, and exquisite interior detailing in stained glass, plaster, and wood. As it gained prestige, the neighborhood became home to a series of distinguished residents, including several mayors, United States congressmen, cabinet members, a Supreme Court justice, and the president of the American Bar Association.

Residents tried various means of protecting exclusivity: Benton Place was laid out as a private street in 1866, and a Lafayette Park security force was hired in 1870. Despite these efforts, the city steadily encroached on the neighborhood. Several blocks east of the park, on land subdivided from Antoine Soulard's estate, German and Czech immigrants soon filled blocks of simple brick tenements. Nearby, cotton factories, breweries, iron foundries, tobacco factories, and flour mills offered employment to these new St. Louisans.

The biggest change, however, was the least foreseen. On May 27, 1896, a devastating tornado roared through the city, leveling whole sections of the Near South Side. St. Louis City Hospital, built at Lafayette and Linn Streets in 1845, was all but destroyed. Churches, factories, businesses, and homes throughout the area were either demolished or badly damaged. The tornado transformed the once beautiful Lafayette Park into a twisted mass of uprooted trees and mangled wrought iron. In its wake, the storm left 306 dead and caused $13 million in damages.

It was a crippling loss for the area, but City Hospital was rebuilt, as were many of the homes in the Lafayette Park area. Still, the park looked barren, and other sections of the Near South Side did not recover. The compounding effects of the tornado and the St. Louis elite's ongoing migration west signaled the beginning of a long, slow decline in the area.

Those who remained in the area faced reduced social services and a dwindling base of business and industry. An influx of lower-income residents, many of them from poorer rural areas, placed greater burdens on the Near South Side's aging housing stock. Federal programs initiated in the depression made money available to attack this problem by subsidizing new housing for the working poor. In 1942, Clinton-Peabody Terrace, a low-rise public housing complex, was constructed near City Hospital. In the mid-1950s, the high-rise apartments of the Darst-Webbe complex were added nearby. These projects, which were intended to improve the area's substandard living conditions, would themselves create new problems for a community struggling to hold itself together.

The construction of Interstates 44 and 55 in the 1960s, which cut through the area with little regard for existing streets and buildings, further hastened the region's decline, fragmenting its once cohesive neighborhoods into separate islands. Ironically, it was this insular quality that ultimately provided the opportunity for reviving the neighborhoods of the Near South Side.

The blocks east of the housing projects provide a case in point. The neighborhood was badly blighted until Ralston Purina Company, a fixture in the area since 1894, formed the LaSalle Park Redevelopment Corporation. Corporate, federal, state, and local funding programs joined together to redevelop the 140-acre historic area. Block after block of restored brick homes now line the streets. Iron street lamps and brick sidewalks recall the neighborhood's nineteenth-century roots; new housing blends in with the old. The strong neighborhood association and a racially and economically diverse population of 2,000 (up from 270 in 1970) attest to the neighborhood's growth.

Lafayette Square also saw a dramatic turnaround—this one spurred by individual homeowners looking for urban ambiance and unbeatable housing values. By the 1960s, prospects for the neighborhood looked bleak: many of the homes were abandoned or deteriorated; a number were converted for use as rooming houses. But as St. Louisans began to rediscover the area and its charms, they capitalized on its distinctiveness to rebuild it in an image that was both historic and new. Like the planners of LaSalle Park's renewal, they carried on the process of building, rebuilding, and redefining neighborhoods that continues not only in the Near South Side and across St. Louis, but also in cities all over America.

❶ CHOUTEAU AVENUE

Chouteau Avenue marks the northern boundary of the Near South Side. The street was named for Auguste Chouteau, who, with Pierre Laclede, founded St. Louis. In 1779, Chouteau purchased a mill, dam, and lake, which he developed into the 100-acre Chouteau's Pond. The pond played an important role in the early development of St. Louis, dividing the city into north and south sides. Chouteau Avenue ran along the south side of the pond.

As the town center became increasingly industrial and polluted, people escaped to the gentle hills above the pond, forming the Near South Side neighborhoods. Chouteau Avenue developed into a fashionable address during the 1850s and 1860s. By the turn of the century, the tree-lined residential street and its gracious homes had given way to rail yards, flour mills, and factories.

❷ LAFAYETTE PARK
Bounded by Mississippi Street and Lafayette, Park, and Missouri Avenues

St. Louis' first developed city park, Lafayette Park was created in 1836 on high ground that was once part of the old French common land. Neighbors planted trees and the city created a military parade ground, but the park remained undeveloped until the park board hired landscaper Maximillian Kern in 1864. Drawing on European trends, he introduced St. Louis to new ideas about park landscaping. Kern re-landscaped the park to form a large lake, ornamental pond, and rocky grotto. The park boasted a bandstand, pavilions, lush foliage, an iron fence, and scores of trees. It became a popular spot for strolls, rides on the swan boats, and concerts. At the peak of its popularity, thirteen gardeners tended the thirty-acre park, which drew thousands of city residents each weekend.

The 1896 tornado leveled all of the trees and most of the ornamental structures. The park failed to recover from the devastation and resulting decline in community interest. However, today the park is the focus of neighborhood preservation and activity. Recently a fundraiser collected fifty thousand dollars to restore the mile of wrought iron fence. Concerts are held every other Saturday in the summer. The police station, built in 1869, is now a museum and visitors' center.

❸ BENTON PLACE
Off Park Avenue between Missouri Avenue and Mississippi Street

In 1866 Julius Pitzman plotted Benton Place for Montgomery Blair around a grove of trees opposite the north gate of Lafayette Park. One of the first private streets in St. Louis, Benton Place became the address of many prominent St. Louisans, including Blair, who served as postmaster general of the United States under Abraham Lincoln. The success of Benton Place led to further development around the park.

❹ PARK AVENUE
Between Mississippi and Grattan Streets

Once the center of Lafayette Square's commercial activity, Park Avenue was nearly empty after its period of decline in the early twentieth century. Since that time, a number of its buildings have been restored and commercial tenants have returned to the avenue. While the close proximity of commercial establishments to exclusive homes caused many residents to move after the turn of the century, today the preservation of buildings and an increase in business activity have helped spark interest in the neighborhood.

❺ ST. LOUIS CITY HOSPITAL
Lafayette Avenue and Linn Street

Established in 1845, St. Louis City Hospital began as a private Catholic hospital that provided its services to the city on a contract basis. After a fire destroyed the original structure in 1856, it was rebuilt and expanded. The 1896 tornado nearly demolished the building, which was rebuilt again and reopened in 1905. Closed in the early 1980s, the once grand structure has no future in sight.

❻ CLINTON-PEABODY TERRACE
1235 South Fourteenth Street

One of St. Louis' earliest attempts to provide affordable public housing, Clinton-Peabody was built in 1942. The two- and three-story row houses predate high-rise public housing construction and have been more successful, but they are not without their share of problems.

The St. Louis City Hospital was rebuilt twice: once after an 1856 fire, and again after the 1896 tornado. The hospital, shown here in the early 1900s, has been vacant since the 1980s. Missouri Historical Society Photograph and Collection.

❼ JOSEPH M. DARST-ANTHONY M. WEBBE APARTMENTS
Bounded by Fourteenth Street on the west, Chouteau Avenue on the north, South Tucker Boulevard on the east, and Lafayette Avenue on the south

Clinton-Peabody and later Darst-Webbe are early examples of how cities built federally subsidized housing to try to deal with increased urban blight and a lack of suitable low-income housing. Of the 515 homes razed for Darst-Webbe, 362 had no toilets and 131 had no running water. In the 1940s and 1950s, slum clearance and new low-cost housing seemed to offer hope for the Near South Side.

The Darst-Webbe apartments were constructed in 1956 and named for affordable housing advocates Mayor Joseph M. Darst and Alderman Anthony M. Webbe. Additions were constructed in 1961. Federal insistence on minimizing land cost for low-cost housing prompted the development of several similar high-rise buildings, including Cochran Gardens and Pruitt-Igoe. Although praised by local leaders and federal housing officials, it soon be came clear that there were too many people in too little space. There also was not enough recreational space, no nearby shopping facilities, and few jobs in the vicinity. Today the complex is sparsely occupied and its fate is still undecided.

❽ RALSTON PURINA COMPANY
Checkerboard Square, 801 Chouteau Avenue

Founded in 1894 by William H. Danforth, Ralston Purina has been a familiar fixture in the Near South Side. The original animal-food processing mill was destroyed in the tornado of 1896. A new mill was constructed at Eighth and Gratiot in 1898. The company later branched out into breakfast cereal and eventually became an internationally known corporation with its famous headquarters at Checkerboard Square.

In the 1960s, when other industries were leaving the area, Ralston Purina started a $2 million funding program for the redevelopment of the LaSalle Park neighborhood. Ralston's support, along with federal, state, and local programs, has revitalized LaSalle Park. The 140-acre LaSalle Park Multiple Resource Area was placed on the National Register of Historic Places in 1983.

❾ PULLIS HOUSE
916 Hickory Street

The iron embellishments that grace many of the area's homes were manufactured by the Mississippi Iron Works, owned by the Pullis family. John Pullis built this home in 1859. Enno Sander, founder of the St. Louis College of Pharmacy, also lived in the home. Preservation work on the house was begun by John Rodabough, author of *Frenchtown*, a history of the Soulard and LaSalle Park neighborhoods.

❿ TURNER'S HALL
1519-1529 South Tenth Street

First located near the Soulard market, the South St. Louis gymnastic club, or *Turnverein*, built this gymnasium in 1881. Growing out of a German movement founded by Friedrich Jahn, *Turnvereins* combined gymnastics with political and social elements to become a major cultural force within St. Louis' German population. This *Turnverein* became a community center,

The century-old Ralston Purina Company is a landmark of the LaSalle Park area and has been instrumental in neighborhood redevelopment. Ralston's checkerboard trademark, evident in this early twentieth-century photograph, is now internationally known. Courtesy of the Ralston Purina Company.

Sister Christine Keethers, D.C., of the Guardian Angel Settlement Association, takes a walk with neighborhood children. Founded in 1859 by the Daughters of Charity of St. Vincent de Paul, the settlement association provides day-care and community services for low-income families. The high-rise buildings of the Darst-Webbe complex are in the background. Courtesy of the Guardian Angel Settlement Association.

offering a lounge, a library, billiards, a theater, chorus rooms, and a bowling alley. In 1981, the brick structure was converted into loft condominiums as part of the redevelopment of LaSalle Park.

⓫ SAINT JOHN NEPOMUK CHURCH
1625 South Eleventh Street at Lafayette Avenue

Established in 1854 as the first Czech Catholic church in North America, Saint John Nepomuk Church served the neighborhood known as Bohemian Hill. The church at one time supported two schools and a print shop, where *Hlas*, the Czech-language newspaper, was printed. The Gothic structure, with its elaborate stained glass, was rebuilt within a year after it was destroyed by the 1896 tornado. The decline in the number of parishioners in the twentieth century was exacerbated by the construction of Interstate 55 in the 1950s.

In 1972, the seven structures comprising the Saint John Nepomuk Parish Historic District were listed on the National Register of Historic Places. The buildings were the Church (1870), the Church Rectory (1870), the Old School (1869), the Print Shop (1844), the Sisters' House (1848 and 1872), Beseda Hall (1892), and the Second School (1884). These buildings provided religious, educational, social, and recreational facilities for St. Louis' nineteenth-century Bohemian community. One of the parish schools has been converted into St. John's Square Apartments.

FOR MORE INFORMATION

Hannon, Robert E., ed. *St. Louis: Its Neighborhoods and Neighbors, Landmarks and Milestones.* St. Louis: St. Louis Regional Planning and Growth Association, 1986.

Wayman, Norbury L. *History of St. Louis Neighborhoods: Lafayette Square.* St. Louis: St. Louis Community Development Agency, 1981.

Rodabough, John. *Frenchtown.* St. Louis: Sunrise Publishing, 1980.

Special thanks to Vernon Thurmer, Kate Carter, Father Joseph Portucheck, Sue Pinker-Dodd, Thomas Keay, Robin Jones and the St. Louis Housing Authority, David Simmons, Eric Sandweiss, Loretta Lipsye, the Ralston Purina Company, Don Kehr, Fonda Fontroy, the Guardian Angel Settlement Association, and the residents of the Near South Side.

HYDE PARK

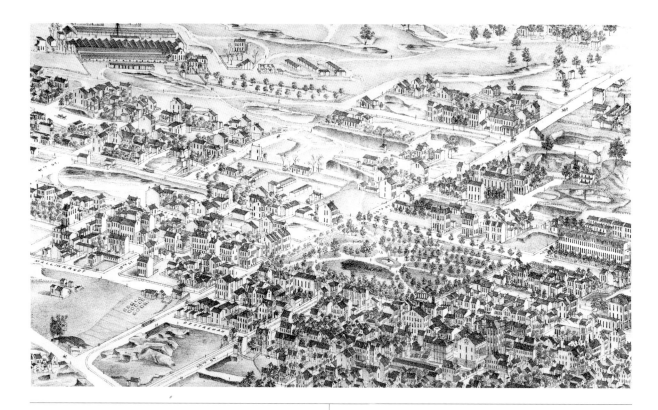

**From St. John Nepomuk Church (Near South Side):
Lafayette Avenue west to Jefferson Avenue. Left (south)
on Jefferson to Interstate 44. Interstate 44 east to Interstate
55/70. Interstate 70 west to Salisbury exit.**

This bird's-eye view of the Hyde Park neighborhood
in 1875 highlights the park, in the lower right, and the
community growing around it. From Richard J. Compton
and Camille N. Dry, *Pictorial St. Louis* (St. Louis, 1876).
Missouri Historical Society Library.

On its surface, the Hyde Park neighborhood looks like
any number of older, urban neighborhoods facing the
familiar inner-city problems of architectural decay,
population decline, and a dwindling commercial base.
Beneath the surface, however, this neighborhood, lying
at the edge of Interstate 70 on the city's north side, has
a distinguished history of its own, separate from that of
the rest of St. Louis. Now, its residents face the task of
building on that history while still staking a claim to
the city that surrounds them.

Hyde Park began as the town of Bremen, a small
settlement on the riverfront founded in 1844. Its name
came from a city in northern Germany that was the
original home of many of the early settlers. They were
enticed to the area by Emil Mallinckrodt, one of the
town's German-born founders; he promised them cheap
land and a hospitable German-speaking environment.
Soon the settlement was so much like his homeland
that Mallinckrodt was moved to comment, "one
believes he is in Germany when he hears *Plattdeutsch*

[low German] and the clatter of wooden shoes in
the streets."

One factor that enabled the town to grow was the
arrival of horse-drawn omnibus service in 1845. The
omnibus line ran from downtown St. Louis to Bremen
and on to the ferry landing at Bissell's Point. The resulting activity brought changes, the most notable one
coming in 1855 when Bremen was annexed by the City
of St. Louis. Though now part of a larger city, Bremen
held on to its local identity. The new focal point was
Hyde Park, created shortly before annexation.

The union with St. Louis brought new public services
and increasing prosperity. The nearby riverfront flourished as a lumber port, and the wharf was covered with
sawmills and lumber yards, giving rise to the trades of
furniture, barrel, and wagon making. By 1866 the Hyde
Park neighborhood boasted three streetcar lines, and
in the decade following the Civil War, the Union
Stockyards, Hyde Park Brewery, and Mallinckrodt
Chemical Works rounded out the area's industrial base.

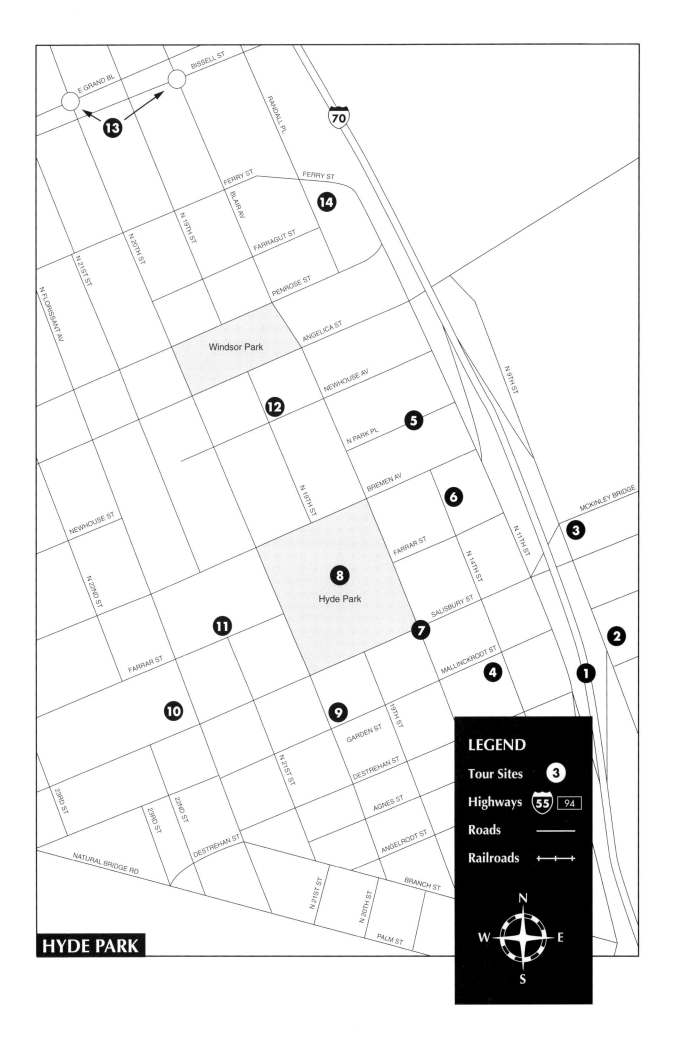

HYDE PARK

Still, despite its close industrial and transportation links to the city, Hyde Park remained a self-contained neighborhood until well into the twentieth century. Workers leaving the industries along the riverfront could stop at the many small shops along Salisbury Street before heading to their homes surrounding the park. Institutions like the North St. Louis *Turnverein,* Clay School, and Holy Trinity Catholic Church, all clustered near the park, were tightly woven into the social fabric of the neighborhood.

In recent generations, internal and external changes have affected Hyde Park much as they have other inner-city neighborhoods. As the descendants of the area's original German immigrants died or left the city for the suburbs, much of the neighborhood's housing stock became rental property. Meanwhile, the decisions of local and federal transportation planners were to have far greater impact on Hyde Park's historical cohesiveness.

For highway planners, the neighborhood was less a place to come home to than it was a space to pass through on the way to other destinations. In making way for a new interstate in the late 1950s, several hundred Hyde Park houses were demolished, with the Bissell Mansion, the area's most historic home, slated for destruction as well. That landmark was spared only after a group of concerned individuals intervened, convincing officials to reroute the highway. Nonetheless, Interstate 70 divided the neighborhood, cutting off Hyde Park's commercial and residential sections from its industrial area east of Broadway.

In the 1970s Hyde Park residents faced a similar challenge as they fought to halt proposals for a north-south distributor highway linking Interstates 44 and 70. The planned highway, which would have cut through the southeastern corner of the neighborhood, was stopped after residents spoke out at public hearings on the issue. Like the earlier battle for the Bissell Mansion, this opposition helped to shore up some of the neighborhood's eroding solidarity.

Today Hyde Park faces the challenges of all urban neighborhoods. Its residents know that recovering their distinctive historical identity is a valuable part of a successful future, but it is only one part. They must also work to be a part of the city, to take advantage of the funding and resources that one neighborhood cannot possibly provide for itself. The former town of Bremen, once autonomous, seeks its due as a full-fledged part of the City of St. Louis.

INTERSTATE 70

Today's busy interstate was planned initially in 1948 as a postwar expressway. In the mid-1950s federal money made the highway possible, and by 1958 the Mark Twain Expressway traversed the Hyde Park neighborhood, dividing the industrial section on the riverfront from the residential area to the west. The highway's construction cut a swath a block or more wide, claiming several hundred houses and stranding the houses to the east.

② INDUSTRIAL DISTRICT
I-70 to Salisbury exit, turn right, then right again at Broadway

Hyde Park's numerous industries grew up along the riverfront. The best known is Mallinckrodt Chemical Works, established in 1867 by the sons of Emil Mallinckrodt, one of the founders of the town of Bremen. Early on, the company produced agricultural chemicals, then branched out into pharmaceuticals and industrial chemicals. The company also refined uranium for the first atomic reaction; between 1946 and 1952, the plant on Destrehan Street was the nation's sole producer of uranium and related products.

Bremen Bank, chartered in 1868, was the first bank to serve the Hyde Park area. The present bank building, at the corner of Broadway and Mallinckrodt, was completed in 1928.

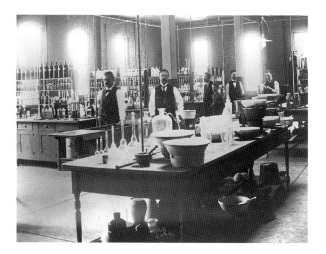

An early interior view of the Mallinckrodt Chemical Works and its research chemists. The company was founded by the three sons of Emil Mallinckrodt in 1867 on their family farmland. Missouri Historical Society Photograph and Print Collection.

❸ MCKINLEY TOLL BRIDGE
Foot of Salisbury Street

The construction of the McKinley Bridge in 1910 furthered Hyde Park's industrial growth by bringing the Illinois Traction System lines to St. Louis. Named for the company's president, William B. McKinley, the bridge provided local access for the Traction System's network of freight lines and carried local streetcars to Granite City. The Traction System evolved into the Illinois Terminal Railroad. Today the McKinley Toll Bridge is used for highway traffic and railroad freight trains.

❹ HOLY TRINITY CATHOLIC CHURCH
North Fourteenth Street at Mallinckrodt Street

Bremen's first church, the Church of the Holy Trinity, was founded as a German-language parish in 1848 and built on land donated by Bernard Farrar and Emil Mallinckrodt. The present structure, the third church building on the site, dates to 1897-98. Designed by Joseph Conradi in a late French Gothic Revival style, the church is set off by twin spires, creating a local landmark. Holy Trinity Church plays an important role in the neighborhood today; its school educates over 260 children from preschool through eighth grade. In 1987, one of the parish priests organized the Trinity Square Association, a neighborhood betterment group, which was renamed the Hyde Park Alliance in 1992.

❺ NORTH PARK PLACE

The blocks to the east, west, and south of Hyde Park were already densely populated by the time Francis Watkins began to develop the area to the north. In contrast to the heavily German population elsewhere in the neighborhood, North Park Place and Bremen Avenue became an enclave for second-generation Americans and natives of England and Ireland. In the 1870s Watkins operated a hotel (now demolished) on North Park Place, just west of 1122-24 North Park Place, an elaborately trimmed double-family brick house built in 1877-78 by stockyard dealer Benjamin F. Cash. In 1881 the prospect of drawing new members from North Park Place prompted Fairmount Presbyterian Church to relocate to the corner of Blair and Bremen Streets, reorganizing there as the Hyde Park Congregational Church. Today the structure is home to the New Shiloh Baptist Church.

❻ CLAY SCHOOL
3820 North Fourteenth Street

Named for statesman Henry Clay, who once owned land in the north St. Louis area, Clay School was established in 1859. It has been located at its present site since 1905. William Torrey Harris, whose educational philosophy would shape the course of public education nationwide, served as superintendent of Clay School in the 1860s. He envisioned the public school as the agent for assimilating immigrants into American society. During Harris' tenure, German-language instruction was introduced in hopes of persuading neighborhood Germans to support the school. Clay School's history as a vital neighborhood institution continues today; in 1992, at a ceremony in Washington, D.C., President Bush presented to the school a National Drug-Free Schools and Communities Award.

❼ SALISBURY STREET

Salisbury Street has long been the business center of the Hyde Park neighborhood. Butchers, grocers, doctors, tailors, shoe salesmen, and midwives all operated on the street, residing on the second floor and serving their clientele from ground-floor shops, ornamented with cast iron. In the late 1970s many buildings were demolished, leaving gaps in the previously complete streetfront. Some of these areas have been converted to green space, and plans are in motion to reclaim some of the vacant buildings for use as community institutions.

❽ HYDE PARK
Bounded by Salisbury and North Twentieth Streets, Bremen and Blair Avenues

In the 1840s, the land that is now Hyde Park belonged to Dr. Bernard G. Farrar, the city's first American-born physician. After Farrar's death, his widow sold the tract, already named Hyde Park, to the City of St. Louis. The city rented out the Farrar's country home, which remained on the site, as a resort hotel and beer garden. Other sections of the park land were leased to vegetable farmers. Hyde Park attracted political meetings and patriotic festivities. On July 4, 1863, a riot erupted when convalescent Union soldiers from the Benton Barracks hospital tangled with Confederate sympathizers. Two people were killed and six others injured when soldiers called in to break up the fight fired into the crowd. Park improvements began in the early 1870s; the landscaping and system of meandering walks soon made the park the centerpiece of the neighborhood. By the 1890s the park was bordered by fashionable row houses, the *Turnverein* hall, and, at the southeastern corner, a fire station, which is still in use.

❾ NORTH ST. LOUIS *TURNVEREIN*
1925 Mallinckrodt Street, overlooking Hyde Park

The North St. Louis *Turnverein* was formed in 1870 as the city's third branch of the Turner organization. The first of its existing buildings was erected at the corner of Salisbury and North Twentieth in 1879. Known primarily as a German gymnastic group, the Turners advocated social and political reforms, including the restriction of child labor. In the 1880s, they worked to establish physical education as part of the St. Louis public-school curriculum. The popularity of the North St. Louis *Turnverein* necessitated a three-story addition to the south end of the original building in 1893. In 1898, a large gymnasium was added, thus filling in the block to Mallinckrodt.

❿ BETHLEHEM LUTHERAN CHURCH
2153 Salisbury Street at North Florissant Avenue

In 1849 Bernard Farrar repeated the offer he had made to the German Catholic community and donated land for the construction of a German Protestant church. This led to the organization of Bethlehem Lutheran Church, which constructed its first building at Nineteenth and Salisbury Streets. In 1893 the congregation built a new church at the present site, but it was used only a few months before being destroyed by fire. The church was rebuilt from the original plans in 1895. Active in the community and immigrant education, Bethlehem became the mother church for six other northside Lutheran churches.

⓫ KREY PACKING COMPANY
North Twenty-first Street at Farrar Street

The Union Stockyards opened at the base of Bremen on the riverfront in 1874. Eight years later the Krey Packing Company was built at the western edge of Hyde Park. Cattle were herded to the Krey plant, passing beside the northern edge of the park, which was fenced along Bremen Avenue to keep out the livestock. By 1906 John Krey's nationally known company employed many Hyde Park residents, who slaughtered several hundred hogs daily for small neighborhood meat shops.

⓬ FRIEDENS UNITED CHURCH OF CHRIST
1908 Newhouse Avenue at North Nineteenth Street

The Friedens congregation began as the German Evangelical Friedens Church in 1858. The current structure replaced the original church building in 1907-8; it dates from 1861. In the two-story school building next door, children received their secular and religious education. Across the street is a building, built in 1907, that was once the Sunday school hall; today it is the home of Friedens Haus, a public-private coalition of community institutions committed to serving the needs of the neighborhood. Friedens Haus operates as a center for after-school activities, including clubs, scouting, tutoring, and a summer day camp for Clay School children. It also sponsors special activities such as an annual Family Day benefiting Clay School and a Drug-Free parade, complete with activities in Hyde Park.

Turnvereins were vital social and cultural centers for the German community in St. Louis. In the Hyde Park neighborhood, the North St. Louis *Turnverein,* formed in 1860, was the city's third such organization. In addition to gymnastics, *Turnvereins* were involved in various political causes. Missouri Historical Society Photograph and Print Collection.

Hyde Park's water towers, one on Grand Avenue (foreground) and the other on Bissell Street (background), are two of only seven such structures remaining in the nation. Photograph by Lester Linck. Missouri Historical Society Photograph and Print Collection.

⑬ WATER TOWERS
East Grand Boulevard and North Twentieth Street (White)
Blair Avenue and Bissell Street (Red)

The Hyde Park neighborhood boasts two of the nation's seven remaining water towers. The white tower, constructed in 1871, regulated surges in the water traveling from the Bissell's Point waterworks to the Compton Hill Reservoir on South Grand. The ornate red-brick tower to the east was designed by William S. Eames and built in 1885-86. Both of these striking neighborhood landmarks are listed on the National Register of Historic Places.

⑭ BISSELL MANSION
4426 Randall Place

This home, considered the oldest remaining brick house in St. Louis, was built in the mid-1820s by Captain Lewis Bissell. Bissell, a veteran of the War of 1812, built the house on a hill overlooking the Mississippi, a site that riverboat pilots came to know as Bissell's Point. In 1958 plans for the construction of the Mark Twain Expressway (Interstate 70) threatened the demolition of the house. A group of concerned St. Louisans negotiated an agreement with the state highway commission, and the highway was rerouted around the mansion. That group became the Landmarks Association of St. Louis. The Bissell Mansion opened as a restaurant in 1978, and today it offers dinner-theater productions.

FOR MORE INFORMATION

Hannon, Robert E., ed. *St. Louis: Its Neighborhoods and Neighbors, Landmarks and Milestones.* St. Louis: St. Louis Regional Planning and Growth Association, 1986.

McCue, George, et al. "Street Front Heritage: The Bremen/Hyde Park Area of St. Louis." *Missouri Historical Society Bulletin* 23 (July 1976), pp. 205-21.

Toft, Carolyn Hewes. *St. Louis Landmarks and Historic Districts.* St. Louis: Landmarks Association of St. Louis, Inc., 1988.

Wayman, Norbury. *History of St. Louis Neighborhoods: Hyde Park and Bissell-College Hill.* St. Louis: St. Louis Community Development Agency, 1980.

Special Thanks to Louise Bauschard, Hyde Park Alliance, Landmarks Association of St. Louis, Inc., Kathy Keeser, John Bratkowski, Rich Roland, Holy Trinity Church, Wendy Krom, and the residents of Hyde Park.

CENTRAL ST. LOUIS: THE NINETEENTH-CENTURY CITY

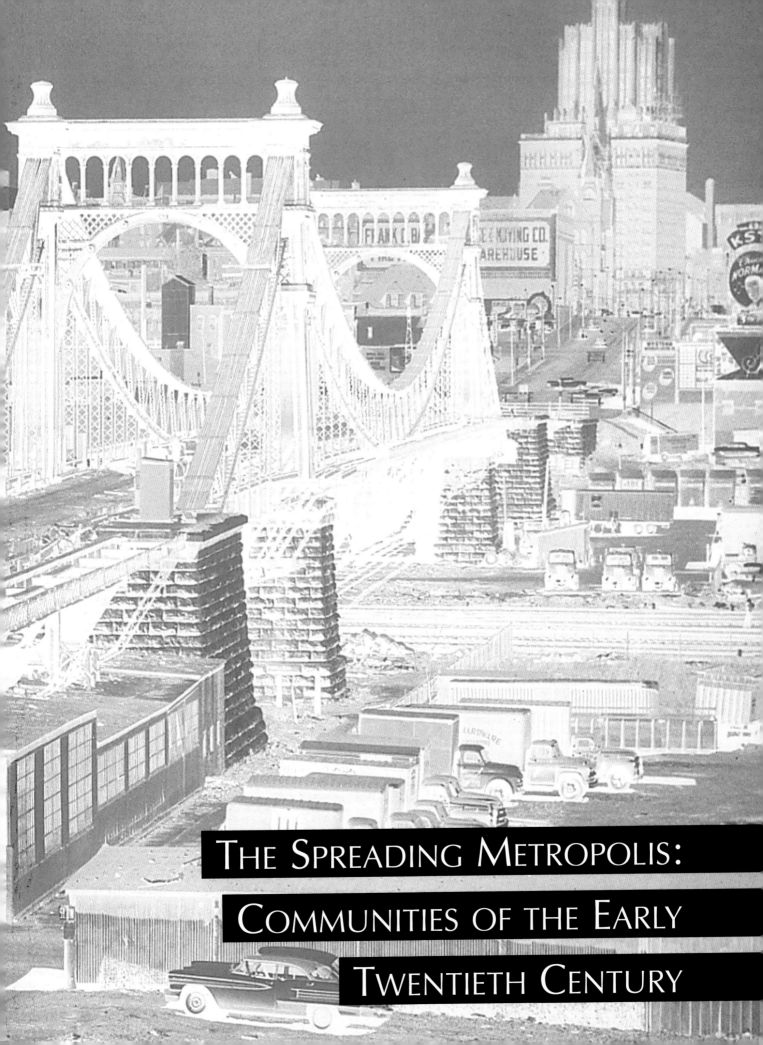

The Spreading Metropolis:

Communities of the Early

Twentieth Century

THE SPREADING METROPOLIS: COMMUNITIES OF THE EARLY TWENTIETH CENTURY

We expect cities to grow. In fact, the concept of "growth" is so wrapped up in our definition of what a city is that we often take it for granted. As a result, the consequences or limitations of growth may not be considered until a community has overreached its resources and finds itself struggling to create newer housing, bigger sewers, or wider streets. The opposite sort of problem occurs when a community places all of its hopes on one industry or one natural resource; the crisis then is often not creating houses, sewers, or streets, but deciding what to do with them when the industry closes or the resources are exhausted and the residents move away to seek greener pastures.

We can be reassured, though, by the fact that growth does not happen by accident. The twelve communities—and one park—of the late nineteenth and early twentieth centuries examined here prove this fact repeatedly. They leave a clear picture of the predictable patterns of growth that shaped the nineteenth-century city and that continue to shape cities and suburbs today.

East St. Louis and Granite City, Illinois, for example, are two communities built of necessity and industry. Nineteenth-century St. Louisans were dependent on the food produced in "Illinoistown," as East St. Louis was then called, and the farmers of Illinoistown were dependent on income from the sale of that food to St. Louis. The construction of the Eads Bridge (1874) and the Merchant's Bridge (1889) helped spur its growth into a major industrial town and railroad center. Similarly, when William and Frederick Niedringhaus needed a less expensive and less environmentally restrictive site for their growing graniteware plant, they created the town of Granite City in the middle of sparsely inhabited farmland.

Since World War II, both East St. Louis and Granite City, once very important to the stability of the metropolitan area, have suffered the same fate as industrial towns across America: lost industry, lost jobs, shrinking populations. But neither has given up. Community centers, colleges, and neighborhood beautification programs are all evidence of the spirit that is helping these communities pull together to meet their new challenges.

Industry guided development in several neighborhoods on the Missouri side of the Mississippi as well.

The Hill and the Grand-Oak Hill and Cheltenham neighborhoods, for example, were developed as industrial sites. Their first residents were immigrant laborers in coal mines, fire brick factories, and other clay-related industries. A walk down the street of almost any St. Louis City neighborhood will demonstrate the importance of brick making to the building of the city; imagining the City of St. Louis without bricks is like imagining Las Vegas without light bulbs.

Other neighborhoods grew out of an escape from industry, not a rush toward it. The role of the sylvan attractions of Forest Park in the city's westward sprawl cannot be underestimated. The city had been creeping in that direction since its inception, but it was the attraction of the park, and the infrastructure that came with it, that drew the city's people—the wealthy at first, and the less well-to-do later—to neighborhoods such as Skinker-DeBaliviere and the Central West End.

But St. Louisans' outward migration was not only to the west; it was to the north as well. There, as in other neighborhoods, the attractions for residents were varied. The Ville, the Fairgrounds-O'Fallon Park neighborhood, and the area now known as Penrose developed for reasons ranging from cultural to recreational to agricultural. As a result, each neighborhood took on its own distinctive characteristics and institutions. The Ville, for example, has been called St. Louis' "cradle of black culture," and it is home to many "firsts" for St. Louis' African American community: the first high school for blacks west of the Mississippi (Sumner High School), the first African American woman millionaire (Annie Turnbo Pope Malone), and one of the first and best hospitals for the care of African American patients (Homer G. Phillips Memorial Hospital).

Ultimately, the fact that cities grow is not nearly as interesting as the way they grow. As you follow the growth of St. Louis—north, south, east, and west—note the thoroughfares, the industries, and the parks that have directed the growth of this city for over two centuries and compare these patterns to the way the city is growing now. Where will the city extend two hundred years from now?

GRANITE CITY, ILLINOIS

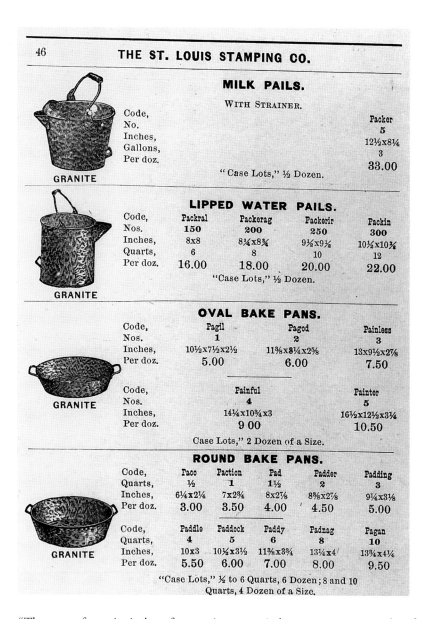

46

THE ST. LOUIS STAMPING CO.

MILK PAILS.
WITH STRAINER.

Code,		Packer
No.		5
Inches,		12½x8¼
Gallons,		3
Per doz.		33.00

GRANITE

"Case Lots," ½ Dozen.

LIPPED WATER PAILS.

Code,	Packral	Packerag	Packerir	Packin
Nos.	150	200	250	300
Inches,	8x8	8¼x8¾	9½x9½	10½x10¾
Quarts,	6	8	10	12
Per doz.	16.00	18.00	20.00	22.00

GRANITE

"Case Lots," ½ Dozen.

OVAL BAKE PANS.

Code,	Pagil	Pagod	Painless
Nos.	1	2	3
Inches,	10½x7½x2½	11⅜x8¼x2⅝	13x9½x2⅞
Per doz.	5.00	6.00	7.50

Code,	Painful	Painter
Nos.	4	5
Inches,	14¼x10¾x3	16½x12½x3¼
Per doz.	9 00	10.50

GRANITE

Case Lots," 2 Dozen of a Size.

ROUND BAKE PANS.

Code,	Paco	Paction	Pad	Padder	Padding
Quarts,	½	1	1½	2	3
Inches,	6¼x2¼	7x2¾	8x2⅞	8⅜x2⅞	9¼x3⅛
Per doz.	3.00	3.50	4.00	4.50	5.00

Code,	Paddle	Paddock	Paddy	Padnag	Pagan
Quarts,	4	5	6	8	10
Inches,	10x3	10½x3½	11⅜x3¾	13¼x4	13¾x4¼
Per doz.	5.50	6.00	7.00	8.00	9.50

GRANITE

"Case Lots," ¼ to 6 Quarts, 6 Dozen; 8 and 10
Quarts, 4 Dozen of a Size.

From St. Louis: Interstate 64 (Highway 40) east, over the Mississippi River. Continue on Interstate 55/70 to Illinois State Highway 203. State Highway 203 north to Granite City. Left at Twentieth Street.

The 1897 catalog for the St. Louis Stamping Works advertised a variety of kitchenware. Testimonials from professors of chemistry promised that these products did not contain anything "injurious to health" and were "safe for cooking, drinking and other purposes." Missouri Historical Society Photograph and Print Collection.

"The story of our city is that of a most important industrial district in the Middle West. Its growth has been aided by the nearness to power and raw materials, transportation facilities and a progressive citizenry." So reads the preface to a history of Granite City written to commemorate the town's fiftieth anniversary in 1946. Granite City's industries, in fact, created their own history, for the town was founded as an industrial complex to support the production of a revolutionary new household product called "graniteware."

Graniteware is the generic name given to lightweight household products manufactured first in Europe and then mass-produced in the United States from the 1870s to the 1950s. An inorganic substance, such as granite, borax, quartz, or feldspar, was dusted and then fused onto a metal surface at temperatures of over fifteen hundred degrees Fahrenheit. The result was an attractive, lightweight product highly resistant to burning, weathering, and discoloration. Unlike tin or cast-iron cookware, graniteware did not rust after being washed.

William F. and Frederick Niedringhaus, two brothers from St. Louis, were the first Americans to patent graniteware. They were already successful manufacturers of it when they began searching for a site to expand their North St. Louis factories: the Granite Iron Rolling Mills, which manufactured sheet iron, and the St. Louis Stamping Company, which produced lightweight, low-cost, enameled sheet-iron kitchenware, such as pots, pans, and cups. Ground granite rock produced a slick surface on these products.

THE SPREADING METROPOLIS: COMMUNITIES OF THE EARLY TWENTIETH CENTURY

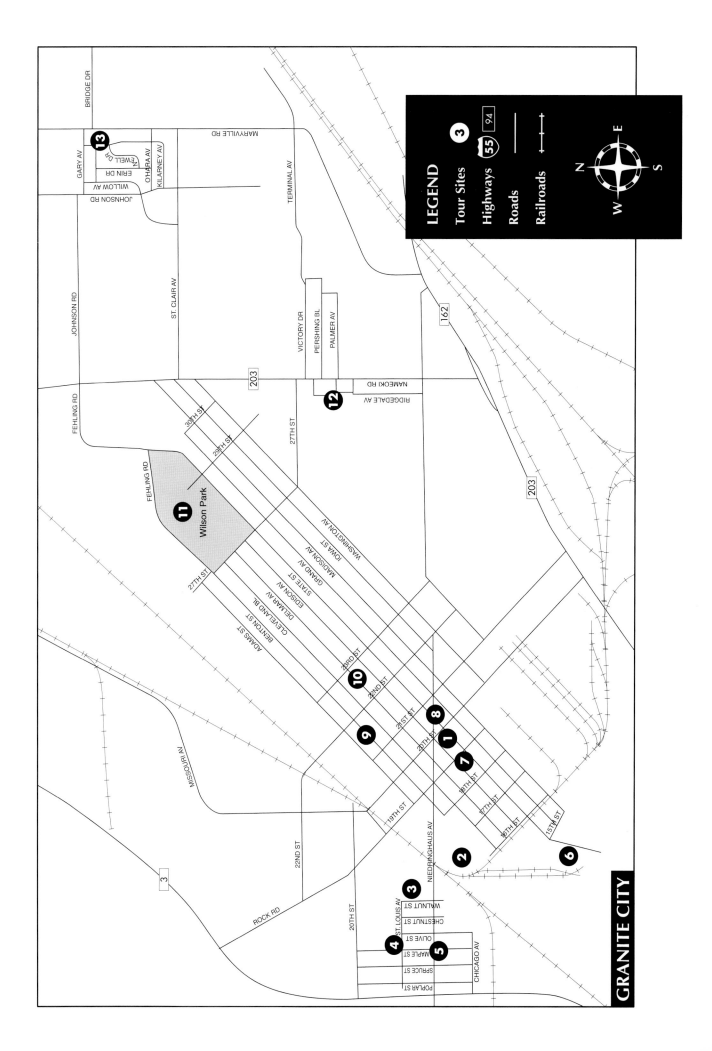

GRANITE CITY

LEGEND

Tour Sites ③

Highways 55 94

Roads

Railroads

Like other St. Louis industrialists, the Niedringhauses decided to set up shop on the Illinois side of the Mississippi. There, the cost for large industrial sites was one-tenth to one-fifth of what it was in St. Louis, rail and river transportation was accessible, and smoke regulations were nonexistent, an important advantage for coal-burning heavy industries such as steel. The site they chose, a farming community called "Kinder Station" about a mile from the Mississippi, was not far from the Illinois side of the new Merchants' Bridge and Venice Ferry landing, allowing an easy commute for workers from St. Louis.

In 1892 the brothers bought thirty-five hundred acres of the highest land in the flood plain, and the following year they hired Julius Pitzman, St. Louis' influential city engineer, to plan their city. Although their families wanted them to call the community "Niedringhaus," the brothers decided to name it after the product that had made them wealthy. In anticipation of a flood of new employees, the Niedringhauses built one hundred brick homes to be sold to their workers.

Even though the Niedringhauses never lived in Granite City, they left their mark on the city's industrial landscape. Their Granite City Steel Works and nearby St. Louis Stamping Works were the town's largest employers through the 1930s. The brothers also helped finance other manufacturing plants, such as the American Steel Foundry and Commonwealth Steel. These plants, in turn, attracted other industries to the area. The Markle Lead Works, Continental Wire Company, and Drummond Box Factory were among the town's earliest major employers. Within a few years, they were joined by the Corn Products Refining Company and Wagner Brewery Company.

Much as its founders envisioned, Granite City quickly boomed. From a population of 992 in 1896, the year of its incorporation, the town had grown to more than 3,000 residents by 1900 and more than 9,000 by 1910. By the late 1940s, the town had 22,000 inhabitants.

Also as the Niedringhaus brothers predicted, most of the industries' employees commuted from St. Louis in Granite City's early years. The majority were American-born or immigrants from northern Europe, particularly Wales and England. Over time, they filled the semiskilled, skilled, and managerial positions at the plants and settled into the new residential neighborhoods northeast of Niedringhaus Avenue. After 1900 thousands of immigrants from Eastern Europe, particularly Bulgaria, moved into the area to fill the need for unskilled labor. Until World War II the town's Eastern European community lived in an isolated enclave on the western edge of town.

Except for the depression years of the 1930s, Granite City's industries continued to grow and diversify. The town enjoyed major residential and school construction booms in the 1920s and 1960s as the city limits expanded into the surrounding farming communities.

Today, Granite City's industrial base has shrunk, as many of its older plants have closed or moved out of the area. After World War II consumers preferred the new aluminum, stainless steel, and glass cookware over graniteware, and the historic St. Louis Stamping Works closed in 1956.

With the town no longer serving as a major magnet for industries, Granite City's population has declined, down from 36,000 in 1970 to just over 32,000 in 1990. At one time there were twenty-one schools in the area; today there are twelve. With the exception of several small retail stores, Granite City's once thriving downtown is full of empty stores.

As the city approaches its centennial year, civic leaders, as well as an active historical society and a downtown neighborhood restoration group, are grappling with these problems. The construction of a downtown bus station, a swimming pool in the city's major park, and a golf course and residential development at the edge of town are several ways the community is trying to bolster its appeal to newcomers as well as old-timers, many of whom now commute to St. Louis. Granite City Steel, now part of National Steel, employs three thousand workers, and the recently reopened American Steel Foundries, after shutting down in the 1980s, employs seven hundred people and is expanding.

Meanwhile, graniteware has become a hot collectible item, as aficionados scour antique shops for the kitchenware that once made Granite City famous.

Many of the workers in the early years of the Granite City Steel Works were of English and Welsh descent. The 1914 *U.S. Census of Manufactures* reported that Granite City had 39 industrial plants and 5,658 persons in manufacturing. Photograph, c. 1914. Courtesy of the National Steel Corporation, Granite City Division.

❶ NATIONAL STEEL CORPORATION, GRANITE CITY DIVISION
1951 State Street

Granite City Steel, built in 1894, dominates the city's industrial landscape. Until 1908, the steel produced here was used exclusively for graniteware products manufactured at the nearby stamping works. After World War I, with the rise in demand for automobiles, refrigerators, metal furniture, washing machines, and other durable consumer goods, Granite City Steel became a major producer of light flat-rolled steel.

The plant is now owned by National Steel, based in Mishawaka, Indiana. Today, Granite City Steel, as it is still called locally, manufactures flat-rolled coil steel, building supplies, pipes, tubing, and wheels for cars and trucks, in addition to other products. With three thousand workers, Granite City Steel is the largest employer in town.

❷ ST. LOUIS STAMPING WORKS BUILDING
1801 Benton Street

This former stamping works plant in Granite City is a mammoth brick structure on a thirty-acre site at the west end of Niedringhaus Avenue. It was the first industrial building erected in Granite City, and its principal product was graniteware. At the stamping works, sheet metal and tin produced by Granite City Steel were cut and then formed into hundreds of products for household use, which were then enameled and shipped to customers all over the world. In 1899, the Niedringhauses formed the National Enameling and Stamping Company (NESCO) by consolidating their stamping works, iron-rolling mills, and steel works with other major American graniteware producers.

As aluminum and glass became popular household items, the demand for graniteware dropped. The stamping works closed in the mid-1950s. Today, the building is used as a warehouse and a steel barrel plant.

❸ AMERICAN STEEL FOUNDRIES
1700 Walnut Street

The American Steel Foundry Company was founded in 1894 by East St. Louis industrialist James G. "Mac" McRoberts, who revolutionized the manufacture of steel castings by using a "green" sand mold, a mixture of sand, clay, and binders. With a patent in hand, McRoberts started a foundry in Granite City with financial backing from the Niedringhauses and other St. Louis businessmen. In 1902 the company became part of a nationwide group of steel foundries. Today, American Steel Foundries, the largest maker of steel castings in the United States, is owned by AMSTED Industries, based in Chicago, and employs seven hundred people in its Granite City plant. Its principal client continues to be the rail industry.

❹ LINCOLN PLACE NEIGHBORHOOD
West end of Niedringhaus Avenue, bounded by Walnut and Poplar Streets and St. Louis and Chicago Avenues

By the early twentieth century, the need for large numbers of unskilled workers in Granite City's industries brought thousands of immigrants from Eastern Europe to the new city. These immigrants settled west of town in an area quickly dubbed "Hungary Hollow." The neighborhood became known as "Hungry Hollow" after the depression of 1908-1909. For many years, the area's population was largely composed of the Bulgarian and Macedonian-Bulgarian community, which at one time was the largest such community in the United States. Most of these immigrants lived in two- and three-story "mercantile houses" run by Bulgarian businessmen who dominated the neighborhood's economic and political life. By World War I, the neighborhood also had become home to Mexican immigrants. In 1916 the newly formed Lincoln Progressive Club, made up neighborhood residents, officially changed the name of its neighborhood to Lincoln Place, in honor of Abraham Lincoln.

The Money Exchange of Hungary Hollow, now Lincoln Place, served the neighborhood's predominantly Bulgarian and Macedonian-Bulgarian population. By 1907 Granite City was home to nearly eight thousand Macedonians. Courtesy of the Granite City Public Library District. L. P. Frohardt, "History of Granite City Slide Picture Presentation."

⑤ LINCOLN PLACE COMMUNITY CENTER
822 Niedringhaus Avenue, between Maple and Spruce Streets

The community center has been an important organization in the Lincoln Place neighborhood since the World War I era, when it was started as a settlement house by Commonwealth Steel to "Americanize" immigrant families with classes in English, citizenship, and hygiene. In the early 1920s, the neighborhood built a new clubhouse at its present location that featured a large auditorium, a gymnasium, classrooms, an office, and an outdoor playground. It sponsored a community band, basketball team, kindergarten, Sunday school, and boys' and girls' clubs, along with Americanization classes. In 1939 the Granite City Park District took over the community center, which still serves as a focal point for the neighborhood.

⑥ COMMONWEALTH STEEL PLANT BUILDINGS
1459 State Street

As Granite City attracted both light and heavy industries, the Niedringhauses provided backing for several new companies. One of these was Commonwealth Steel, which was eventually bought by St. Louis businessman Clarence H. Howard and two of his old school chums to produce steel castings for railroad cars. By 1928, nearly all locomotives and passenger cars built in the United States were using Commonwealth Steel products. The following year the company was purchased by General Steel Casting Corporation.

At one time Commonwealth Steel, as it is still known, employed over five thousand people. Closed since the 1970s, the site is now owned by National Steel, which leases the space to various metal processors.

⑦ WASHINGTON AIRDOME AND THEATER SITE
Madison County Transit Bus Depot, Nineteenth Street, between Delmar Avenue and State Street

The Washington Airdome, an outdoor theater built in 1911, was a popular venue for live entertainment, movies, labor rallies, and political meetings and campaigns. After air conditioning became possible in movie theaters, a new indoor theater replaced the airdome in the 1930s. It featured an auditorium with more than seventeen hundred seats.

Until the 1970s, this stretch of Nineteenth Street was a thriving retail and entertainment district. The Washington Street Theater closed in 1977 as downtown Granite City declined with the rising popularity of new shopping centers in the outlying sections of town. In 1993 the Madison County Transit District built a bus depot on the site.

⑧ TRI-CITIES LABOR TEMPLE
State Street, between Twentieth Street and Niedringhaus Avenue

Granite City has always been a strong union town. Since 1920 union members have used the Tri-Cities Labor Temple as a meeting hall and place for social gatherings. The three-story brick building houses numerous meeting halls, union offices, and a large auditorium. Once used for dances and post-meeting "smokers," the auditorium today is mostly used for mass meetings. Granite City Steel and American Steel Foundries are still heavily unionized, although workers at the town's second-largest employer, St. Elizabeth Medical Center, are not.

⑨ ORIGINAL WORKERS' DUPLEX HOUSES
Benton Street, between Twenty-first and Twenty-second Streets

This block features some of the original brick homes the Niedringhauses built for their blue-collar employees in the 1890s, half of which were "double cottages." Advertisements in real estate catalogs appealed to potential home buyers with the promise of jobs, assuring that "the largest manufacturing concerns in the West will be in Granite City."

⑩ "SILK STOCKING ROW"
Cleveland Boulevard, between Niedringhaus Avenue and Twenty-third Street

As the city expanded toward Wilson Park, Granite City's elites moved with it. The newer homes between Twenty-third Street and the park—only one block from the workers' duplexes on Benton Street—reflect this migration, with the tree-lined Cleveland Boulevard featuring large Victorian- and Edwardian-era homes. Many of these homes have been carefully restored.

⑪ WILSON PARK
Bounded by Twenty-seventh Street, Benton Street, Fehling Road, and State Avenue

Wilson Park was opened in 1923 on seventy acres in what was then the northwestern edge of Granite City, a product of the city's 1921 park district. Heavily used by the people of Granite City, the park today has four outdoor basketball courts, two regulation baseball fields, a new swimming pool, an all-weather ice-skating rink, tennis courts, flower gardens, and picnic facilities.

Commonwealth Steel, makers of steel castings for railroad cars, once employed five thousand people at its Granite City plant. Commonwealth's closing in the 1970s was a major loss for the community. Despite such set-backs, Granite City continues to be a proud manufacturing center. Courtesy of the Granite City Public Library District.

12 KIRKPATRICK HOMES
Nameoki Road, between Edwards Street and Victory Drive

This two-story apartment complex, built by the U.S. Housing Authority in 1941 to ease the wartime housing shortage, was named for M. E. Kirkpatrick, mayor of Granite City from 1935 to 1942. Controversy surrounded the selection of the site, part of which was on land that had been donated for a cemetery. The Kirkpatrick Homes are among the earliest examples of public housing in the St. Louis area.

13 OLD SIX MILE MUSEUM
3279 Maryville Road

This museum, housed in a nineteenth-century farmhouse, was created by the Old Six Mile Historical Society, named for the Six Mile Prairie, the farming community whose western section was sold to the Niedringhauses for their new town. The community was so named because it was approximately six miles from St. Louis. By the early twentieth century, Granite City's industries, businesses, and houses had swallowed up much of the area's farmland. The fully restored 1830s-era farmhouse contains a display of graniteware on the second floor. The museum is open on Sunday, 1:00 to 4:00 P.M., from May through December.

FOR MORE INFORMATION

Beuttenmuller, Doris Rose Henle. "The Granite City Steel Company: History of an American Enterprise." *Missouri Historical Society Bulletin* 10 (January 1954), pp. 135-55, 199-282.

DeChenne, David L. "Hungry Hollow: Belgian Immigrant Life in Granite City, Illinois, 1904-1921." *Gateway Heritage* 11 (Summer 1990), pp. 52-61.

———. *Labor and Immigration in a Southern Illinois Mill Town, 1890-1937.* University Microfilms International, Ann Arbor, Mich., 1989.

Engelke, Georgia. *Old Six Mile: An Early History of Granite City.* Granite City, Ill.: Old Six Mile Historical Society, 1976.

Granite City Public Library. *History of Granite City, 1896-1946.* Vol. 1. Granite City, 1953.

Special thanks to Georgia Engelke and Elmer Stille, R. C. Bush, Joe Juneau and Diane Ribbing, Jeanette L. Kampen, Louisa Bowen, Irv L. Strauss, Granite City mayor Ron Selph, Granite City city clerk Dave Williams, former Granite City city clerk Robert W. Stevens, Bob Maxwell and Norman B. Jones, Marge Burdge, Betty Meszaros, Lorna Eavenson and Diane Simon, Jerry Gura, Chris, Norma Gaines, David DeChenne, Robert Lauenstein, Tomea Kirchoff, Pat Adams, Sharon Smith, Anne Woodhouse, Eric Sandweiss, Kathy Corbett, Kris Runberg Smith, and the residents of Granite City.

THE SPREADING METROPOLIS: COMMUNITIES OF THE EARLY TWENTIETH CENTURY

EAST ST. LOUIS, ILLINOIS

From Granite City: State Highway 203 south to Interstate 55/70. Interstate 55/70 south/west to East St. Louis Third Street exit. Straight on Third Street to Broadway. Left (south) to Eighth Street. Right (west) to the State Community College.

The riverfront in East St. Louis, where twenty-two rail lines formed a major transportation hub, was once an island. The Eads Bridge, spanning the Mississippi at the top of this photograph, was an important link with St. Louis and the west. Photograph by W. C. Persons. Missouri Historical Society Photograph and Print Collection.

East St. Louis once flourished as the result of its strong ties to St. Louis and the surrounding region. In fact, the city, which bustled in the 1920s as the nation's second-busiest railroad hub, was founded because it was a prime undeveloped site directly across the river from St. Louis. In recent decades, however, East St. Louis has been cut off from the region, left isolated as major industries closed or relocated, taking East St. Louisans' jobs with them. Today, the city that for so long focused on its economic ties to St. Louis, is beginning to look internally for the necessary resources to recover.

East St. Louis dates back to the 1790s, when James Piggott built a five-mile timber and rock road northward from Cahokia through the Grand Marais, a vast swamp on the Illinois flood plain known as the American Bottom. At a point opposite St. Louis, Piggott built a ferry landing and began transporting people across the river in 1797. Piggott's road brought settlers to the American Bottom. Soon the village of Illinoistown was laid out there.

Economic ties quickly formed after a transportation link to St. Louis was established. Beginning in the late 1830s, coal mined in the Belleville bluffs was transported on a crude railroad over the Grand Marais, and to St. Louis by ferry. By 1841 farmers who worked the fertile flatland near Illinoistown produced most of the cattle, vegetables, and fruit consumed by St. Louisans.

Illinoistown's role in the region had started to solidify by the mid-nineteenth century, and the city was incorporated in 1859. In 1861 the townspeople voted to change the town's name to East St. Louis, an act which emphasized the community's relationship with its neighbor

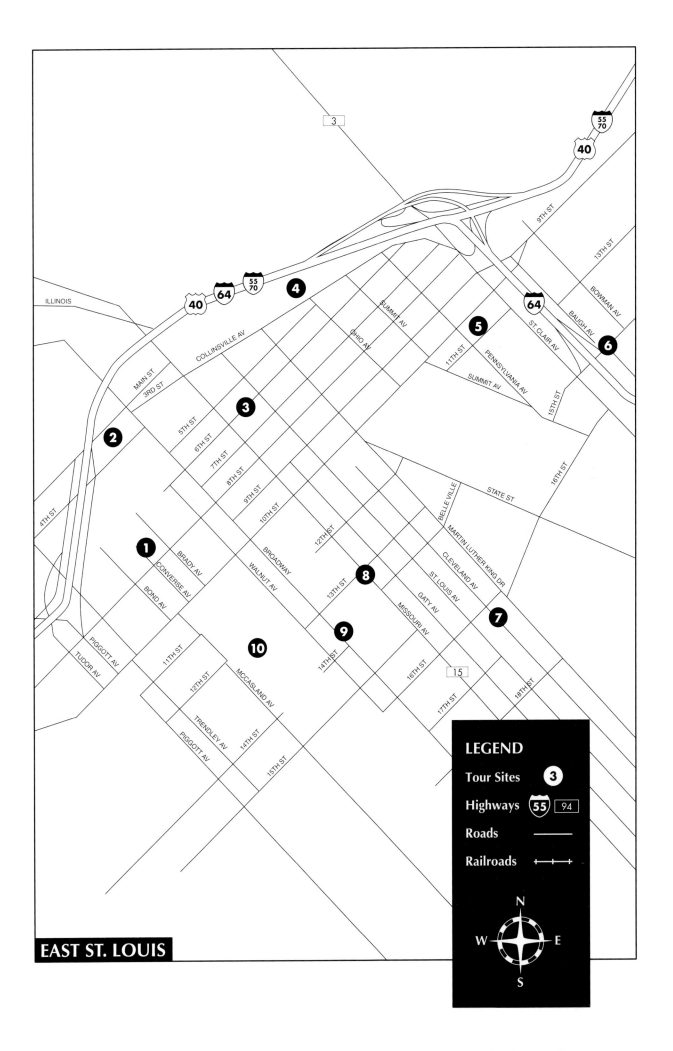

EAST ST. LOUIS

LEGEND

Tour Sites ③

Highways 🛡55 ▢94

Roads ———

Railroads ┤─┼─┼─

across the river. Industries attracted by the availability of land soon developed in and around East St. Louis, beginning with the National Stockyards, a venture organized in 1871 by investors from St. Louis, where there was no suitable, undeveloped tract of land on which to locate the business. By the end of the nineteenth century, East St. Louis had gained the nickname "the Pittsburgh of the West." New plants and factories hummed with activity, producing steel, aluminum, chemicals, glass, flour, soap, and paint pigments. The opening of the Eads Bridge in 1874 and Merchant's Bridge in 1889 facilitated shipment of these products to St. Louis and Western markets.

The booming economy attracted a diverse ethnic mix of Eastern European immigrants and African Americans from the South, who migrated to the city in search of employment. The changing population, combined with decades of municipal political corruption and long-smoldering labor frustrations, erupted in July 1917, when mobs of white residents attacked African Americans, leaving at least forty-seven people dead.

In spite of its internal problems, East St. Louis' leaders continued to focus outward, confident of the city's standing as a great industrial center. But while its industries provided jobs for residents, the largest companies were located outside the city limits and thus did not pay taxes to East St. Louis. Of all American cities with more than fifty thousand residents in 1920, East St. Louis was the second poorest. With the onset of the depression, East St. Louis' industrial base faltered and many industries closed.

Although the resumption of industrial production during World War II buoyed East St. Louis, nine of its major industries closed between 1950 and 1964. Most middle-class whites and many African Americans left the city, and the population dropped by half. Today the city's shrunken tax base not only means a dearth of jobs, but has also severely hindered East St. Louis' ability to provide basic services for residents.

In addressing its problems, the city, which for so long relied on its connections to other places, is now beginning to focus inward. East St. Louisans have renewed their commitment to their city. Community and church groups developed "Operation New Spirit," a neighborhood beautification program. In one community, local institutions and concerned citizens are joining forces to create a cultural redevelopment district, which will showcase the city's achievements in physical surroundings, the arts, and education. East St. Louisans have changed their form of government to a city-manager system in hopes of creating a more efficient city government. Riverboat gambling aboard the Casino Queen draws patrons from both sides of the river, generating several million dollars in revenue each year for the city. East St. Louis' future continues to brighten as new developments take shape, including plans for additional attractions along the riverfront.

❶ STATE COMMUNITY COLLEGE
601 James R. Thompson Boulevard

Motorists headed north on Interstate 64 pass the State Community College (SCC), a large brick building near the highway. The future of the twenty-five-year-old school is the focus of a current community debate. Because the state of Illinois cut off subsidies to the college in 1993, SCC faces a serious financial dilemma. Nearby Belleville Area College has developed a merger plan under which it would absorb SCC. However, East St. Louisans who are proud of the college and want it to remain independent are countering the plan with one of their own. Their proposal calls for a tax to be levied on the gambling riverboat Casino Queen, with half the revenue going to the college and the remainder toward development in East St. Louis and neighboring communities. East St. Louisans will go to the polls to determine SCC's future.

Flames from fires ignited during the 1917 race riot could be seen from as far away as Belleville. This view shows the East St. Louis Public Library, which suffered severe damage during the riot. Photograph by Underwood and Underwood. Missouri Historical Society Photograph and Print Collection.

❷ 1917 RACE RIOT SITES
Third and Fourth Streets, south of Broadway

One of the bloodiest racial conflicts in the nation's history took place in this area in early July 1917. During the 1910s, East St. Louis' black population grew rapidly as African Americans migrated from rural areas. White stockyard, packing plant, and factory workers perceived these new members of the community—who could be hired at lower wages—as a threat to their livelihoods.

When employees at the Aluminum Ore Corporation went on strike in April 1917, the company brought in strikebreakers, some of whom were black. Their strike defeated, white workers blamed the black strikebreakers. The racial tension was reinforced when white labor leaders protested black migration in a city council meeting a few weeks later, resulting in a flurry of sporadic rioting.

East St. Louis' smoldering racial problems came to a head on the night of July 1. The trouble started when a group of whites drove through a black neighborhood, shooting into their homes at random. The detectives who were dispatched to investigate the shooting encountered a crowd of black residents. Probably mistaking the detectives for more drive-by shooters, the residents fired on the detectives' car, killing them both. When news of their deaths reached white residents, rioting erupted in the city. On July 2, mobs of whites started pulling black citizens off of streetcars to be clubbed and stoned. Mobs invaded Third and Fourth Streets, south of Broadway, the same area they had attacked in May, and set black families' homes afire. When residents tried to escape the flames, armed whites shot them. The final toll was grim: at least thirty-nine blacks and eight whites were killed, and over three hundred buildings, many of them homes, were destroyed. Estimates contend that nearly four thousand blacks left East St. Louis for good soon after the riot. Following the riot trials were held; while eleven blacks went to prison for shooting the detectives, only four whites were convicted of murder.

❸ LINCOLN HIGH SCHOOL
(SECOND CHANCE SHELTER)
240 North Sixth Street

At its founding in 1886, Lincoln School was a combined elementary and high school for African American students. The school was named for President Abraham Lincoln, whose 1863 Emancipation Proclamation freed all slaves living in the states in rebellion against the Union during the Civil War. The school moved to 1100 East Broadway when the Lincoln building became the headquarters for the East St. Louis Board of Education in 1909. Today the original building is used as a halfway house.

❹ COLLINSVILLE AVENUE

Collinsville Avenue, East St. Louis' main commercial thoroughfare, was a significant site long before the city's founding. Recently archaeologists from Southern Illinois University unearthed evidence that around A.D. 1100 a large Indian settlement, with as many as forty-five mounds, flourished in what is now downtown East St. Louis. The largest of the mounds was located on a spot now occupied by a commercial building at 431

Collinsville. Dirt from the mounds was later used as fill for dikes, levees, and roads.

To prevent destruction from flooding—a frequent occurrence in East St. Louis—Mayor Melbern M. Stephens devised a plan in 1887 to raise the grade level of principal downtown streets, including Collinsville Avenue. Crews of workmen unloaded rock and dirt brought in on railroad flatcars. After ten years of work, the streets were nearly twenty feet higher than before. Property values skyrocketed as a result.

By the turn of the century, Collinsville Avenue had grown into the city's premier business and entertainment district. The Seidel Apparel Company, still a downtown landmark, opened in 1905. By the 1920s, five theaters graced Collinsville Avenue, including the $1 million Majestic, built by Harry Redmon in 1928. The opulent Majestic, the city's first talking picture palace, served as

Dating to the 1920s, the Spivey Building continues to dominate the downtown skyline. The building, which can be seen from the East St. Louis MetroLink stop, served for a time as the State Community College. It is now vacant. Photograph by W. C. Persons, Missouri Historical Photograph and Print Collection.

East St. Louis' main entertainment attraction until it closed in the 1970s. The theater building continues to overshadow the pawn shops, shoe stores, and taverns that line Collinsville Avenue today.

⑤ KATHERINE DUNHAM DYNAMIC MUSEUM
1005 Pennsylvania Avenue

After coming to East St. Louis in 1967 to teach at Southern Illinois University, renowned dancer, choreographer, and activist Katherine Dunham not only founded a performing arts training center there but also created a curriculum in dance anthropology. In the late 1970s, a group of Dunham's supporters acquired the Judge Maurice Joyce Mansion to serve as the Katherine Dunham Museum. Dunham Company performance costumes, African and Caribbean folk and contemporary art, original paintings by Dunham, and various musical instruments are all on display in the museum. It is open by appointment. Call (618) 271-3367 for information.

The area around the museum is part of a historic district once known as "Quality Hill." In the 1900s many well-to-do East St. Louisans, including mayors and prominent businessmen, lived in mansions that lined Pennsylvania and Summit Avenues. A fifteen-block cultural redevelopment district is planned for the neighborhood. A coalition of ten East St. Louis organizations and institutions, including the Katherine Dunham Centers for the Arts and Humanities, is pulling the district together around the Hughes Quinn-Rock Junior High School. Educational and cultural programs will be developed in the school and other neighborhood institutions, buildings will be refurbished, and landscaping will be completed. The neighborhood is planned to serve as a model for other East St. Louis communities.

⑥ IMMACULATE CONCEPTION LITHUANIAN CATHOLIC CHURCH
Fifteenth Street and Baugh Avenue

Immaculate Conception Catholic Church is one of the last ethnic parishes remaining in East St. Louis. Lithuanians fleeing Russian oppression immigrated to the United States in large numbers in the late nineteenth century. Attracted by plentiful jobs in the coal, steel, and meat-packing industries, many settled in the neighborhoods of northern East St. Louis. A group of Lithuanians who wanted to worship in their native language organized Immaculate Conception Parish in 1895 and built their first frame church in 1897. Fire destroyed the church in 1943, and services were held in the basement until the new church, a distinctive structure designed by Lithuanian architect Jonas Mulokas, was completed on the same site in 1955.

The "Quality Hill" district of East St. Louis, today the location of the Katherine Dunham Dynamic Museum, was a popular area for prominent East St. Louisans. This house, which stood at 802 Summit Avenue, was the home of Paul W. Abt, president of the First National Bank of East St. Louis. Missouri Historical Society Photograph and Print Collection.

The neighborhood around the church was integrated and within walking distance of the stockyards and packing plants. Jazz musician Miles Davis lived there as a child. Davis recalls the community as being ethnically mixed, "with Jews and Germans and Armenians and Greeks living all around us."

⑦ JUDGE BILLY JONES ELEMENTARY SCHOOL
1601 Cleveland Street

First called Monroe Elementary, this school's name was changed to honor Judge Billy Jones in 1987. The first African American associate judge in the Twentieth Judicial Circuit Court of Illinois, Jones received national attention in 1949 when he challenged the existing "separate but equal" policy by taking African American children into nine all-white public schools. Later, Jones filed a suit on behalf of the NAACP that was successful in integrating public schools in East St. Louis and Sparta and Cairo, Illinois. Jones consulted for several 1952 United States Supreme Court school desegregation cases, culminating in the court's 1954 landmark *Brown v. Board of Education, Topeka, Kansas* decision. Jones was also president of the Illinois NAACP and the National Bar Association. Judge Billy Jones Day, held annually on the third Monday in September, honors this important civil rights pioneer.

8 ORR-WEATHERS APARTMENTS
1300 Missouri Avenue

This twenty-two-acre housing project built in 1960-61 consists of two high-rise buildings and thirty-nine low-rise buildings, with a combined total of 588 living units. In the mid-1980s, two other high-rises were closed when funds scheduled for their renovation were misappropriated.

The housing project honors two prominent African American East St. Louisans: Louis Orr, city attorney, and Dr. Henry H. Weathers, Jr., a heart surgeon. Both were members of the housing board. Dr. Weathers, a well-known physician in East St. Louis, had his office near Thirteenth Street and Missouri Avenue. The city purchased his office site after his death to serve as the site of a public housing development. Louis Orr urged officials to name the development after Dr. Weathers, but Orr died before the buildings could be named. In order to honor both men, the city dedicated the buildings as Orr-Weathers Apartments in 1963.

9 MACEDONIA BAPTIST CHURCH
1335 East Broadway

Macedonia Baptist Church moved to its present site at Fourteenth and Broadway in 1929. Macedonia, originally known as the First Colored Baptist Church, dates to 1863, when it was established on Carr Island. The church's name has been changed twice: first to Macedonia Colored Baptist, and finally to Macedonia Baptist of East St. Louis, Inc.

10 LINCOLN HIGH SCHOOL (NEW)
1211 Bond Avenue

Lincoln High School moved to this site, its third location, in 1950. Among the school's well-known graduates is Olympic gold medalist Jackie Joyner-Kersee, who graduated from Lincoln High in 1980. Kersee was a member of Lincoln track teams coached by Nino Fennoy, which won Illinois Class AA championships in three consecutive years: 1978, 1979, and 1980. Other famous Lincoln graduates include jazz trumpeter Miles Davis. Today Lincoln High School has one of the premier high school jazz ensembles in the nation.

FOR MORE INFORMATION

Baldwin, Carl R. "East St. Louis History," in *History of St. Clair County, Illinois.* Vol. 2. Comp. by St. Clair County Genealogical Society. Dallas, Tex.: Curtis Media Corp., 1992.

English, W. Edward. *The Good Things of East St. Louis.* Mascoutah, Ill.: Top's Books, 1992.

Wright, John A. *Discovering African-American St. Louis: A Guide to Historic Sites.* St. Louis: Missouri Historical Society Press, 1994.

Yelvington, Ruben L. *East St. Louis, The Way It Is, 1990.* Mascoutah, Ill.: Top's Books, 1990.

Special thanks to Norman Ross, East St. Louis Chamber of Commerce, Katherine Dunham Centers for the Arts and Humanities, East St. Louis Business and Economic Development Office, Kirsten Hammerstrom, and the residents of East St. Louis.

MIDTOWN

From Lincoln High School (East St. Louis): Broadway north to Main. Right on Main to Interstate 55 south. Interstate 55 across the Mississippi. Continue on Interstate 64 (Highway 40) to the Forest Park Boulevard/ Grand Boulevard exit. Turn right on Grand to enter the city's Midtown area.

The Shubert-Rialto, on Grand just south of Olive, opened in 1912 as a vaudeville house called the Princess Theatre. The first theater built in the neighborhood, it operated under many names before it was razed in the late 1970s. Photograph by W. C. Persons. Missouri Historical Society Photograph and Print Collection.

Midtown St. Louis has undergone many changes since its heyday as a theater and commercial district in the first half of this century. In the 1920s the area rivaled downtown as the heart of the city. Tradition held that everyone in St. Louis passed by the corner of Grand Boulevard and Olive Street at some time. By the 1960s, that was no longer the case. Highway 40 had bypassed the neighborhood, and streetcars no longer brought in the shoppers and theatergoers who had once made it prosper. Businesses and theaters closed, residents moved out, and the neighborhood fell into disrepair. During the past twenty years, a series of redevelopment efforts have been implemented to carve out a new identity for Midtown, one which builds on its past rather than merely seeking to duplicate it.

Although today Midtown is the geographical center of St. Louis, the area was largely rural before 1850. An 1855 ordinance expanded the city's boundaries to just slightly west of Grand, and by 1864, the Missouri Railroad Company's horse car line ran out Olive to the new limits. In 1867 the Grand Avenue Railway Company ran a line on Grand from the old water tower at North Twentieth Street south to Meramec. These routes, which were electrified in the 1890s, formed a transit crossroads at Grand and Olive. An enterprising turn-of-the-century press agent proclaimed the Grand-Olive intersection to be "fifteen minutes from anywhere"—Baden, Carondelet, a downtown office, or an uptown home were but a short streetcar ride away.

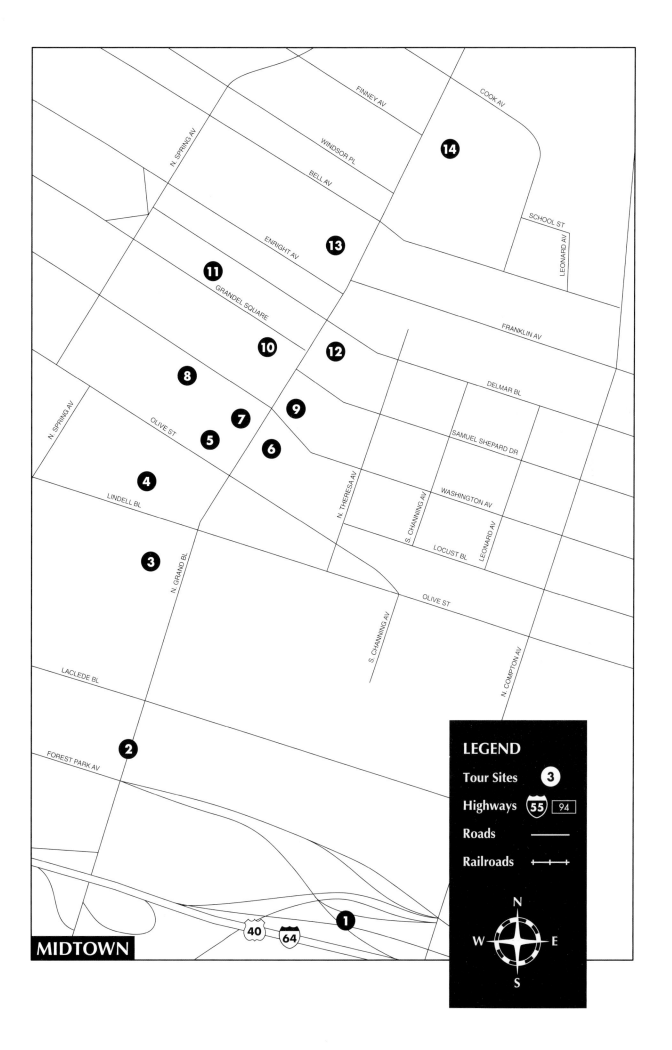

MIDTOWN

LEGEND

Tour Sites ③

Highways 55 94

Roads ——

Railroads ┼┼┼

The Midtown we recognize today began to take shape in the 1880s when Saint Louis University moved into its new campus at the corner of Grand and Lindell. The 1912 opening of the Princess Theatre, a vaudeville house on Grand just south of Olive, marked the beginning of Midtown's theatrical era. The Princess was joined by other theaters in the 1910s and 1920s, including the St. Louis Theatre (now Powell Hall) and the most opulent of all, the Fox, at Grand and Washington. Dance palaces and jazz clubs added to the neighborhood's nightlife. But Midtown was more than an entertainment district. During the 1920s St. Louis' oldest and most exclusive clubs and fraternal organizations erected imposing buildings along Lindell and Grand. The easily accessible location also appealed to professionals, with some fifteen hundred doctors and dentists locating their offices there by the late 1920s. Most conspicuous among the commercial establishments that lined surrounding streets were the deluxe auto showrooms, which attracted shoppers from around the city.

Ironically, it was the automobile that also took people out of Midtown in the 1950s, when theaters, stores, and professional offices began to relocate in less crowded outlying areas. When the Grand Avenue Viaduct was razed in 1960 as part of the Mill Creek Valley slum clearance project, the north-south streetcar service that had made Midtown the heart of the city was ended as well. By the late 1960s, the newly completed Daniel Boone Expressway (Highway 40) allowed traffic to bypass Grand altogether as it passed through the Mill Creek Valley out to St. Louis County.

Still, some institutions remained committed to redeveloping the area. Saint Louis University, the Third Baptist Church, the Scottish Rite, and the St. Louis Symphony Orchestra all played important roles in revitalizing the Midtown area. In 1972 Saint Louis University Chancellor Rev. Paul Reinert founded the Midtown Forum, an organization that worked to bring businesses and low-income housing back to Midtown.

The redevelopment efforts that began with the Midtown Forum eventually helped lead to the formation of Grand Center, Inc., in 1987. Grand Center is a private, not-for-profit organization formed to create a secure urban neighborhood by building and supporting visual and performing arts facilities in the area. Among Grand Center's accomplishments are the Grandel Square Theatre (St. Louis' first new theater in twenty years) and an innovative streetlighting plan that highlights the area's architecture as it enhances security.

Grand Center's approach to redeveloping the Midtown area builds on the neighborhood's proud history as a theater district. The organization's success may catalyze other aspects of Midtown's economic development, as well as provide a model for other St. Louis neighborhoods.

❶ MILL CREEK VALLEY

Named for a creek that ran from Vandeventer and Market streets to the Mississippi River, the Mill Creek Valley stretched from Twentieth Street west to Grand Boulevard, and from Olive Street south to the railroad tracks. A fashionable place of residence in the mid-nineteenth century, by the beginning of this century the area had become a mix of mansions, tenements, shops, businesses, factories, dance halls, taverns, clubs, churches, schools, and other institutions. At the honky-tonk district along Chestnut and Market streets near Twentieth, Scott Joplin and other musicians played ragtime music at nightclubs like Tom Turpin's Rosebud Cafe. Mill Creek Valley was home to a large African American population, which grew dramatically after World War II due to a large migration from the rural South.

By 1954 the area's population of twenty thousand people was nearly 95 percent African American. In that year, city voters approved a massive bond issue that included plans to redevelop Mill Creek Valley. In 1959 demolition of housing and structures in the 465-acre area began forcing thousands of St. Louisans to move elsewhere. The completion of the Daniel Boone Expressway in the late 1960s brought traffic streaming through the former Mill Creek Valley. North of the highway, St. Louis University expanded its campus onto land cleared in the redevelopment, while the Laclede Town and the Grand Towers apartments provided some housing to replace the old. Today, MetroLink riders who pass through the old Mill Creek Valley see no traces of the heavily populated, bustling neighborhood of the early twentieth century.

The Grand Avenue Viaduct spanned the railroad tracks in Mill Creek Valley from 1890 until it was torn down in 1960. Streetcar service along Grand in Midtown was ended when the viaduct was razed. Here the northern half of the bridge has been dismantled. Photograph by Irv Schankman. Missouri Historical Society Photograph and Print Collection.

Streetcar lines intersected at Grand and Olive, making it a bustling corner for businesses like Liggett's Rexall Drugs and F. W. Woolworth's. Photograph by W. C. Persons. Missouri Historical Society Photograph and Print Collection.

❷ GRAND BOULEVARD

In the 1850s real estate agent Hiram Leffingwell envisioned a grand boulevard that would extend the length of the city to mark St. Louis' western boundary. The new street was realized in the 1870s, and transportation routes, first in the form of horse-drawn omnibuses and later as electric trolleys, led to Grand's development as a commercial thoroughfare. In spite of the loss of the trolley system, Grand Boulevard continues to be an important link for the city's north and south sides, and was vital to the Midtown area's development as a commercial and entertainment district.

❸ SAINT LOUIS UNIVERSITY
Grand Boulevard at Lindell Boulevard

Founded in 1818, Saint Louis University has long been an anchoring institution for the Midtown community. The school moved from its crowded site at Ninth and Washington to its new campus at Grand and Lindell in 1888, and the landmark St. Francis Xavier Church, also called "College Church," was completed in 1898. The university acquired the Samuel Cupples House on West Pine Boulevard in 1946. This 49-room Romanesque Revival mansion—a vestige of the era when opulent residences graced Midtown—now contains the university's art center. In 1962, the college purchased 22.5 acres of slum-cleared property in the Mill Creek Valley Redevelopment Area, to the east of Grand Boulevard. Several classroom buildings, lecture halls, and an athletic field have since been constructed on the site. Recently the university acquired the former St. Louis Club building on Lindell for use as graduate school offices. In the early 1980s, University Chancellor Paul C. Reinert formulated the City Center Redevelopment Corporation's master plan for revitalizing Midtown's cultural and

commercial district. The university remains deeply involved in the redevelopment of Grand Center and the Midtown community as a whole.

❹ SCOTTISH RITE CATHEDRAL
3633 Lindell Boulevard

Built in 1924, the Scottish Rite Cathedral is a monumental building with an imposing two-hundred-foot frontage. Designed by St. Louis architect William B. Ittner, the building's construction required the demolition of several mansions. In the early 1970s, the Scottish Rite, a Masonic organization, became active in the Midtown Forum, a coalition of Midtown businesses and institutions that together worked to redevelop the neighborhood and bring new businesses into the area. The Scottish Rite continues to play an integral role in Grand Center's redevelopment.

❺ CONTINENTAL BUILDING
3615 Olive Street

The twenty-two-story Continental Building has towered over its Midtown neighbors since its completion in 1929. Also designed by William B. Ittner, the Art Deco skyscraper originally housed the Continental Insurance Company, while the Grand National Bank operated on the building's ground floor. Ed Mays, the banker and insurance executive who built the Continental for $2 million, lived with his family in an opulent three-story penthouse apartment on the premises. Implicated in a robbery of the Grand National Bank, Mays lost control of the bank, insurance company, and the building in 1934. For the next forty years the Continental passed through a succession of owners, but since 1974 it has been unoccupied. Today, Grand Center, Inc., has the option to buy the property for future restoration.

6 VAUGHN GALLERY AND CULTURAL CENTER
524 North Grand Boulevard

Organized in 1977, the Vaughn Gallery and Cultural
Center began as a cultural enrichment program of the
Urban League. Ermalene Lovell Vaughn contributed
funds for the establishment of the center in memory
of her husband, Dr. Arthur N. Vaughn. The Vaughn
Cultural Center is a neighborhood-based organization
that brings the resources of the regional arts institutions
into the North St. Louis community. The center houses
a gallery for exhibition by African American artists
and promotes appreciation and understanding of black
history and culture by sponsoring cultural events
and activities.

7 FOX THEATRE
527 North Grand Boulevard

When it opened in 1929, the Fox Theatre—with 5,060
seats—was the second largest theater in the country.
William C. Fox, theatrical magnate and founder of
Twentieth Century Fox, built the theater as part of his
motion picture empire. Its eclectic design, combining
Moorish, Far Eastern, and Indian motifs, features ele-
phants, lions, and scimitar-wielding rajahs that enliven
the lobby and sides of the stage. The Fox was privately
purchased in 1981 and has undergone extensive renovation, including installation of state-of-the-art sound,
lighting, and stage equipment. Today the Fox presents
major touring theatrical productions and concerts. Tours
of the theater are available. Call 534-1678 for information.

8 SHELDON CONCERT HALL
3646 Washington Avenue

Completed in 1912, this building is a memorial to
Walter L. Sheldon, who organized the St. Louis Ethical
Society in the 1880s. The Ethical Society, which used
the building as its meeting house until 1966, began as
a quasi-religious organization that stressed intellectual
freedom and philanthropic actions. After the Ethical
Society's move to the county, the Sheldon was used as
a church until 1985, when a concert promoter took
over the building. After extensive renovation, the
Sheldon reopened the following year as a concert hall.
The Sheldon's auditorium is nationally known for its
fine acoustics. The Sheldon Arts Foundation took over
building operations in 1991, and—with plans for
expansion—recently acquired the building just west
of the Sheldon.

9 THIRD BAPTIST CHURCH
620 North Grand Boulevard

Organized in 1850, the Third Baptist Church has
been located at its present site since 1885. The church
remained on Grand as the Midtown area became more
commercialized. In 1950 the current Third Baptist
Church was built around the older building. A leader
in the redevelopment of the Midtown area, the church
is dedicated to remaining in the neighborhood and often
opens its large facilities for use by community groups.

10 GRANDEL SQUARE THEATRE
3610 Grandel Square

This building was dedicated in 1884 as the First
Congregational Church. In later years, Methodist
and Pentecostal congregations owned the Romanesque
Revival church. A two-year, $4.5-million renovation
project converted the church into a 470-seat theater,
which opened in the fall of 1992 and is currently the
main stage home of the St. Louis Black Repertory
Company and a venue for other performing arts productions. Founded in 1976, the St. Louis Black Repertory
Company strives to heighten social and cultural aware-
ness of the African American perspective through the
performing arts.

11 URBAN LEAGUE OF METROPOLITAN ST. LOUIS
3701 Grandel Square

Formed in 1910, the St. Louis chapter of the Urban
League was the first interracial social organization in
the city. The organization was originally formed to assist
African American migrants moving from the rural South
to the St. Louis area in search of jobs. Throughout its
history, the Urban League has aggressively addressed
such problems as segregation, discrimination, and unemployment while advocating improved housing, cultural
resources, and health-care facilities. The Grandel Square
Building, the Urban League's headquarters since 1981,
previously housed the John Berry Meachum Branch of
the St. Louis Public Library.

12 POWELL SYMPHONY HALL
712 North Grand Boulevard

Powell Symphony Hall, home of the St. Louis Symphony
Orchestra, was built in 1925 as the St. Louis Theatre by
the firm of Rapp and Rapp of Chicago. For nearly forty
years, this theater presented vaudeville and motion pictures until the Symphony purchased the building in the
mid-1960s. In 1966, the St. Louis architectural firm of
Wedemeyer, Cernik, & Corrubia undertook a $2 million

renovation effort that included replacing the seats, refurbishing the dressing rooms, and redesigning the orchestra shell. The old theater was renamed to honor manufacturer Walter S. Powell, whose widow, Helen Lamb Powell, contributed extensively to the hall's renovation. In moving to Powell Hall, the St. Louis Symphony has returned to its old neighborhood near its original location at the former Odeon Theatre, where the orchestra was in residence from the turn of the century until it moved to the Kiel Auditorium in 1934. The Symphony's residence at Powell Hall, and its strong support of the Grand Center redevelopment project, demonstrates the organization's commitment to the Midtown neighborhood.

⑬ VANDEVENTER PLACE

At the close of the nineteenth century, the area bounded by Delmar Boulevard (then Morgan), Jefferson Avenue, the Mill Creek Valley, and Vandeventer was a tree-lined community of over eighteen hundred homes, interspersed with fine gardens and exquisite churches. The pinnacle of prestige in St. Louis addresses was Vandeventer Place, an exclusive private neighborhood laid out in 1870 by Julius Pitzman. The neighborhood ran west from Grand between Enright and Bell. Nationally renowned architects, including H. H. Richardson, designed elegant mansions for some of the city's most influential residents. Commercial development in Midtown and the opening of newer private places in the Central West End led to the end of Vandeventer Place's reign. In 1947 the Veterans Administration razed the east end of Vandeventer Place, from Grand to Spring, and built the John C. Cochran Veterans Administration Hospital. Not far from the hospital, the Blumeyer Housing Project, which offered low-income public housing to some of the many families displaced from Mill Creek Valley, opened in the late 1960s.

Today, one of the goals of the Grand Center redevelopment effort is to create a mixed-use neighborhood with performing and visual arts facilities, offices, stores, and residences. Following renovation, the fifteen-story University Club building, long a meeting place for the city's oldest social organization, reopened in 1986 with eighty-three apartments and commercial space on the ground floor.

⑭ ST. ALPHONSUS LIGUORI (ROCK) CHURCH
1118 North Grand Boulevard

Established in the late 1860s as a parish for Irish immigrants, St. Alphonsus' congregation today is predominantly African American. Its nickname, the "Rock" church, may stem from its being one of the first churches in St. Louis built of quarry stone. The St. Louis firm of Conradi and Schrader did much of the work on the

Vandeventer Place, an exclusive private place established in the 1870s, was home to many of the city's most prominent businessmen. This view shows the east gate looking west from Grand, where the Veteran's Administration Hospital stands today. The gates were re-erected near the Jewel Box in Forest Park. Missouri Historical Society Photograph and Print Collection.

church including constructing the steeples, which were added to the structure in 1894. St. Alphonsus, today known for its outstanding gospel choir, uses African American traditions in its music and liturgical style.

FOR MORE INFORMATION

Eberle, Jean Fahey. *Midtown: A Grand Place to Be.* St. Louis: Mercantile Trust Company, 1980.

Wayman, Norbury L. *History of St. Louis Neighborhoods: Midtown.* St. Louis: St. Louis Community Development Agency, 1980.

Wright, John A. *Discovering African-American St. Louis: A Guide to Historic Sites.* St. Louis: Missouri Historical Society Press, 1994.

Special thanks to Thom M. Digman, Laurel Meinig Brewster, Grand Center, Inc., Opal Morris, Third Baptist Church, Eric Sandweiss, Katharine Corbett, Duane Sneddeker, Kirsten Hammerstrom, David Schultz, Katie Velasco, and the residents of Midtown.

THE SPREADING METROPOLIS: COMMUNITIES OF THE EARLY TWENTIETH CENTURY

Grand-Oak Hill

From St. Alphonsus Liguori (Rock) Church (Midtown): Grand Avenue south to Arsenal Street. (You will pass the entrance to the Shaw neighborhood, the next chapter, just after crossing Interstate 44.) Arsenal right (west) to South Kingshighway Boulevard.

Several communities make up the Grand-Oak Hill neighborhood, including Parkside South. This area features an eclectic mix of housing, as evidenced by the varying roof lines in this 1934 view, taken at Alfred and Hartford. Photograph by Richard Moore. Missouri Historical Society Photograph and Print Collection.

A walk through the Grand-Oak Hill neighborhood, which extends west from Grand to Kingshighway and south from Arsenal to Chippewa, reveals little of the subterranean wealth on which this community was built. Once a rural outpost, home to immigrant miners and farmers, the area's quarries and fields were leveled for house lots, and its streets were soon populated with merchants and middle-class homeowners. The neighborhood's character has continued to change. With rapidly growing Southeast Asian and Eastern European communities, it is one of the most ethnically diverse areas of the city.

In the late eighteenth century the area west of Grand between Arsenal and Chippewa made up part of the *Prairie des Noyers,* an area of rich agricultural land divided into long, narrow strips called common fields. In 1805, as the *Prairie des Noyers* fields were being divided further and sold, the Russell family purchased a large tract of the land. It was here that they built their estate, Oak Hill. Around 1820 James Russell discovered a vein of coal on the property. The "Gravois coal diggin's," as the area was soon known, became an important source of fuel for the growing city. Although the coal deposits were exhausted by the 1880s, the Parker-Russell Mining Company maintained a lucrative business quarrying fire clay from its mines. The arrival of the St. Louis, Oak Hill and Carondelet (later Missouri Pacific) Railroad in 1885 helped extend the company's markets at the same time that it brought other industries to the area.

GRAND-OAK HILL

LEGEND
Tour Sites ③
Highways (55) 94
Roads
Railroads

N E S W

Tower Grove Park

ARSENAL ST
KEMPER AV
CONNECTICUT ST
FYLER AV
PARKER AV
FAIRVIEW AV
POTOMAC ST

KINGSHIGHWAY BL

LACKLAND AV
JUNIATA ST

ALFRED AV

MORGANFORD RD

BECK AV

HARTFORD ST
JUNIATA ST
CONNECTICUT ST
WYOMING ST
HUMPHREY ST
UTAH ST
MCDONALD AV

CONNECTICUT ST
WYOMING ST

UTAH PL

GRAND BL
GRACE AV

SPRING AV

GUSTINE AV

ROGER PL

OAK HILL AV

BENT AV

POTOMAC ST

THOLOZAN AV

GRAVOIS AV

CHIPPEWA ST

Although Welsh and British immigrants originally came to work in the mines, after 1850 a newer generation of German-born settlers prospered as truck farmers and merchants. The Germans built their own church and school, creating a community life of their own that, in time, overtook that of their predecessors. Oak Hill changed along with its population. The community, which had been considered a suburb, became part of St. Louis when the city limits expanded westward in 1876.

The arrival of public transit service in the early 1900s brought major changes to the character of the neighborhood. The Tower Grove branch of the Union Depot Railroad extended its electric trolley line westward along Arsenal Street to Kingshighway. Subdivisions sprang up near the streetcar track, and homes were built on former farmland. Neat rows of single- and two-family brick homes in the vicinity of Grand and Arsenal contrasted sharply with the frame cottages of miners who lived in "The Alley" between Beck and Chippewa, near Kingshighway.

The improved transit system spurred commercial development along the neighborhood's main streets. Businesses and banks lined South Grand by the 1920s. Shoppers could catch a streetcar to bakeries, drug stores, tailor shops, meat markets, and movie theaters on South Grand. Development on Kingshighway took a different course. There, large industrial lots, the former sites of fire brick companies along the railroad line, hampered development of the kind of small-scale shopping district that had formed along South Grand. Commercial development along Kingshighway catered to automobile rather than streetcar traffic.

Today the Grand-Oak Hill neighborhood continues to adapt to changing times. The Grand-Oak Hill Community Corporation, the umbrella organization for the neighborhood, is rehabbing a historic storefront building to serve as a community center. Along the eastern edge of the neighborhood more than thirty new businesses have opened on South Grand, revitalizing a commercial district that had seriously declined. Many of the new businesses are specialty stores and restaurants owned and operated by Asian-American immigrants, mainly from Vietnam. Others, owned by Thais, Filipinos, Arabs, and Germans, make shopping on South Grand an international experience. As new groups move to the area and contribute to the community, the faces of Grand-Oak Hill continue to change, as they have throughout the neighborhood's history.

The frame shaft house was a familiar sight around the neighborhood. The structure housed the machinery that lifted clay and miners from the underground workings. Photograph by Richard Gruss. Missouri Historical Society Photograph and Print Collection.

❶ SOUTH KINGSHIGHWAY BOULEVARD

Long one of St. Louis' important thoroughfares, Kingshighway originated in the eighteenth century as an outer road, running just beyond the fields surrounding what was then a colonial village. Its name is derived from the French phrase *Route de Roi*, literally "the king's highway." For generations Kingshighway lay undeveloped. In the mid-nineteenth century the discovery of coal led to the opening of the Russell coal mines along the thoroughfare. Still, as late as 1874 most of the area along South Kingshighway remained farmland, but it would not remain so for long. By the turn of the century, press-brick plants had opened at the clay deposits along the road, and Kingshighway improvement was soon proposed as part of a citywide dress-up for the 1904 World's Fair. But substantial residential and business development did not take place along this stretch of the road until the late 1920s, when realty companies, feed stores, construction companies, and service stations opened on South Kingshighway. The opening of the Southtown Famous-Barr department store and its spacious parking lot in 1951 (demolished in 1994) characterized South Kingshighway as a commercial thoroughfare easily accessible by automobile. Today the street is lined with automobile dealerships, service stations, auto parts stores, and drive-in restaurants.

2 AMERICAN NATIONAL CAN COMPANY
3200 South Kingshighway Boulevard

The streamlined buildings of the American National Can Company plant give motorists on Kingshighway a hint of the neighborhood's industrial district along the railroad line. In 1942 American Can moved from north St. Louis to this location, formerly occupied by the Superior Brick Company. The U.S. Navy took over the can company during World War II, converting it into a torpedo-making plant known as Amertorp Defense. Workers made more than seven thousand torpedoes there before the plant returned to container manufacturing in 1946. In the mid-1950s the plant expanded, adding a warehouse, storage facilities, and new rail spurs from the Missouri-Pacific railway tracks to the south. These changes allowed the company to receive and process longer strips of tin and steel plate. At its peak in the 1970s, American Can employed one thousand people who produced millions of beer and beverage cans annually for Anheuser-Busch and other companies. Today the company's 450 employees primarily manufacture coffee cans.

3 CHURCH OF THE HOLY FAMILY
4125 Humphrey Street

The Church of the Holy Family was founded in 1898 as a German-language parish. For the first year the 125-family parish rented a home on Wyoming Street to serve as a church and school. In 1899 a new church building was opened on Humphrey Street. This church housed the congregation until the present structure, at the corner of Humphrey and Oak Hill, was built in 1926. The Romanesque-style church is constructed of variegated granite, which lends an imposing appearance. The present Holy Family School, at 4132 Wyoming, was completed in 1941. Today the school serves 310 students from kindergarten through the eighth grade. In 1963 a parish center was built at 4141 Humphrey. The center includes a gym, a kitchen, and a variety of meeting rooms.

Holy Family Parish was part of a neighborhood ecumenical group comprised of several local churches which together spearheaded the effort to form the Grand-Oak Hill Community Corporation in 1972. Father David Rauch of Holy Family Church served as the community corporation's first president. The church remains active in the organization today.

4 OAK HILL PRESBYTERIAN CHURCH
4111 Connecticut Street

Oak Hill Presbyterian Church was organized in 1895. The members built their first frame church at the corner of Bent Avenue and Humphrey. After a fire destroyed the building in 1907, the small congregation bought a lot for a new church at the corner of Oak Hill and Connecticut. The church and chapel were built in four sections as money was raised; they finally were completed in 1919. In those days corn fields made up the area around Arsenal, Hartford, and Oak Hill to Gustine. Congregants wore boots to church in order to negotiate the muddy streets. Church membership grew with the neighborhood, doubling between the years 1940 to 1945. In 1950 the church acquired the eleven-room house to its west for use as Sunday school classrooms. Three years later construction began on an educational building that provided even more classroom space and linked the church to the house. Today Oak Hill Presbyterian's 220-family congregation is spread throughout the metropolitan region. Since 1974 the church has rented out the house at 4115 Connecticut to the American Indian Center of Mid-America, an organization which provides social services to the local Native American community.

5 HORACE MANN SCHOOL
4047 Juniata Street

Horace Mann School, named for the nineteenth-century educator, has served the Oak Hill community since 1902, making it the oldest remaining school building in the neighborhood. The Tudor Revival building was designed by prominent St. Louis architect William B. Ittner. The extremely narrow lot upon which the school was to be built posed a challenge to Ittner, whose design, a variation of his typical "open plan," is specially suited to the site. Mann School, along with several other Ittner-designed schools around St. Louis, was recently added to the National Register of Historic Places.

6 DICKMANN BUILDING
3115-3117 South Grand Boulevard

The six-story, Art Deco Dickmann Building near the corner of Grand and Arsenal is an example of the ongoing change that characterizes the South Grand business district. Built in 1926 to house the Joseph F. Dickmann Real Estate Company, scores of doctors and dentists also occupied the building's 107 offices. In 1946 the Queen's Work Press purchased both the Dickmann Building and the corner building next door for use as a printing plant. The press published booklets, pamphlets, and the national *Queen's Work* magazine, the journal for the

Gravois had long been a main thoroughfare when this photograph of L. L. Coryell's service station was taken in the 1930s. Coryell's attracted customers with gasoline prices advertised as "always less" and the added inducement of free cake and coffee on Saturdays. Photograph by Richard Gruss. Missouri Historical Society Photograph and Print Collection.

Sodality of Our Lady, a Catholic religious society. After the Dickmann Building had stood vacant for a decade, the New Apostolic Church bought it in 1970 and rented space to various tenants, including Siegfried's IV Restaurant. Today Richard Deutsch owns the building, which now houses offices and a futon company.

❼ SOUTH GRAND BOULEVARD

In 1874 South Grand from Arsenal to Chippewa was open land dotted with a few houses. The area near Grand and Gravois featured a greater degree of development, due to Gravois' longer history as a transportation route. Rapid development in the early 1900s brought bakeries, drug stores, saloons, tailors, butchers, music schools, doctors, and dentists to the boulevard. Grand experienced a decline in the late 1960s, when most of the businesses lining the street closed. In 1974 the Jay International Food store opened, specializing in Asian foods. Jay, at 3172 South Grand, received a contract from the nearby International Institute of St. Louis to provide foods for the incoming Asian refugees that the institute aided in resettlement. Jay's acted as an anchor store for Asian development in the area, and today South Grand features Vietnamese, Thai, and Filipino restaurants as well as a host of ethnic markets and specialty shops. Most recently, chain stores, including Streetside Records and the St. Louis Bread Company, have opened in the area, drawn by the successful business climate. Much effort has been made to revitalize South Grand. Store owners and their families work extremely long hours in order to establish their businesses. The South Grand Business Association, which coordinates and promotes commercial development in the district, sponsors Summerfest, an annual celebration of the area's distinct multicultural character.

❽ TOWER GROVE HEIGHTS SUBDIVISION
Bounded by Arsenal Street, Grand Boulevard, Utah Place, and Gustine Street

In the late 1880s much of the land in this area, including the Russell tract, was subdivided and housing was built on the former farmland. The Tower Grove Heights subdivision opened in 1905 after a streetcar line was extended west on Arsenal to Kingshighway. The Connecticut Realty Company financed the development and left its mark on the subdivision with three street names: Hartford, Connecticut, and Humphrey, after Humphrey Green, president of the realty company. Deed restrictions in the subdivision required the construction of two-story homes set back uniformly from the street. Blocks were divided in rows of spacious, forty-foot-wide lots, which sold for about forty dollars per front foot. Houses and duplexes in the subdivision went for four to six thousand dollars, a higher than average price for the time. Utah Place, at the southern edge of Tower Grove Heights, was designed as an especially attractive street with fine houses and a tree-lined median. By 1918 a number of physicians, building contractors, and architects lived on Utah, along with many families of German descent. The Tower Grove Heights Neighborhood Association, one of Grand-Oak Hill's neighborhood organizations, represents residents in the subdivision. Residents from Morganford west to Kingshighway belong to the Parkside South Neighborhood Association. The Grand-Oak Hill Community Corporation serves residents throughout the entire Grand-Oak Hill neighborhood.

9 SOUTH SIDE NATIONAL BANK
3606 Gravois Avenue

South Side National Bank, at the intersection of Grand and Gravois, marks an important site in the community. The area became a popular stopping point after 1860, when a grocery and saloon opened there. These establishments catered to farmers who took their produce into town via Gravois. When Grand Avenue opened in the 1870s, the intersection became the center of a rapidly developing north-south thoroughfare. Streetcar lines ran along Grand and Gravois by the early 1890s, bringing more people to the district. In 1907 the Farmers and Merchants Trust Company opened at the intersection. The original Farmers building was replaced with a new structure in 1914. This building still stands at the southeast corner of Grand and Gravois. Farmers merged with the South Side Trust Company, founded by Adolphus Busch in 1891, to form the South Side National Bank. South Side's ten-story art deco building opened in 1929.

FOR MORE INFORMATION

Boyer, Mary Joan. "The Old Gravois Coal Diggings." *The Tri-City Independent,* (Festus, Mo.), 1952.

Hannon, Robert E., ed. *St. Louis: Its Neighborhoods and Neighbors, Landmarks and Milestones.* St. Louis: St. Louis Regional Planning and Growth Association, 1986.

Wayman, Norbury. *History of St. Louis Neighborhoods: Oak Hill-Morganford.* St. Louis: St. Louis Community Development Agency, 1981.

Special thanks to Grand-Oak Hill Community Corporation, Oak Hill Presbyterian Church, St. Louis Public Schools, Landmarks Association of St. Louis, Inc., Eric Sandweiss, David Schultz, Kirsten Hammerstrom, and the residents of the Grand-Oak Hill neighborhood.

A long-time neighborhood institution, the South Side National Bank opened its landmark ten-story building in January 1929, proudly displaying a sign which read, "We believe in the future of Grand and Gravois." Missouri Historical Society Photograph and Print Collection.

SHAW

The long, even blocks and uniform architectural character of the Shaw neighborhood point to a fact that is
easily overlooked: this is a suburban tract development.
If that phrase conjures up something quite different
from what we find in this pleasant urban neighborhood,
the reason is the unique history of nineteenth-century
St. Louis real estate development. In neighborhoods like
Shaw, it was the builder, the developer, and the speculator who have exercised a firmer hand than the architect
or the city planner.

The circumstances behind the eventual appearance
of the Shaw neighborhood are as old as the city itself. The
streets of Shaw lie atop a portion of the *Prairie des Noyers,*
an extensive common field laid out in 1769 between
today's Grand Boulevard and Kingshighway. Their paths
coincide with the forty-arpent property divisions (approximately 192 feet wide and a mile-and-a-half long) that
were typical of colonial St. Louis. Ownership of the individual fields was gradually consolidated through the years.
One who amassed a large estate in this manner was
Henry Shaw. Another important landowner was Mary
Tyler, who inherited most of the property from present-
day Shaw south to Botanical. Tyler left this property
undeveloped for forty years, even after it had been incorporated into the city limits. The land was simply too
distant and too poorly served by transportation lines to
interest most home buyers of the time.

In 1887, Mary Tyler sold her property to the Western
Investment and Improvement Company. The following
year, the company announced a residential development
of unprecedented size and scope: twelve hundred lots in
the new Tyler Place Subdivision. An 1888 advertisement
claimed that the "proposed new rapid transit line will
furnish quick transportation . . . by which residents in
Tyler Place may go and come at leisure at a rate of speed

double that now furnished any other section of the city
or by any other mode of transportation." Developers also
touted the proximity of Tower Grove Park, Reservoir
Park, and Shaw's Garden.

The real catalyst for development came in August
1889 with the opening of the Grand Avenue Viaduct
following four years of construction. With the south
side long isolated from the central city by the Mill
Creek Valley, property owners there had to travel east
to Jefferson Avenue to cross the railroad tracks. This
isolation limited interest in the Tyler Place property to
wealthy families that could afford the leisurely commute.
With the completion of the Grand Avenue Viaduct and
the extension of the streetcar lines, the commute was
suddenly within the reach of the average wage earner.
On May 11, 1889, the *Spectator* predicted that "with
this communication between the north and south ends
established, a boom in real estate is sure to follow."

Most of the property in Tyler Place was sold at auction on June 9 and 10, 1890. The auctioneers offered
fifty-seven thousand linear feet along fourteen streets
and avenues without limit or reserve. Terms included
one-third cash down with the balance due within two
years at 6 percent interest. Advertisements promised
freedom from the "smoke, heat and noise of the more
thickly populated districts" and boasted that "being on
the highest ground in the city, [the neighborhood] pos-
sesses natural drainage."

The People's Cable Railway and John Scullin's Electric
Line brought over ten thousand people to the real estate
auction. By the end of the sale, over forty-six thousand
frontage feet had been sold for a total of $1.4 million.
Owners and speculative builders soon transformed the
countryside. In the depression decade of the 1890s,
about four hundred residences were erected in the area;

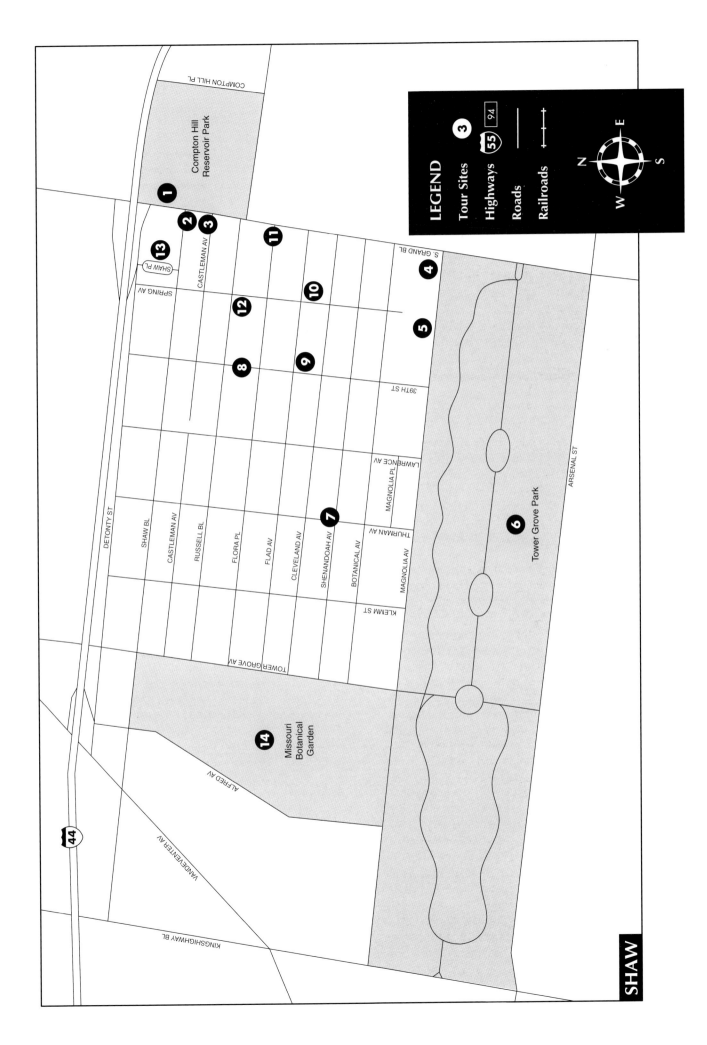

SHAW

in the decade that followed, another thousand were built. Deed restrictions in Tyler Place established a uniform building line and limited construction to two-story brick buildings. Housing styles ranged from Romanesque and Georgian Colonial to English Tudor mansions, at a cost of around five thousand dollars each.

In the 1920s, many two- and four-family flats went up in the Shaw neighborhood. Although the area's single-family homes attracted some wealthy families, most households were headed by middle-income wage earners who labored in the downtown business district or in the shops and institutions along Grand Boulevard.

The buildings of Tyler Place and the surrounding Shaw neighborhood demonstrated the response of resourceful contractors and architects to the financial demands of the real estate market. They built for profit. But their success depended on creating solid, attractive housing in a setting that offered middle-class families relief from the crowds and dirt of the central city. As St. Louisans continued their exodus from downtown, Tyler Place suggested the brightness of a suburban future. Today, its streets speak just as eloquently to the attractions of what now seems a distinctly urban past.

❶ COMPTON HILL WATER TOWER
Reservoir Park, Grand and Russell Boulevards

The Compton Hill Water Tower, at 179 feet high, is a distinctive landmark for motorists driving along South Grand and Interstate 44. Designed by Harvey Ellis and made of limestone and brick, the water tower regulated water pressure to neighborhood homes from 1899 until about 1929. The adjacent Compton Hill Reservoir has been in use since 1871. One of only seven remaining water towers in the United States, the Compton Hill Water Tower is listed on the National Register of Historic Places.

❷ WARNER MANSION
1905 South Grand Boulevard

Architect Theodore Link designed this ornate house for St. Louis lumber baron Erastus Herrick Warner in 1888. The remarkable interior of the structure reflects Warner's interest in hardwood and its ornamental use. The exterior is an amalgam of late nineteenth-century styles, featuring a massive Romanesque Revival entrance and three-story tower. Built before extensive development came to the Shaw neighborhood, the Warner Mansion is one of the few survivors of South Grand's elegant era.

❸ SAUM HOTEL-APARTMENTS
1919 South Grand Boulevard

The Saum Hotel, overlooking the Compton Hill Water Tower and Reservoir Park, offered guests deluxe accommodations when it opened in 1926. Designed by brothers Frank J. and Thomas P. Saum, the eight-story building, one of the neighborhood's two high-rises, featured a lounge, restaurants, and shops on its first floor. The seven upper stories boasted 112 apartments, as well as an eight-room penthouse and roof garden with a panoramic view of the city.

❹ BEAUVAIS MANSION (MEMORIAL HOME, INC.)
3625 Magnolia Avenue

The central portion of this building is a three-story Greek Revival mansion built about 1867 for René Beauvais, a St. Louis silversmith and jeweler of French-Canadian heritage. After Beauvais' death in 1882, the St. Louis Women's Christian Association opened the mansion as a home for the elderly. They named it the Memorial Home, in honor of the Civil War soldiers who were among the home's first residents. Four additions to the original structure went up between 1885 and 1918. In 1984, the Memorial Home, a not-for-profit organization, opened a new facility at the rear of the property. Today, the restored mansion is used for social functions and resident activities.

❺ MISSOURI SCHOOL FOR THE BLIND
3815 Magnolia Avenue

The Missouri School for the Blind began as a private charitable institution in 1851, with the state assuming responsibility for its operation four years later. It had several homes in St. Louis before moving to its present site in 1906. In 1860, owing largely to the efforts of trustee Simon Pollack, the school became the first in the nation to adopt the Braille system. The school currently has approximately one hundred students, from age five through twenty-one.

❻ TOWER GROVE PARK
Bounded by South Grand Boulevard, Arsenal Street, and Kingshighway and Magnolia Avenues

A visitor to Tower Grove in 1892 called the park "one of the most beautifully artistic and classically adorned places of its kind." It dates to 1868, when Henry Shaw deeded 276 acres of his country estate to the City of St. Louis for use as a park; he insisted that it be governed by an independent board of commissioners, of which he would be a life member. In this way, Shaw and the

commissioners retained control over the park's development. Unlike Forest Park, with its relative wildness, Tower Grove was designed in the Gardenesque style, based on Shaw's knowledge of European parks and landscape architecture. The park's architecture, including Turkish and Chinese pavilions, carefully enhances the beauty of the natural plantings. Marble busts of classical composers surround the park's Music Stand, itself a colorful piece of Victorian splendor. One of the best-preserved Victorian parks in the United States, Tower Grove is among only four urban parks to be declared National Historic Landmarks.

❼ BICYCLEWORKS
4069 Shenandoah Avenue

This corner storefront is the home of BicycleWORKS, an innovative and educational youth program begun in 1988 by Roy Bohn. Neighborhood children, ages nine to fourteen, can participate in activities that add up to a community-based alternative education. They can earn bicycles of their own by completing twenty-five hours of bike repair and maintenance training, along with five to ten hours of neighborhood service, such as participating in block clean-ups and working in community gardens. Located in storefront space donated by the St. Margaret of Scotland Housing Corporation, BicycleWORKS sells the bicycles participants have recycled. Call 664-0828 for more information.

❽ THIRTY-NINTH STREET

In the early part of the century, Thirty-ninth Street was the gateway to the Shaw community. It bustled with activity as shoppers arrived on the Lindell Railway streetcar and headed off to visit the district's butchers, bakers, barbers, tailors, grocers, and shoe salesmen. When the streetcar lines were eliminated, however, the street altered in character. The Thirty-ninth Street Redevelopment Corporation, composed mainly of Shaw neighborhood residents, is working to redevelop the street in a way that

The Shaw neighborhood continues to thrive, thanks to the enthusiasm of its residents. The innovative youth program BicycleWORKS, for example, offers neighborhood children the chance to earn bicycles of their own. Photograph by Roy Bohn. Courtesy of BicycleWORKS.

complements the surrounding residential area. It has razed some of the older commercial buildings and landscaped the lots as green space.

9 ST. MARGARET OF SCOTLAND CATHOLIC CHURCH
3854 Flad Avenue

St. Margaret of Scotland Catholic Church, created out of the need for an English-speaking parish north of Tower Grove Park, held its first services in a vacant storefront at the corner of Russell Boulevard and Thirty-ninth Street in 1900. The present church opened in 1907. The parish population peaked at around ten thousand members in the 1940s and early 1950s. St. Margaret's School, at 3964 Castleman, serves 272 students from preschool through the eighth grade. The church was instrumental in organizing the St. Margaret of Scotland Housing Corporation, which plays a vital role in attracting developers and coordinating development activity within the neighborhood.

10 TEMPLE APARTMENTS (FORMERLY B'NAI EL TEMPLE)
3666 Flad Avenue

This is the oldest surviving structure built for a Jewish congregation in St. Louis. The building began its long and varied history in 1906, when it was dedicated as B'nai El Temple, with a membership of nearly two hundred families, many of them middle-class merchants and professionals of German descent from the Tyler Place subdivision. The congregation moved to a West End site

in 1930, and the Compton Heights Christian Church rented the building until it was sold in 1944 to St. Margaret of Scotland Catholic Church for use as a parish school. St. Margaret's occupied the building until 1969, when ownership passed to the St. Louis Board of Education and the structure became Sherman Branch School. In 1982 developers converted the former temple into apartments, retaining the building's original exterior in recognition of its status as a National Historic Place.

11 FLORA PLACE GATE
Flora Place

Designed in the late 1890s, Flora's east-end gateway marks the entrance to a six-block-long private place. Henry Shaw envisioned the street as a fitting approach west from Grand Avenue to the entrance of his Missouri Botanical Garden on Tower Grove Avenue. Flora Boulevard became a private street in 1897, when its south-side owners joined forces with the trustees of Shaw's Garden, holders of the north-side title, to improve the street in the manner established by the stylish Vandeventer Place in the city's Midtown area. Improvements to Flora Place, including paving, curbs, sewers, trees, and shrubbery, totaled $100,000.

12 TYLER PLACE PRESBYTERIAN CHURCH
2109 South Spring Avenue

Organized in 1896, the Tyler Place Presbyterian Church is the only neighborhood institution to retain the name of the subdivision. The congregation met at several houses in the neighborhood until 1901, when the first

Shaw opened the Missouri Botanical Garden on the grounds of his estate in 1859. This statue of Juno once stood in a sunken garden, or parterre, near the garden's main gate on Flora. Photograph by EMIL Boehl. Missouri Historical Society Photograph and Print Collection.

services were held in the present church. In 1927 workmen blasted a basement into the church's solid rock
foundation to create additional space. The church
sanctuary recently underwent renovation.

⓭ SHAW PLACE
Off Shaw Boulevard

Henry Shaw developed Shaw Place from land originally
part of the *Prairie des Noyers*, the French common field.
Shaw engaged his friend, architect George I. Barnett,
to help with the planning, and together they designed
a tiny private place with ten two-story, red-brick rental
houses. The rental property provided an endowment for
the Missouri Botanical Garden. In 1915, the trustees of
the garden sold Shaw Place for $55,000. The following
year, deed restrictions establishing single-family use and
private-street status were adopted. In the 1960s, Shaw
Place gained a cast iron fountain, *Leda and the Swan*, a
legacy from Vandeventer Place.

⓮ MISSOURI BOTANICAL GARDEN
4344 Shaw Avenue

The Missouri Botanical Garden, known also as Shaw's
Garden, after its creator, Henry Shaw, is one of the
earliest American botanical gardens devoted to both
the display of living plants and scientific research. Shaw,
an Englishman, loved the gardens of his homeland, and
in 1859 opened his own garden at his country estate,
Tower Grove. The garden quickly became a popular
St. Louis attraction, drawing some fifty thousand visitors
in 1868. The garden features numerous greenhouses,
formal rose gardens, a Japanese garden, and the world-
famous Climatron, a geodesic dome housing tropical
vegetation. Also on the grounds are Shaw's country
residence, known as Tower Grove House, and his town-
house, moved to the garden after his death. The Missouri
Botanical Garden is open daily from 9:00 A.M. until
5:00 P.M. Call 577-9400 for more information.

FOR MORE INFORMATION

Harris, NiNi. *A Grand Heritage: A History of the St. Louis
Southside Neighborhoods and Citizens.* St. Louis:
DeSales Community Housing Corporation, 1984.
Toft, Carolyn Hewes. *St. Louis Landmarks and Historic
Districts.* St. Louis: Landmarks Association of
St. Louis, 1988.
Wayman, Norbury L. *History of St. Louis Neighborhoods:
Shaw.* St. Louis: St. Louis Community Development
Agency, 1981.

Special thanks to the Shaw Neighborhood Improvement
Association, Lisa Suggs, Roy Bohn, Martha Riley, Estelle
Vosen, Karen Goering, Kris Smith, Eric Sandweiss, Jane
Anton, Tyler Place Presbyterian Church, and the resi-
dents of the Shaw neighborhood.

THE HILL

From the Missouri Botanical Garden (Shaw): Shaw Boulevard west to Marconi Avenue. Marconi left (south) to Wilson Avenue.

The Christy Fire Clay Company at South Kingshighway south of Chippewa Street was one of the many major clay mines in the area that employed Hill residents from the late nineteenth to mid-twentieth centuries. Photograph by Dr. William G. Swekosky. Swekosky Photo Collection, School Sisters of Notre Dame.

To many people in the St. Louis area, the Hill is an Italian neighborhood known for its nationally acclaimed restaurants, specialty groceries and bakeries, tiny "shotgun" houses, and fire hydrants proudly painted red, white, and green, the colors of the Italian flag.

Yet these elements of the community just touch the surface, for this fifty-square block area in South St. Louis is not merely one of the city's purest ethnic neighborhoods, but among its most stable, tightly woven communities. Throughout its history, both out of necessity and choice, the Hill's staunchly Italian Catholic identity has been the glue that has held this neighborhood together.

The history of the Hill goes back to pre–Civil War years, when the discovery of clay deposits in the area brought thousands of immigrants—Germans and Irish mostly, but later Italians—and African Americans to the remote slopes above Manchester Avenue between Kingshighway Boulevard and Hampton Avenue. In the years after the Evens and Howard Fire Brick Company

and clay mines opened in 1854-55, more than a dozen brick and tile factories sprang up along the banks of the River Des Peres to support the new industry.

Reflecting the strong presence of Germans and African Americans in the early stages of settlement on the Hill, the German St. Aloysius Gonzaga Parish and the African American Pattison Avenue Baptist Church were the earliest churches established in the neighborhood. But from the 1880s until 1924, when the National Origins Act virtually shut the door on immigration from southeastern Europe, Italian immigrants swelled their ranks and eventually outnumbered the other groups.

The first Italian immigrants were predominantly men who lived in boarding houses. As they arranged for their family members and friends to join them in St. Louis, the area changed from a mining camp to an Italian immigrant neighborhood. These early immigrants lived in the northern edge of the area around Pattison, Northrup, and Shaw Avenues. Gradually the community

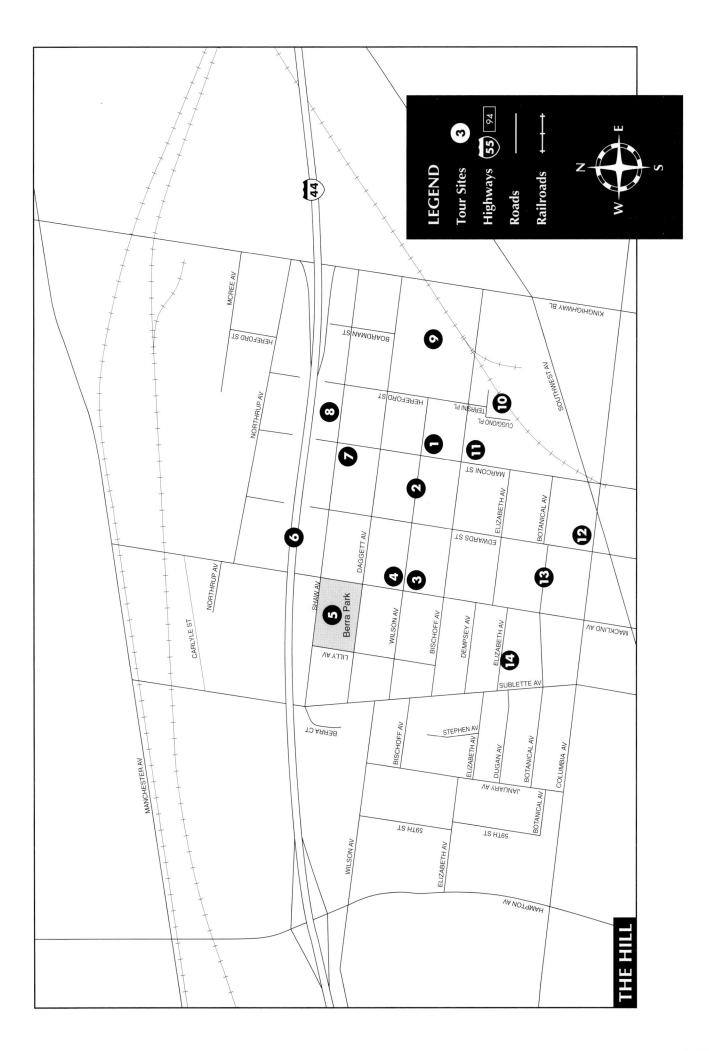

THE HILL

spread south to Daggett, Wilson, and Bischoff Avenues. Non-Italians dubbed the neighborhood "Dago Hill." The Italians called it "*La Montagna*," "the mountain." As its name implies, the Hill remained remote from the rest of St. Louis, helping to solidify its strong ethnic identity.

This insularity was due, in part, to its location. Surrounded by clay mines, factories, railroad tracks, and the River Des Peres, the community had to learn to be self-sufficient.

In the process, the Hill also developed into a vibrant Italian neighborhood, a place where one could work, buy Italian specialty foods and breads, share a drink at the corner tavern, meet future mates at one of the many Italian social clubs, and attend church and school without ever leaving the neighborhood. It was a neighborhood filled with small wooden and brick shotgun homes, symbols of permanence and stability. By 1930 59 percent of the homes on the Hill were owner-occupied, compared to 32 percent citywide.

Of course, the Hill is no longer the isolated enclave it once was; the Italian population has shrunk to 70 percent of the residents, and most of the second- and third-generation Italians have moved out of the neighborhood. But the Hill has retained a cohesiveness that goes beyond the painted fire hydrants, annual Columbus Day parades, and the many popular restaurants and Italian grocery stores that dot the neighborhood. This is still a neighborhood where childhood friends meet for lunch, where most people know all of their neighbors, and where businesses have been operated by the same families for generations.

Even many of those who have moved away for newer, greener pastures in the county eventually return. They have their children baptized at St. Ambrose Church, open up businesses in buildings that once housed taverns and corner stores, and, when possible, buy old property to renovate or rebuild so they can move back to the old neighborhood.

As the Hill's population ages, the neighborhood is working to assure that these old ties continue through the fourth and fifth generations and that the community retains its historic ethnic character. While they recognize that outsiders bring much needed business to the Hill, many long-time residents yearn for the days before the rest of St. Louis "discovered" their neighborhood in the 1960s and 1970s.

Yet even as they complain about the increased noise, traffic jams, and parking problems, the community welcomes newcomers, especially those who want to live there for the same reasons that the natives find it difficult to leave. Hill residents know that you don't have to be Italian to appreciate the enduring community that their parents and grandparents created here.

① ST. AMBROSE CHURCH
5130 Wilson Avenue

Since its origins more than ninety years ago, Sant'Ambrogio (St. Ambrose) Church, named after the first bishop of Milan, has been the heart and soul of the Hill community. Not until 1903 did the Hill's Italian Catholic community even have its own church, the first St. Ambrose, a small wooden frame structure built on this site in 1903. In 1907, St. Ambrose was recognized as a separate parish.

The Lombard-Romanesque church that stands on this corner today was built in 1926, five years after the original church burned to the ground. Designed by architect Angelo Corrubia, St. Ambrose's terra cotta and red brick are the very materials that provided work for the Italian community during the Hill's early years. The adjacent St. Ambrose School opened in 1915. Along with the Henry Shaw School, the only public school on the Hill, St. Ambrose has educated several generations of the neighborhood's families.

② SHOTGUN HOUSES
Wilson Avenue, between Marconi Avenue and Edwards Street

Shotgun houses, the earliest houses in the neighborhood, were built during the early years of the twentieth century. These narrow, single-family, three-room homes, concentrated in the older sections of the Hill east of Macklind Avenue, were built "shotgun" style, so named because if someone had fired a shot through the front door, the bullet would have passed straight through the living room, bedroom, kitchen, and out the back door.

Most of the Hill's earliest Italian immigrants lived in boarding houses within walking distance of clay mines and factories. These two houses on Pattison Avenue facing north are in the oldest section of the Hill. Photograph by Dr. William G. Swekosky. Swekosky Photo Collection, School Sisters of Notre Dame.

3 SACRED HEART VILLA
2108 Macklind Avenue, between Wilson and
Bischoff Avenues

During the Great Depression, St. Louis, like the rest of the country, suffered a loss of industrial jobs. On the Hill, many wives and daughters became the sole supporters of their families. By 1940, approximately 35 percent of the neighborhood's women held jobs, the majority in the Liggett and Myers Tobacco Company on Tower Grove Avenue. The Sacred Heart Villa, a convent, kindergarten, and day nursery run by the Apostles of the Sacred Heart (known then as the Missionary Zelatrices), was built to serve the needs of these families. Opened in 1940, the three-story building and its spacious grounds were designed by Angelo Corrubia, the same architect who designed St. Ambrose Church. Though it consistently has a long waiting list, Sacred Heart Villa continues to care for the Hill's young children.

4 CLUB CASINO SITE (NOW DUPLICATING SYSTEMS)
2024 Macklind Avenue

Among the special qualities of the Hill's residents are their strong family ties and commitment to the neighborhood. Many businesses, like Tony Ranciglio's blacksmith shop, the Missouri Baking Company, Spielberg Furniture Company, Fair Mercantile Company, Volpi Italian Foods, and John Viviano and Sons Retail Groceries, have been family-owned and operated for generations. Less obvious are the commercial buildings throughout the neighborhood, whose businesses have changed while the buildings themselves have stayed within the family. The building on the northeast corner of Macklind and Wilson avenues is a prime example. Back in the 1940s and 1950s, it was home to the Club Casino, a nightclub that attracted people from all over St. Louis by featuring live entertainment, food, and dancing. The DiBartola family lived upstairs from the club. Today the building is owned by Ron DiBartola, who runs Duplicating Systems, a company that provides duplicating and printing equipment to customers throughout the city.

5 BERRA PARK
Bounded by Macklind, Daggett, Lilly, and Shaw Avenues

Berra Park, the major park on the Hill, is named for the late Louis "Midge" Berra, the popular alderman and boss of the Twenty-fourth Ward in the 1940s and 1950s. Berra is credited with helping many Italians in the community get jobs at a time when discrimination was rampant. During his twenty-five-year tenure, Berra acted as the community's major spokesperson and benefactor.

The five-acre park, called Vigo Park when the land was purchased by the city in 1945, was renamed in 1965. It has served as a gathering place for neighborhood festivals and fundraising picnics, as well as being home to the neighborhood baseball league and annual summer day camp run by the Shaw Community Center (Shaw School).

6 INTERSTATE 44 OVERPASS
Between Pattison and Shaw Avenues, west of
Edwards Street

In the early 1970s, the integrity of the Hill neighborhood was threatened when the new Interstate 44 was built. The highway cut a wide swath through the middle of the community, taking 98 homes in its path and cutting off 450 residents from the heart of the neighborhood. One of those buildings demolished was the African American Pattison Avenue Baptist Church, established in 1897.

Led by Father Salvatore Polizzi, then pastor of St. Ambrose Church, the community organized a campaign to build an overpass over the interstate to reconnect the two sections of the neighborhood. Having been rebuffed in Jefferson City, Hill representatives took their case to Washington, D.C., offering the U.S. Treasury Department $50,000 raised entirely by the community for an overpass. According to witnesses, when the Hill learned it would get its overpass, the bells of St. Ambrose rang.

7 BIG CLUB HALL SITE
Southwest corner of Shaw and Marconi Avenues

The North Italian-American Mercantile Company, better known as the "Big Club," was organized in 1913 by northern Italian immigrants, most of whom came from Lombardy. Transferring the Italian tradition of men's social clubs to St. Louis, several generations of neighborhood men gathered here to play cards and bocce (a game similar to lawn bowling) and enjoy a glass of beer. Its original name reflects the identification most of the Hill's early residents had with northern Italy. Through the years the north-south dichotomy disappeared, and Big Club Hall evolved into a community center for all Hill Italians. It was used as a sports and political center, for social occasions such as weddings and dances, and as a food cooperative. The club bought the building at Shaw and Marconi in 1929. In January 1994, the members sold their building to a photographer, who now uses it as a studio.

⑧ HILL 2000 OFFICE
5129 Shaw, between Marconi Avenue and Hereford Street

The Hill 2000 organization grew out of the Improvement Association of the Hill. When Hill 2000 was established in 1970, its motto was "improve not move." Hill 2000 works closely with St. Ambrose Church and neighborhood residents to improve the Hill neighborhood in the areas of housing, crime prevention, resident-business relationships, communication within the community, and the needs of its aging population.

Along with housing improvement projects, Hill 2000, now housed in a former barber shop, ran "Hill Days," a major annual fundraiser for its programs as well as a celebration of the neighborhood. Today, Hill 2000 sponsors the Sick and Elderly Program, annual family picnics, crafts fairs, and a winter festival.

⑨ QUICK MEAL STOVE COMPANY (MAGIC CHEF) SITE
2100 Kingshighway Boulevard, bounded by Kingshighway Boulevard, Daggett and Bischoff Avenues, and Hereford Street

The Quick Meal Stove Company opened its huge plant on the Hill in 1910 and began making Magic Chef oven ranges in 1929. Along with McQuay-Norris Company, a manufacturer of piston rings and engine parts, Quick Meal was a major neighborhood employer until it closed in the mid-1950s. In the 1920s and 1930s, the company employed more than one hundred workers from the neighborhood, reinforcing the Hill's tradition of living and working in or near the neighborhood. The site, now partially vacant, is occupied by various manufacturing facilities.

⑩ ST. AMBROSE PLACE
South of Hereford Street and Bischoff Avenue

Initially an industrial and commercial neighborhood, the Hill became a residential neighborhood as Italian immigrants, and eventually their families, moved to the area to work in the clay mines, brick plants, and other nearby industries. As a result, the neighborhood has a checkerboard of zoning regulations. St. Ambrose Place, a modern subdivision of single-family, two-story homes, was built in the late 1980s to accommodate the need for new

housing in the neighborhood. Built on a vacant lot in the middle of an industrial zone, the property was rezoned to allow for residential development. Although criticized for its density, the subdivision is frequently cited as one way the Hill has tried to solve the shortage of new housing, keep residents in the neighborhood, and attract new families to the Hill.

⑪ ITALIA-AMERICA BOCCE CLUB
2210 Marconi Avenue

In keeping with Italian immigrants' long tradition of belonging to social clubs, the Italia-America Bocce Club is an important gathering point for the Hill's Italian community. Members and their guests can relax over a drink and a game of bocce. Community fundraisers and wedding receptions are held in the spacious dining and reception area. The club, originally on Manchester Avenue, moved to its present site in the early 1990s. The completely remodeled building was originally the shower room for the now empty McQuay-Norris plant next door. The new headquarters for the Bocce Club demonstrates how Hill residents buy vacant buildings in their neighborhood for community-based purposes.

⑫ COLUMBIA THEATER (COLUMBIA SHOW) SITE
Northeast corner of Edwards Street and Columbia Avenue

As with other immigrant groups in the U.S., the Hill Italians were introduced to the larger American culture outside of their neighborhood primarily through the movies. The Columbia Show opened as a vaudeville

The 1931 eighth grade graduating class of the Henry Shaw School lines up for a class photo in front of the Missouri Baking Company. The bakery was started on the Hill by Stefano Gambaro and Franco Arpiani after the 1904 St. Louis World's Fair. It was called the Missouri Bakery because it was not fashionable to have an Italian-sounding name at the time. From the collection of Joann Arpiani.

Volpi's salami factory, c. 1910. This Italian specialty food store, which opened on the Hill in 1902, was started by John Volpi, who brought in his brother-in-law, Gino Pasetti, as a business partner. Like many Hill businesses, Volpi's has stayed in the family; it is now owned and run by Armando Pasetti, who started out as an apprentice for his uncles in 1938 and took over the business in 1958. Photograph reprinted with permission of the collection of Armando Pasetti.

theater in 1925 and featured the new talking pictures of Hollywood's emerging movie industry. After the theater shut down in the early 1970s, the building was used as a racquetball club. In 1987 an architect/artist from outside the neighborhood bought the site, then gutted and renovated it for a living quarters and studio. In such ways, many new residents are helping to stabilize the neighborhood while bringing new life to the Hill.

13 ITALIAN EVANGELICAL CHURCH SITE
5343 Botanical Avenue, between Macklind Avenue and Edwards Street

Religious institutions have always played an important part in the Hill community. Since 1921, the small Italian Protestant community has been served by the Italian Evangelical Church, founded by Italian Protestant minister Peter Ottolini. First located on Edwards Street, the church relocated to its present site in 1929. Only a handful of Hill residents belonged to the church; most congregants commuted to the church from other neighborhoods. In keeping with its immigrant history, the church is now home to a Korean Baptist church.

14 LAWRENCE PETER "YOGI" BERRA AND JOE GARAGIOLA BOYHOOD HOMES
5447 Elizabeth Avenue (Yogi Berra) and 5446 Elizabeth Avenue (Joe Garagiola)

Organized sports have played an important role in the Hill's immigrant community. As Gary Ross Mormino points out in *Immigrants on the Hill*, organized sports helped bridge the gap between feuding Italian factions, transforming their animosity into creative competition.

Two of baseball's greats and among the Hill's most famous celebrities, Yogi Berra and Joe Garagiola grew up across the street from each other. After Berra signed on with the New York Yankees in 1943 and Garagiola debuted with the St. Louis Cardinals in 1941, each helped break the stereotypical ethnic caricatures of Italian-Americans held by those living outside the Hill.

FOR MORE INFORMATION

Mormino, Gary Ross. *Immigrants on the Hill: Italian-Americans in St. Louis, 1882-1982.* Urbana: University of Illinois Press, 1986.

Toft, Carolyn Hewes, ed. *The Hill: The Ethnic Heritage of an Urban Neighborhood.* St. Louis: Washington University Social Science Institute, 1975.

Wayman, Norbury L. *History of St. Louis Neighborhoods: The Hill.* St. Louis: St. Louis Community Development Agency, 1978.

Special thanks to Cathy Ruggeri-Rea, Alderman Robert Ruggeri, Joann Arpiani, John and Rose Marie Bianchi, Ida Galli, Sister Linda, Sister Felicetta, Orestes Zioia, Mary Ronzio, Whitey Colombo, Carol Savio, Martin Spielberg, Theresa Ranciglio, Anthony Ranciglio, Rita Merlotti, Frances Marino Grana, Rudolph Torrini, Armando Pasetti, Joe Thele of Operation Conserve, Father Thomas Santen of St. Ambrose Parish, Monsignor Salvatore Polizzi of St. Roch's Parish, Joe Torrisi of the Shaw Community Center, Marilyn Farrario of the St. Louis Public Library's Kingshighway branch, Peggy DiBartola, Ron DiBartola, Mary Seematter, Kris Runberg Smith, Kathy Corbett, Eric Sandweiss, Kathy Petersen, Charles Brown, Duane Sneddeker, and the residents of the Hill.

THE SPREADING METROPOLIS: COMMUNITIES OF THE EARLY TWENTIETH CENTURY

THE CHELTENHAM NEIGHBORHOODS

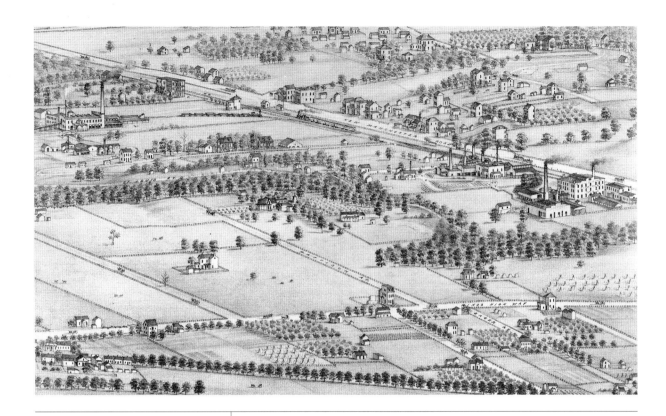

From the Berra and Garagiola homes (The Hill): East on Elizabeth Avenue to Macklind Avenue. Macklind left (north) to Manchester Road. Manchester left (west) to Sulphur Avenue.

The neighborhoods south of Forest Park were still rural when Compton and Dry created this image in 1876. However, the scattered growth shows promise for the neighborhoods of Cheltenham, Clayton-Tamm, Hi-Pointe, and Franz Park. From Richard J. Compton and Camille N. Dry, *Pictorial St. Louis* (St. Louis, 1876). Missouri Historical Society Library.

In 1852, when the Pacific Railroad extended its line to Cheltenham, Missouri, the community was still idyllic countryside. It lay five miles west of downtown, with Kingshighway the boundary on the east and New Manchester Road framing the south. The River Des Peres wandered lazily through the valley, and oak and papaw trees covered the hillsides. There was little in the way of settlement except the Sulphur Springs Hotel, scattered farmhouses, and a few homesteads.

The railroad access soon transformed the rural countryside, for a spate of factories sprang up along the tracks. The earliest and largest of the enterprises was the Laclede Fire Brick Company, which had begun in 1844 but expanded rapidly with the coming of the railroad. The Evens and Howard Fire Brick Company opened a factory in 1855, with Mitchell Clay Manufacturing following close behind.

Eventually about a dozen companies dealing with clay products centered in Cheltenham, making the name synonymous nationally with fire brick. Accessible transportation, the availability of high-quality clay, and an immigrant labor force enabled companies to produce the cheapest fire brick in the country.

The industry's raw material came from the Cheltenham seam, a thick layer of hard white clay running from 5 to 120 feet below the hills. Typically, the mines ran as deep as 65 feet, following the seam of clay. First the hard clay was blasted, then a crew of four diggers, five car fillers, and a mule driver would bring out up to forty tons a day. Some clay was mined from large open pits. Companies weathered the clay for a period ranging from six months to seven years before it was mixed and molded. Rows of coal-fired beehive kilns dried the fire bricks, which were then shipped by rail to points throughout the country.

In addition to the excellent fire brick, the factories turned out tile and sewer pipe, products in sharp demand during this period of nationwide industrial

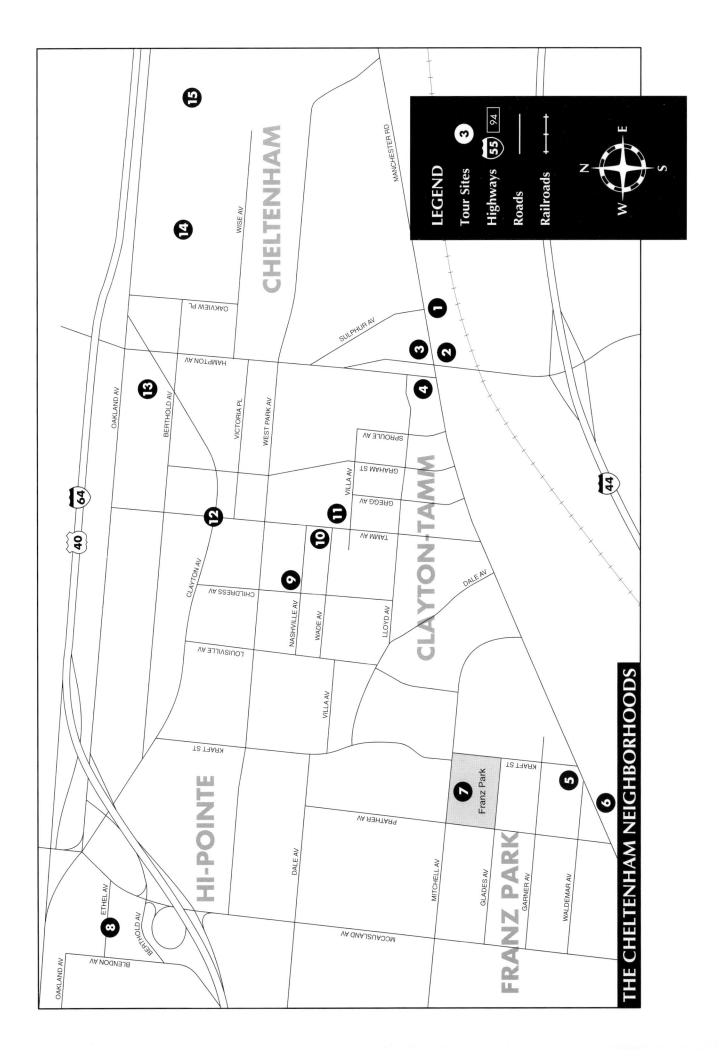

THE CHELTENHAM NEIGHBORHOODS

growth and rapidly expanding urban infrastructures. By 1889 the area produced more sewer pipe than any other region in the nation. Another clay product, terra cotta, proved more fickle in quality than fire brick; only one company in Cheltenham, the Winkle Terra Cotta Company, manufactured it on a large scale. The company successfully combined the fire-brick clay with other types to create decorative tile work that adorned homes such as those on Portland Place, as well as such downtown landmarks as the Wainwright Building.

Irish, Italian, German, and Polish immigrants came to work in the mines and factories. They built homes along Manchester Road, then progressed north toward Oakland and spread westward, hopscotching around the mines and pits. Especially along Clayton and Tamm, small businesses multiplied to serve the growing community. In 1860, the Catholic diocese established a mission, which grew into St. James the Greater Parish. The Cheltenham public school opened in 1868, and another was built further west in 1870.

By World War II, most of the mines had shut down and the brickyards had closed. Subdivisions were built over the mines and pits, and other industries occupied the railroad rights of way. But the early industry had left a strong legacy. It dictated the patchwork housing pattern that makes this area distinct in St. Louis—and it helped create stable neighborhoods that continue to attract new residents.

❶ SULPHUR SPRINGS HOTEL SITE
Sulphur Avenue and Manchester Road

Famous mountain man William Sublette built guest quarters in the 1830s on Manchester Road near his house. He hoped to take advantage of sulphur springs said to have healing qualities. The resort, briefly fashionable to early St. Louisans, never proved financially successful; it deteriorated as industry grew in the area. By 1872 the St. Louis *Times* reported that the "cottage and spring have both fallen into bad repute and the odor of one is nearly as bad as that of the other." It burned three years later.

❷ CHELTENHAM RAILROAD STATION SITE
Manchester Road and
Hampton Avenue

Until the late 1980s, the train station at Manchester and Hampton carried the first and last namesake of Cheltenham. The Pacific Railroad terminated at what was then known as Sulphur Springs in December 1852. The name was borrowed from Cheltenham Cottage, owned by the manager for the Sulphur Springs resort and named for his English birthplace. The area was still known as Cheltenham even after it become a part of St. Louis in 1876. When the station was torn down in the 1980s, the last visible reminder of the independent community of Cheltenham went with it.

WHAT'S IN A NAME OR A NEIGHBORHOOD

The clay industry and such businesses as St. Louis Smelting and Refining Company and Scullin Steel drew immigrants to Cheltenham, now defined as the area around Hampton and Manchester, behind the Arena. From there, housing expanded west and north.

First called West Cheltenham, for at least one hundred years the Clayton-Tamm neighborhood has been known commonly as Dogtown, a name the area's businesses eagerly display. Neighborhoods farther west, Hi-Pointe and Franz Park, take their names from local landmarks.

Groups from these various enclaves work cooperatively through such organizations as the Triad Housing Corporation and the Forest Park Community League. Although periodic efforts have been made to link the neighborhoods together under one name—South Forest Park, Forest Park Southwest, and Oakland have been suggested—none has gained acceptance. But by whatever name, the area remains a strong working-class neighborhood, proud of its heritage and its future.

❸ ICARIAN COMMUNITY
Manchester Road and
Hampton Avenue

The Icarians, a group of French immigrants, bought the Sulphur Springs resort area and the Sublette home in 1857. In Cheltenham, they hoped to reestablish the Utopian community they had known in Nauvoo, Illinois, under leader Etienne Cabet, a social theorist and reformer. The group tried to live a communal life, but to survive economically most followers took outside jobs. Fever and "veritable epidemics" constantly plagued followers' health, caused by the nearby polluted River Des Peres. Sickness, financial mismanagement, and internal dissension drained the community. In March 1864 the last Icarian families left Cheltenham.

❹ GRATIOT SCHOOL (CONTINUED EDUCATION)
Hampton Avenue and Manchester Road

Gratiot School pays tribute to the first white owner of the neighborhood lands. In 1798 French immigrant Charles Gratiot received deed to a three-square-mile land grant stretching from Kingshighway to Big Bend. At his death in 1817, the Gratiot League Square was divided, a process that would continue to shape land development through the twentieth century.

❺ SCULLIN STEEL HEADQUARTERS (NOW COPYING CONCEPTS)
6691 Manchester Road

In addition to brickworks, heavy industries like Scullin Steel and St. Louis Smelting and Refining Company found homes along the railroad tracks on Manchester. Founded by John Scullin, a noted nineteenth-century

railroad builder and magnate, Scullin Steel was part of the Cheltenham landscape for decades. Like many St. Louis industries, Scullin shifted its focus during World War II from its primary business—manufacture of railroad cars and parts—to munitions manufacturing. The plant was closed in 1981 and its main office, still proudly labeled "Scullin Steel," converted to other usage.

❻ ST. LOUIS MARKETPLACE
6548 Manchester Road

The forty-one acre St. Louis Marketplace is situated on the former site of the Scullin Mill. A successful example of the pooling of public and private money, the strip mall boasts a mixture of large chain stores and smaller specialty stops. The Midland Group, which developed the site in the early 1990s, used the mall's convenient city location as a major selling point; many of its tenants had previously focused their new stores on the county, not the city. The railroad tracks that had previously serviced Scullin Steel had to be moved for the project, further evidence of changing land use.

❼ FRANZ PARK
Prather Avenue between Glades Avenue and Mitchell Avenue

The only city park in the area, Franz Park gives its name to the surrounding neighborhood. A gift to the city from E. D. Franz in 1915, the park continues to host local sports activities.

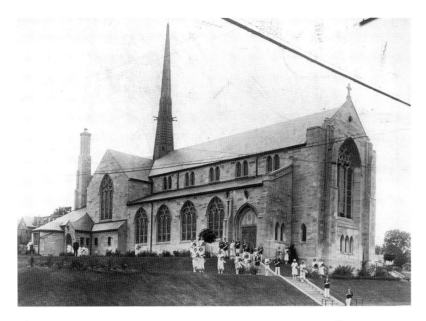

8 HI-POINTE NEIGHBORHOOD
McCausland Avenue and Clayton Road

The Hi-Pointe neighborhood takes its name from the elevation, the highest in St. Louis. Many people associate the Hi-Pointe Cinema with the area, but most of the neighborhood is residential. Home owners have long fought neighborhood intrusions, from commercial zoning changes in the 1910s to the expansion of Oakland Avenue and construction of Highway 40.

9 UTAH HOUSE
Childress Avenue and Nashville Avenue

For its exhibit at the Louisiana Purchase Exposition, the state of Utah built a frame house to encourage settlement in the young state, then only sixteen years old. After the Fair the house was moved to its present location on the northeast corner of Childress and Nashville. Many of the Fair's workers and craftsmen found housing in the neighborhoods south of the park, and at the Fair's end new housing developed along Oakland. Many of the homes of Hi-Pointe and Franz Park were built in part from wood salvaged from the exposition.

10 ST. JAMES THE GREATER
Tamm Avenue and Wade Avenue

Perched on "Dry Hill" overlooking the neighborhood, St. James the Greater began as a mission in 1860. The early priests were all Irish born, a reflection of the origin and culture of many families in the area. The parish was also home to Italians and Germans. The present church, styled after the Gothic cathedral in Ireland, was dedicated October 7, 1928.

11 ST. JAMES SCHOOL
Tamm Avenue and Wade Avenue

Attempts to maintain a Catholic school in the neighborhood failed until four Dominican nuns arrived in 1902. They lived and taught seventy children in a six-room cottage until the school building was completed several years later. A surge in new housing and the post–World War II baby boom prompted the current school building in 1950. St. James–sponsored athletic teams played an important role for neighborhood children, interesting them in sports like boxing, soccer, and baseball.

12 CLAYTON AND TAMM INTERSECTION

Since the turn of the century, the Clayton and Tamm intersection has remained the heart of the neighborhood business district. Lehman Hardware Store has served the neighborhood from the time George Lehman opened the doors in 1909. Through several name changes, a drugstore has occupied the opposite corner since 1913. Others businesses providing neighborhood services have come and gone throughout the years. Today customers from all parts of the city enjoy the district's restaurants.

13 DEACONESS HOSPITAL
Oakland Avenue and Hampton Avenue

Deaconess Hospital moved west from midtown in 1928, building a new 225 bed facility at the fringe of the city. In the 1960s and again in the 1980s, hospital officials made decisions to remain in the city, expanding facilities instead of relocating. Much of the hospital's early work and history is credited to the Deaconess Sisterhood, a Protestant order that helped change the profession of nursing through their vows of service. In the 1930s, 130

The Forest Park Highlands was a popular attraction from 1896 until the early 1960s. St. Louis Community College at Forest Park was constructed on the site two years after the Highlands burned down in 1963. Missouri Historical Society Photograph and Print Collection.

sisters served as the hospital's sole nursing staff; their nursing school was one of the finest in the region. The order quit recruiting in the 1950s.

⓮ ST. LOUIS ARENA
5700 Oakland Avenue

Built in 1929, the Arena suffered a shaky financial beginning. In 1931, Arena owners tried to attract a new audience by installing ice-making equipment for hockey. But as teams practiced before a game the next year, they noticed that the ice was getting softer. On investigation of the ice-making equipment, the engineer found that the Arena had not paid its electric bill. Undaunted, the owners took advantage of a St. Louis cold snap and opened the doors and windows in the massive building, freezing the ice along with those early fans. The Arena served as home for the St. Louis Blues hockey team and hundreds of concerts, conventions, and shows until it was closed with the opening of the new downtown Kiel Center in 1994. As of this writing, the fate of the St. Louis Arena is not known.

⓯ ST. LOUIS COMMUNITY COLLEGE AT FOREST PARK (FORMER SITE OF THE FOREST PARK HIGHLANDS)
Oakland Avenue west of Macklind Avenue

Although this site has been the home of St. Louis Community College at Forest Park since 1966, many St. Louisans still remember it as home of the Forest Park Highlands. Opened in 1896 as beer garden, the Highlands became the largest amusement park in the area thanks to its nearness to the 1904 World's Fair. It boasted several of the fair's leftovers, including a bandstand created from the former Japanese gates. The streetcar deposited adventure-loving crowds, who came to enjoy the entertainment and to ride coasters like the Racer Dip and the Mountain Ride. Like its counterparts across the country, the Highlands' popularity dwindled after the Second World War. Little spirit was left by the time a fire destroyed much of it in 1963.

The Forest Park campus of St. Louis Community College was the first to be built after passage of a $47 million bond issue that created the Junior College District in 1965. Currently, nearly seven thousand St. Louisans attend the Forest Park campus each semester. Other St. Louis Community College campuses are in the suburbs of Ferguson and Kirkwood.

FOR MORE INFORMATION

Brooks, George R. "Some New Views of Old Cheltenham." *The Bulletin of the Missouri Historical Society* 22 (October 1965), pp. 32-34.

Hannon, Robert E. *St. Louis: Its Neighborhoods and Neighbors, Landmarks and Milestones.* St. Louis: St. Louis Regional Planning and Growth Association, 1986.

O'Connor, Rev. P. J. *History of Cheltenham and St. James Parish.* St. Louis: St. James Parish, 1937.

Wayman, Norbury L. *History of St. Louis Neighborhoods: Oakland & Clifton.* St. Louis: St. Louis Community Development Agency, 1980.

Special thanks to Joe Thele, Father David Rauch, John Raniero, Juanita Turin, Bob Pierce, Frank Mead, Dina Young, and the residents of the Cheltenham, Clayton-Tamm, Franz Park, and Hi-Pointe neighborhoods.

THE SPREADING METROPOLIS: COMMUNITIES OF THE EARLY TWENTIETH CENTURY

FOREST PARK

This engraving from the park commissioner's first report in 1875 shows the park's early pastoral nature. Sheep were used to graze the park grounds. Engraving by Camille N. Dry. Missouri Historical Society Photograph and Print Collection.

Since 1876, Forest Park, with its 1,293 acres of public space, has been the communal "backyard" of St. Louis, providing an arena for local groups to debate their different views about the role parks should play in urban life. As a result, decisions about the park's use have rarely been smooth ones. Recent controversies over the need for more parking, the proposed expansion of Highway 40, and admission charges for the park's institutions are just the latest manifestations of an old pattern.

The very formation of the park sparked the initial dispute. The chosen site, almost two miles west of the city limits then near Grand Boulevard, was a forty-minute carriage ride from downtown, making the transportation cost well beyond the reach of the ordinary citizen. Additionally, the proposal for Forest Park put its size at three times that of New York's Central Park, which struck many St. Louisans as excessive. In the end, the park was reduced to half the proposed size, and a new railroad route made it more accessible to the central city.

Controversy and compromise did not end with the opening of the park. The question of how St. Louisans wished to use their new amenity—and which of them had access to the park—had a real effect on its evolving landscape. Forest Park's original 1876 design emphasized scenic plantings, which served for passive, leisurely enjoyment. Its more active spaces, such as the winding carriage drives or the hippodrome for horse racing, primarily benefited wealthier residents. Not until 1885, when the streetcar lines were extended to the park, did Forest Park become accessible to greater numbers of St. Louisans. Then, as the park enjoyed wider use, it became a place for active recreation. By the 1890s, it was crisscrossed with bicycle paths, baseball diamonds, and lawn tennis courts. On its newly expanded lake, parkgoers boated in the summer and skated in the winter.

By the turn of the century, St. Louisans' fondness for their park had grown so much that proposals to use it as the site for the Louisiana Purchase Exposition stirred great controversy. Neighborhood associations, labor groups, and individual politicians argued that the World's Fair would deny St. Louisans free access to their park and damage the grounds. In the end, a compromise

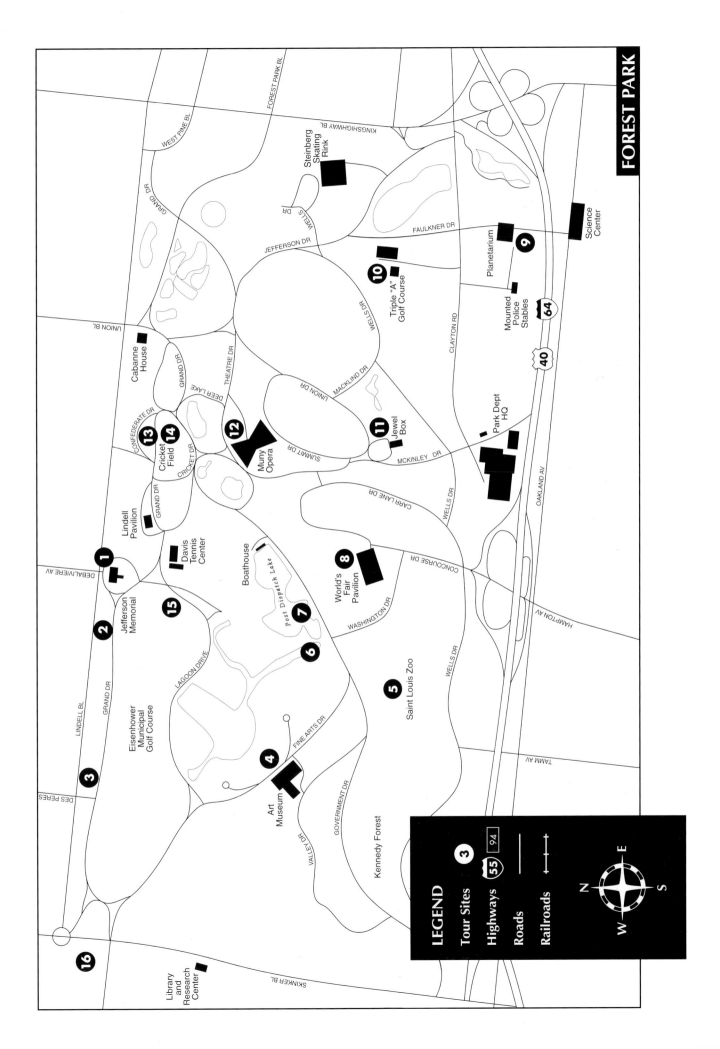

FOREST PARK

LEGEND

Tour Sites   ③

Highways   🛡55   94

Roads

Railroads

N E S W

Library and Research Center

⑯

Eisenhower Municipal Golf Course

③

DES PERES

LINDELL BL

GRAND DR

②

Jefferson Memorial

⑮

LAGOON DRIVE

Davis Tennis Center

Lindell Pavilion

①

DEBALIVIERE AV

Cabanne House

UNION BL

GRAND DR

CONFEDERATE DR

⑬ ⑭

Cricket Field

CRICKET DR

DEER LAKE

THEATRE DR

GRAND DR

WEST PINE BL

FOREST PARK BL

GRAND DR

KINGSHIGHWAY BL

Steinberg Skating Rink

WELLS DR

JEFFERSON DR

⑩

Triple "A" Golf Course

FAULKNER DR

⑨

Planetarium

Science Center

Mounted Police Stables

64

40

CLAYTON RD

WELLS DR

MACKLIND DR

UNION DR

⑫

Muny Opera

SUMMIT DR

⑪

Jewel Box

MCKINLEY DR

Park Dept HQ

CARR LANE DR

WELLS DR

OAKLAND AV

HAMPTON AV

Boathouse

Post Dispatch Lake

⑦

⑥

⑧

World's Fair Pavilion

WASHINGTON DR

CONCOURSE DR

Saint Louis Zoo

⑤

WELLS DR

④

Art Museum

FINE ARTS DR

GOVERNMENT DR

VALLEY DR

Kennedy Forest

TAMM AV

SKINKER BL

was negotiated: only the western half of the park was used for the fair, keeping the eastern half open to visitors free of charge. In addition, a city ordinance required the exposition company to fully restore the park following the fair.

The park restoration brought with it a renewed debate over the best use of this public space. The exposition company retained George E. Kessler, the chief landscape architect of the fair, to oversee the restoration. Kessler emphasized the careful preservation of the natural scenery, which he believed would allow "rich and poor alike" to enjoy the "quiet repose of the country."

Kessler's view held sway until 1911, when Dwight F. Davis became city park commissioner and advocated an entirely different philosophy. A progressive reformer and enthusiastic amateur athlete, Davis believed that recreation would promote health and build character in the city's youth. He maintained that "if we can't have the grass and the people in our parks, let's sacrifice the grass." By 1930, Davis' legacy of golf courses, tennis courts, and other athletic facilities had given the park the contours we recognize today.

Still, Forest Park was not a park for all St. Louisans. Until 1923, African Americans were barred from its golf courses; it was not until the 1940s that these citizens won full access to park facilities. Even then, the St. Louis Amateur Athletic Association (Triple "A") was allowed to maintain members-only facilities on park grounds for two additional decades.

Today, more St. Louisans than ever before can claim Forest Park as their own. This means, perhaps, that the challenge of making the park a truly "public" place is greater than at any time in the past. But the park's history as a place where disputes and controversies have been solved by negotiation serves as a model—not only for defining the future of this vital green space, but for solving the problems that face the city as a whole.

❶ JEFFERSON MEMORIAL BUILDING (THE MISSOURI HISTORY MUSEUM)

The Jefferson Memorial Building, home of the Missouri Historical Society, opened in 1913 as the first national monument to President Thomas Jefferson. A statue of Jefferson, located in the loggia, commemorates his role in the nation's 1803 purchase of the Louisiana Territory from France. The building was constructed by the Louisiana Purchase Exposition Company, using funds from the 1904 World's Fair. It marks the site of the fair's main entrance.

The Missouri Historical Society, which has occupied the building since its opening, operates the Missouri History Museum, a public museum dedicated to collecting and interpreting the history of the St. Louis community. In 1991, the Historical Society opened its Library and Research Center in the former United Hebrew Temple on South Skinker Boulevard, just west of the park.

❷ RIVER DES PERES

Although the River Des Peres flows through Forest Park along Lindell Boulevard, today's observer would be hard-pressed to discover its course. In the early 1900s, the river, frequently the scene of floods, was regarded as an open sewer, and a section of its channel was boxed in to hide it from World's Fair visitors. Following a severe flood, which swamped the bear pits at the zoo and left the Jefferson Memorial Building an island surrounded by water, a 1923 bond issue provided funds to turn the river into a sanitary sewer. In the park, the river was rerouted into the shape of a horseshoe, roughly following Lindell Boulevard and Kingshighway, then was buried in a thirty-two-foot-wide cement sewer pipe.

Along with increased numbers of parkgoers, the 1890s brought a change in recreational taste. Active sports, such as lawn tennis, became very popular among both men and women. Missouri Historical Society Photograph and Print Collection.

❸ BICYCLE PATH

Bikers, runners, and roller bladers compete today for space on this seven-and-one-half-mile trail, which encircles the park. It dates to 1898, when a cinder path was opened in answer to the nationwide bicycle craze. When interest in bicycling dwindled in the 1910s, the path was converted into a bridle path for horseback riders. Then, in 1968, the bridle path was paved over, becoming a bicycle path once again.

❹ ST. LOUIS ART MUSEUM

The Art Museum was the first of the park's free, public institutions. It is housed in the only surviving building from the 1904 Louisiana Purchase Exposition, the former Palace of Fine Arts. After the Fair, the building was occupied by Washington University's School and Museum of Fine Arts, which was open to the public. This museum proved to be a popular attraction, especially among working-class visitors, who flocked there by the thousands each Sunday. In 1909, the City Art Museum (later the St. Louis Art Museum) was created, to be housed in the building and supported by a recently passed property tax. The new tax, which had won endorsement from the Central Trades and Labor Union, meant that admission to the museum was free.

❺ ST. LOUIS ZOOLOGICAL PARK

In his first report in 1875, Park Superintendent M. G. Kern sketched out a plan for a zoo in Forest Park. The institution he described was to be a place of public instruction and amusement, open to all free of charge.

In the 1890s, the Forest Park Zoological Association, a private organization, raised funds to acquire and house animals. The zoo's small collection grew larger and more exotic when many animals brought to the city for the World's Fair exhibits were left behind. The giant bird cage from the federal government exhibit became a popular attraction. Park Commissioner Dwight Davis, whose reforms stressed structured, supervised recreation, urged that the zoo be moved elsewhere in the city, rather than "destroy a portion of [the] existing park properties." Despite such opposition, in 1916 city voters adopted a special zoo tax, which raised funds for new buildings and maintained the free-admission policy.

The bear pits at the zoo, cast using molds of limestone bluffs found near Herculaneum, Missouri, received national recognition when they opened in the early 1920s. Photograph by W. C. Persons. Missouri Historical Society Photograph and Print Collection.

❻ FRIEDRICH LUDWIG JAHN MEMORIAL

This memorial is one of the numerous local monuments erected by diverse groups as a way to remember their heritage. It commemorates Friedrich Ludwig Jahn, the German founder of the *Turnverein*, an international gymnastic and fraternal society. Dedicated in 1913, the monument rests on the site of the German pavilion from the 1904 World's Fair. Commissioned by the local *Turnvereins*, the memorial was designed by Robert Cauer and includes three bronze figures. The two smaller figures were recently restored by Forest Park Forever, a group dedicated to the revitalization of the park.

❼ POST-DISPATCH LAKE

This lake takes its name from the *St. Louis Post-Dispatch*, which, in 1894, conducted a campaign to raise funds for the expansion of Peninsular Lake, then popular for ice-skating and boating. In an era before the instigation of governmental relief measures, the financial Panic of 1893 had left many St. Louisans unemployed. The newspaper's campaign netted enough money to employ some six thousand men for a four-month period. Today, canoes and paddle boats are available for rent on the lake.

❽ WORLD'S FAIR PAVILION

This pavilion, located on Government Hill, is one of several park structures commemorating the 1904 World's Fair. It was erected in 1910 by the Louisiana Purchase Exposition Company as part of the World's Fair site reconstruction. Built as a refreshment pavilion, it occupies the former site of Charles Schweickardt's Cottage Restaurant, which, in pre-fair days, held the exclusive right to sell refreshments in the park. One of the park's few formally landscaped areas, Government Hill features floral patterns and hillside stairways designed by landscape architect George E. Kessler.

❾ ST. LOUIS SCIENCE CENTER (MCDONNELL PLANETARIUM)

The choice of a site for the McDonnell Planetarium in Forest Park touched off a controversy over the use of park space for new buildings. In the end, the planetarium, completed in 1963, was built on the site of the recently razed Mounted Police Station. *Architectural Forum* magazine described the planetarium as "looking like some strange craft spun down to earth from outer space." In 1984, the city sold the planetarium to the Museum of Science and Natural History, which soon reopened the building as the St. Louis Science Center. A few years later, the Science Center's plans for expansion

again met with the familiar opposition over the use of park space. A compromise was achieved when, in 1991, the Science Center's new building opened on Oakland Avenue, just south of the park but connected to the planetarium building by a highway overpass and tunnel.

❿ ST. LOUIS AMATEUR ATHLETIC ASSOCIATION (TRIPLE "A")

Private clubs have been located in Forest Park since its early years. The St. Louis Amateur Athletic Association began as a private club organized in the park in 1897. The club built its own tennis courts and golf course for the exclusive use of its members, paying no rent to the city despite some early objections that this use of park land was inappropriate. The objections intensified in later years when Triple "A," as a private club, was not subject to the city's ordinance prohibiting racial discrimination. The controversy reached a head in 1962, when the Board of Aldermen passed an ordinance prohibiting the exclusive use of park property by a private club. The city and the club then hammered out an agreement in which anyone who applied for membership would be accepted, with non-members allowed to use athletic facilities on a fee basis.

⓫ JEWEL BOX

The Jewel Box, a floral display house opened in 1936, is one of a number of park projects undertaken with public funds aimed at providing employment during the Great Depression. Officially named the St. Louis Floral Conservatory, it was built with a federal Public Works Administration grant, along with funds contributed by the City of St. Louis. When federal funding for the Jewel Box dropped off, the city instigated a nominal admission charge to help support the institution.

⓬ MUNICIPAL THEATRE ASSOCIATION (THE MUNY)

The Municipal Theatre Association has its roots in an enormous theatrical production called the Pageant and Masque, performed in 1914 to commemorate the 150th anniversary of St. Louis' founding. On a stage built over part of the Grand Basin opposite Art Hill, a cast of seven thousand reenacted scenes from the city's history. Civic leaders saw the show as a chance to unite a city split not only by racial and ethnic differences, but also by political divisions lingering from the defeat of a proposed 1911 city charter. Charlotte Rumbold, secretary of the city's Public Recreation Commission, summarized the hoped-for benefits of the pageant with the motto, "If we play together, we will work together." Some 400,000 people saw the show during its four-day run. Proceeds from the

Pageant and Masque were used the following year to produce a play at a natural amphitheater near Art Hill. That theater, soon known as the Municipal Open Air Theatre and later popularly shortened to the Muny, was made permanent in 1917.

⓭ CONFEDERATE MEMORIAL

During the Civil War, St. Louisans, along with other citizens of the border state of Missouri, were divided in loyalty between the Union and the Confederacy. This memorial features a bronze relief of a young man leaving home to fight for the Confederacy—a subject that was still controversial in 1914, when the monument was erected. After much debate, the city council accepted the monument, with the stipulation that it be maintained by its sponsor, the Confederate Monument Association of St. Louis. No other monument in the park was encumbered by such an ordinance. Eyeing the Confederate Memorial from directly across the cricket field to the south is a statue of Union general Franz Sigel, an irony that captures forever the divisiveness of the Civil War.

⓮ GENERAL FRANZ SIGEL STATUE

This statue, just south of the Confederate Memorial, was dedicated in 1906 as a memorial to German Union general Franz Sigel and the many German Americans who fought for the Union during the Civil War. It was the first addition to the park following the 1904 World's Fair. General Sigel led a regiment of U.S. Volunteers in the 1861 capture of Camp Jackson, and quickly became a hero among St. Louis' German population, though his military career following Camp Jackson was less accomplished. A St. Louis elementary school is also named for the general, as are towns in Illinois and Pennsylvania.

⓯ MUNICIPAL GOLF COURSES AND DWIGHT F. DAVIS TENNIS CENTER

Dwight F. Davis, St. Louis Commissioner of Parks from 1911 until 1930, left his mark on Forest Park in the form of numerous athletic facilities for organized sports like golf and tennis. A strong believer in the value of amateur athletics, Davis planned a public golf course in Forest Park as "a means of healthful exercise and amusement" for those unable to pay membership fees in clubs. The open lawn in the northwest part of the park, formerly the site of many World's Fair buildings, was transformed into a nine-hole golf course in 1912. (Fire hydrants installed during the fair still dot the golf course.) That same year, Davis, also a tennis enthusiast, built thirty-two tennis courts, which soon became so crowded that gaslights were added to allow nighttime

play. The founder of tennis' prestigious Davis Cup, Davis was memorialized in 1966 when the city opened the Dwight F. Davis Tennis Tournament Center in the park adjacent to the golf course.

⓰ WASHINGTON UNIVERSITY
West of the Park across Skinker Boulevard

Washington University, founded in 1853 as the Eliot Seminary, announced plans to move its campus from its downtown location at Seventeenth and St. Charles Streets to this property just west of the park in 1894. The university built Brookings Hall in 1901, and Ridgley Library was completed the following year. However, the university delayed occupying its new campus until 1905 in order to lease the buildings to the Louisiana Purchase Exposition Company. Washington University is now one of the nation's most recognized research universities.

FOR MORE INFORMATION

Loughlin, Caroline, and Catherine Anderson. *Forest Park.* Columbia: Junior League of St. Louis and University of Missouri Press, 1986.
Report of the Commissioners of Forest Park, 1875. St. Louis, 1876.
Winter, William C. *The Civil War in St. Louis: A Guided Tour.* St. Louis: Missouri Historical Society Press, 1994.

Special thanks to Caroline Loughlin, Forest Park Forever, Eric Sandweiss, Katharine T. Corbett, and the friends of Forest Park.

Skinker-DeBaliviere

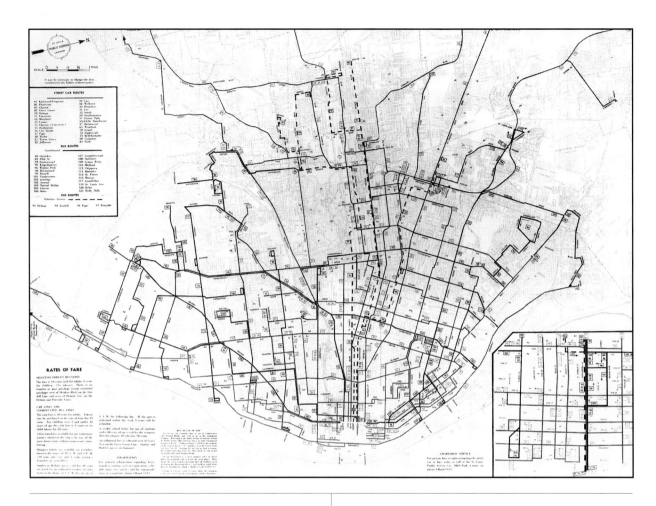

From Washington University (Forest Park): Skinker Boulevard to Forest Park Parkway. Forest Park Parkway right (east) to DeBaliviere Avenue. DeBaliviere left (north) to Waterman Boulevard. Waterman left (west) to DeGiverville Avenue.

Good access to public transportation encouraged the development of the Skinker-DeBaliviere neighborhood. This 1940 streetcar and bus route map shows that the neighborhood was directly served by four streetcar and three bus routes. Missouri Historical Society Photograph and Print Collection.

Until the early twentieth century, the area that is now the Skinker-DeBaliviere neighborhood—bounded by Skinker, Lindell, DeBaliviere, and Delmar—was mostly open farmland, interrupted only by the meandering River Des Peres.

But in the late nineteenth century, two events transpired that radically altered the landscape and opened the door for rapid residential development. The first was the opening of Forest Park in 1876, and the second was the announcement that Washington University—which had been located at Seventeenth and St. Charles Streets since 1857—would move to its current location just west of Skinker Boulevard after the turn of the century.

These two events, in addition to the June 28, 1901, selection of Forest Park as the site of the Louisiana Purchase Exposition, set off a flurry of speculation. That year, the Parkview Realty and Improvement Company, a somewhat mysterious consortium of investors and developers, began buying parcels of farmland for residential development. One of the largest, the Kingsbury family's farm, comprised land that now lies between Delmar Boulevard and Forest Park Parkway, extending west and east of the Skinker-DeBaliviere neighborhood. The Catlin Tract, another of the company's holdings, lay between present-day Lindell Boulevard and Forest Park Parkway. For the fair, the Parkview Company leased the

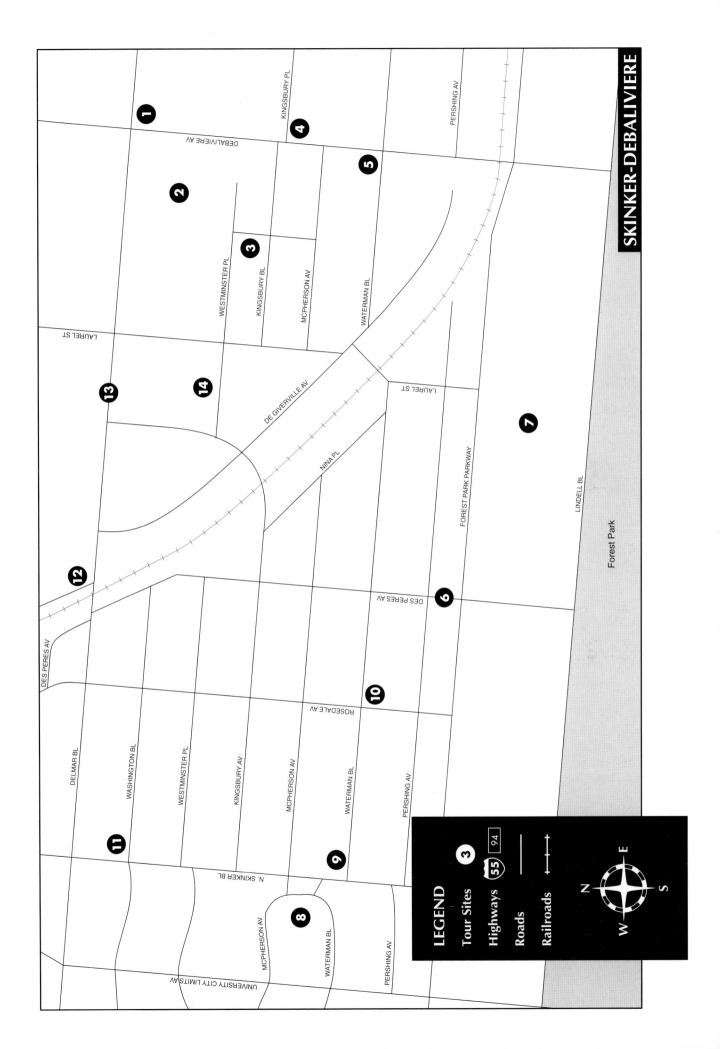

SKINKER-DEBALIVIERE

LEGEND

Tour Sites ❸

Highways 🛡55 94

Roads ——

Railroads +++

N E S W

Forest Park

western portion of the Catlin Tract to the Louisiana Purchase Exposition Company for the installation of the Pike, one of the fair's most popular attractions.

A few years after the fair, promoters used the beauty and tranquillity of the park—as well as the infrastructure of sewers and streetcar lines that had been installed for the fair—to attract well-to-do residents to new developments. The Catlin Tract was subdivided and sold as deep lots for exclusive housing, and attractive subdivisions such as Julius Pitzman's Parkview and the two less exclusive Washington Heights subdivisions were opened. The building boom, which lasted from about 1907-16, gave the Skinker-DeBaliviere neighborhood the intriguing mix of stately mansions, multifamily apartments, and modest family homes that it enjoys today.

Throughout the first half of the twentieth century, the Skinker-DeBaliviere neighborhood was a self-contained area of tree-lined streets featuring a school for the many children in the area and three churches. A bustling commercial life developed in the area, with shops and new apartment buildings clustered around streetcar transfer points. Residents could come back from any part of the city by streetcar, stop at their neighborhood butcher or sundries shop, and carry their purchases the few blocks home. In 1930 businesses along the DeBaliviere strip included a candy store, meat market, cleaners, pharmacy, beauty shop, barber shop, pharmacy, two shoe repair shops, and two markets.

However, many changes came to the neighborhood with the rise of the private automobile and highway system in the 1940s and 1950s. The many walk-up shops along DeBaliviere Avenue gave way to businesses that provided off-street parking for customers, while businesses that could not adapt as easily struggled to keep going. Meanwhile, on-site owners of apartment buildings began to move further west, becoming "absentee landlords" and allowing their property to fall into disrepair.

In response to these new challenges, the Skinker-DeBaliviere Community Council was founded in 1966 to revitalize the community. This interfaith alliance realized the many attractions the neighborhood still held—Forest Park, Washington University, a uniquely urban atmosphere—and used them to draw people back to the neighborhood. Their efforts were helped recently with the addition of MetroLink stops near the Forest Park Parkway and DeBaliviere intersection and at the old Wabash Railway station on Delmar. The Skinker-DeBaliviere neighborhood thus stands as proof that committed residents can counteract even the allure of suburbanization.

A. Moll Grocer Co. was located at Delmar and DeBaliviere. Many small businesses such as this one, often clustered around streetcar transfer points, prospered in the neighborhood during its boom years of 1907-16. Missouri Historical Society Photograph and Print Collection.

❶ DELMAR-DEBALIVIERE BUILDING
5654 Delmar Boulevard

Designed by Isadore Shank in 1928, this richly textured building with black and red terra-cotta panels currently houses the Stella Maris Day Care Center on the first floor and efficiency apartments above.

❷ BI-STATE BUS FACILITY
DeBaliviere Avenue and Delmar Boulevard

This bus maintenance complex was designed in 1986 by Ripley Rasmus for Mackey Associates. A postmodern clock tower faces DeBaliviere. A power house for the St. Louis Public Service Company still stands on the northeast corner of the property.

❸ KINGSBURY SQUARE
Kingsbury Boulevard west of DeBaliviere Avenue

These newly constructed twin homes have a turn-of-the-century flavor. Kingsbury Square was considered to be the first new subdivision built in the city for twenty years; its 1979 plan called for one hundred units arranged around a park complete with a bandstand.

4 CROSSROADS SCHOOL
500 DeBaliviere Avenue

Crossroads, a private school for grades seven through twelve, occupies a renovated former supermarket building on the one-time site of the Winter Garden. A popular west-end sports facility, the Winter Garden featured roller skating from 1904-16 and ice skating beginning in 1926. Originally constructed as the Jai Alai Courts for the 1904 World's Fair, the Winter Garden building was razed in 1963.

5 DORR AND ZELLER BUILDING
401 DeBaliviere Avenue

This building was designed by Preston J. Bradshaw in 1922 for the Dorr and Zeller catering firm. In 1929 they advertised "weddings and parties on short notice" and invited people to visit their beautiful chocolate shop and ice cream parlor at DeBaliviere and Waterman. It currently houses the Central West End Bank.

6 RIVER DES PERES (DES PERES AVENUE)

In the early days of the neighborhood, the River Des Peres was a popular recreational site. But it was also an eyesore and a danger. The river—which became more and more of an open sewer as development increased—was boxed in to hide it from the sight of visitors to the 1904 World's Fair. Worse yet, in 1915 a catastrophic flood claimed eleven lives and damaged more than one thousand homes in the St. Louis area, leading to the passage of a major bond issue to contain and control the river. Today the river flows underground, roughly beneath the street that bears its name.

7 THE CATLIN TRACT
Bounded by Lindell Boulevard on the south, Forest Park Parkway on the north, Skinker Boulevard on the West, and Union Boulevard on the east.

The area known as the "Catlin Tract" was part of the flurry of real estate development brought about by the World's Fair. In 1901, the Parkview Realty and Improvement Company, in anticipation of the fair, purchased the Catlin Tract, a strip of land immediately to the north of the park, and the area west of Skinker that would become Julius Pitzman's Parkview subdivision. Approximately sixty acres of the one-hundred-acre tract lie within the boundaries of the Skinker-DeBaliviere neighborhood.

When the fair was finally in place, the Catlin Tract was leased to the Louisiana Purchase Exposition Company. It was here that one of the most popular attractions of the fair, the Pike, was installed. Among other things, the Pike featured Jim Key, the horse that did math; a display ambitiously called "Creation and the Hereafter"; and daily reenactments of the Boer War and the Galveston flood. The land was subdivided after the fair for residential development; the mansions that now grace the property are a result of the covenant that required that homes built on the tract cost no less than five thousand dollars.

8 PARKVIEW PLACE
Bounded by Skinker Boulevard, Westgate Avenue, and Millbrook and Delmar Boulevards

Lying half in the City of St. Louis and half in University City, Parkview Place is the largest and last subdivision built by prominent St. Louis developer Julius Pitzman. Most of the 250 homes were built between 1906 and

The Pike, one of the most popular attractions of the 1904 World's Fair, was installed along the Catlin Tract, a piece of land purchased by the Parkview Real Estate Company in 1901 and leased to the Louisiana Purchase Exposition. Missouri Historical Society Photograph and Print Collection.

1914. The curving, tree-lined streets were promoted in 1906 as an unsurpassed residential district. Because of the excellent location, the advertisement continued, "Parkview property will be benefited by the hundreds of thousands of dollars which will be spent in beautifying Forest Park and the grounds of Washington University." The Parkview District was added to the National Register of Historic Places in 1986.

9 GRACE METHODIST CHURCH
Skinker and Waterman Boulevards

Designed in 1896 by Theodore Link and Alfred Rosenheim as Lindell Avenue Methodist Church, this structure was originally located on the southwest corner of Lindell and Newstead. Following the westward movement of its congregation, the church was actually taken down and rebuilt at the Skinker location between 1913 and 1914. The congregation of Grace Methodist Church continues to be a vital force in the Skinker-DeBaliviere neighborhood.

10 ST. ROCH'S CATHOLIC CHURCH
Waterman Boulevard and Rosedale Avenue

The rapid growth of the neighborhood led to the June 1911 purchase of land at the corner of Rosedale and Waterman for a neighborhood Catholic church. The first Mass was celebrated in a rented storefront at 6008 Kingsbury. St. Roch's School was completed in 1912 and served both as a school and church until this brick-and-stone Gothic church, designed by Lee and Rush, was completed in 1922. Along with the Baptist and

The Delmar Air Dome, an outdoor theater, was located at 5923 Delmar from 1912-21. Missouri Historical Society Photograph and Print Collection.

Methodist congregations in the neighborhood, St. Roch's helped found the Skinker-DeBaliviere Community Council in 1966.

11 NEW COTE BRILLIANTE CHURCH OF GOD
Washington and Skinker Boulevards

William B. Ittner designed this church building in 1918 as the fourth home of the Delmar Baptist Church. In 1990 the congregation moved to a new location on Clayton Road, and the Washington and Skinker church was sold to New Cote Brilliante Church of God.

12 DELMAR STATION, WABASH RAILWAY COMPANY
Delmar Boulevard and Des Peres Avenue

The Wabash Railway was one of the most popular methods for people getting to and from the 1904 World's Fair, as well as a major mover of people to points further north. Its stop for the Fair was at the present-day Forest Park Parkway and DeBaliviere intersection near the current Forest Park MetroLink stop. The Delmar Station building was closed as a train station in 1970, but it is currently enjoying new life as office space.

13 DELMAR BOULEVARD

Over the years, numerous theaters, houses of worship, restaurants, beauty parlors, cleaners, and other neighborhood services have been located on Delmar Boulevard. The Delmar Air Dome, located at 5923 Delmar from 1912 until 1921, offered outdoor theater. By the 1930s the avenue housed both the Pershing and the Pageant Theaters. Near Skinker, the Brith Sholom Congregation, founded in 1907, worshiped at 6166 Delmar until 1959. The building is currently occupied by Olivet Baptist Church. A Vaad Hoeir, the organization responsible for overseeing rituals in the Orthodox Jewish community, was located at 6128 Delmar.

14 HAMILTON SCHOOL
5819 Westminster Place

The rapid development of the Skinker-DeBaliviere neighborhood made it necessary to house 377 students in portable buildings at the corner of Hamilton and Washington during the 1914-15 school year. The twenty-four room brick and stone building, designed by Rockwell M. Milligan, was completed in the 1917-18 school year and immediately served 772 pupils.

FOR MORE INFORMATION

Harleman, Kathleen M., Georgina B. Stewart, and Susan K. Tepas. *The Neighborhood: A History of Skinker-DeBaliviere.* St. Louis: Skinker-DeBaliviere Community Council, 1973.

Loughlin, Caroline, and Catherine Anderson. *Forest Park.* Columbia: University of Missouri Press, 1986.

McCue, George, and Frank Peters. *A Guide to the Architecture of St. Louis.* Columbia: University of Missouri Press, 1989.

Savage, Charles C. *Architecture of the Private Streets of St. Louis.* Columbia: University of Missouri Press, 1987.

Toft, Carolyn Hewes. *St. Louis: Landmarks and Historic Districts.* St. Louis: Landmarks Association of St. Louis, 1988.

Urban Oasis: 75 Years in Parkview, A St. Louis Private Place. St. Louis: Boar's Head Press, 1979.

THE CENTRAL WEST END

From Hamilton School (Skinker-DeBaliviere): West on Westminster Place to Skinker Boulevard. Skinker left (south) to Lindell. Lindell left (east) to Kingshighway Boulevard. Kingshighway left (north) to Westmoreland Place.

Private places, such as Westmoreland Place, shown here, formed the original core of the Central West End neighborhood. The success of Westmoreland and Portland Places, plotted in the 1880s, led to the creation of other private streets in the area. Photograph by Emil Boehl, c. 1900. Missouri Historical Society Photograph and Print Collection.

Is it possible for a city's wealthy citizens to create an urban enclave, isolated from noise, pollution, and other urban problems? In the nineteenth century, St. Louis' business and social elite learned that the answer to this question is "Probably not—at least, not forever." Each time they attempted to insulate themselves from St. Louis' industries and transportation systems, the very "problems" they had helped to create, the city managed to creep up on them. As St. Louis spread rapidly westward from the Mississippi, the wealthy stayed just ahead of the city's creeping border, leaving behind their once bucolic neighborhoods at Chouteau's Pond, Lucas Place, Lafayette Park, and Vandeventer Place.

By the late nineteenth century, the city's final western edge had become St. Louis' last setting for an upper-class enclave. As early as 1885, real estate ads offered land in the area east of Forest Park with promises of property "that never depreciates" because of its proximity to the park, major streetcar lines, and the wealthy neighborhoods nearby. In this largely rural section of the city, those who had made their fortunes in distilling, flour milling, chemicals, iron and steel, textiles, utilities, tobacco, and shoe manufacturing built palatial

mansions in the most extensive cluster of private places in St. Louis: Portland and Westmoreland Places, Fullerton's Westminster Place, Kingsbury Place, Washington Terrace, Pershing Place, Hortense Place, and Lenox Place. Along with Lindell Boulevard, they formed the original core of the Central West End.

Residents of these private streets were determined to avoid the mistakes of earlier years. Much as their predecessors had done, they used strict covenants to govern and protect their enclaves "in perpetuity." Annual fees helped pay for street, sidewalk, and center-parkway maintenance and street lighting. Minimum costs for houses were specified ($7,000 for Westmoreland Place, $6,000 for Portland Place, and $10,000 for Hortense Place and Westminster Place). Yet residents also used their wealth and influence to control the surrounding environment. In the absence of zoning restrictions (St. Louis did not get its first zoning code until 1918), they bought the adjacent Rock Island Railroad yards to set aside for luxury apartments and hotels and made certain that the Wabash Railroad did not lay above-ground tracks or allow railroad-related industries in the vicinity.

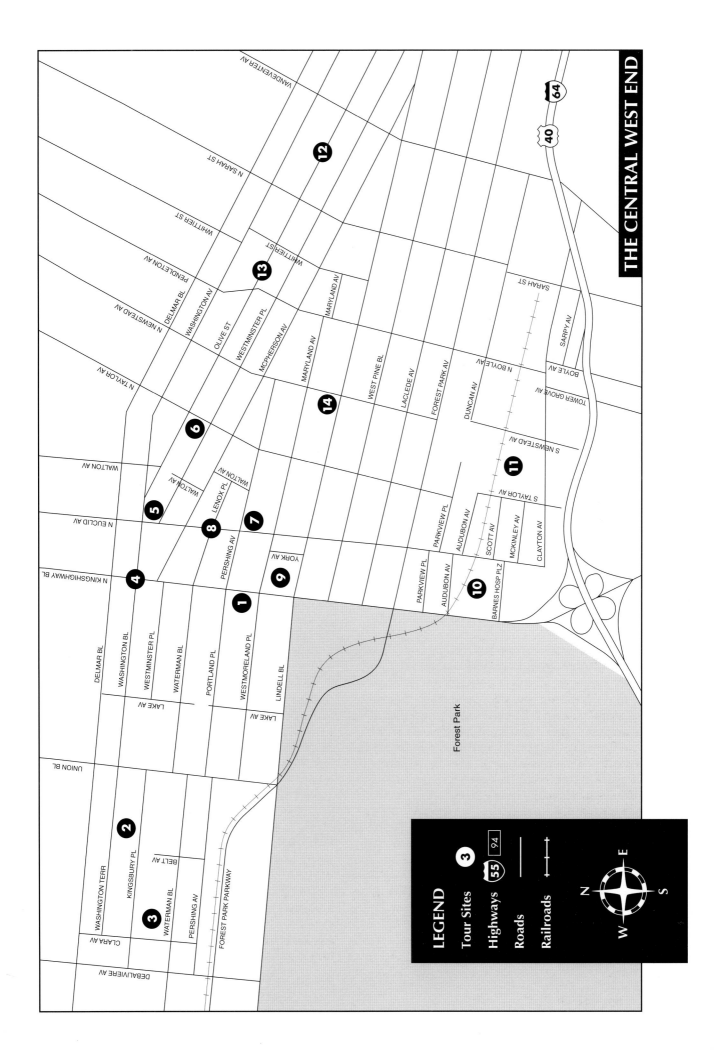

THE CENTRAL WEST END

LEGEND
Tour Sites ③
Highways 55 94
Roads
Railroads

N
W E
S

Forest Park

This arrangement worked for more than half a century. From the end of the nineteenth century to the post–World War II years, St. Louis' wealthy families were comfortably concentrated here, and they dominated the social tone and commercial life of the neighborhood. Siblings and cousins built homes on adjacent lots, while parents built homes for their adult children.

By World War I, the neighborhood had begun to change as the city's middle classes also moved west. Electrified streetcars and commuter trains made both Forest Park and the West End neighborhood accessible to these families, and modest single-family homes and multifamily apartment buildings soon filled the area, providing a friendly buffer for their wealthy neighbors.

Until the late 1950s, the West End was predominantly a white upper- and middle-class neighborhood. Following the 1948 *Shelley v. Kraemer* U.S. Supreme Court decision stating that racially restrictive covenants could not be enforced by state courts, African Americans began moving into areas of St. Louis that had previously been closed to them. This court case, combined with large-scale urban renewal programs and the resulting shortage of housing, radically changed the racial makeup of the neighborhood. By 1960 African Americans made up 30 percent of the population. (Today that figure is about 38 percent.) As the newspapers ran stories about "creeping blight" and "increased crime in the mansion areas," many middle-class and affluent residents sought sanctuary in St. Louis County.

However, the story doesn't end there. The Central West End is no longer an area dominated by wealthy families trying to shut their eyes on the rest of the city. Today the Central West End is an economically and racially diverse community whose residents celebrate urban living and work hard to stabilize and maintain what they consider to be the most vibrant area in St. Louis.

As in many other St. Louis neighborhoods, security is an important issue. Neighborhood block captains are working closely with their aldermen and precinct police. As part of a special tax district, property owners in one section of the neighborhood have voted to increase their taxes to pay for supplementary security patrols.

As the properties have aged, neighborhood improvement plans have been addressing the problems of derelict and vacant buildings. Since the 1970s, individuals committed to urban living, along with large-scale redevelopment projects, have helped renovate, upgrade, or replace these properties.

In 1974, the area of the Central West End bounded roughly by Lindell on the south, Westminster and Washington on the north, Boyle on the east, and DeBaliviere on the west was designated as the Central West End City Historic District. It is one of twelve local historic districts in St. Louis created to maintain both the architectural and social heritage of designated neighborhoods.

Although the area has a mix of rental and owner properties, the shortage of affordable housing is an important issue for moderate- and low-income families and senior citizens on fixed incomes, who have watched neighborhood housing prices rise since the 1980s. Moreover, many families in the area who are looking for alternatives to public schools find that private education is not always available or affordable.

Yet even with these problems, most who live in the Central West End agree that they would not choose to live anywhere else. Like the St. Louisans who created the original neighborhood, today's Central West Enders are firm believers in taking control of their environment to make it a better place for everyone who lives there.

❶ PORTLAND PLACE AND WESTMORELAND PLACE
North of Forest Park between Kingshighway and Union Boulevards

Portland Place and Westmoreland Place were developed in the late 1880s and 1890s by the Forest Park Improvement Association. The first of the neighborhood's private places designed as exclusive residential oases for St. Louis' business and political elite, Portland and Westmoreland Places were planned by St. Louis' city engineer, Julius Pitzman. The neighborhood's private places have helped attract visitors and new residents to the Central West End.

❷ WASHINGTON TERRACE AND KINGSBURY PLACE
North of Forest Park between Union Boulevard and Clara Avenue

Washington Terrace and Kingsbury Place were opened for development by the Bell Realty Company in the late nineteenth and early twentieth centuries. The clock tower at the Union Boulevard entrance to Washington Terrace was designed by Harvey Ellis, while Thomas P. Barnett designed the beaux-arts gateway at the Union Boulevard entrance to Kingsbury Place. Appealing to wealthy families' desire to escape the city's industrial pollution, early advertisements promised a location free from the "smoke and noxious gases generated and thrown out by factories."

❸ DEBALIVIERE PLACE REDEVELOPMENT AREA
Bounded by Pershing Avenue and Delmar Boulevard, DeBaliviere Avenue, and Union Boulevard

Considered the western anchor of the neighborhood's extensive redevelopment efforts, DeBaliviere Place was developed by Leon Strauss and his Pantheon Corporation between 1979 and 1988.

DeBaliviere Place was St. Louis' first large-scale renovation project by a private real estate development company. It includes about fifteen hundred units, a mixture of town houses, condominiums, and rental units.

4 "HOLY CORNERS"
Kingshighway Boulevard at the intersections of Washington Boulevard, McPherson Avenue, and Westminster Place

The Central West End's many historic institutions have helped stabilize the neighborhood. A prime example is the cluster of buildings on Kingshighway known as "Holy Corners," so named because most are religious institutions.

In 1903 St. John's Methodist Church on Washington Boulevard was designed by St. Louis architect Theodore Link, who also designed Union Station. The former Second Baptist Church on McPherson Avenue is now home to the Life Cathedral Baptist Church. Across the street from Life Cathedral, the former Temple Israel is now the Angelic Temple of Deliverance. At Westminster Place, the First Church of Christ, built in 1904, housed the first Christian Science congregation west of the Mississippi. The Tuscan Temple, built in 1907 and 1908 at Westminster Place, continues to serve as headquarters for the Tuscan Lodge No. 360 A.F. & A.

5 TRINITY EPISCOPAL CHURCH
Euclid Avenue and Washington Boulevard

Founded in 1900, this church relocated to the Central West End in 1910. An important community gathering point, Trinity Episcopal is heavily involved in neighborhood programs, including educational and recreational activities for young people. Its location in the Olive/Washington "Triangle" area has served as an important anchor for the neighborhood.

6 SECOND PRESBYTERIAN CHURCH
Westminster Place and Taylor Avenue

The congregation of the Second Presbyterian Church, organized in 1838, first built a church at Fifth and Walnut streets in 1840, relocated to Seventeenth Street and Lucas Place in 1870, and built its Romanesque Revival church in the Central West End at the turn of the century. Theodore Link designed its main sanctuary. Like Trinity Episcopal, Second Presbyterian has been very active in neighborhood preservation efforts and provides important social services to the community.

7 EUCLID AVENUE BUSINESS DISTRICT
Between Delmar Boulevard and Forest Park Avenue

The Central West End's major business district is actually three commercial nodes, each with its own story. Today Euclid Avenue features restaurants and shops catering to a mix of neighborhood residents, other St. Louisans, and out-of-town tourists.

In the early twentieth century, the Euclid/McPherson area was the major shopping district for its wealthy neighbors. By the 1950s, it had evolved into St. Louis' "Greenwich Village" and by the late 1970s also featured stores devoted to the counterculture.

For years the Maryland Plaza area was *the* premier shopping area in St. Louis until its most famous tenants, Saks Fifth Avenue and Montaldo's, moved to Plaza Frontenac in the 1970s. The Maryland Plaza Redevelopment Corporation has overseen much of the renovation on Maryland Plaza west of Euclid.

The Euclid and Laclede section developed as a neighborhood shopping area as the nearby Washington University Medical Center expanded.

8 HORTENSE PLACE AND LENOX PLACE
Between Pershing and McPherson Avenues, west (Hortense Place) and east (Lenox Place) of Euclid Avenue

Hortense Place was established in 1900 by Jacob Goldman, a cotton manufacturer who decided to create his own private place after being refused admittance to Portland and Westmoreland places because he was Jewish. Goldman named the street after his daughter. The more modest Lenox Place was developed in 1903. Many of its original inhabitants were the children of Westmoreland and Portland Place residents.

9 CHASE HOTEL BUILDING AND PARK PLAZA APARTMENT COMPLEX
Kingshighway Boulevard between Lindell Boulevard and Maryland Plaza

The Chase Hotel, dating from 1922, and the Park Plaza Hotel, designed in 1929, were St. Louis' premier hotels and luxury apartments in the mid-twentieth century.

Combined in 1961 as the Chase-Park Plaza, by the 1970s the complex employed over one thousand people and hosted fifteen thousand conventioneers. In the popular Chase Club, St. Louisans heard entertainers like Frank Sinatra and Tony Bennett.

By the 1980s, the hotel complex was losing out to new and renovated hotels downtown. In 1989, the Chase Hotel closed. The recently renovated Park Plaza has been converted to luxury apartments and offices.

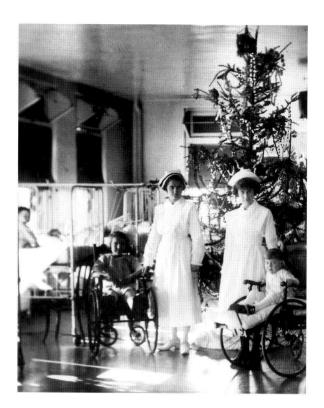

This 1923 photograph shows a ward at Children's Hospital, now part of the Washington University Medical Center. The medical center, through the Washington University Medical Center Redevelopment Corporation, has played a major role in the revitalization of the Central West End. Courtesy of the Bernard Becker Medical Library, Washington University School of Medicine.

⑩ WASHINGTON UNIVERSITY MEDICAL CENTER
Kingshighway Boulevard between Forest Park Avenue and Interstate 64 (Highway 40)

Washington University Medical Center has been an important stabilizing force in the Central West End since the World War I era, when the Washington University Medical School moved to its present site from Locust and Eighteenth Streets, the new Barnes Hospital opened, and St. Louis Children's Hospital relocated from Jefferson Avenue. In the late 1920s, Jewish Hospital moved from Delmar and Union Boulevards, and the medical complex has been expanding ever since.

A turning point for the neighborhood came in the 1970s, when Washington University Medical Center chose to stay at its present site rather than relocate to St. Louis County. Today, Barnes, Jewish, and Children's Hospitals are part of a newly merged health system that also includes Christian Health Services and Missouri Baptist Healthcare System/Missouri Baptist Medical Center.

⑪ WASHINGTON UNIVERSITY MEDICAL CENTER REDEVELOPMENT CORPORATION AREA
Bounded roughly by Lindell Boulevard on the north, Manchester Avenue south of Interstate 64 (Highway 40) on the south, Kingshighway Boulevard and Euclid Avenue on the west, and Boyle Avenue on the east.

Formed in 1974, the Washington University Medical Center Redevelopment Corporation was formed to upgrade and stabilize thirty-eight square blocks in the medical center's surrounding neighborhood.

The corporation buys up dilapidated or underused properties and sells them to developers, helps relocate displaced residents, and works with the city to improve streets and lighting and make other improvements.

One example is Laclede Place, a two-block area in the 4300 and 4400 block of Laclede Avenue to the west and east of Newstead Avenue. Other projects provide housing for low-income families and senior citizens and apartments to accommodate the needs of disabled residents.

⑫ WESTMINSTER PLACE REDEVELOPMENT AREA
Bounded roughly by Washington Boulevard on the north, McPherson Avenue on the south, Boyle Avenue on the west, and Vandeventer Avenue on the east.

The newest large-scale redevelopment project in the Central West End was developed by Richard D. Baron and his St. Louis-based McCormack Baron and Associates, whose renovated buildings have also been important to the redevelopment of the Shaw neighborhood and Soulard as well as urban areas across the country.

The Westminster Place residential project, begun in 1986, includes rental units, condominiums, and single-family homes. The two blocks of Olive Boulevard and Westminster Place between Vandeventer and Boyle avenues are showcases for this development.

Immediately to the west is the historic Fullerton's Westminster Place. The poet T. S. Eliot's parents lived at 4446 Westminster Place; two blocks to the west, at 4633 Westminster Place, is the former apartment of playwright Tennessee Williams. Novelist Kate Chopin lived at nearby 4232 McPherson Avenue.

⑬ GASLIGHT SQUARE SITE
Olive Street between Whittier Street and Boyle Avenue

Rising from the ruins of the devastating February 1959 tornado that ripped through sections of the Central West End and north St. Louis, Gaslight Square became St. Louis' premier hot spot in the 1960s. The district was home to the Crystal Palace, the Golden Eagle saloon, Smokey Joe's Grecian Terrace restaurant, the Laughing Buddha coffeehouse, Gaslight Bar, Jimmy

At its height in the early 1960s, Gaslight Square was the hottest dining, music and entertainment spot in St. Louis. Today its former venues are boarded-up buildings or empty lots. Missouri Historical Society Photograph and Print Collection.

Masucci's Opera House, the Three Fountains restaurant in the historic Musical Arts Building, and other entertainment and dining establishments.

Many St. Louisans theorize about why Gaslight Square had declined by the 1970s. Most agree that the tight parking and a rise in crime in the surrounding area drove many customers away. Today boarded-up buildings and vacant lots are all that remain.

14 CATHEDRAL OF ST. LOUIS (NEW CATHEDRAL)
4431 Lindell Boulevard at Newstead Avenue

Along with the Central West End's private places and the Euclid Avenue shopping district, the Cathedral of St. Louis is a major stopping point for out-of-town visitors and St. Louisans alike. The presence of the mother church of the Roman Catholic Archdiocese of St. Louis has helped regenerate the Lindell Boulevard area.

In 1896, Archbishop John Kain bought the present site at Lindell and Newstead to replace the old cathedral at the riverfront, and a new parish was organized. The architectural firm Barnett, Haynes & Barnett was hired to design the new edifice. Groundbreaking ceremonies finally got underway in 1907, and a cornerstone was laid

the following year. The New Cathedral was completed in 1914, when it received its title, Cathedral of St. Louis.

The Byzantine and Romanesque cathedral features a 227-foot dome and one of the most outstanding collections of mosaics in the Western Hemisphere.

FOR MORE INFORMATION

Goell, Suzanne, ed. *The Days and Nights of the Central West End*. St. Louis: Virginia Publishing Company, 1991.

Hunter, Julius K. *Kingsbury Place: The First Two Hundred Years*. St. Louis: The C.V. Mosby Company, 1982.

———. *Westmoreland and Portland Places: The History and Architecture of America's Premier Private Streets, 1888-1988*. Columbia: University of Missouri Press, 1988.

Levitt, Rachelle L., ed. *Cities Reborn*. Washington, D.C.: Urban Land Institute, c. 1987.

McConachie, Scot. "The 'Big Cinch': A Business Elite in the Life of a City: St. Louis, 1895-1915." Ph.D. diss., Washington University, 1976.

Toft, Carolyn Hewes. *St. Louis Landmarks and Historic Districts*. St. Louis: Landmarks Association of St. Louis, 1988.

Wayman, Norbury L. *History of St. Louis Neighborhoods: Central West End*. St. Louis: St. Louis Community Development Agency, 1980.

Special thanks to Jack Byrne, David Koch, Barbara Quinn, Jeffrey L. Fister, Jeffrey Drane Kimbrell, Mary Bartley, Dan McGuire, Terry Kennedy, Joe Roddy, O. G. Harris, Charlotte Lawton, Tom Hoerr, Michelle Swatek, Anne Spencer, Richard D. Baron, Gene Kilgen, John Roach, Nancy Ferrell, Judy Woolsey, Anne McAlpin, Paul Anderson, Mary Lou Storment, Rev. William , Rev. James T. Telthorst, Karen Duffy Peter Rothschild, Barry Leibman, Lucy Vassia, Shirley Hunt, Joyce Littlefield, Kris Runberg Smith, Kathy Corbett, Eric Sandweiss, Mary Seematter, Duane Snedekker, Deborah Brown, Charles Brown, and the residents of the Central West End.

PENROSE

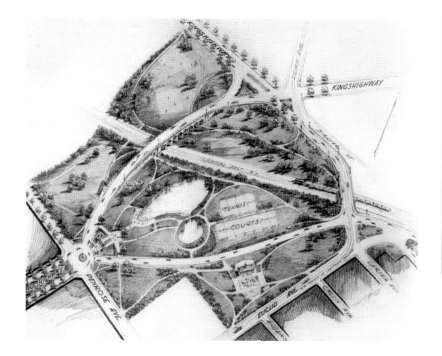

From the Cathedral of St. Louis (Central West End): West on Lindell Boulevard to Kingshighway Boulevard. Kingshighway right (north) to Natural Bridge Road.

This early rendering of Penrose Park shows how the park was designed around Kingshighway Boulevard, an important transportation route since the eighteenth century. Missouri Historical Society Library.

In the early nineteenth century, the area that now makes up the Penrose neighborhood was characterized more by land speculation than by actual settlement. The land took its name from Clement B. Penrose, whom Thomas Jefferson appointed land commissioner in 1805. Penrose lived on a nearby estate and was one of the region's prime land investors. Another early landowner was statesman Henry Clay, a shaper of the Missouri Compromise.

Penrose did not take on the contours of a community until the late 1880s, when farmers and dairymen, mostly of German heritage, moved their families into the area. By 1900, the community, though still relatively rural, was sufficiently settled to boast two German churches, St. Engelbert's Catholic Church and Salem German Evangelical Church.

With the 1920s, commercial development and transit lines raised land values around the northern edges of St. Louis. Most of Penrose's subdivisions date from that era, when rows of single-family brick homes sprang up along Euclid, Shreve, and Lee avenues. Although some of these subdivisions were the work of outside investors, others were developed by longtime residents, a prime example being the area around Steinlage Drive, a street named for a local German family in the dairy business.

The early 1960s were years of transition for Penrose. As older residents moved out, African American families moved in. The well-constructed houses were ideal for moderate-size families, offering many their first opportunity for home ownership. Middle- and upper-income

African Americans, including teachers, nurses, and city and government employees, made Penrose their new home. A significant number came from the Ville, located to the southeast and long the city's premier African American neighborhood.

As Penrose's African American population increased from 33 percent in 1960 to 95 percent in 1970, African American institutions helped solidify the neighborhood. St. Peter's AME Church relocated to the corner of Shreve and Margaretta in 1962. In 1974, the Julia Davis Branch Library, its name honoring the well-known St. Louis educator, opened on Natural Bridge Avenue.

Soon residents began to organize, showing their commitment to community improvement. One of their first tasks was to define exactly where Penrose began and ended. Choice, not history, became the factor for deciding neighborhood boundaries—Kingshighway on the west, Natural Bridge on the south, Newstead on the east, and Interstate 70 on the north.

In 1981 Penrosians joined forces with St. Engelbert Church to create a chapter of Neighborhood Housing Services, a non-profit partnership of residents, businesses, and government. By 1989 NHS had made nearly $1 million in home improvement loans, much of it to senior citizens with modest incomes. Today the Penrose Self-Reliant Neighborhood Association, an outgrowth of NHS, rehabs and invests in existing structures.

In addition, Penrose boasts several neighborhood safety and social programs. One such effort is the local Community-Oriented Policing (COPs) program,

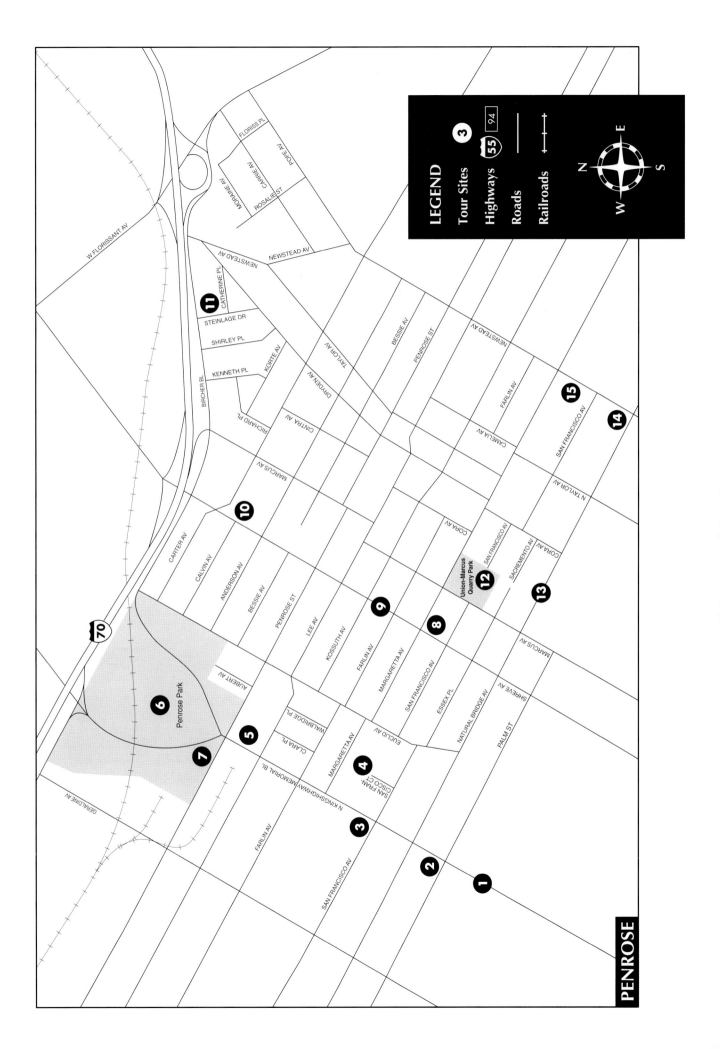

PENROSE

through which patrolmen have become a highly visible part of the community. The Penrose Neighborhood Festival, held each June in Penrose Park, is a much-anticipated event, bringing together local residents and visitors from all around St. Louis.

Penrose's strength today lies in the dedication of its residents, many of whom have lived in the neighborhood for thirty years or more. Through "choice," they have redefined their community, building an atmosphere of cooperation and improvement. Here, as elsewhere in St. Louis, the idea of "neighborhood" comes as much from human spirit as from streets and landmarks.

❶ NORTH KINGSHIGHWAY BOULEVARD

Although envisioned in the early part of the twentieth century as a broad parkway linking the city's major parks, stretching from Carondelet Park in the south to O'Fallon park in the north, with Tower Grove Park and Forest Park in between, Kingshighway Boulevard did not achieve its present design until 1923. The tree-lined Memorial Plaza between Martin Luther King Boulevard and Penrose Street now offers a pleasing combination of beauty and utility.

❷ FREDERICK N. WEATHERS POST OFFICE
3415 North Kingshighway Boulevard

In 1986, Congress authorized this post office, which is named in honor of St. Louisan Frederick N. Weathers. Weathers, an African American businessman, had a long career in politics and social groups. As a Democratic committeeman for the Eighteenth Ward for twenty-eight years, he worked hard to promote African Americans in city government and helped to add an affirmative action clause to the charter of the St. Louis Board of Police Commissioners. Weathers was also a longtime board member of the NAACP, the Urban League, and the YMCA.

❸ REXALL CORPORATION HEADQUARTERS
3901 North Kingshighway Boulevard

This manufacturing plant served as the headquarters of the Rexall Drug Company from 1922 until its closing in 1985. Best remembered as a franchiser of drug stores, Rexall had ten thousand branches throughout the country in 1960. The company also turned out nearly twenty-three hundred different kinds of drugs, medicines, and cosmetics from its seven-story Kingshighway plant. At its peak in the 1970s, Rexall employed one thousand workers. The building is currently used as storage space, with plans underway for its adaptive reuse.

❹ SAN FRANCISCO COURT
Off San Francisco Avenue

This small cul-de-sac, with its attractive single-story brick homes, was developed in 1957, much later than most of the area around it. Although close to busy Kingshighway, San Francisco Court is a quiet street, its feeling of seclusion enhanced by the absence of through traffic on San Francisco Avenue.

These stockclerks are working in the warehouse of the Rexall Drug Company, which had its headquarters in Penrose from 1922 to 1985. The Rexall building is currently being used as storage space. Photograph by W. C. Persons. Missouri Historical Society Photograph and Print Collection.

Swimming is but one of the athletic and recreational activities offered at Mathews-Dickey Boys Club, founded in 1959. The Boys Club was recently chosen as the training site for the St. Louis Rams. Courtesy of the Mathews-Dickey Boys Club.

❺ SCULLIN SCHOOL
4160 North Kingshighway Boulevard

Scullin School, which serves students from kindergarten through fifth grade, is named for John Scullin, the St. Louis businessman and railroad magnate who founded the Scullin Steel Company. The school opened in 1928 in response to the neighborhood's population growth.

❻ PENROSE PARK
North Kingshighway Boulevard at Penrose Street

Penrose Park, a fifty-acre site acquired by the city in 1910, was designed to be the hub of the Kingshighway Boulevard system in the northwestern part of the city. As such, the designers had to work around existing industrial features, a challenge not encountered in the laying out of the city's more idyllic parks; the site was bordered by an industrial district to the west and bisected by the Terminal Railroad line. Rather than meandering drives, like those in Forest Park, the roads in Penrose Park channeled traffic to specific destinations.

Today the park is an integral part of the neighborhood. Each June it hosts the Penrose Neighborhood Festival. The park features tennis and handball courts, softball fields, and the St. Louis area's only regulation velodrome, a one-fifth-mile asphalt oval with banked curves used for bicycle racing. (The velodrome can be seen from the Kingshighway viaduct.)

❼ MATHEWS-DICKEY BOYS CLUB
4245 North Kingshighway Boulevard

The Mathews-Dickey Boys Club began in 1959 with a meeting between Martin L. Mathews and Hubert "Dickey" Ballentine, coaches of a neighborhood baseball team. The two men then began to organize additional

athletic teams, their goal being to keep boys on the playing fields and off the streets. As the number of players grew, Mathews and Ballentine secured a small storefront building to serve as a clubhouse. The present facility, built in 1981, covers twelve acres of ground and houses athletic, recreational, educational, and cultural-enrichment activities, along with offices, meeting space, and classrooms. The club began programs for girls in 1986, offering education, arts and culture, personal development, and athletics. Today the club serves more than forty thousand youths, ages six to eighteen, from throughout the St. Louis metropolitan region, and in 1995 it was chosen as the training site for the St. Louis Rams football team.

❽ ST. PETER'S AFRICAN METHODIST EPISCOPAL (AME) CHURCH
4730 Margaretta Avenue

The St. Peter's congregation was formed in 1847 by a group of north St. Louisans from St. Paul AME Church. In 1866, they built their first church at the corner of Elliott and Montgomery. The congregation remained at that site, rebuilding three times after storm damage, until moving to the present site in 1962. The building, dating from 1898, originally housed the Salem Evangelical and Reformed Church, a German congregation that had worshiped in Penrose since 1886. St. Peter's AME Church is the second oldest African Methodist Episcopal church west of the Mississippi.

Today St. Peter's AME serves about five hundred congregants. The church's outreach programs include Faith House, a shelter for babies born with drug addictions; Project Home Again, a housing-search program for families recently out of shelters; and Cooperative Congregational Outreach, a job training and employment-search program.

9 SHREVE AVENUE

Shreve Avenue is named for Henry Shreve, a well-known steamboat builder and operator who, in the mid-1800s, retired to a nearby three-hundred-acre estate. In the early 1900s, the street was the quiet home of Penrose's two oldest churches, Salem Evangelical (now St. Peter's AME) and St. Engelbert Catholic. By the late 1920s, Shreve had become a busy commercial street, dotted with German-owned grocery stores, barber shops, bakeries, and florists, as well as a dry goods store and a hardware store. Many of these small shops remained for decades, before finally bowing to the growth of chain stores and the change in shopping patterns. Today Shreve Avenue is a mixed residential and commercial street, featuring apartment buildings, hair salons, a bakery, and a dry cleaning establishment.

10 ST. ENGELBERT CATHOLIC CHURCH AND SCHOOL
4336 Shreve Avenue

St. Engelbert's parish was organized by a small group of area residents in early 1891. Later that year, the first church was dedicated on a six-acre site at Shreve and Carter avenues. The present church, built in 1926, is a Tudor Gothic edifice designed by architect Henry P. Hess. The church's beautiful stained-glass choir window was created by St. Louis artist Emil Frei. St. Engelbert's parochial school, for students from kindergarten through eighth grade, opened in 1891. It moved to the present building at 4720 Carter Avenue in 1930.

Originally a German church, St. Engelbert's congregation is now mostly African American, its nine hundred members coming from Penrose, Normandy, Florissant, and North County. St. Engelbert is active in community outreach programs through the St. Vincent de Paul Society and the Father Tolton Catholic Charities Outreach Center. St. Engelbert Church works closely with the Penrose neighborhood organizations on a variety of community-based projects.

11 STEINLAGE DRIVE

This street, off Bircher Boulevard, was developed in the late 1920s as part of Steinlage's Subdivision. The Steinlages, a German family involved in the dairy business, had lived and worked in the neighborhood since the 1880s. The brick homes on this street are some of the finest in the community.

12 EUGENE "TINK" BRADLEY PARK
Marcus Avenue at San Francisco Avenue

Eugene O. "Tink" Bradley served as Twenty-first Ward Alderman from 1965 until his death in 1981. From November 1979 through November 1980, Bradley served as the acting president of the St. Louis Board of Aldermen, the first African American to serve in this post. Bradley, who was a social worker before beginning his political career, also served on the board of directors of the St. Louis Urban League.

13 NATURAL BRIDGE AVENUE

Natural Bridge, one of north St. Louis' most traveled thoroughfares, is named for the natural stone bridge that once crossed Rocky Branch Creek. The bridge was near present-day Twenty-third and Palm Streets, several blocks east of Fairgrounds Park. First laid out in the 1840s, the road stretched from West Mound Street in St. Louis to Normandy. When civic boosters in the 1930s feared that Lambert-St. Louis airport was being outstripped by the Kansas City airport, a short-lived movement to change the name from Natural Bridge to Airport Road sprang up to increase St. Louisans' interest in their own airport.

The high volume of traffic along Natural Bridge Avenue led to the development of commercial strips and auto-oriented facilities, including service stations and automobile dealerships. The old Northwestern Hotel, built in the 1920s near North Euclid, catered to motorists passing through the Penrose neighborhood. Today, Natural Bridge is a popular location for drive-in businesses, including many fast-food restaurants.

14 JULIA DAVIS BRANCH LIBRARY
4415 Natural Bridge Avenue near North Newstead Avenue

The Julia Davis Branch Library, which opened its new building in February 1993, honors Dr. Julia Davis, whose initial gift of $2,500 in 1961 was used to begin the St. Louis Public Library's Julia Davis Research Collection on African American History and Culture. Dr. Davis, a well-known educator and historian, graduated from Sumner High School and Stowe Teachers College. She taught in the St. Louis Public Schools from 1913 until 1961, spending thirty-one of those years at Simmons School in the Ville.

The library, built on land donated by Commerce Bank, is a fifteen-thousand-square-foot structure with capacity for fifty thousand books. Designed by architect Russell Lewis, the building features a 120-seat auditorium and two meeting rooms. The new library houses the Dr. Julia Davis Research Collection and also offers computers and educational software for public use.

FOR MORE INFORMATION

Hannon, Robert E., ed. *St. Louis: Its Neighborhoods and Neighbors, Landmarks and Milestones.* St. Louis: St. Louis Regional Planning and Growth Association, 1986.

Wayman, Norbury L. *History of St. Louis Neighborhoods: Fairground.* St. Louis: St. Louis Community Development agency, 1981.

Wright, John A. *Discovering African-American St. Louis: A Guide to Historic Sites.* St. Louis: Missouri Historical Society Press, 1994.

Special thanks to Carol Clounch, Pearl Hawkins, Bob Cole, Lawrence Hamilton, George Kirkland, Alderwoman Sharon Tyus, Rev. Anthony G. Siebert, St. Peter's AME Church, and the residents of Penrose.

New development continues in the Penrose neighborhood, which takes pride in its quality housing. Here, members of Neighborhood Housing Services break ground for a new house in eastern Penrose. Courtesy of Neighborhood Housing Services of St. Louis, Inc.

15 ASHLAND SCHOOL

3921 North Newstead Avenue

The present Ashland School stands on the site of the original school building, constructed in 1874, in what was then a rural area called Elleardsville. For years the only public school in the area, Ashland took its name from statesman Henry Clay's home county in Kentucky. Clay had been involved in land speculation and in the 1840s owned the Old Orchard Tract, a large piece of property that is now Calvary Cemetery. The present Ashland School, built in 1909, serves students from preschool through fifth grade. Designed by prominent St. Louis school architect William B. Ittner, the building bears his signature ornamental detailing.

FAIRGROUNDS-O'FALLON PARK

**From Ashland School (Penrose):
Right (south) on North Newstead
Avenue to Natural Bridge Road.
Natural Bridge left (east) to
North Grand Boulevard.**

The annual, week-long St. Louis Fair was the high point of St. Louis social
life from 1856 until 1902. Tens of thousands of visitors came to the fair every
year, including the Prince of Wales, later King Edward VII, who visited here
in 1860. Engraving by J. P. Davis. Missouri Historical Society Photograph and
Print Collection.

The North St. Louis neighborhoods that lie beside the
Fairgrounds and O'Fallon Park have a unique place in
the cultural and recreational life of St. Louis. Since the
mid-nineteenth century, the area that extends from the
corner of Grand Boulevard and St. Louis Avenue west
to Fair Avenue and north to Broadway has been home
to some of the city's most important public spaces. Here,
at what was once the edge of town, St. Louisans came
to relax and to play. Whether attending the annual fair,
going to a Cardinals game, or taking a scenic drive, their
trip began with a ride north on Grand Boulevard.

St. Louisans today think of Grand as the street that
neatly cuts through the middle of the city. In the 1760s,
however, this route marked the eastern edge of the
Grand Prairie common field, a set of narrow, east-west
strips laid out in the colonial period for agricultural use.
The Grand Prairie was so far from the village of St. Louis
that huts were built there for overnight stays. The common field area (which extended from St. Louis Avenue

on the south, to Carter Avenue on the north, and from
Grand west to Newstead and Marcus avenues), is what
we know today as the Fairgrounds neighborhood. Its
location, for so long at the periphery of the city, helped
to determine the kinds of institutions that gave the
neighborhood its original character.

In 1855 the extension of St. Louis' boundaries put
the city limits just west of Grand. Within a few years
horse-drawn omnibuses carried passengers from the central city out to the fairgrounds on the edge of Grand.
Development in the area began in 1856, when the
St. Louis Agricultural and Mechanical Association purchased a fifty-acre site at the northwest corner of Grand
and the Natural Bridge Plank Road. The association, a
private group dedicated to boosting St. Louis commerce,
bought the land from one of its members, Colonel John
O'Fallon, who had extensive holdings in the area. The
site became the home of the St. Louis Agricultural and
Mechanical Fair, an annual week-long event that drew

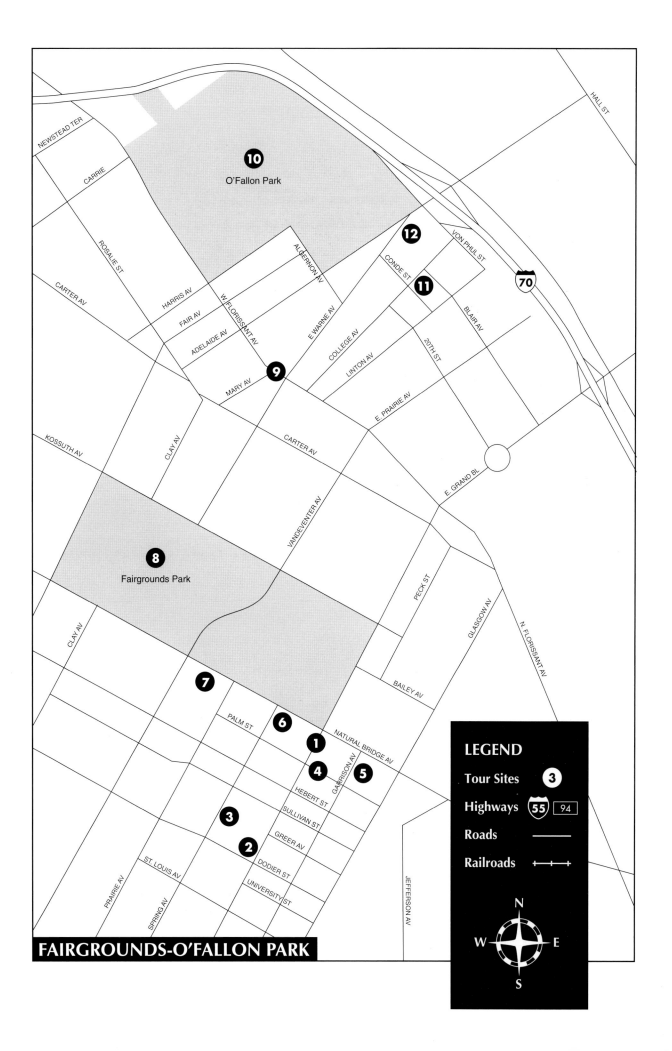

FAIRGROUNDS-O'FALLON PARK

LEGEND

Tour Sites ③

Highways 🛡55 94

Roads

Railroads ┼┼┼┼

N
W E
S

thousands of visitors from the city and outstate Missouri. Manufacturers exhibited and sold their latest inventions and farmers vied over whose livestock would be chosen the fair's best. For entertainment, fairgoers visited the floral hall, fine arts hall, and sideshow tents.

Like the fair, Sportsman's Park, established in 1866 at the northwest corner of Grand and Dodier Street, was also a private enterprise. Chris von der Ahe, a German-born grocer and saloonkeeper, bought the park in 1881, hoping that baseball games would draw patrons to his nearby establishment. As the "boss president" of the St. Louis Browns, von der Ahe dictated how the team should be run, and added to his profits by scheduling games on Sundays and selling liquor in the ballpark.

O'Fallon Park, in contrast to these private institutions, was a public space. Opened in 1876 as part of the city park system, O'Fallon Park offered visitors winding roadways for scenic drives, a picturesque lake, and an observation tower with a dramatic view of the Mississippi River. Unlike the fair or Sportsman's Park, O'Fallon Park was created for passive recreation; it was a place designed more for contemplation than competition.

The community's popular attractions and easy access to streetcar facilities encouraged early residential development. Subdivisions sprang up near the eastern edge of the fairgrounds in the 1860s, and the area continued to develop into the early 1900s. As the city developed other recreation areas, however, the Fairgrounds-O'Fallon Park community gradually lost its identity as an entertainment center. By the late 1960s, people drove their own cars downtown to the new Busch Stadium to cheer on the Cardinals instead of riding the streetcar up Grand.

Today, as Fairgrounds and O'Fallon Park struggle with the problems that face all urban neighborhoods, residents are organizing to preserve their community. Door-to-door petition drives led to the creation of a number of one-way streets in O'Fallon Park, a measure that reduces traffic on residential streets. Fittingly, the Fairgrounds and O'Fallon Park neighborhood organizations, both just a few years old, are focusing their efforts on revitalizing their parks as places for recreation. Vital public spaces gave the Fairgrounds-O'Fallon Park community its unique historic identity and may well prove essential to its future.

❶ NORTH GRAND BOULEVARD

North Grand Boulevard was vital to the popularity of the Fairgrounds and Sportsman's and O'Fallon Parks, as it offered an easy way for people from the city to get to the then-remote recreational area. More importantly, the road encouraged residential development and commerce. Even though the streetcars no longer run north along Grand, and even though Busch Stadium has now moved downtown, North Grand continues to be an important link between North St. Louis and the city to the south.

❷ HERBERT HOOVER BOYS' CLUB (FORMERLY SITE OF SPORTSMAN'S PARK)
2901 North Grand Boulevard

The site of the Herbert Hoover Boys' Club has been used as a place to play since the first baseball diamond, known as the Grand Avenue Ball Grounds, was laid out here in 1866. It was renamed Sportsman's Park in 1876, when it became the home of the St. Louis Browns.

Sportsman's Park, at Grand and Dodier, was the home of the St. Louis Cardinals from 1920 until 1966. When the ball club was moved to the new Busch Stadium downtown, August A. Busch, Jr., donated the site of the old stadium to the Herbert Hoover Boys' Club. Missouri Historical Society Photograph and Print Collection.

An arts and crafts program is one of the many activities available to members of the Herbert Hoover Boys' Club, located on the former site of Sportsman's Park. Herbert Hoover Boys' Club.

Chris von der Ahe bought the team in 1881, and as the "boss president" of the Browns he guided them to four pennants from 1885 through 1888.

The Cardinals joined the Browns at Sportsman's Park in 1920. The 1934 Cardinals, known as the Gashouse Gang and led by Frank Frisch, Leo Durocher, Pepper Martin, and Dizzy Dean, earned the National League pennant with their gritty and aggressive play. Ten years later, the Cardinals defeated the Browns in St. Louis' first and only streetcar series. In 1953 August A. Busch, Jr., bought the Cardinals and Sportsman's Park, which he renamed Busch Stadium. The last game was played at the stadium in May 1966, one hundred years after the first ball diamond had been laid out on the site.

But five months before the Cardinals played their last game there, August A. Busch, Jr., donated the site for a new boys' club, still in its planning stages. Named for President Herbert Hoover, longtime Chairman of the Board of Boys' Clubs of America, the club opened in June 1967. The boys' club serves youths ages six to eighteen, most of whom live in the neighborhood. It offers a wide range of programs designed to enhance self-esteem and promote academic, physical, and social development. Members receive homework assistance, attend theatrical events, and participate in arts and crafts programs. The boys' club offers team sports including baseball, basketball, and football, as well as individual sports such as karate and aquatics. For more information call 652-8300.

3 CARTER CARBURETOR
2840 North Spring Avenue

For many years this was the site of Carter Carburetor's main plant, where workers manufactured carburetors, fuel pumps, oil filters, and other car parts. During World War II, when automobile production was curtailed, Carter partially converted to manufacture shell fuses for the War Department. Like numerous other local war industries, Carter Carburetor was the site of labor protests. In August 1942 several hundred men and women marched from Tandy Park in the Ville neighborhood to the Carter plant, protesting the company's reluctance to hire African American employees.

In the early 1980s Carter Carburetor became Carter Automotive Company, Inc. Today its fifty-eight employees produce fuel pumps for the Chrysler Corporation.

4 PALM STREET

Before its development as a residential street, Palm, between Glasgow and Grand, was the site of the Lindell Amusement Park, a private recreational ground rented to organizations for outings from the early 1870s until it closed in the 1890s. In the late 1910s, a predominantly German American population lived in the large single- and two-family homes on Palm, reflecting the population of much of the neighborhood at that time. Today Palm Street is a cul de sac. This change was intended to reduce through traffic on the street and help residents maintain control over their section of the neighborhood.

5 CENTRAL VISUAL AND PERFORMING ARTS HIGH SCHOOL (FORMERLY YEATMAN HIGH SCHOOL)
3616 North Garrison Avenue

Upon its opening in 1904, Yeatman was the only high school in North St. Louis. Named for St. Louis philanthropist James E. Yeatman, it was rechristened Central High School in 1927 after Central's building was destroyed by a tornado. In 1988 the school became the Central Visual and Performing Arts High School, a magnet school offering its students programs in drama, vocal and instrumental music, visual arts, dance, and fashion.

6 FAIRGROUNDS HOTEL
Natural Bridge and North Spring Avenue

Built in 1927, the eight-story Fairgrounds Hotel served as quarters for members of the Cardinals and the Browns, who played at Sportsman's Park, just four blocks away. Stan Musial and his family lived at the hotel during his first few seasons with the Cardinals in the 1940s. After the demolition of Sportsman's Park, the hotel was converted into Fairgrounds Manor, a four-hundred-bed extended care nursing home. In 1983 the building was renovated and reopened as Drew Towers, with sixty-five apartments for senior citizens and the disabled.

7 BEAUMONT HIGH SCHOOL
3836 Natural Bridge Road

Named for early St. Louis surgeon William Beaumont, Beaumont High School stands on the former site of National League Park, where the St. Louis Cardinals played from 1899 until their move to Sportsman's Park on Grand Boulevard in 1920. The city bought the ballpark in 1920 and, six years later, built the largest school in St. Louis. The faculty and students of Yeatman High School moved from their old building to the larger Beaumont High in 1926. The school, which serves fourteen hundred students, recently reopened following a complete renovation. Beaumont High School has received local, state, and national awards for its science programs.

8 FAIRGROUNDS PARK
Bounded by Natural Bridge Road, Fair Avenue, Kossuth Avenue, and North Grand Boulevard

In 1855 a group of St. Louis businessmen formed the St. Louis Agricultural and Mechanical Association for the purpose of offering an annual trade fair. The first St. Louis Fair opened on October 13, 1856, and ran for one week. Manufacturers displayed their latest inventions, and farmers from outstate brought their best livestock and produce, competing for huge premiums. Outside the fair's entrance gates were sideshow tents featuring such curiosities as the Snake Charmer and the Educated Pig.

Fifteen to twenty-five thousand people a day flocked to the fairgrounds during fair week, most of them by way of the horse-drawn omnibus line on Grand. St. Louis schools and businesses closed on "Big Thursday" of every fair week so that everyone might attend.

Over the years, three hundred buildings were constructed for the fair, including a twelve-thousand-seat amphitheater, a mechanics' building, a floral hall, and livestock halls. In the 1870s a zoo was constructed in the southeast corner of the fairgrounds. The bear pit structure, dating to 1876, is the only building remaining from the fair.

In 1884 the fairgrounds received a blow from the opening of the Exposition Hall downtown, which was built expressly for the purpose of displaying machinery and manufactured products. With the upcoming 1904 Louisiana Purchase Exposition, interest in the annual St. Louis Fair dwindled, and the last fair at the fairgrounds took place in 1902.

The city purchased the abandoned fairgrounds in 1908, and after removing the Fair's structures, reopened the site as Fairgrounds Park in 1909. In the 1910s, the former location of the amphitheater was rebuilt into a five-acre swimming pool. When African American children challenged their exclusion from the pool in 1949, sporadic rioting took place in the Fairgrounds neighborhood. The following year, two thousand St. Louisans rioted over the Park Department's decision to allow African American children to use the pool.

Today, Fairgrounds Park continues to be a focal point for the neighborhood. The Fairgrounds Community Development Organization has plans for a skating rink in the park and a bicycle path around the park's perimeter.

Until 1950, African American children were denied the right to use the pool at Fairgrounds Park. Here, a father asks the pool superintendent to admit his sons. The boys were refused entry. Photograph by Ed Meyer. Missouri Historical Society Photograph and Print Collection.

9 WEST FLORISSANT AVENUE

Florissant Avenue has long been a vital thoroughfare in the O'Fallon Park community. The road linking St. Louis with Florissant, a major grain supplier, grew to be an important commercial street. In the 1910s, neighborhood residents could board a streetcar to visit the district's doctors, dentists, tailors, grocers, butchers, and barbers, as well as shoe stores, bakeries, and dry goods stores.

10 O'FALLON PARK
Bounded by West Florissant Avenue, Harris Avenue, Algernon Street, Adelaide Avenue, Interstate 70, and East Taylor Avenue

Unlike Fairgrounds and Sportsman's Parks, O'Fallon Park did not begin as a private venture. The City of St. Louis created it from the estate of John O'Fallon, who owned over six hundred acres of land in the area. In the 1850s, O'Fallon built a country house, named Athlone after his ancestral home in Ireland, overlooking the Mississippi River. In 1875, ten years after O'Fallon's death, the city purchased 166 acres of the estate from his heirs for use as a park. O'Fallon Park, like Carondelet Park in the south, was created as a compromise for St. Louisans who resented the long buggy ride to Forest Park, then under development. O'Fallon became a popular park for scenic drives and picnics. The lake, added in the 1890s, gave rise to boating.

In the 1960s, the park's uninterrupted view of the Mississippi was blocked when the Missouri Highway Department routed Interstate 70 through the park, paving over forty acres of athletic fields. Today efforts are underway to revitalize O'Fallon Park. The O'Fallon Community Development Organization has worked to clean up the park and designate one-way streets to cut down on the amount of through traffic. Plans are in the works to renovate the boathouse and bring back boating and other lake activities.

11 KULAGE HOUSE
1904 College Avenue

In the 1830s, Saint Louis University acquired the area roughly bounded by Warne, Carter, Linton, and Broadway with the intention of building a new campus there. For over forty years the land served as the college farm until the University subdivided it and moved to its present site at Lindell and Grand. Joseph and Maria Kulage purchased the land from the University and established a brick manufacturing business there in the 1880s. Their home, built in 1906, is distinctive for its unusual stone-faced organ tower, which houses a church-sized organ with nearly seventeen hundred pipes.

12 MOUNT GRACE CHAPEL OF PERPETUAL ADORATION
1438 East Warne Avenue

Established in 1928 through an endowment from Maria Kulage, the convent is the home of the Holy Spirit Adoration Sisters, also known as the Pink Sisters, for the color of the habits they wear. Part of a contemplative order, the Pink Sisters rarely go beyond the walls of the convent. Most of their day is spent in prayer; there is round-the-clock prayer in the chapel.

FOR MORE INFORMATION

Hannon, Robert E., ed. *St. Louis: Its Neighborhoods and Neighbors, Landmarks and Milestones.* St. Louis: St. Louis Regional Planning and Growth Association, 1986.

Wayman, Norbury. *History of St. Louis Neighborhoods: Fairground.* St. Louis: St. Louis Community Development Agency, 1978.

———. *History of St. Louis Neighborhoods: Hyde Park and Bissell-College Hill.* St. Louis: St. Louis Community Development Agency, 1980.

Wright, John A. *Discovering African-American St. Louis: A Guide to Historic Sites.* St. Louis: Missouri Historical Society Press, 1994.

Special thanks to James Williams, Lewis Collins, Mary Taylor, Debra Burtis, Herbert Hoover Boys' Club, Wendy Krom, and the residents of the Fairgrounds and O'Fallon Park neighborhoods.

THE VILLE

From Mount Grace Chapel of Perpetual Adoration (Fairgrounds-O'Fallon Park): East Warne Avenue south to Kossuth Avenue. Kossuth right (west) to Newstead Avenue. Newstead left (south) to Martin Luther King, Jr., Drive.

Established in the Ville in 1910, Sumner High School provides a focal point for the community. Sumner's excellent reputation has attracted many new residents to the Ville. Photograph by David Schultz.

The Ville, St. Louis' cradle of black culture, reigned for decades as the city's premiere African American neighborhood. Today, the area—bounded by Dr. Martin Luther King Drive, Taylor Avenue, St. Louis Avenue, and Sarah Street—still thrives on the same impassioned commitment of its community members and institutions. Schools, churches, and social service organizations combine to create a close-knit, supportive community.

The Ville originally belonged to Charles M. Elleard, a florist and horticulturist who maintained a conservatory and greenhouses on the tract. A small town known as Elleardsville grew up around the nursery; St. Louis annexed the area in 1876. In the late nineteenth century, Elleardsville (later shortened to "the Ville") attracted German and Irish immigrants, along with some African Americans. The neighborhood's first black institution, Elleardsville Colored School No. 8 (later renamed Simmons School), opened in 1873; St. James African Methodist Episcopal Church was organized in 1885, further establishing an African American presence in the community.

Sumner High School, the first high school for black students west of the Mississippi, moved to the Ville in 1910 after a group of concerned citizens petitioned the board of education for the relocation of the school from its site in the central business district. Thanks to the Ville residents' continuing commitment to education, the John Marshall School opened as an intermediate school in 1918, and the Charles Henry Turner School for the handicapped was founded in 1925. These institutions, combined with Sumner High School's Normal School for teacher training, lent the Ville distinction as one of the few St. Louis communities in which black residents could attend school from kindergarten through professional training.

While educational and religious institutions helped to draw residents into the Ville, other factors went to work to shape the neighborhood. In 1911, some parts of the city adopted race restrictive covenants that forbade property owners to sell, rent, or lease any property to blacks or other minorities. The Ville was surrounded by streets with these covenants; as an unrestricted neighborhood, it soon became a desirable place for black residents. Between 1920 and 1950, the number of African Americans in the Ville increased from 8 to 95 percent of the total population. Small, single-family homes sprang up, mixed with such family businesses as Wardlow's Grocery Store, Morgan's Drug Store, and Velars Dry Goods Store. The Ville had become a self-contained community.

In 1917, Annie Turnbo Pope Malone, a self-made millionaire, established Poro College, a manufacturing plant and training school for agents selling her line of beauty products. Poro College provided nearly two hundred jobs for Ville residents and served as a social center for the neighborhood. Homer G. Phillips Hospital, the largest institution in the Ville from its opening in 1937 until its controversial closing in 1979, employed more than eight hundred people at its peak. Many black doctors from across the nation performed their internships and residencies at the hospital, which provided health care for St. Louis' black community.

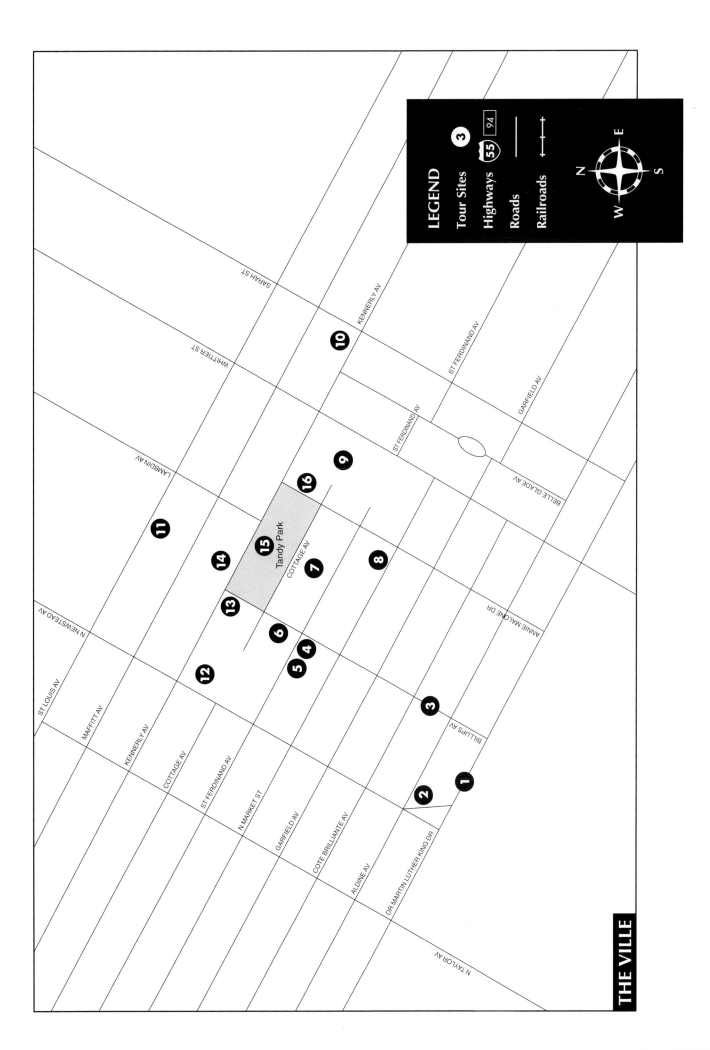

THE VILLE

LEGEND

Tour Sites ③
Highways 55 94
Roads
Railroads

N E S W

In the landmark 1948 *Shelley v. Kraemer* case, the Supreme Court ruled that restrictive covenants were unconstitutional. African Americans could no longer be denied the right to own property on the basis of race. Many residents moved out of the Ville into other parts of St. Louis; between 1950 and 1970, the total population in the Ville dropped by nearly 38 percent.

Today, the residents of the Ville are committed to recapturing the spirit of the neighborhood's bright past. In 1985 the Ville Apartments, a 110-unit complex of frame and brick buildings, opened for residency. Neighborhood groups such as the Martin Luther King Business Association, the Greater Ville Historic Development Corporation, and the Ville Historic Preservation Corporation have ongoing area clean-up and rehabilitation programs. Community churches, educators, and graduates of local schools have joined forces to revitalize the Tandy campus area in the heart of the Ville.

Finding a new use for the former Homer G. Phillips Hospital has been a special neighborhood goal. Recently, the Annie Malone Children and Family Service Center received a grant from the Community Development Agency to rehabilitate the Nursing School building for use in the center's independent living program. Additional plans for recycling the hospital include converting the upper stories to housing for senior citizens or those needing limited care and developing a cultural gallery and a trauma center on the lower floors.

❶ DR. MARTIN LUTHER KING DRIVE (FORMERLY EASTON AVENUE)

In 1972, Easton Avenue and a portion of Franklin Avenue were renamed Dr. Martin Luther King Drive as a tribute to the Baptist clergyman and civil rights activist who was slain in 1968. In East St. Louis, Veterans Bridge became Dr. Martin Luther King Bridge.

❷ JOHN MARSHALL ELEMENTARY SCHOOL
4322 Aldine Avenue

Built in 1900, Marshall Elementary is the only school in the Ville area not originally intended for African American students. In 1918, Marshall became an intermediate school for African Americans. It has served the area as an elementary school since 1927.

❸ BILLUPS AVENUE (FORMERLY PENDLETON AVENUE)

This street takes its name from Kenneth B. Billups, a musician, teacher, and Sumner alumnus who served as chairman of Sumner High School's music department and founded the Legend Singers. He later became director of music for the St. Louis Public Schools. Opera star Grace Bumbry was one of Billups' most successful students.

Running west of Sumner High School on a section that was formerly part of Pendleton, Billups Avenue extends from Kennerly on the north to Martin Luther King Drive on the south.

❹ PORO COLLEGE SITE
Southwest Corner, St. Ferdinand Avenue and Billups Avenue

Annie Turnbo Pope Malone, one of Missouri's first self-made millionaires and the nation's first black woman millionaire, established Poro College in the Ville in 1917. At the college, agents in Malone's hair-care and beauty business were trained in the use and distribution of the company's products. The three-story building occupied an entire city block and housed many facilities, including instructional departments, offices, an auditori-

Annie Malone established Poro College (shown here in 1927) to "hold aloft the ideals of dignity, beauty, industry, thrift, efficiency and godliness" for African American women. Missouri Historical Society Photograph and Print Collection.

um, a dormitory, dining room, sewing shop, emergency first-aid rooms, and an apartment for the Malones. By the 1920s, Poro College provided nearly two hundred jobs for Ville residents, including many students from nearby Sumner High School.

After Malone moved her enterprise to Chicago in 1930, the building became a hotel; later it was home to the Lincoln University Law School. Today, the Poro College corner is the site of the James House, 4310 St. Ferdinand Avenue, a senior-citizen apartment complex sponsored by St. James African Methodist Episcopal Church.

❺ JAMES HOUSE
4310 St. Ferdinand Avenue

In 1970 St. James African Methodist Episcopal Church constructed the James House, the first church-developed housing project in St. Louis. The ten-story apartment building at Billups and St. Ferdinand is part of an Office of Housing and Urban Development "turnkey" project. St. James AME raised $45,000 toward the construction of the project, which now houses over two hundred self-sufficient senior citizens.

❻ ST. JAMES AFRICAN METHODIST EPISCOPAL CHURCH
4301 St. Ferdinand Avenue

St. James AME Church, established in 1884, was built to serve African Americans moving into the Ville. Its first structure, a frame chapel at Pendleton and St. Ferdinand, was replaced by the present brick church at 4301 St. Ferdinand. St. James AME helped finance the building of the James House across the street from the church, at the former site of Poro College. Working with the Vaughn Cultural Center, St. James is an important supporter of community activities.

❼ SUMNER HIGH SCHOOL
4248 West Cottage Avenue

Opened in 1875 as the first African American high school west of the Mississippi, Sumner High School is named for Senator Charles Sumner, who in 1861 became the first prominent politician to call for full emancipation. The high school moved from its first location at Eleventh and Spruce Streets to Fifteenth and Walnut Streets in 1895. In 1910, after a group of citizens petitioned the board of education to move the school away from the saloons and pool rooms near its downtown location, the school was moved to its present site.

Over the years, Sumner High has served as a cornerstone of the neighborhood, attracting some of the brightest, most talented members of St. Louis' African American community. Prominent Sumner High School graduates include entertainer Tina Turner, opera singers Grace Bumbry and Robert McFerrin, activist Dick Gregory, actor-singer Robert Guillaume, U.S. Minister to Liberia Lester Walton, educator Julia Davis, tennis great Arthur Ashe, musician David Hines, and newscaster Julius Hunter.

William B. Ittner designed the red brick, Georgian Revival building. In 1988 the school was added to the National Register of Historic Places.

❽ ANTIOCH BAPTIST CHURCH
West North Market Street and Annie Malone Drive

The Antioch Baptist Church, incorporated in 1884, is one of the oldest Protestant churches in the Ville. The present church building, at Annie Malone Drive (formerly Goode Avenue) and North Market, dates from 1920. Reverend James E. Cook, one of Antioch's most memorable pastors, gained recognition for his direction of the Pine Street YMCA and his activity in the civil rights movement. The church continues to play a vital role in community life.

Until it closed in 1979, Homer G. Phillips Hospital offered a wide variety of training programs and served as a center for the education of African American doctors, nurses and medical personnel. Photograph by W. C. Persons. Missouri Historical Society Photograph and Print Collection.

9 HOMER G. PHILLIPS MEMORIAL HOSPITAL
2601 Whittier Street

When Homer G. Phillips Hospital was dedicated in 1937, it was the largest and best health care facility in the world committed to the care of African American patients and the training of African American doctors and nurses. Homer G. Phillips was an African American attorney who almost single-handedly led the battle for approval of the $87 million bond issue to build the hospital. Phillips died in 1931, shot by an unknown assailant one year before the hospital's construction began.

In addition to serving the community, Homer G. Phillips Hospital offered internship programs in the areas of internal medicine, urology, pediatrics, obstetrics and gynecology, general surgery, pathology, radiology, otolaryngology, ophthalmology, and neuropsychiatry. The hospital was closed in 1979. The building, designed by Albert A. Osberg, won listing with the National Register of Historic Places in 1982.

10 ST. MATTHEW'S PARISH COMPLEX
2715 North Sarah Street

St. Matthew's, located on Sarah Street between Kennerly and Maffitt Avenues, serves as testament to the one-time presence of Irish Catholics in the Ville. Built in several phases, the complex consists of a Gothic Revival church (1907) designed by Joseph Conradi, a rectory, a school building (1902-25), and a garage adorned with a glazed brick shamrock. The school building has found a new purpose as housing for the elderly. Since August 1986, St. Matthew's has been listed on the National Register of Historic Places.

11 SIMMONS ELEMENTARY
4318 St. Louis Avenue

The first black institution in the Ville was the two-room Simmons Elementary School. The school opened in 1873 as Elleardsville Colored School No. 8, ten years after blacks gained the legal right to education in Missouri. By 1877 the white teachers had been replaced by black teachers, who also served in administrative positions. The school was renamed in 1891 for Dr. William J. Simmons, a Baptist clergyman, educator, and author. The present Simmons School building, constructed in sections from 1899 to 1930, is the work of prominent architect William B. Ittner.

12 THE VILLE APARTMENTS
Kennerly and Newstead Avenues

Construction of the Ville Apartments, a 110-unit complex on North Newstead, was completed in 1985. This new housing complex represents an important step in the redevelopment of the inner core of the historic Ville area. Along with the extensive rehabilitation of older homes in the area, these apartments give the Ville a substantial boost toward its goal of revitalizing the residential community.

13 TURNER MIDDLE SCHOOL
2615 Billups Avenue

When the Sumner Normal Department expanded to form Stowe Teacher's College (named for Harriet Beecher Stowe), the building that now houses Turner Middle School was constructed to house the new college. Designed by George W. Sanger and constructed in 1940 at what was then 2615 Pendleton Avenue, the building served in this capacity until 1954. In that year, segregation ended in St. Louis Public Schools and Stowe merged with Harris Teachers College. The middle school now housed in the building is named for Charles Henry Turner, a black scientist who taught at Sumner High from 1908 to 1922.

14 TURNER MIDDLE BRANCH
4235 West Kennerly Avenue

Turner Middle Branch opened in 1925 as Charles Turner Open Air School for Handicapped Children, the first school of its kind for blacks in the United States. The school served both disabled and tubercular children. As an open air school, it allowed children with tuberculosis to take in fresh air year round, but as a result students often had to dress warmly. The school charged no tuition and offered a standard curriculum to its physically challenged students. In place of stairs, the school featured ramps and rails. The school was phased out in 1960-61, a number of years after the passage of desegregation laws. The school building now houses non-handicapped classes for Turner Middle School.

15 TANDY COMMUNITY CENTER AND PLAYGROUND
4206 Kennerly Avenue

Tandy Community Center opened in 1938 as a Public Works Administration project during the depression. The center's name honors Captain Charlton Hunt Tandy, an African American Civil War veteran and captain of "Tandy's St. Louis Guard," a state militia

Elleardsville, as the Ville was first known, attracted many German and Irish immigrants. This glazed brick shamrock on a wall near the garage at St. Matthew's Church is a visual reminder of the neighborhood's Irish past. Photograph by David Schultz.

FOR MORE INFORMATION

Schoenberg, Sandra, and Charles Bailey. "The Symbolic Meaning of an Elite Black Community: The Ville in St. Louis." *Missouri Historical Society Bulletin* 23 (January 1977), pp. 94-102.

Smith, JoAnn Adams. *Selected Neighbors and Neighborhoods of North St. Louis.* St. Louis: Friends of Vaughn Cultural Center, 1988.

Toft, Carolyn Hewes, ed. *The Ville: The Ethnic Heritage of an Urban Neighborhood.* St. Louis: Social Science Institute Ethnic Heritage Studies, Washington University, 1975.

Wayman, Norbury L. *History of St. Louis Neighborhoods: Grande Prairie.* St. Louis: St. Louis Community Development Agency, , 1979.

Wright, John A. *Discovering African-American St. Louis: A Guide to Historic Sites.* St. Louis: Missouri Historical Society Press, 1994.

composed of African American volunteers recruited by Tandy. After the Civil War, Tandy was instrumental in the founding of Lincoln University in Jefferson City. Tandy Park, a 5.6-acre playground, has numerous sports facilities, including the tennis courts where champion Arthur Ashe once practiced.

16 ANNIE MALONE CHILDREN AND FAMILY SERVICE CENTER
2612 Annie Malone Drive

Sarah Newton founded the St. Louis Colored Orphans' Home in 1888 as an institution for orphans or neglected and dependent children. The home moved from Twelfth Street to its current site in 1922. Annie Malone donated money to fund the construction of the new facility, which was named for her in 1946. Neglected and abused children can seek refuge at the Service Center, and troubled families can seek counseling there. Medical and social services, crisis intervention services, and a youth volunteer program are also part of its services.

The former Homer G. Phillips Hospital nurses' residence has now been reutilized by the center as housing for an independent living project. Funding comes, in part, from the United Way and from proceeds from the annual Annie Malone May Day Parade.

SUBURBS:

POST–WORLD WAR II DEVELOPMENT

SUBURBS: POST–WORLD WAR II DEVELOPMENT

Suburb. To our contemporary thinking, the very word conjures images of conformity and monotony, row after row of identical houses in a forever expanding Levittown. While there is an element of truth to this perception—the familiar pattern can be seen in modern-day planned residential "developments"—the truth about what is "suburban" and what is not is much more complicated.

To begin with, many of the neighborhoods discussed in the preceding sections at one time served the same function as today's suburban neighborhoods. The private streets of the the Near South Side, Midtown, and the Central West End, for example, were first envisioned as places where people could escape the congestion and clamor of the city. It was only as transportation systems developed that these areas, once accessible primarily to the wealthy because of the cost in time and money of traveling to them, began to open up to the less prosperous. As this happened, in conjunction with legal cases that challenged the fairness of housing practices in the private neighborhoods, their air of exclusivity subsided.

Fittingly, transportation in the form of the railroads and streetcars also enabled the development of four of the suburbs discussed in this section. University City, Webster Groves, Kirkwood, and Ferguson all grew up along publicly accessible transportation lines. It is no accident that all four of these small cities still cherish emblems of their railway past: University City's Delmar Loop and Webster Groves', Kirkwood's, and Ferguson's standing train stations now link the cities symbolically as they once linked them—and St. Louis—literally.

Another thing to keep in mind is that suburbs often grow in ways that mirror, on a smaller scale, the growth of the larger city. Some parts of suburbs become more "desirable" than others, just as some parts cities do; there are very few suburbs that are homogenous in terms of race, socioeconomic level, or class. Similarly, suburbs often find themselves involved in the same kinds of controversies and arguments that take place in the city. Much can be learned, for example, by comparing the

response of Webster Groves and the city's Hill area to the construction of Interstate 44. In each case, the communities gathered together to protect their own interests, and in each case compromise was reached. In Webster Groves, the highway was routed through only part of the community and then along an existing rail line, thus reducing the destruction of housing; on the Hill, the citizens rallied to construct a highway overpass, thus preserving the cohesiveness of their community. Similar comparisons can be drawn between any neighborhood in the county and any neighborhood in the city; the two sides of the city-county fence are not as different as residents sometimes like to think.

Finally, even though all of these suburbs have their origins in the nineteenth century, it is impossible to talk about suburban development without mentioning the post–World War II exodus out of the city. A city such as Manchester, whose roots stretch back into the early nineteenth century, is a good example of the phenomenal growth of suburbs that occurred with the development of the interstate highway system, the rise of the automobile, and the introduction of government home-buying incentives in the 1940s and 1950s. In the forty years after its incorporation as a city in 1950, Manchester's population has tripled, and anyone who braves the traffic on Manchester Road can testify to the incredible commercial success of the area.

Of course there are many more suburban communities than the five discussed in these sections, but these five can be seen as prototypes. All but Manchester were specifically planned as "suburbs"; their developers followed an impulse to build, from the ground up, ideal communities—communities where those who could afford to could escape the city while remaining linked to it. It is an impulse that continues to shape St. Louis' urban landscape to this day.

UNIVERSITY CITY

From St. Louis City: Interstate 64 (Highway 40) west to Clayton Road/Skinker Boulevard exit. Right (north) onto Skinker Boulevard. Continue past Forest Park to Pershing Avenue.

From St. Louis County: Interstate 64 (Highway 40) east to McCausland Avenue exit. Left (north) on McCausland. Continue on Skinker Boulevard past Forest Park to Pershing Avenue.

The Magazine Building, now the University City Hall, is a center of both national and local pride in this photograph. Courtesy of the University City Public Library Archives.

University City, a vibrant community of forty thousand people on the western boundary of St. Louis, has a cosmopolitan character more typical of a city than a suburb. An eclectic mix of cafés, ethnic restaurants, bookstores, specialty shops, cultural institutions, and places of worship line its commercial districts. Within its neighborhoods, a range of housing accommodates people from every economic level. The city's population, which includes many students and faculty from neighboring Washington University, is made up of a wide age range and broad ethnic mix.

Since it was founded at the turn of the century, this suburban city has faced many traditionally urban problems. Like many older communities, it has been forced to redefine itself, as some residents and businesses have left for newer suburbs. Yet through the years University City residents have maintained their commitment to creating an active, cohesive community—and this commitment has become a hallmark of University City life.

The first vision of University City came from Edward Gardner Lewis, a Connecticut entrepreneur who founded the city in 1902. He bought an unincorporated eighty-five-acre tract of high land on Delmar Boulevard and built a publishing plant for his popular *Woman's Magazine* and other publications. Lewis dreamed of developing a model city based on the principles of the City Beautiful movement, which emphasized urban design and planning. The octagonal City Hall (originally the magazine's headquarters) and the nearby Lion Gates convey a piece of Lewis' vision for the new city. (A model of Lewis' never-completed plan for the Civic Plaza, which included replicas of the Parthenon and the Taj Mahal, is on display in City Hall.) Lewis laid out the University Heights One subdivision himself, applying

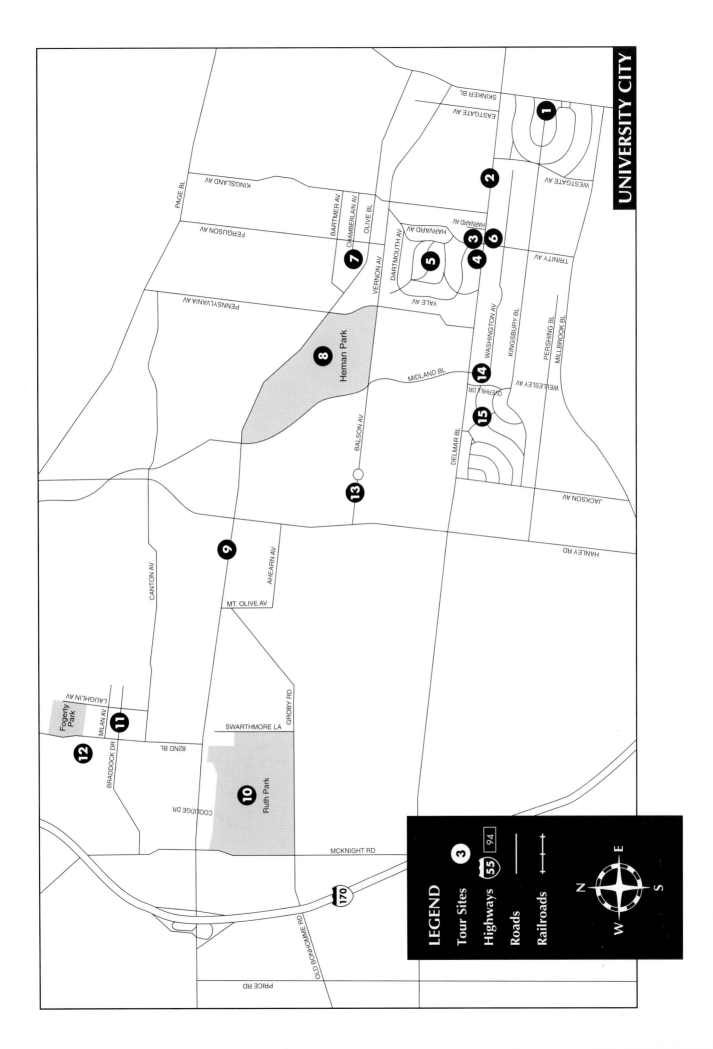

the principles of modern landscape architecture and planning to its hillside site.

Expanding his vision for the city, Lewis founded the American Woman's League, a national women's organization, and the People's University, an outgrowth of the league that offered courses in such fields as law, medicine, and the arts. Proclaiming University City the nation's center of art and education, Lewis brought together talented ceramists, sculptors, and artists in his Academy of Fine Arts (now the Lewis Center, 725 Kingsland). But his empire was short-lived. In 1912, six years after Lewis incorporated University City and became its first mayor, he left for California under allegations of business misdealings. Subsequent city leaders shared some of Lewis' vision, but lacked his utopian ambitions. The city was left with a half-realized dream.

In 1931 Harland Bartholomew, the most prolific city planner of his day, was hired to turn Lewis' vision into a more practical plan. Bartholomew set guidelines for future subdivisions and emphasized recreational space. By 1945 University City's thirteen parks represented one-third of all park acreage in St. Louis County.

Education has also formed a key part of the civic vision that has guided the city's growth. Around 1915 University City was one of the first places in the country to develop a junior high school system. The district's tradition of excellence drew a wide and shifting variety of ethnic groups to the schools: Jewish students made up more than 70 percent of the student body by 1960, and African Americans accounted for a similar proportion two decades later. The intervening years brought times of controversy, as the schools made the transition to full racial integration. Today, the community is still deeply concerned about its schools, and school board elections are the most hotly contested political races in the area.

The commercial vision for University City has come to life through a close alliance of business and the arts. Nowhere is this union more visible than in the revitalization of the Delmar Loop area. In its Delmar gallery, the Craft Alliance has exhibited its artists' works since 1970. The St. Louis Symphony Community Music School has been recognized as one of the finest professional schools in the nation. Blueberry Hill restaurant, the Market in the Loop, the newly renovated Tivoli Theatre, and other area businesses have led the commercial renewal of this vital strip.

But University City's historic commitment to diversity is not only evident in its shops, restaurants, churches, and cultural institutions; most important, it is also reflected in the faces of the people who live there. This diversity continues to enrich the civic vision that has distinguished the city from its earliest days.

 PARKVIEW

Bounded by Skinker Boulevard, Westgate Avenue, and Millbrook and Delmar Boulevards

The Parkview subdivision, located one-third in the City of St. Louis and two-thirds in University City, was plotted in 1905. It is the last and largest private place designed by Julius Pitzman, a Prussian immigrant who served as the chief engineer of Forest Park and also designed more than forty private places in St. Louis. Pitzman's design for Parkview combined the private place concept with the ideas of the landscape park movement. He avoided the common rectangular grid pattern by bending streets into horseshoe curves. Pitzman is believed to have introduced the concept of selling residential lots under deed restrictions that limited them to single-family occupancy and made lot holders the owners of their streets and alleys. In Parkview, an upper-middle-class subdivision, residents were required to spend at least $4,000 to $7,000 constructing their homes.

② DELMAR LOOP

Delmar Boulevard, between Eastgate and Kingsland Avenues

The Delmar Loop—so called because the streetcars of the Delmar line made a U-turn on Delmar at Heman Avenue—has long been a main attraction in University City. In the early 1900s the Delmar Racetrack (the entrances to which gave Eastgate and Westgate avenues their names) and the Delmar Gardens Amusement Park drew crowds of visitors. By 1911, both the racetrack and amusement park had closed. They were soon replaced by spacious apartment buildings and many shops such as grocery stores, bakeries, Kosher butchers, stylish clothing stores, and shoe stores. In the early 1960s, an urban renewal project set tough new housing codes and some old buildings were razed. While apartments in the Loop attracted college students, new apartment buildings, like Parkview Towers, provided homes for the elderly and disabled. A new generation of businesses, including Blueberry Hill, Paul's Books, and Streetside Records, opened in the Loop, bringing new activity to the area. The new University City Public Library, completed in 1969 at Delmar and Kingsland, helped anchor the neighborhood, while the Tivoli Theatre, a local landmark since 1924, was recently renovated after being threatened with demolition. Also along Delmar on the Loop is the St. Louis Walk of Fame, which features bronze stars and placques honoring famous St. Louisans such as Miles Davis, Vincent Price, and Betty Grable.

❸ UNIVERSITY CITY CITY HALL
(THE MAGAZINE BUILDING)
Delmar Boulevard at Harvard Avenue

A walk around the ornate city hall and adjacent buildings gives present-day observers a sense of E. G. Lewis' grand vision for his city. The five-story octagonal tower was constructed in 1903 as the Magazine Building, the executive office building for Lewis and the staff of his popular *Woman's Magazine.* Elaborately decorated inside and out, the building features an Italian marble spiral stairway and eight murals on the lobby ceiling depicting stages of Lewis' life and career. The building became the city hall in 1930. On the north side of the Magazine Building, Lewis built one of the world's largest press room buildings, with nine huge presses, each able to produce 300,000 copies per hour. This building now serves as the Police and Fire Department Annex.

❹ LION GATES
Delmar Boulevard at Trinity Avenue

These two massive concrete felines, the symbols of University City, have served as what E. G. Lewis called "the gates of opportunity" since they were erected in 1909. Lewis commissioned Hungarian-born sculptor George Julian Zolnay, who directed the art department of the Louisiana Purchase Exposition, to design the sculptures marking the entrance to the new city's residential area. For many years the sculptures were thought to be a pair of lions, a male and a female, but recent research into the models used by Zolnay reveals that the northern sculpture is probably a tiger. In 1989, new cats were cast in polymer concrete from molds of the originals.

❺ UNIVERSITY HEIGHTS ONE SUBDIVISION
Bounded by Delmar Boulevard, Yale, Dartmouth, and Harvard Avenues

This subdivision is the only one of several planned residential developments that E. G. Lewis actually brought into being. Lewis purchased the site—a hillside sloping down from the north side of Delmar to the River Des Peres—in 1902. During the 1904 World's Fair, the area from Princeton to Cornell Avenues served as Camp Lewis, a tent city funded by Lewis for those subscribers to his publications who needed a place to stay while visiting the fair.

Lewis designed the subdivision with great care, constructing a wax model of the site in order to experiment with different landscape designs. The subdivision's streets curve gently, forming K- and Y-figures instead of right angles; they resemble a landscaped park more than an urban residential neighborhood. While private streets typically excluded the lower classes, Lewis provided for a range of income levels. Houses built at the top of the hill had to cost more than those on the slope of the hill.

❻ CENTER OF CONTEMPORARY ARTS
(B'NAI AMOONA SYNAGOGUE)
524 Trinity Avenue

The B'nai Amoona Synagogue, built in 1948-50, was one of the first synagogues in the United States to depart from the traditional Moorish and Byzantine styles of synagogue design. Designed by the world-famous modernist architect Erich Mendelsohn, the complex included a series of one-story education buildings arranged around a higher, curved sanctuary. To provide for fluctuations in attendance, Mendelsohn placed moveable doors in the sanctuary; when opened they expanded the seating capacity from six hundred to fifteen hundred. The B'nai

Amoona congregation, organized in 1885, moved to a new location in West County in 1987. Today the complex is the home of the Center of Contemporary Arts (COCA), which offers arts education classes for adults and children and serves as a performance place for many arts groups. The B'nai Amoona complex is listed on the National Register of Historic Places.

❼ SUTTER-MEYER HOUSE
6826 Chamberlain Court (turn left on Chamberlain from Ferguson)

The Sutter-Meyer House, built about 1873, is the oldest known residence in University City. The Sutter family, emigrants from Germany, operated a large dairy farm from 1850 near present-day Olive and Ferguson. By the 1860s, a small community had grown up in the vicinity of the farm, and in 1887 the tiny settlement of Sutter, Missouri, was granted its own post office. The farmhouse, sold in 1875 to Roman Meyer, also a German-born farmer, is the last remaining building of the Sutter settlement.

❽ HEMAN PARK
Bounded by Pennsylvania and Vernon Avenues, Midland and Olive Boulevards

Heman, University City's largest park, was established in 1923 and named for Mayor August Heman, who served from 1913 to 1920. As a depression relief measure, the park's swimming pool—completed in 1933—was constructed entirely by hand, allowing the city to employ

The scenic railway, an early form of the roller coaster, was a popular attraction at the Delmar Gardens Amusement Park on the loop of the Delmar streetcar line until the park was closed in the early twentieth century. Photograph by EMIL Boehl. Missouri Historical Society Photograph and Print Collection.

the maximum number of workers. The park also features tennis courts, a skating rink, and a community center.

❾ OLIVE BOULEVARD

From the early nineteenth century, Old Bonhomme Road, later renamed Olive Boulevard, connected the riverfront in St. Louis to Howell's Ferry on the Missouri River. The road became a market route as settlers began farming the lands along Olive. Stanhope's Dairy operated on the site of present-day Heman Park in the early days when Hanley Road was a cow path. Mile houses along Olive offered refreshment for travelers, and during Prohibition a number of speakeasies carried on the tradition. By the late 1920s thriving businesses catered to traffic along the road; one wagon repair shop, for example, turned into an auto body shop with the coming of the automobile. Today, a transition is taking place along Olive Boulevard, as Chinese-American entrepreneurs open restaurants and specialty shops along the western section of Olive.

❿ RUTH PARK
Along McKnight Road south of Olive Boulevard

Ruth Park, a nine-hole municipal golf course, is named for University City's ambitious and controversial mayor Eugene D. Ruth, Jr., who served from 1926 until 1933. The city created the park from farm land it purchased in 1929. During the depression, the city's Board of Aldermen levied a five-cent tax on golfers who played at the park to finance a relief program for unemployed citizens.

⓫ WALTON TERRACE

The Walton Terrace subdivision, located between Eighty-second Boulevard and Laughlin Avenue, was laid out in 1948 by the Milton Construction and Supply Company in response to the postwar demand for housing. These small brick ranch houses originally sold for about thirteen thousand dollars. The Daniel Boone Elementary School on Eighty-second Boulevard opened in 1952, as more families moved to northwest University City in the years after World War II.

⓬ ST. JOSEPH INSTITUTE FOR THE DEAF
1483 Eighty-second Boulevard

The St. Joseph Institute for the Deaf was organized nearly a century before it moved to University City in 1935. Two Sisters of St. Joseph, who had learned sign language in France, began classes for the deaf in Carondelet in 1837. The school had several homes in St. Louis before

By 1928, the area around the Delmar Loop—seen in the right half of this photograph—was filled with apartment and commercial buildings. Photograph by Eugene Taylor. Courtesy of the University City Public Library Archives.

relocating to its present site. In 1966 the building was enlarged with a new addition. Today the school has 110 students ranging from preschool through grade eight.

⑬ UNIVERSITY CITY EDUCATION DISTRICT
7400 Balson Avenue

University City High School, designed in the art deco style by the firm of Trueblood and Graf, opened in 1930. It replaced the combined junior and senior high school that had been located in the Fine Arts building at 725 Kingsland Avenue. Since the 1931 master plan for University City by civic designer Harland Bartholomew called for the grouping of public buildings at certain key locations, Jackson Park Elementary School, designed by William B. Ittner, opened in 1933, next to the high school on Balson Circle. The city widened and landscaped Balson Avenue as part of a scenic road system connecting the schools with Jackson Park to the south. In 1937 the construction of Hanley Junior High School at the western end of Balson Avenue completed the education district. The junior high school closed in 1981. Its site is being redeveloped as University Place, a private subdivision of single family homes and townhouses.

⑭ FIRST PRESBYTERIAN CHURCH
7200 Delmar Boulevard at Overhill Drive

First Presbyterian Church, the first Protestant church organized in St. Louis, was established in 1817; many of St. Louis' Presbyterian congregations began as branch congregations of this church. The church had relocated three times from its original site at Fourth and St. Charles before its last move to University City in 1927. Developer Cyrus Crane Willmore encouraged the congregation to buy the site at 7200 Delmar in his new University Hills subdivision. The English Gothic church was designed by architects LaBeaume and Klein.

⑮ UNIVERSITY HILLS
Bounded by Pershing and Delmar Boulevards, Wellesley and Jackson Avenues

Passing through the massive iron gates on Purdue Avenue and up steep and winding drives, motorists enter University Hills, a subdivision that has been called "an almost perfect realization of the architectural and planning ideals of the 1920s." Its developer, Cyrus Crane Willmore, drew on designs for earlier subdivisions, particularly E. G. Lewis' University Heights One. The winding streets in University Hills represent a clever adaptation to the topography of the hillside. Like Lewis' subdivision, University Hills was divided into districts of differing minimum costs to provide for residents from a range of economic levels. Many homes are designed in the Tudor Revival style, though Georgian-, Renaissance-, and Spanish-style dwellings provide an architectural mix. Willmore took Lewis' ideas one step further by adding multifamily and commercial buildings along Delmar and Pershing. The City Plan Commission and its consultant, Harland Bartholomew, assisted with the commercial zoning, and the addition of Flynn Park School at the southeastern end of the subdivision in 1924 helped solidify the neighborhood.

FOR MORE INFORMATION

Harris, NiNi. *Legacy of Lions: A History of University City.* University City: Historical Society of University City, 1981.

Longo, Jim. *A University City Album: Remembrances and Reflections of Seventy-five Years.* University City: Citizens Committee for the Seventy-fifth Anniversary, 1981.

Special thanks to Judy Little, Linda Ballard, Lorine Compton, Esley Hamilton, and the residents of University City.

SUBURBS: POST-WORLD WAR II DEVELOPMENT

WEBSTER GROVES

From University Hills (University City): Delmar Boulevard east to Big Bend Boulevard. Big Bend right (south) to Lockwood Avenue. Lockwood to Bompart Avenue.

St. Louis publisher Nathan D. Thompson lived in this stylish Queen Anne home at Swon and Jefferson. In the late 1880s and 1890s, Thompson, who helped bring about the incorporation of Webster Groves, built a number of large homes on speculation, hoping to attract other successful businessmen to Webster Groves. Photograph by John W. Dunn. Missouri Historical Society Photograph and Print Collection.

In 1892 the developers of Webster Park, a well-to-do community in what would soon become part of the City of Webster Groves, promoted their development as the "Queen of the Suburbs." In the century since then, Webster Groves' tree-lined streets and abundance of single-family homes have often been used as selling points by developers and real estate agents. This tranquil, suburban image has at times given Webster residents a strong, positive sense of civic identity. At other times, however, the image has blurred the realities of life in this diverse community.

Webster Groves' location on the Pacific Railroad line led to its development as a suburb. In the late nineteenth century, overcrowding, congestion, and unhealthy conditions in cities like St. Louis led some urban residents to leave the city for quieter, more bucolic surroundings. The Webster Park and Tuxedo Park subdivisions were designed to appeal to city-dwellers with the means to move out of St. Louis. Businessmen and professionals took up residence in these communities, raising families in a country-like atmosphere while commuting by train to their jobs downtown.

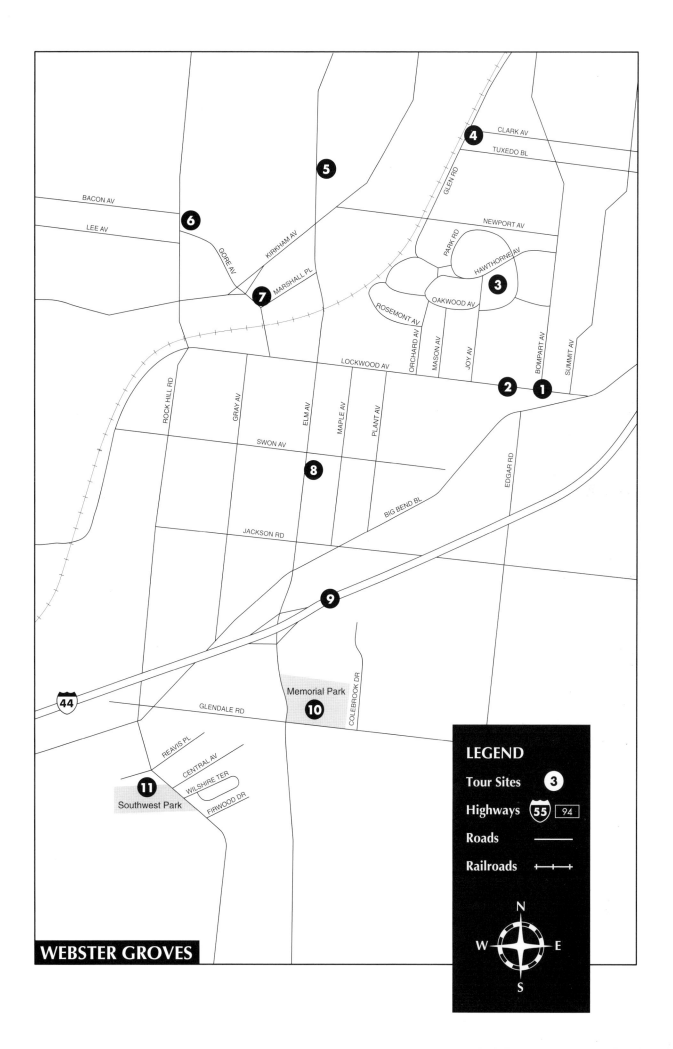

WEBSTER GROVES

LEGEND

Tour Sites   ③

Highways   55   94

Roads   ——

Railroads   +—+—+

The "Queen of the Suburbs" image that developers cultivated in the 1890s persisted well into the twentieth century. However, the same vision that made Webster Groves appear a desirable place to live at the turn of the century was placed in a completely different context in more recent years. The 1966 CBS documentary *16 in Webster Groves* examined the city through the lives of its high school students, presenting the community as materialistic, provincial, and insulated from the social upheavals of the day. Similarly, former Webster resident Jonathan Franzen's 1988 novel, *The Twenty-Seventh City,* depicts a similar community of well-to-do families, living in comfortable homes and tending carefully groomed lawns far away from the problems of urban life.

Yet, as Webster residents themselves have long maintained, the reality behind the "Queen of the Suburbs" is more complex than such accounts would suggest. The city, in fact, had its origins as five separate communities along adjacent railroad lines. In 1853, the Pacific Railroad began to make stops at Webster College; a village also called Webster soon grew there. Tuxedo Park and Webster Park, two 1890s residential communities, were also served by station stops on the Pacific Railroad route. South of these three stations, near Big Bend Boulevard, the South Pacific (later Frisco) Railroad made stops at Old Orchard Station and Selma Station. Together, these five railroad stops, arranged like beads on a string, became the core of residential and commercial development in the area. In 1896, with no utilities or services of their own, the communities incorporated as the City of Webster Groves. The city soon developed its own public services, and new streetcar lines linked Webster Groves with St. Louis.

Incorporation did not automatically make Webster Groves a homogeneous community, however. Residents of the Old Orchard community, feeling that incorporation had raised their taxes but failed to provide the hoped-for services, wanted to disincorporate in 1901. Today, even though no formal boundaries divide the city, a variety of neighborhood organizations look out for the interests of each neighborhood.

Webster's image belies not only the geographic diversity of the town, but also its economic diversity. The city is not solely the wealthy commuter suburb that early developers planned for. Like other suburban towns, Webster Groves has its share of unemployed and low-income residents. Webster–Rock Hill Ministries, an ecumenical social services agency, offers a range of programs for those in need, including counseling, emergency food programs, legal services, and educational programming for adults.

Another way in which the residents of Webster Groves have proven that they can act together as a community can be seen in the recent passage of an $8.8 million bond issue to improve Memorial Field. Supporters formed a volunteer citizens' committee to campaign for the bond issue's passage, while numerous city organizations and businesses joined in. Representatives from all the city's neighborhoods urged support for it, and residents took part in community meetings to offer their comments on the proposal. Total community involvement proved successful; the bond issue passed by a two-to-one margin.

The diversity of Webster Groves becomes apparent as soon as one looks beyond the images that have governed our view of the city for one hundred years. The "Queen of the Suburbs" faces the same problems as other small communities. Its success as a livable community comes not from the affluence or insulation that image-makers described, but from continued success in bringing many small communities together toward common goals.

❶ EMMANUEL EPISCOPAL CHURCH
9 South Bompart Avenue

Emmanuel Episcopal Church stands on land donated by Richard and Angelica Lockwood, whose summer home stood nearby. The cornerstone was laid in 1866, the same year that the Presbyterian, Congregational, and First Baptist Churches were founded in Webster Groves. In 1951 Emmanuel Church took part in the Webster Groves Ministerial Alliance, which petitioned the Webster Groves City Council to reopen the municipal swimming pool as an integrated facility. Today, Emmanuel Church engages in a variety of outreach programs, including an emergency food supply center and a number of youth activities.

❷ WEBSTER UNIVERSITY AND EDEN THEOLOGICAL SEMINARY
470 and 475 East Lockwood Avenue

Webster University has its roots in a girls' preparatory school founded by the Sisters of Loretto in 1898. The Loretto College and Academy, an outgrowth of the preparatory school, opened in 1916 as the first Catholic women's college in Missouri. Its name was changed to Webster College in 1924, and later to Webster University. Under Sister Jacqueline Grennan, then college president, Webster severed its church connections and became a lay college in 1967. Conrad Hilton gave the college $1 million for the construction of the Loretto-Hilton Center for the Performing Arts. The theater, which opened in 1966, houses the Repertory Theatre of St. Louis, the Opera Theatre of St. Louis, and Webster University's Conservatory of Theatre Arts.

Across the street from Webster University is the Eden Theological Seminary, founded in Marthasville, Missouri, in 1850. After relocating for a period in Wellston, the seminary moved to Webster Groves in 1924. Eden began as a small college for German-born students of the Evangelical faith. Since the 1960s the school has been supported by the United Church of Christ.

Many Webster Park residents commuted to work in St. Louis from the Webster Park Station. Annie E. Door, who posed for this photo in 1900, served as ticket taker at the station from 1896 until the station closed in 1950. Courtesy of the Webster Groves Historical Society.

❸ WEBSTER PARK
Bounded by Lockwood, Bompart, and Newport Avenues and the Missouri Pacific Railroad

The Webster Park neighborhood began in 1892 as a private subdivision developed by the Webster Real Estate Company and designed by landscape architect Elias A. Long. An 1892 promotional brochure, titled "Webster: Queen of the Suburbs," extolled the advantages of residence in Webster Park, noting the benefits that the "democratic family" derived from the "vigor and endurance" of country life. The booklet described Webster Park's large lots and curving, tree-lined streets in pastoral imagery designed to appeal to well-to-do city residents. No less a lure to the neighborhood was the Webster Park Railroad station, constructed by the Missouri Pacific Railroad on land purchased from the subdivision's developers. Since most Webster Park residents commuted to work in downtown St. Louis, having a depot within a few minutes' walk was necessary to the development's success. Most of the houses in Webster Park were built between the 1890s and 1920s. The subdivision is no longer private; the City of Webster Groves now maintains the roadways.

❹ TUXEDO PARK STATION
643 Glen Road

The Tuxedo Park Station is the last commuter station still standing between St. Louis and Kirkwood. In 1890 railroad promoter Lilburn McNair bought a two-hundred-acre site to create an exclusive commuter suburb named Tuxedo Park, after the original Tuxedo Park outside of New York City. McNair sold the Missouri Pacific

Railway a lot for the Tuxedo Park Station for the token sum of one dollar. Over the years, the station's ten daily eastbound trains served hundreds of businessmen, shoppers, and families who lived nearby. Missouri Pacific discontinued commuter service in 1961 and gradually tore down all of its small frame commuter stations. The stone Tuxedo Park Station was spared and used by the railroad for equipment storage. In 1980, the City of Webster Groves saved the station, the only example of Richardsonian Romanesque architecture in Webster Groves, from demolition. The city was given ownership of the building in 1983.

❺ NORTH WEBSTER

North Webster, the area between Rock Hill Road and Kirkham Avenue, is an African American community with roots that stretch back to the Civil War era. In 1866, the First Baptist Church was established on Shady Avenue, just west of Gore. The church housed the first public school in Webster Groves, and African American children attended class there from the year the church was built. The school continued in various buildings and was named Douglass School, after abolitionist Frederick Douglass, in 1895. North Webster, an unincorporated area, evolved into a self-contained community with a credit union, African American–owned grocery stores, a drugstore, and fire company. In 1918, the Missouri Supreme Court, in a case brought by North Webster residents, ruled that school districts must educate their African American students. As a result, the Webster Groves district paid tuition for North Webster teens to attend Sumner High School in St. Louis' Ville neighborhood. A high school was added to Douglass in 1925 that drew students from St. Louis and Franklin counties.

Douglass High School closed in 1954 after the U.S. Supreme Court's decision in *Brown v. Board of Education*. Students then attended Webster Groves High School. The Douglass School building was renovated in 1983 and converted to Douglass Manor (546 North Elm Avenue), a community center with apartments for the elderly.

In 1960, North Webster was annexed by Webster Groves amid concerns from North Webster residents that their sense of community might be lost in the process. Residents today still express concerns that at times the city neglects North Webster. With funding from the Community Development Block Grant program, and a growing sense of civic commitment to the neighborhood, the City of Webster Groves is facing the challenge of providing for a diverse community.

After the closing of the train station, the downtown express bus picked up passengers nearly every five minutes at this stop during morning rush hours. Courtesy of the Webster Groves Historical Society.

6 EDGEWOOD CHILDREN'S CENTER
(THE ROCK HOUSE)
330 North Gore Avenue

The Rock House, possibly the oldest building in Webster Groves, was built in 1852 as the Webster College for Boys. Named for statesman Daniel Webster, the school was founded by Dr. Artemus Bullard, a Presbyterian minister. By 1853 the Pacific (later the Missouri Pacific) Railroad, which ran west to Kirkwood, made a stop near the school, and soon a village grew up around the station. Shortly before the Civil War a post office was established there and the village became known as Webster Groves. Although the college closed at the beginning of the war, the Rock House served for many years as an orphanage. The name of the institution was changed to the Edgewood Children's Center in 1943. Today the old Rock House serves as the center's adminis-tration building. The Edgewood Children's Center provides care and treatment for seventy-two behaviorally disordered children from age five through seventeen.

7 ROLLING RIDGE NURSERY (FORMERLY HENRY SCHULZ FEED COMPANY)
60 North Gore Avenue

In 1893 Henry Schulz started a feed and grain business in Webster Groves. Schulz later expanded into the moving and storage business. His venture proved so successful that the Missouri Pacific Railroad built a spur to accom-modate his needs. Schulz was also a garden enthusiast,

and his legacy continues in the Rolling Ridge Nursery, a garden center established by his daughter and son-in-law in the feed-company building in 1959. Today Schulz's grandson, James F. McMillan III, runs the business located in the historic Old Webster Business District.

8 CENTRAL WEBSTER HISTORIC DISTRICT
Bounded by Gray, Lockwood, Plant, Swon, and Maple Avenues, and Jackson Road

The Central Webster Historic District is a fourteen-block residential area in the geographic center of Webster Groves. Most of its nearly three hundred buildings are single-family frame houses built between the 1860s and the 1920s for middle- and upper-middle-class suburban commuters. This community, with its fashionable hous-es, expansive lawns, and tree-lined streets, came to embody the neighborhood ideal represented by Webster's "Queen of the Suburbs" image. In addition to private homes, a number of organizations have located in the area. In 1911 a cabin was built on Elm Avenue for the Webster Groves Boy Scouts, one of the first Boy Scout troops organized in the United States. The Monday Club, organized in 1887 as a women's literary and social club, built its meeting hall at 37 South Maple in 1911. In 1984, when plans to widen Elm Avenue into a four-lane boulevard threatened to destroy the nostalgic atmosphere of the area, residents countered with a "Save the Heart of Webster" campaign, creating a local historic district with guidelines for preservation. Their fight was successful and the highway plan was withdrawn. The district was added to the National Register of Historic Places in 1985.

9 INTERSTATE 44

Planning for an interstate highway through southwestern St. Louis County began in 1958. Within a year, contro-versies erupted over the route the highway should follow. Overflow crowds attended public hearings at Kiel Auditorium, urging the Missouri Highway Commission to locate the highway somewhere other than in their own communities. The Association of Webster Groves Property Owners advocated a route that would run along Watson Road instead of through Webster Groves. In the end, part of the road was cut through the middle of Webster Groves, parallel to the Frisco Railroad. Two hundred homes in Webster were lost in the construction of the interstate.

Students wore their best on graduation day at Douglass School in North Webster, which for many years was the only African American high school in St. Louis County. Courtesy of the Webster Groves Historical Society.

⑩ MEMORIAL PARK
Elm Avenue and Glendale Road

Established in 1948, Memorial Park has been the scene of many community debates. The plan for a park with a swimming pool, bath house, and athletic facilities was introduced in 1945 as part of the Webster Groves Post-War Program. The pool soon became the focus of controversy when African American residents were refused entry during its first summer in 1950. After a court decision mandating integration, attendance at the pool declined so severely that the loss of ticket revenue forced its closing for two years. In the spring of 1953, the *Webster News Times* and a coalition of local churches urged residents to support the opening of the pool, and the now integrated facility reopened that summer. More recently, residents passed an $8.8 million bond issue to fund a new pool, an indoor ice rink, and new tennis courts. Support for the bond issue was gathered by a volunteer citizen's committee made up of representatives from all of Webster Groves' neighborhoods.

⑪ HAWKEN HOUSE
1155 South Rock Hill Road

Christopher Miller Hawken built this house in 1857. The home originally stood on a one-hundred-acre tract of farmland at what is now 9442 Big Bend Boulevard, near Grant Road. In the late 1960s, when the Hawken House was in danger of being razed, the Historical Society of Webster Groves bought the house. With $46,000 in pledges and a matching grant from the federal government, the society restored the house and moved it a half-mile to its present location. The house is open for tours on weekends from March 1 to mid-December. The History Center, adjacent to the Hawken House, is the repository of the archives of the Webster Groves Historical Society and is open by appointment.

FOR MORE INFORMATION

Ambrose, Henrietta, and Ann Morris. *North Webster: A Photographic History of a Black Community.* Bloomington: University of Indiana Press, 1993.

Kate Moody Collection, Missouri Historical Society.

Niesen, Andy. "Webster Groves Historical Trail." N.p. Webster Groves, 1992.

Start, Clarissa. *Webster Groves.* Webster Groves: City of Webster Groves, 1975.

Swift, Wilda H., and Cynthia S. Easterling. *Webster Park: 1892-1992.* N.p. Webster Groves, 1993.

Special thanks to Rev. Charles Rehkopf, Webster Groves Historical Society, Mayor Glenn Sheffield, Council Member Henrietta Ambrose, Webster-Rockhill Ministries, and the residents of Webster Groves.

KIRKWOOD

From Hawken House (Webster Groves): North on South Rock Hill Road to Watson Road. Watson left (west) to Lindbergh Boulevard. Lindbergh right (north) to 1201 South Kirkwood Road.

Visitors to Kirkwood will find that this view through downtown—looking north along what is now Kirkwood Road—looks remarkably similar to this 1936 scene. Photograph by W. C. Persons. Missouri Historical Society Photograph and Print Collection.

Today, trains pass through the heart of Kirkwood just as they have for 140 years, bringing traffic to a standstill at the intersection of Argonne Drive and Kirkwood Road. The story of the trains is intertwined with the story of Kirkwood, a commuter suburb of nearly 27,300 located southwest of St. Louis. The city began its life as a stop on the Pacific Railroad.

The first stirrings of a community came in the mid-nineteenth century when two real estate agents, Hiram Leffingwell and Richard S. Elliott, purchased land around a proposed railroad route and touted the development of a suburb. When their efforts generated interest, the site was dubbed Kirkwood, after James P. Kirkwood, the Scottish chief engineer of the Pacific Railroad. Land sales began in 1853, coinciding with the first passenger service from St. Louis. The Kirkwood line was the only railroad operating in Missouri at that time.

As the first residential commuter suburb west of the Mississippi, Kirkwood offered advantages over life in St. Louis. A devastating cholera epidemic, coupled with the great fire of 1849, had vividly dramatized the dangers of a congested city. Kirkwood, with its high elevation, healthy climate, and spacious lots, offered a defense against the spread of fire and disease, appealing to well-to-do city residents.

Socially, the move from St. Louis to this fledgling suburb reflected a new set of ideals stemming from the growth of the middle class. Many who benefited from the expansion of business and industry in the late 1800s found Kirkwood a haven from the noisy, impersonal world of the city. The old row house of the walking city lost its appeal as society placed more and more emphasis on privacy. The new community offered single-family homes with broad, open lawns on tree-shaded streets.

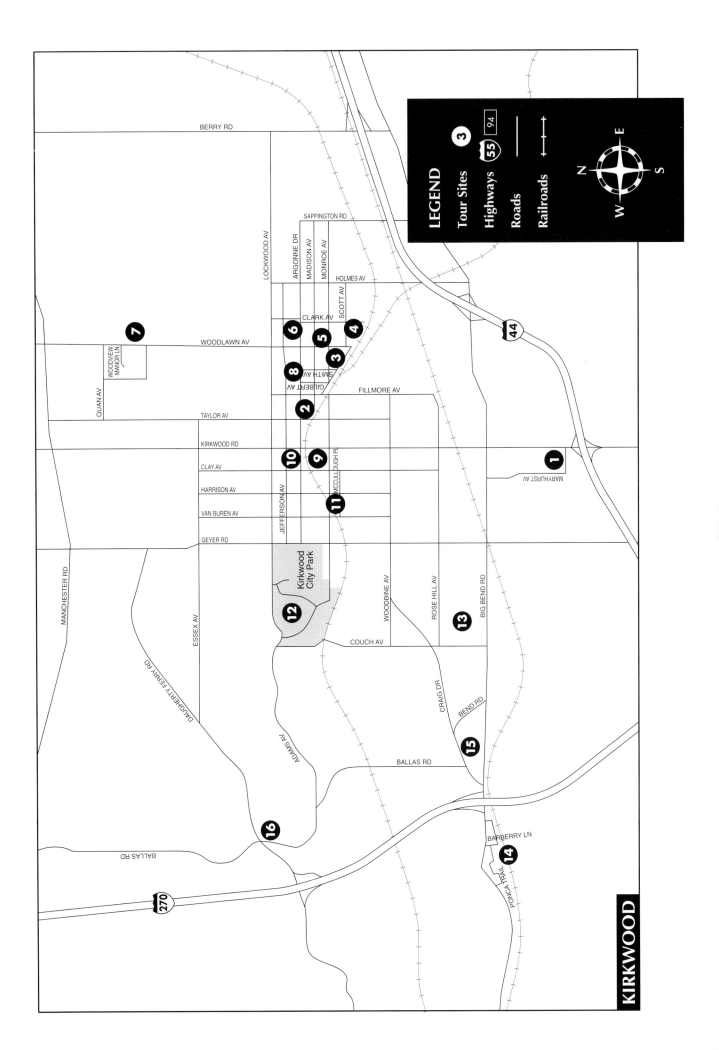

In physical layout, Kirkwood varied a great deal from St. Louis. The relatively unplanned growth of streets in the city did not suit the suburb. Kirkwood's developers plotted the streets in a rectangular grid, with lots reserved for the railroad depot and the Kirkwood Hotel. Blocks were divided into quarter sections of more than one acre each. Families could purchase an entire block, creating an estate of five acres.

As an early suburban town, Kirkwood was far more closely connected to the life of the central city than are the suburbs of recent years. Economically, educationally, and culturally it maintained strong ties to St. Louis. Jobs, schools, and the theater were downtown—just a forty-minute train ride for Kirkwoodians.

From Kirkwood's earliest days, deed restrictions limited commercial activity; no slaughter houses, soap factories, or dram shops were allowed. Today, a thriving Kirkwood continues to plan its growth as a city. Recent activities include the annexation of Meacham Park, formerly an unincorporated area near Kirkwood and Big Bend Roads. Named for its developer, E. E. Meacham, who plotted it in 1892, Meacham Park is an African American neighborhood settled by Kirkwood service workers. Public and private agencies and resident groups have joined forces to work toward community improvement in Meacham Park.

In 1989, Kirkwood was selected as one of ten cities in the Missouri Main Street Program, which is aimed at revitalizing and maintaining healthy downtown business districts. The program emphasizes economic restructuring, with incentive programs for new and existing businesses as well as for the beautification of the downtown area. Design projects include the enhancement of the Kirkwood train station—a fitting symbol of the city, both past and present. Proud of their heritage, Kirkwoodians, through projects like the Main Street Program, are striving to preserve the distinct historic character of their city.

❶ BROWNHURST
1201 South Kirkwood Road

Around 1880, wealthy St. Louis manufacturer Daniel S. Brown bought a 140-acre tract in Kirkwood in an effort to escape the city smoke that interfered with his hobby of horticulture. He built this huge country home of wood shingle and limestone in the Romanesque style popularized by H. H. Richardson. About forty acres of the estate were devoted to flower gardens, conservatories, and greenhouses. Brown assembled a fine collection of rare and beautiful palms, ferns, and orchids. When a coal shortage during World War I put greenhouse heating at risk, Brown donated many specimens to the Missouri Botanical Garden. They became the basis for the garden's now-famous orchid collection.

❷ ELIOT UNITARIAN CHAPEL (FORMERLY GRACE EPISCOPAL CHURCH)
106 South Taylor Avenue

Grace Episcopal Church, built in 1860 in the Gothic Revival style, is the earliest surviving church in Kirkwood. In 1854 H. I. Bodley, a lay reader, conducted St. Louis County's first Episcopal services in his home. Later a parish was organized, and the church, designed by Robert S. Mitchell, was constructed at a cost of twelve thousand dollars. In its early days Grace Episcopal Church served as a landmark, signaling passengers aboard the Pacific Railroad trains that they were thirteen miles from St. Louis. Eliot Unitarian Chapel bought the church in 1960. The building gained listing on the National Register of Historic Places in 1982.

Kirkwood pioneer and manufacturer Daniel S. Brown had forty acres of gardens, conservatories, and greenhouses at Brownhurst, his Kirkwood estate. His orchid collection became the basis for the orchid collection in the Missouri Botanical Garden. Missouri Historical Society Photograph and Print Collection.

3 WISCONSIN HOUSE
415 Scott Avenue

This house, constructed as the Wisconsin hospitality house for the Louisiana Purchase Exposition in 1904, originally overlooked the giant bird cage in Forest Park. Built at a cost of $14,750, the house won a grand prize because it "nearest fulfilled the ideal State home." After the fair the house was transported, most likely by rail, to Kirkwood, where it was reconstructed as a residence, minus some of the original porches and pavilions.

4 HAZARD HOUSE
401 Clark Avenue

This Victorian Vernacular house, built in 1875, belonged to Rebecca Naylor Hazard, a noted nineteenth-century social reformer. During the Civil War, Hazard cared for soldiers and newly freed slaves in St. Louis as a member of the Ladies Union Aid Society and the Freedmen's Relief Society. Following her war work, Hazard began to explore questions of women's legal and political status. In 1867 she helped organize the Woman Suffrage Society of Missouri. The American Woman's Suffrage Association, a national organization, elected her president in 1878. Hazard died in her home in 1912 and is buried in Bellefontaine Cemetery.

5 SEVEN GABLES
503 East Monroe Avenue

Despite its name, this Tudor Revival house actually has ten gables. It was built about 1913 for Judge Enos Clarke. The grounds covered a full block and enclosed a vast formal garden with beds of roses, peonies, and zinnias set in patterns of circles, stars and crescents. The garden was the scene of many Kirkwood social gatherings.

6 MCLAGAN HOUSE, FORMERLY HISTORY HOUSE
549 East Argonne Drive

Built in the 1860s in the Italianate style, this house deceives the eye; its wood siding is cut and beveled to resemble stone, the standard—though costly—material for houses of this type. Since its construction for the McLagan family, the house has boasted a long list of distinguished residents. Charles Black, publisher of the *Clayton Argus*, bought the property in 1879 and lived there until 1904, when Ethan Allen Taussig and his wife, Edith, both renowned opera singers, moved into the house. The Taussigs sold the home in 1924 to Phil Rau, a dry goods merchant and amateur entomologist who published studies of the mining bees he kept in the lawn behind the house. The members of the O. G. Saller

family were the next tenants of the house, living there until 1972. The property then passed to the Kirkwood Historical Society, which operated it as History House, with public access to the library and exhibit areas. In 1992 the house became a private residence once again.

7 WOODLAWN AVENUE/WOODVIEW MANOR LANE

Woodlawn Avenue, long one of the premier streets of Kirkwood, exemplifies the suburban ideal of spaciousness. Named after an 1860s mansion near Monroe Avenue, Woodlawn boasts many fine homes built by prominent citizens. The Kirkwood (later Woodlawn) Country Club, established in 1914, occupied the area just west of the street from Gill to Seekamp avenues. When the country club failed to survive the depression, the grounds were developed as subdivisions. Streets named Bogey, Fairway, and Par give testimony to the land's earlier use. Woodview Manor Lane, a recent development, demonstrates a use of space much different from the gridlike street pattern of Kirkwood's commercial center; its design, a gently angled cul-de-sac, provides privacy and a pleasant sense of seclusion.

8 PEMBERTON-MUNROE HOUSE
345 East Argonne Drive

This house, built about 1876, is an example of middle-class Victorian architecture. Its tower and brackets identify the house as an adaptation of the Italianate style. Like the McLagan house, the wood siding is carefully fitted to give the appearance of cut stone. The George C. Burr family bought the house in 1888. The present owners, the Pemberton and Munroe families, have resided there since 1918.

9 KIRKWOOD TRAIN STATION
Argonne Drive at Kirkwood Road

The Kirkwood train station, the symbol of the city, was completed in 1893. It occupies the site of the first depot on the Missouri-Pacific line, which opened in 1853. At the turn of the century nearly all the men living in Kirkwood held jobs in St. Louis and commuted daily, boarding one of the fourteen trains bound for the city. Today Amtrak's River Cities line offers early morning service to St. Louis. The station, built in the Richardsonian Romanesque style, is listed on the National Register of Historic Places.

10 COULTER FEED STORE BUILDING
113 West Argonne Drive

Joseph Coulter established the Coulter Feed Company about 1904. After operating at a site now known as 113 North Kirkwood Road, he moved to this location in 1912. Though the building presently houses other types of businesses, it retains the distinctive checkerboard design and painted advertisements from its feed-store days.

11 OLIVE CHAPEL AFRICAN METHODIST
EPISCOPAL (AME) CHURCH
301 South Harrison Avenue at Monroe Avenue

Organized in 1853, Olive Chapel was the second church founded in Kirkwood. For many years a circuit rider served the congregation. In 1867 Olive Chapel housed Kirkwood's first public school for African Americans. In 1923 the church bought the present building, dating to 1896, from the former Friedens Evangelical Lutheran Church.

The historic Olive Chapel AME Church, built in 1896, features beautiful stained glass windows. Photograph by David Schultz.

12 KIRKWOOD CITY PARK
Bounded by Geyer Road, Adams, Monroe, and Couch Avenues

Unlike St. Louis, which set aside acreage for public parks beginning early in the nineteenth century, Kirkwoodians for many years felt no need for a sizable park. The abundance of woods, fields, and streams within walking distance met residents' recreational needs. Only after the closing of the Woodlawn (formerly Kirkwood) Country Club did efforts at establishing a public park begin in earnest. Parcels of property were acquired over time, and by 1950 the present ninety-one-acre Kirkwood Park was assembled. Tennis courts, baseball diamonds, an amphitheater, rifle range, senior citizens' center, wading pool, and picnic areas provide a range of activities for park visitors.

13 ST. LOUIS COMMUNITY COLLEGE AT MERAMEC
Big Bend Boulevard at Geyer Road

In 1965, voters in St. Louis and St. Louis County approved a $47 million bond issue—the largest bond issue for education in the nation's history—to create the Junior College District. Three community college campuses were funded: Florissant Valley in Ferguson, Forest Park in St. Louis, and Meramec in Kirkwood. The Meramec campus, erected on the site of the former St. Joseph College, was completed in 1971. Its current enrollment of nearly fourteen thousand students is the highest of the three campuses.

14 MERAMEC HIGHLANDS HISTORIC DISTRICT
Ponca Trail and Barberry Lane

Meramec Highlands opened in 1895 as a summer resort catering to affluent St. Louisans. The resort included a 125-room luxury hotel, a dance pavilion called the Sunset Pagoda, a boathouse, and a bath house. Advertisements touted the health benefits of water from a nearby sulphur spring and the alkaline-saline baths that offered "the greatest curative effect in diseases of the blood and nervous system." The St. Louis-San Francisco (Frisco) Railroad serviced Meramec Highlands, dropping off visitors on the steps of Frisco station at the end of Barberry Lane. After the 1904 World's Fair, the Highlands' popularity waned and the resort closed in 1912. A fire destroyed the hotel in 1926. Frisco Station and thirteen rental cottages transformed into residences on Ponca Trail are all that remain of Meramec Highlands.

The Meramec Highlands Hotel was the centerpiece of the summer resort which enticed vacationers at the turn-of-the-century. The hotel was destroyed by fire in 1926, but the rental cottages used by visitors to the Highlands still exist as residences along Ponca Trail. Missouri Historical Society Photograph and Print Collection.

⑮ QUINETTE CEMETERY
Old Big Bend Boulevard at Ballas Road

This small tract of land has served as a cemetery for African Americans since before the Civil War. The original landowner allowed his slaves and others nearby the use of the tract as a graveyard. The Olive Chapel AME Church later purchased the site. Burials took place until the early 1950s, but no official records exist, partly because many of those interred were indigents. The cemetery was sold in 1987.

⑯ RUSSELL KRAUS HOUSE
120 South Ballas Road

This house, one of only two in the St. Louis area designed by Frank Lloyd Wright, was built in 1951 for artist Russell Kraus and his wife, Ruth. Triangular in design, the house follows the contours of the hill on which it is built. Both the house and furniture, much of which was also designed by Wright, avoid right angles. The bricks were specially made to fit the design. The house, still a private residence, sits secluded from the road.

FOR MORE INFORMATION

Dahl, June Wilkinson. *A History of Kirkwood, Missouri, 1851-1965.* Kirkwood, Mo.: Kirkwood Historical Society, 1965.

Hannon, Robert E., ed. *St. Louis: Its Neighborhoods and Neighbors, Landmarks and Milestones.* St. Louis: St. Louis Regional Planning and Growth Association, 1986.

Kirkwood Historical Society. *Kirkwood Historical Review.* 1961 to the present.

Kirkwood Landmarks Commission. *Guide to Kirkwood Landmarks.* Kirkwood, Mo.: Kirkwood Landmarks Commission, 1989.

Special thanks to Rosalind Williams, Rod Lake, Irm Messmann, Rep. Michael Gibbons, Mayor Marjorie B. Schramm, and the residents of Kirkwood.

MANCHESTER

This view of Manchester, taken in the early 1900s from the hilltop where St. John United Church of Christ now stands, looks to the north, showing the village in the valley below. Courtesy of the Old Trails Historical Society.

Drivers stuck in traffic at the intersection of Woods Mill and Manchester Roads may blame their predicament on a road system ill-equipped to deal with heavy suburban traffic, but this particular intersection is more than just a challenge to a driver's patience. For nearly two hundred years, from its beginning as a coach stop on the road to Jefferson City to its days as a farming community and its later expansion as a West County suburb, the City of Manchester has been a focal point for the needs of the surrounding area.

Manchester, the oldest settlement on Manchester Road, owes its existence to the presence of a sulphur spring, not far from the present-day Woods Mill–Manchester Road intersection, which was a natural stopping place for travelers to refresh themselves and their animals. In 1800 Bryson O'Hara built a workshop near the spring, where he made ox yokes, oxbows, and axe handles from trees found in the nearby woods. By 1820 the settlement had a store, a blacksmith shop, a saddlery, a tannery, and a tavern. Missouri statehood in 1821 brought more horse and wagon traffic through the

village along the road to the new capital, Jefferson City. Tradition holds that in its early years the settlement was called Hoardstown, after an early resident. In 1825 another resident renamed the town after his hometown, Manchester, England.

Most residents of the Manchester area made their living as farmers, raising crops to sell in St. Louis and buying supplies in the city that village merchants did not stock. They carried their produce to a two-story market house on the Market Street wharf, causing Manchester Road to be known originally as Market Street Road as it extended west from Market Street in St. Louis. In the 1850s Manchester lost some of its east-west road traffic after the extension of the Pacific (later Missouri Pacific) Railroad to Valley Park, situated to the south of Manchester. However, the new importance of Valley Park also promoted the development of a north-south axis through Manchester to supplement its existing east-west orientation.

Even before the railroad passed nearby, Manchester had become something more than a way station on the

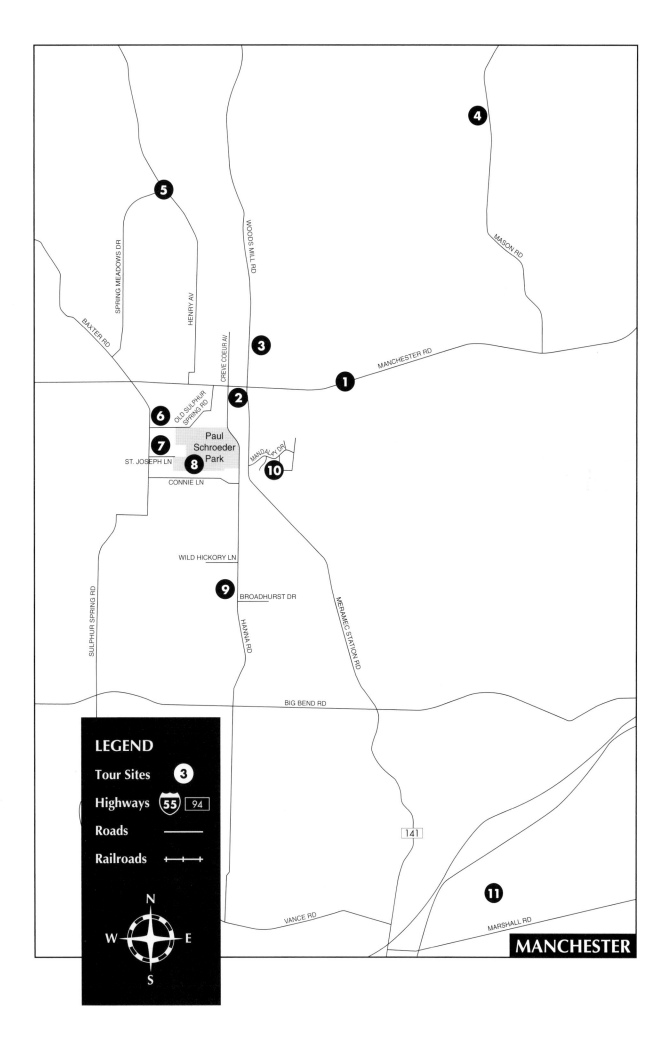

LEGEND

Tour Sites **3**

Highways **55** 94

Roads ———

Railroads +—+—+

N
W E
S

MANCHESTER

road to Jefferson City. Elijah P. Lovejoy, St. Louis' well-known abolitionist minister, wrote to his supervisor in 1834 that Manchester "for its wickedness has acquired the name of Sodom." In 1837, however, the village lost some of its freewheeling atmosphere when it added a church to its twelve log houses, several businesses, and school.

In the next few decades Manchester grew to be more self-sufficient, developing its own small industries, including a brewery, grist mill, cigar manufacturing business, soda water factory, and construction company. Within a generation Manchester also had its own cultural institutions. The Männerchor, a German men's singing society, performed at Sänger Hall, Manchester's first cultural building, which opened in 1881. With the construction of the Lyceum in 1894, Manchester could boast two public halls devoted to instruction and culture. Its identity as a self-contained community was assured.

Manchester retained its small-town identity through the first half of the twentieth century. However, by 1950 postwar prosperity and growth had led St. Louisans to move to newly developed subdivisions springing up around West St. Louis County. Manchester, with its established community and commercial core, attracted extensive residential development. The community incorporated in 1950, and its population more than tripled between 1960 and 1990. Historically a focal point for neighboring areas, Manchester easily assumed its new role as an expanding suburban center.

Today residential development has filled Manchester's boundaries. If the community is to continue to grow, and if it hopes to gain a larger share of the county tax pool, it must annex surrounding unincorporated land. Drivers are also feeling the pinch; the State Highway Department has plans for widening Highway 141 to ease the traffic on Woods Mill Road near Manchester Road. However, these proposals threaten to eliminate Manchester's commercial district to the east of the present highway.

More than a mere traffic tie-up, motorists can read the history of a community in the busy intersection of Woods Mill and Manchester Roads. For instance, amid the stores and shops, drivers can also see the Lyceum, a building that was once Manchester's cultural center. There the community gathered to see plays or watch movies. The building is now home to the City Hall, where council members plot a course for their community into the twenty-first century. This intersection and the Lyceum building embody Manchester's civic slogan, "Proud Past, Bright Future."

Some longtime Manchester residents remember the days when the intersection of Manchester and Woods Mill was a dirt crossroads. It is now one of the busiest intersections in the area; a recent study revealed that ninety-seven thousand cars pass this spot in a twenty-four-hour period. Courtesy of the Old Trails Historical Society.

❶ MANCHESTER ROAD

Known variously as *La Rue Bonhomme*, Market Street Road, and later Missouri Highway 100, this important road is traditionally known as Manchester Road—named after the oldest settlement along the route. The heavily traveled road was originally an Indian trail that led west from the Mississippi River. Indians, and later white settlers, refreshed themselves at the mineral spring, which can still be seen at a park near the intersection of Manchester and Woods Mill Roads. Manchester Road was first called *La Rue Bonhomme* by French fur traders, but as area farmers began taking their produce east to St. Louis the road was renamed Market Street Road because it was an extension of St. Louis' Market Street. In 1835 the Missouri General Assembly established Manchester Road as the first official state road in St. Louis County because it ran west from St. Louis to the state capital, Jefferson City. With state funding, the road has expanded from a narrow, muddy trail to a four-lane, concrete highway. Today the City of Manchester retains little control over the road despite the fact that it continues to be the community's main thoroughfare.

❷ THE LYCEUM
14318 Manchester Road

Turn-of-the-century travelers on Manchester Road knew they had reached Manchester when they drove their wagons by the large, two-story, barn-red Lyceum building at the edge of the road. By the 1890s, Manchester, long closely tied to St. Louis, was beginning to develop as its own community. The Lyceum building, a Manchester landmark, came to embody the transformation taking place in community. The Lyceum was built in 1894 by John Straszer, the founder and president of the First National Bank of Manchester. Straszer's name for his building is a Latin word designating a place for public education and entertainment, but he also intended the structure to be a place of business. The first floor contained a tin shop operated by John's two sons, David and Edward Straszer, while the second floor held an auditorium used for public dances, village meetings, and dramatic productions. The building's exterior, which resembles brick, is actually made of tin siding manufactured by the Straszer family. In the early 1900s the Lyceum became Manchester's own theater—no longer did residents have to go to St. Louis to be entertained. In 1928, the upstairs of the Lyceum was transformed into a movie theater. When the State Highway Department's plans to widen Manchester Road threatened demolition of the building, the Lyceum's owners decided to move it back from the road. Over the years the Lyceum has housed such businesses as an ice cream parlor, an upholstery store, and even an indoor roller skating rink. The City of Manchester purchased the then-vacant building in 1980. Gerhardt Kramer, a St. Louis architect, extensively renovated the assembly hall; the first floor shop walls were torn down, the outside of the building was painted gray, and the second floor was cleaned and recarpeted. The Lyceum, once used for civic gatherings, now houses the city council chambers and the mayor's office. The structure appears in the official logo for the city of Manchester.

❸ MANCHESTER UNITED METHODIST CHURCH
129 Woods Mill Road

Motorists on Highway 141 approaching the busy Manchester Road intersection pass by what appears to be a small, quiet, country church. Built in 1859, the Manchester United Methodist Church is a county landmark that, in its own physical expansion, reflects Manchester's growth from a rural village to an expanding suburb. The congregation, formed in 1827, built its first church on the present site in 1837, then replaced it twenty-two years later with the Greek Revival chapel that stands today. A twelve-room educational building was added to the west of the chapel in 1965, and three years later a two-story brick sanctuary was built. Today the congregation numbers over thirty-six hundred worshipers from all over the greater St. Louis area, making this the largest United Methodist church in the state. Early congregants included farmer Kenneth Shotwell, whose tombstone in the cemetery adjoining the church is embellished with carvings of agricultural scenes—a telling juxtaposition with the highway, which stands a few feet away.

❹ JARVILLE (RENARD-QUEENY HOUSE)
1723 Mason Road

Built in 1853 by Hyacinthe Renard, Jarville has had a diverse history of owners and tenants. Renard, who came to St. Louis from Belgium in 1816, married Marie Louise Papin, the granddaughter of Marie Therese Chouteau, the grande dame of St. Louis French society. Jarville is a Greek Revival–style house designed on a more modest scale than a city home. Successive owners operated a farm at Jarville. Then, in 1931, Edgar and Ethel Queeny purchased the home and its three-hundred-acre estate. Queeny, president of the Monsanto Company, sold Jarville in 1962, and seven years later St. Louis County purchased the estate for the creation of a park. Ethel Queeny gave $1 million for park development, and Edgar M. Queeny Memorial Park was dedicated in 1974. Since 1987 Jarville has housed the Dog Museum, which preserves and exhibits dog art and artifacts and includes a library of books about dogs. The museum is open Tuesday through Saturday from 9:00 A.M. until 5:00 P.M., and Sunday from 12:00 P.M. until 5:00 P.M. Call 821-3647 for more information.

Manchester United Methodist Church, built in 1859, exemplifies the growth of West County as a suburban residential region. The church, seen here at its original size, has been enlarged twice. Today the church has the largest United Methodist congregation in the state. Courtesy of the Old Trails Historical Society.

SUBURBS: POST-WORLD WAR II DEVELOPMENT

5 BACON HOMESTEAD
Henry Avenue at Spring Meadows Drive

This L-shaped log house, built about 1840, is all that remains of the 380-acre farm owned by William Bacon and his son James. The farm stretched along both sides of Henry Avenue and Woods Mill Road south of Clayton Road and had a number of log cabins, outbuildings, and barns. The remaining log house is believed to be a composite of two structures; the structure facing Spring Meadows Drive appears to have been relocated to this site. Today the Old Trails Historical Society operates a local history museum in the Bacon Homestead.

6 ST. JOHN UNITED CHURCH OF CHRIST
Old Sulphur Springs Road

Organized in 1860 as the United Evangelical Church of Manchester, St. John United Church of Christ was a German institution from its beginning, complete with a German-English school conducted in the church building. The name Saint Johannes Evangelical Church was adopted in 1866, and services were held in German until 1928. The church acquired the hilltop site on Sulphur Springs Road and built a new church there in 1952, overlooking Manchester in the valley below. The foundation of the first church, built in 1868, lies in the cemetery to the north of the present church. North of the cemetery, near Grand Glaize Creek, is a cave, hand dug from the hillside in the early 1850s. A local brewery stored barrels of beer in the cave, which, legend holds, also served as a hiding place for the townspeople during the Civil War when Union and Confederate Army troops passed through the area. In 1979 St. John United Church of Christ and Joseph Seibert donated the cave and surrounding ground to the City of Manchester. Today the site is Seibert Park.

7 ST. JOSEPH CATHOLIC CHURCH
567 St. Joseph Lane

The congregation that worships in this modern brick and steel structure first gathered in a Manchester barn in 1839. In that year a group of Irish settlers moved to Manchester from St. Louis and founded St. Malachy's Catholic Mission, named in honor of one of Ireland's patron saints. Visiting priests came on horseback from St. Louis to serve the mission. St. Malachy's first church was a stone structure completed in 1851. As Manchester changed, so did the church. Its name changed to St. Joseph in 1865, and the influx of Germans to the area necessitated the construction of a larger church in 1893. As families moved to West County after World War II, the suburban populace swelled the membership of St. Joseph's from five

hundred families in 1959 to more than eighteen hundred in 1973, requiring yet another, larger church to be built. The present structure, dedicated in 1975, seats a thousand. Today the St. Joseph congregation is the largest in the St. Louis Archdiocese, numbering 2,960 families from the Ballwin-Manchester area.

8 PAUL A. SCHROEDER PARK
359 Old Meramec Station Road

Since its dedication in 1969, this forty-four-acre park has served most of Manchester's recreational needs. Developed on farmland once owned by the Shotwell family, the park features a swimming pool, lighted tennis courts, a playground, baseball diamonds, and nature trails. The small log structure on the northern side of the park was relocated from the Baxter homestead, built in the early nineteenth century near Baxter and Clayton Roads. In 1983 the park was renamed in honor of Paul A. Schroeder, a lifelong resident of Manchester and the community's first superintendent of parks. The fountain at the park's entrance was dedicated in the fall of 1992 as part of Manchester's annual homecoming celebration.

9 PARKWAY SOUTH HIGH SCHOOL
801 Hanna Road

Built in 1976 in response to the rapid population growth in southwestern St. Louis County, Parkway South was the fourth high school created in the Parkway School District. The district, named after the Daniel Boone Parkway (Highway 40), which passes through its center, was formed in 1954, when three local school districts were consolidated to produce enough money and students to support a high school. Until the opening of Parkway Central Junior-Senior High School in 1957, Manchester students attended high school in Maplewood. Today over twenty-two thousand students attend the Parkway School District's twenty-five schools, giving the district the largest enrollment in the county.

10 MANDALAY SUBDIVISION
Enter at Mandalay Drive and Highway 141

This self-contained neighborhood of ranch houses built in the mid-1950s is one of Manchester's first subdivisions. Mandalay was developed by A. Sydney Johnson, a local developer. In the 1950s Manchester began to take shape as the suburb we recognize today. As subdivisions like Mandalay were being developed, the village invested in its infrastructure and services, including new street lights, sewer lines, fire hydrants, and trash removal. As early as 1951 property owners in and around the village began asking for annexation by Manchester.

11 VALLEY PARK
Southeast of Manchester on Highway 141

To the south of Manchester is Valley Park, where the Meramec railroad station linked Manchester to the world by rail. There, passengers could board one of as many as twenty-four daily trains to and from St. Louis. Into the 1960s, when the automobile had replaced the train as the primary means of transportation, residents of Manchester and other nearby communities went to Meramec Station to pick up deliveries from mail-order companies. At the turn of the century, the community of Valley Park flourished as an industrial center. Its railroad station and proximity to the Meramec River provided the transportation links to support a plate-glass factory, a milling company, a bottling works, and a sand and gravel company. A devastating flood in 1915, the first in a cycle of floods that continues to the present, forced many industries to close, and Valley Park survived as a tourist town for years. Day-trippers escaping the summer heat of St. Louis rode the train to Valley Park and swam, canoed, or fished in the river. Valley Park still contends with flooding, but it has a stable and growing industrial base.

FOR MORE INFORMATION

André, R. Miriam. *Moving Forces in the History of Old Bonhomme: The Manchester, Missouri, Area.* Manchester: C. E. Biggs and R. Miriam André, 1982.

Hannon, Robert E., ed. *St. Louis: Its Neighborhoods and Neighbors, Landmarks and Milestones.* St. Louis: St. Louis Regional Planning and Growth Association, 1986.

Old Trails Historical Society. *Along the Trail.* Vols. 1 and 2 (1969, 1972).

Special thanks to Til Keil, Old Trails Historical Society, Mayor Frank McGuire, Dee Wangerin, Manchester United Methodist Church, St. Joseph Catholic Church, Eric Sandweiss, Katharine T. Corbett, and the residents of Manchester.

FERGUSON

From Valley Park (Manchester): Highway 141 north to Manchester Road. Manchester right (east) to Interstate 270. Interstate 270 north to North Florissant Road exit. North Florissant Road right (south) to January-Wabash Park.

Along with commuter trains, streetcars helped transform Ferguson into a middle-class rail and streetcar suburb of St. Louis. The streetcars stopped running in the early 1950s, and the streetcar loop shown here is now a municipal parking lot. Missouri Historical Society Photograph and Print Collection.

Since its founding over one hundred years ago, the City of Ferguson has changed from a small town centered on a rail depot to a modern suburban community of over twenty-two thousand covering five times the area it did in 1894.

Like other St. Louis suburbs, such as Webster Groves and Kirkwood, Ferguson's early history was shaped by the railroad. The city, in fact, takes its name from William B. Ferguson, who in 1855 deeded part of his property as a right-of-way for the North Missouri Railroad Company (the Wabash, St. Louis and Pacific Railroad Company). With an eye toward the future growth of the area, Ferguson stipulated that the railroad create a train stop on his land and name it after him.

Ferguson Station became a major stop for both freight and cross-country passenger trains. Like the town's

founder, most early residents were wealthy landholders from the South and East, whose legacies remain in the names of many of the town's original streets. In 1876 the Wabash began construction of a spur line linking Ferguson directly to St. Louis' Union Depot downtown, and in the years that followed Ferguson changed from a rural community into a rail suburb of St. Louis. The town's population grew from 185 in 1880 to 1,200 in 1894, the year it incorporated; this growth accelerated even more after a new streetcar line was installed in 1900. The town also had a small African American community, including many former slaves of Thomas T. January, part of whose estate became January-Wabash Park.

By the early twentieth century, Ferguson had outgrown its city limits, and it expanded further through a series of annexations from 1904 to the mid-1980s.

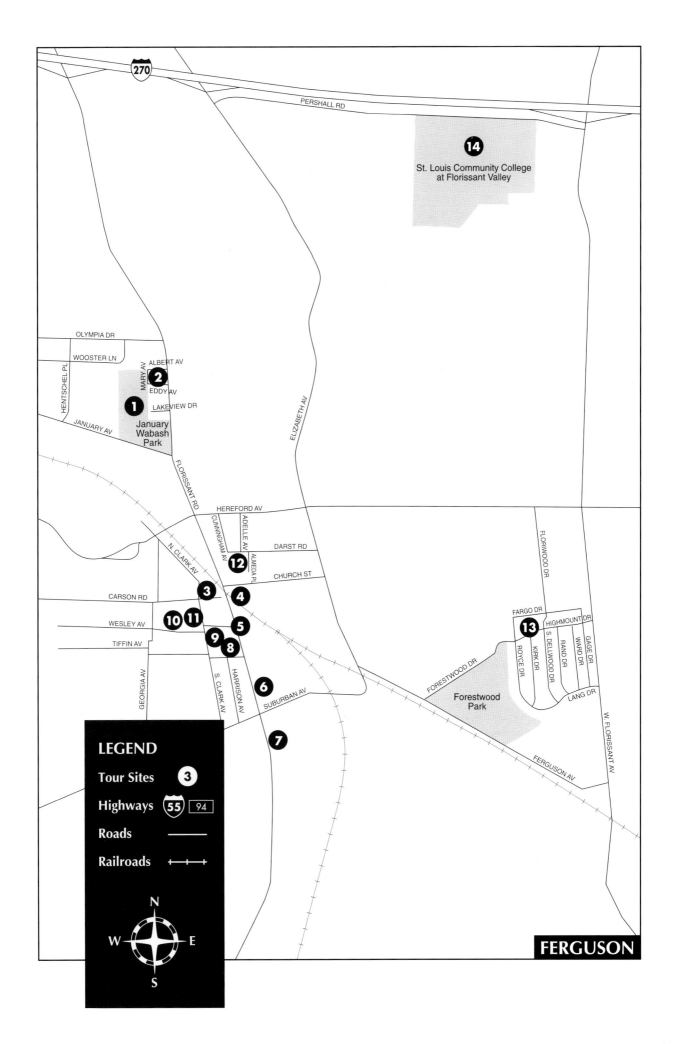

270

PERSHALL RD

14
St. Louis Community College
at Florissant Valley

OLYMPIA DR

WOOSTER LN

HENTSCHEL PL

ALBERT AV

MARY AV

2

EDDY AV

1

LAKEVIEW DR

JANUARY AV

January
Wabash
Park

FLORISSANT RD

ELIZABETH AV

HEREFORD AV

CUNNINGHAM AV

ADELLE AV

DARST RD

N CLARK AV

12

ALMEDA PL

CHURCH ST

CARSON RD

3

4

WESLEY AV

10 11

5

TIFFIN AV

9

8

GEORGIA AV

S. CLARK AV

HARRISON AV

6

SUBURBAN AV

7

FLORIWOOD DR

FARGO DR

HIGHMOUNT DR

13

S. DELLWOOD DR

RAND DR

WARD DR

GAGE DR

ROYCE DR

KIRK DR

LANG DR

FORESTWOOD DR

Forestwood
Park

W. FLORISSANT AV

FERGUSON AV

LEGEND

Tour Sites   3

Highways   55   94

Roads

Railroads

N
W   E
S

FERGUSON

The open fields and farms that once surrounded the town were gradually filled by new residential subdivisions that were no longer an easy walk to downtown. By the end of World War II, most Ferguson residents chose the convenience of automobiles over trains and streetcars. After the commuter trains stopped running in the late 1940s and Northland Shopping Center opened in 1955, downtown Ferguson ceased to be the retail and commuting center of the city.

Nevertheless, like many other St. Louis County communities, Ferguson boomed during the postwar era. Many of the recent arrivals worked at nearby McDonnell Aircraft, Universal Match, and the newly relocated Emerson Electric Company.

Although the neighborhoods close to downtown have retained their historic character, most people in Ferguson live in modern subdivisions and travel to the outlying malls for their recreational and shopping needs. The community has also become increasingly diverse.

Its once small African American community now makes up 25 percent of the city's population, although minorities are still underrepresented on Ferguson's city council and community boards.

Over the last twenty years, Ferguson's population has declined as its residents have moved into newer suburbs in West St. Louis County. The city is trying to stem this outward flow and attract newcomers through special zoning for new and affordable housing and through home repairs, grants, and loans sponsored by the Ferguson Neighborhood Improvement Program. Approximately 41 percent of these grants and loans have gone to racial minorities.

As the city has expanded and changed, Old Ferguson has remained the geographical, if not the social and economic, center of Ferguson. Its downtown and historic rail depot are reminders of Ferguson's rich railroad heritage. After all, like most of St. Louis' suburban communities, the railroad put Ferguson on the map.

This series of photographs shows the evolution of January Lake and the nearby clubhouse in January-Wabash Park, north of downtown Ferguson. The clubhouse presently houses the offices of the Parks and Recreation Department. Courtesy of the City of Ferguson Parks and Recreation Department.

The Ferguson Depot was built in 1885. At one time, six trains left every morning from Ferguson Station en route from St. Charles to the Union Depot in downtown St. Louis. Courtesy of the Ferguson Historical Society.

❶ JANUARY-WABASH PARK
North Florissant Road and January Avenue

This park, owned by the City of Ferguson, was once part of the estate of Thomas T. January, a settler from Kentucky who bought a thousand acres of land in the area in the 1840s. His estate included a race track, a small pond, and a brick mansion with a wine cellar.

Important to Ferguson's early railroad history, January served as director of the Location and Construction Committee of the North Missouri Railroad Company (the Wabash, St. Louis and Pacific Railroad Company) in the 1850s. The railroad contracted with January to enlarge the pond so it could lay an underground pipe to carry water directly from the pond to a water tank on the west side of the tracks.

After January's death in 1886, his son Charles sold 19 1/2 acres of the family property to the railroad, and it was eventually developed as a recreational area for railroad employees and their families. In 1948 the City of Ferguson bought the land from the railroad to be used as a public park.

❷ MOUNT OLIVE MISSIONARY BAPTIST CHURCH SITE
North side of Eddy Avenue, west of North Florissant Road

Ferguson's nineteenth-century residents included a small African American community that in 1880 built a church on land Thomas January had given to his former slaves after the Civil War. Baptisms were held in January's pond.

Demolished in the 1980s, Mount Olive served African Americans in both Ferguson and Kinloch until the First Baptist Church of Kinloch was built. Since World War II, Ferguson's African American community has grown, as residents from St. Louis have moved into North County suburban communities. Today, Ferguson's African Americans make up 25 percent of the population.

❸ FERGUSON DEPOT
North Clark and Carson Road, west of North Florissant Road

The depot on this site was built in 1885. Once the heart of Ferguson, it housed the first Protestant church services in town, was responsible for sounding the public alert system, and blasted its whistle to announce the end of two world wars. When the Wabash spur was completed in the late 1870s, six commuter trains ran through the station each day, in addition to daily trains to Kansas City and points further west. A reminder of Ferguson's railroad origins, the depot has been empty since the mid-1960s. In July 1994, Norfolk Southern, its last owner, officially gave the depot to the city of Ferguson.

❹ BINDBEUTEL BUILDING
Southeast corner of North Florissant Road on Church Street

The Bindbeutel Building—actually three buildings—was built in 1895. The last remnant of Ferguson's nineteenth-century business district, the buildings enjoy new life today as one of the anchors of the Church Street commercial district, part of Ferguson's original downtown. Fred Bindbeutel, a grocer, bought the buildings in 1903. Bindbeutel's Meat Market was located in the center building. The area that is now City Hall property was once used for slaughtering livestock for the market.

By the 1970s, with downtown Ferguson fallen by the wayside, the Bindbeutel Building had become sadly neglected. The buildings were bought and rehabilitated in the 1980s by local realtor David Pope as a major part of the revitalization of the old downtown. The Bindbeutel Building is on the National Register of Historic Places.

❺ FERGUSON STREETCAR LOOP SITE
North Florissant Road and Spot Drive

Like Ferguson's commuter railroad, the streetcar helped bring an influx of city-weary residents to Ferguson. The original Ferguson-Kirkwood streetcar line started operating in 1900. Its tracks ended in front of the frame building next to the original Graf and Case Realtor's office on South Florissant Road. After stopping, the driver manually reversed all the passenger seats for the return journey south. By 1915, a loop was installed to eliminate this tedious procedure.

The streetcar stopped running in the late 1950s. Today, all traces of the old streetcar loop are gone, and the site is now the location of Ferguson's municipal parking lot.

❻ CABOOSE PARK
222 South Florissant Road

In an effort to recapture and popularize its railroad heritage, the City of Ferguson opened Caboose Park in 1987. The complex features two restored cabooses, a 1941 Great North and a 1921 Louisville-Nashville. These cabooses function as a museum and site for tours and meetings. Caboose Park also features a station platform between the railroad cars, benches, and children's playground. Everything on the site was donated to the city by the Ferguson Station Business Association.

❼ VERNON ELEMENTARY SCHOOL SITE
East side of North Florissant Road, approximately 100 yards south of Maline Creek

In 1887 the Ferguson School District bought land for a one-room school to serve the community's African American children, but the new Vernon Elementary School was closed after only a few months when attendance dropped off. The remaining students then traveled by train to Normandy, where they attended classes in the old Grace Lutheran Church on Lucas and Hunt Road. In 1927, a two-room Ferguson school for African American students was built at 5764 Mable Avenue. This school closed in 1967.

❽ 101 TIFFIN AVENUE
West of North Florissant Road, near Harrison Avenue

This house is the former residence of Mary Priscilla Tiffin Thomas and her husband, David P. Thomas. It was built by her father, Henry Harrison Tiffin, a farmer and cattleman as well as a member of one of Ferguson's oldest families. The Ferguson Landmarks Commission has named the house a Century Home, a designation reserved for buildings that are at least as old as the city's incorporation. Like many other Century Homes in Old Ferguson, the property remained within the original family throughout most of its history. This building is currently a private residence.

❾ ONE-ROOM SCHOOL SITE
110 South Clark Avenue, near Wesley Avenue, west of North Florissant Road

Originally built in 1867 on the south side of Wesley Avenue as Ferguson's first school for white children, this former one-room schoolhouse was moved to its present location in 1877. It was used as a school until 1880, when Central School was built nearby. The exterior has been updated, and a screened-in porch has been added. Today, the old schoolhouse is a single-family residence and has been designated a Century Home by the Ferguson Landmarks Commission.

❿ CENTRAL ELEMENTARY SCHOOL
201 Wesley Avenue, between Georgia and South Clark Avenues, west of North Florissant Road

Central School, built in 1880 on two acres of land purchased from Ferguson's founder, William Ferguson, replaced the old one-room school for white children. The new school originally included two classrooms on the first floor and a village hall on the second. Initially used as an elementary school, Central School was turned into a two-year high school in 1896 and St. Louis County's first four-year high school in 1903. Additions have been added to the original school, which is once again an elementary school. The school is listed on the National Register of Historic Places.

⓫ MASONIC LODGE (FERGUSON MASON LODGE #542 A.F. AND A.M.)
25 South Clark Avenue, near Central School and the railroad tracks

The Masonic Lodge, a two-story brick and stone building with stained-glass windows, was built as the permanent home of the Ferguson Mason Lodge in 1926. In its early years, the dining room on the building's lower level had a stage at one end and served as Ferguson's first indoor movie theater. The lodge hall is on the main level.

After the 1870s, Ferguson became a popular suburban retreat for commuters to St. Louis. Many of the Victorian-era homes, such as these on North Florissant Road, can still be seen in the older neighborhoods. Missouri Historical Society Photograph and Print Collection.

⑫ 114 DARST ROAD
East of North Florissant Road, near Almeda Place

This home was the property of Adam Deichmiller, a Ferguson blacksmith and carriage builder. Completed in 1867, the house is the oldest remaining brick building within the original city limits of Old Ferguson. It was constructed in stages, with the wooden rear section completed first. The brick front was added a few years later. This house has been designated a Century Home by the Ferguson Landmarks Commission.

⑬ LANG-ROYCE NEIGHBORHOOD
West of West Florissant Avenue, off Highmount Drive

This 1950s-era neighborhood southeast of Old Ferguson is typical of the many post–World War II residential neighborhoods built in Ferguson. No longer within walking distance of the old railroad station and streetcar loop, these newer areas developed into automobile-dependent suburbs.

⑭ ST. LOUIS COMMUNITY COLLEGE AT FLORISSANT VALLEY
3400 Pershall Road, south of Interstate 270, between West Florissant Avenue and Elizabeth Avenue

After voters in St. Louis City and County approved a $47 million bond issue for a Junior College District in 1965, Ferguson was chosen as one of three sites for a new community college. Completed in 1970, the St. Louis Community College at Florissant Valley campus (formerly St. Louis Junior College) is a major source of job training and retraining for residents in Ferguson and North County. Today, the 108-acre campus educates nearly nine thousand students.

FOR MORE INFORMATION

The Ferguson Historical Society. *Ferguson: A City Remembered.* Ferguson: Ferguson Historical Society, 1994.

Montgomery, Jean, Irene Smith, Ruth Brown, and Carol Rehg. *Ferguson: The First 100 Years.* St. Louis: Nutwood Publishing Company, 1994.

Smith, Irene Sanford. *Ferguson: A City and Its People.* Ferguson: Ferguson Historical Society, 1976.

Special thanks to Mark Etling, Ferguson mayor Michael H. James, Ferguson city manager Robert B. Burns, Dorris Carter, Ruth Brown, Irene Sanford Smith, Barbara Tipsword, Ron Penoyer, Charles Grimm, Jean Dean, Esley Hamilton, Dave Halloran, Dave Smith, the Ferguson Historical Society, the Ferguson Landmarks Commission, Eric Sandweiss, Kathy Corbett, Kris Runberg Smith, Charles Brown, Duane Sneddeker, and the people of Ferguson.

SUBURBS: POST-WORLD WAR II DEVELOPMENT

COMMUNITIES BEYOND:

PLACES TO VISIT, PLACES TO LIVE

COMMUNITIES BEYOND:
PLACES TO VISIT, PLACES TO LIVE

For most visitors to or residents of St. Louis, the four sites discussed in this final section of Where We Live—Alton and Elsah, Illinois, Kimmswick, and the Augusta-Weldon Spring area—are just that: sites. They are places to visit during those first crisp, cool days of fall, when the leaves along the river banks start to change colors, or during the long days of summer, when the oppressive heat of the city seems to dare residents to stay amid the asphalt and carbon monoxide.

But they are not usually thought of as places to live.

Unless, of course, you are among the thousands of people who *do* live in these communities. Then they are places just like any other in this book: places with histories deeply enmeshed in the enterprises that have made this region into what it is today: river traffic, railroading, manufacturing, and, yes, tourism.

On the Illinois side of the Mississippi, just northeast of St. Louis, you will encounter the City of Alton. Like many cities along the Mississippi, Alton got its start as a steamboat port, but it went on to achieve notoriety for a number of important events. Site of the lynching of abolitionist Elijah Lovejoy in 1837, the Lincoln-Douglas debate in 1858, the deaths by smallpox of thousands of Confederate war prisoners in 1863, and the home of Thirteenth Amendment author Lyman Trumbull, the Alton area's past is indicative of the deep-seated tensions that divided the nation in the nineteenth century. In the twentieth century, the city has become home to "urban refugees," people seeking refuge from hustle and bustle in Alton's restored Victorian homes, antique shops, and scenic setting. A new bridge, a riverboat casino, and a nationally televised reenactment of the Lincoln-Douglas debate in 1994 have drawn more visitors—and residents—to this town on the Mississippi.

Up the Mississippi on the Great River Road lies the Village of Elsah. Betrayed by the nineteenth-century promises of both river and rail traffic, Elsah stands as a testament to individualism. Its second life was granted to it by Principia College, a private Christian Science insti-

tution that occupies over two thousand acres high above the riverfront, and the opening of the Great River Road. The college and the River Road maintain Elsah as a living place, populated by people who enjoy the town's unique character and subtle charms.

On the other side of the river, south of St. Louis along Interstate 55, is the small town of Kimmswick, Missouri. The Kimmswick area gained early notoriety in 1839 when the skeleton of an American mastodon was discovered there. When the town of Kimmswick was officially founded in 1859, it quickly became a successful industrial and transportation center, which had the additional attraction of a park to draw tourists from St. Louis. Modern-day visitors no longer hop on a ferry to get to Kimmswick, but get to Kimmswick they do, as it has become an important center for the preservation of historic buildings.

To the northwest, along Highway 94, is the Augusta-Weldon Spring area. The history to be found in the small communities of this region—Weldon Spring, Defiance, Matson, and Augusta—goes back almost two hundred years and includes the home of frontiersman Daniel Boone as well as several less famous but not less colorful characters. The town of Defiance, for example, was named by settlers to indicate their opinion of local landowner (some would say "landgrabber") Richard Matson. Wineries, the Katy Trail, rolling bluffs, and hard-to-find small-town atmosphere are a few of the attractions that draw visitors to these communities today.

As you explore these communities beyond the metropolitan area, on either side of the Mississippi, keep in mind that they are not simply "sites"; they are living, breathing places, places where people still like to put their feet up at the end of the day, happy to be home again.

ALTON, ILLINOIS

From St. Louis: Interstate 270 north to State Highway 367. State Highway 367 north to U.S. Route 67 north. U.S. Route 67 to Alton. After crossing the Clark Bridge, turn left onto Landmarks Boulevard. Right at the first light (Ridge Street) to Fifth Street. Fifth Street right to Vine.

This 1848 depiction of Alton by the German writer and artist Henry Lewis shows Alton's unique topography. Its location at the confluences of the Mississippi, Illinois, and Missouri Rivers, combined with its natural harbor, helped make Alton a steamboat center in the pre–Civil War era. Lithograph by Henry Lewis. Missouri Historical Society Photograph and Print Collection.

Alton, Illinois, twenty-five miles north of St. Louis, prides itself on being different. Located on the north side of the Mississippi River—the only place where the Mississippi flows from west to east—it has always been set apart from the surrounding area. And like their town, the people of Alton consider themselves a world apart, especially from St. Louis.

The area's first European settler was a Frenchman, Jean Baptiste Cardinal, who ran a short-lived fur trading post on the site of present-day Alton in the late eigh-

teenth century. The town's official founder, Rufus Easton, a land speculator who also happened to be the postmaster general of St. Louis, saw the site as the perfect location for a steamboat landing, which he named after his son, Alton. Although Rufus Easton never lived there, he started a passenger ferry line service between Alton and Missouri in 1818.

Alton grew rapidly in the 1830s, thanks to a growing steamboat trade with New Orleans and St. Louis. In 1837 it was incorporated as a city. "The

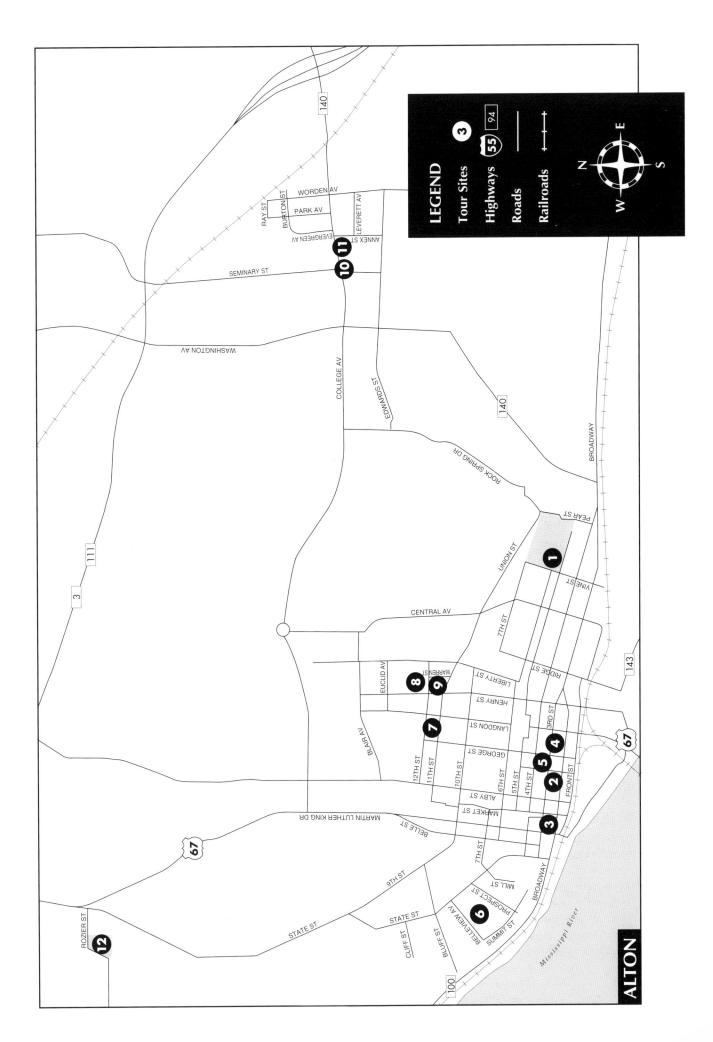

ALTON

rapid development of the City of Alton from its original condition to its present prosperous state is not easily matched in enterprising Western America," observed Henry Lewis, a German writer, in 1848. "The city has wide, attractive streets, several excellent houses of worship, and numerous mercantile establishments which do an extensive business."

The same year Alton incorporated, Elijah Lovejoy, the abolitionist minister and editor of the Alton *Observer,* was murdered by a mob of pro-slavery sympathizers; his printing press was tossed into the Mississippi. Lovejoy's murder tarnished Alton's reputation, and the demise of the steamboat era put a damper on its economic growth.

But Alton bounced back as a commercial center. By the 1850s its first railroad station had renewed the riverfront as travelers from the north disembarked on their way to St. Louis by ferry. Alton's close proximity to Missouri also made it a logical stopping point for the Underground Railroad. Today, many of the area's African Americans can trace their families back to the pre–Civil War years.

In the late nineteenth and early twentieth centuries, Alton's location on the river as well as its excellent railroad facilities attracted heavy industries. The companies became the area's largest employers and helped mold Alton's social classes and neighborhoods. Wealthier families built palatial mansions high on the hills and bluffs, while working-class families lived in more modest dwellings in the gullies below. By 1895 Alton's largest employer, Illinois Glass Company (Owens-Illinois, Inc.), employed twenty-four hundred people. By 1912 the Alton Manufacturing District along the riverfront boasted 102 industries, and that number continued to grow into the 1920s.

The face of Alton started to change in the 1950s. Many of the area's industries shut down, their plants obsolete and too expensive to renovate. Symbolic of this trend, Owens-Illinois, Inc., closed its major shop in 1983. Like other downtown areas across America, Alton's once bustling retail district suffered with the opening of a new outlying shopping center. Several historic buildings, including the 1860s-era Union Railroad Station, were torn down.

During those same years, newcomers poured into Alton, urban refugees from Chicago and St. Louis, young families who fell in love with the Victorian-era houses, tree-lined streets, pockets of woods, and tiny city parks. Most commuted to jobs in St. Louis or at Southern Illinois University at Edwardsville; others opened small businesses in the area. Rejuvenated by the newcomers' appreciation for their town, Altonians organized to preserve their architectural heritage and history. Thanks to local preservationists' efforts, three neighborhoods and eleven buildings were placed on the National Register of Historic Places, and one building was listed as a National Historic Landmark.

Alton continues to redefine itself as it celebrates its past. Downtown's "Antique Row" has helped revitalize the area, and the Alton Belle Casino, opened in September 1991, employs 840 people and brings additional visitors to the area. The new Clark Bridge, opened in January 1994, offers easier access between Alton and the St. Louis area, and plans are in the works for a new parklike setting along the riverfront. But even as the gap between Alton and "that town" to the south closes, Altonians see their home as an alternative to, never a suburb of, St. Louis.

Elijah Lovejoy was shot to death in the old Godfrey-Gilman warehouse. Lovejoy and his companions used the warehouse as a fortress in an attempt to defend themselves. The assassination site is at the foot of William Street at Broadway. Missouri Historical Society Photograph and Print Collection.

A turn-of-the century grocery store at 311-313 West Second Street (now Broadway). This stretch of Broadway currently houses antique shops. Courtesy of the Alton *Telegraph*.

❶ LOVEJOY MONUMENT AND GRAVE SITE
ALTON CEMETERY
Fifth and Monument Streets

This ninety-foot monument, a symbol of freedom in memory of Alton's most famous martyr, the abolitionist editor of the Alton *Observer*, was created by St. Louis architect Louis Mullgardt and sculptor Robert P. Bringhurst. The monument was dedicated on November 8, 1897, sixty years after Elijah P. Lovejoy's death at the hands of a pro-slavery mob. Local funds were raised to pay for the monument; a state grant from the Illinois legislature helped pay for the construction. Lovejoy is not buried at the monument, but seventy-five yards north of it.

Every year on the anniversary of Lovejoy's death, Altonians gather at Lovejoy's grave site and pledge to create a better community and world. The Lovejoy Monument is the tallest monument in the state of Illinois.

❷ ELIJAH P. LOVEJOY PRESS
IN THE LOBBY OF THE ALTON *TELEGRAPH*
111 East Broadway

After Elijah P. Lovejoy was murdered, the mob broke apart his press and threw it into the Mississippi River. The lobby of the *Telegraph* houses the remains of this press, recovered from the river in 1915. The *Telegraph*, originally called the Alton *Observer*, first started publishing in 1836, a year before Lovejoy's death. In 1837 the *Observer* reported the "lamentable occurrence" as follows: "It is with deepest regret that we stop the press in order to state that, at a late hour last night, an attack was made by a large number of persons, on the Warehouse of

Messrs. Godfrey, Gilman & Co., for the purpose of destroying a press, intended for the revival of the Alton *Observer*; which, shocking to relate, resulted in the death of two individuals—the Rev. E. P. Lovejoy, late Editor of the *Observer*, and a man named Bishop. Seven others were wounded; two severely, and the others slightly."

❸ LINCOLN-DOUGLAS DEBATE MARKER
Broadway and Market Streets

Altonians were proud to host the seventh and final debate between Abraham Lincoln and Stephen Douglas on October 15, 1858. Lincoln, a Republican, and Douglas, a northern Democrat, were battling for a seat in the U.S. Senate. The event was one of the largest political events to be held in Alton, and reports stated that more than six thousand spectators showed up. The debate took place on a platform in front of the newly completed city hall, which was destroyed by fire in 1924. Although Douglas won the senatorial seat, two years later he lost the presidential election to Lincoln.

❹ "ANTIQUE ROW"
Broadway, from State Street to George Street and one or two blocks away from Broadway in either direction

Alton's antique district has brought visitors to the area and revitalized the city's downtown, which suffered a major exodus of retail stores after the Alton Square shopping center opened in 1978. Many of the shops are housed in nineteenth-century buildings like the Kendall Cracker Factory at 201-207 East Broadway. Before the 1993 flood inundated Alton, the district included more than fifty shops. One year after the flood, most had reopened, and with the opening of the new Clark Bridge, Alton hopes to attract additional retailers to its downtown.

⑤ ENOS APARTMENTS
325 East Third Street

From the 1830s through the Civil War, Alton was a major stop on the Underground Railroad, which provided safe passage for escaped slaves from the Confederacy and the border state of Missouri. According to legend, one stop on the Underground Railroad was the Enos Apartments, whose basements included a series of rooms and passageways fifteen feet below street level. In 1910 the building was bought by a Dr. Enos, who turned it into a sanitarium.

⑥ CHRISTIAN HILL HISTORIC DISTRICT
On the Mississippi River bluffs immediately west of the central business district, bounded by Broadway, Belle, Seventh, Cliff, Bluff, and State Streets.

One of Alton's three neighborhoods listed on the National Register of Historic Places, the Christian Hill Historic District features homes dating back to Alton's early years in the 1830s. In the 1970s residents of Christian Hill were among the first activists to fight for the preservation of Alton's historic homes.
    Christian Hill's name originated when the new SS. Peter and Paul Catholic Church was built on State Street in the 1850s. The site of the old Catholic Church across town was sold to the Unitarians. The church's new location became known as "Christian Hill," while the old location was labeled "pagan."
    Among the neighborhood's most significant structures is the Lucas Pfeiffenberger House at 708 State Street. Pfeiffenberger was one of the most important Alton architects and served as mayor of Alton for four successive terms. The remains of the old state penitentiary are also located here.

⑦ MIDDLETOWN HISTORIC DISTRICT
With Henry Street as its "spine," this district extends north to Twentieth Street, west to the Belle-Alby corridor, and east to Central Street.

The largest of Alton's historic districts, Middletown features 1830s merchants' homes, baronial mansions built by late nineteenth-century industrialists, and small houses constructed by German immigrants who settled in the area in the 1840s and 1850s. The Lyman Trumbull House is located in Middletown, as are the Haskell Playhouse and the Samuel Wade House. The latter was the home of one of Alton's earliest settlers.

⑧ HASKELL PLAYHOUSE
1211 Henry Street

Listed on the National Register of Historic Places, this tiny replica of a Victorian-era home was built around 1880 by Dr. and Mrs. William A. Haskell and was designed by famed Alton architect Lucas Pfeiffenberger. The Haskells built the house for their only daughter, Lucy, who died of diphtheria in 1889. Today the house is part of Haskell Park and is used for educational and recreational purposes by the Alton Park and Recreation Commission. The original Haskell House is long gone.

⑨ LYMAN TRUMBULL HOUSE
1105 Henry Street

This house, located on one of the main streets of Alton's Middletown Historic District, was named as a National Historic Landmark in 1975. It was once the home of Senator Lyman Trumbull, author of the Thirteenth Amendment, which abolished slavery. The house was built around 1820. Senator Trumbull lived here from 1855 to 1873. Like many other homes in Alton, the Lyman Trumbull House was designed to accommodate its hillside location by having its dining room, kitchen, and a secondary entrance in the basement.

⑩ UPPER ALTON HISTORIC DISTRICT
Approximately two miles northeast of Alton's central business district, along Seminary Street, College, Leverett, and Evergreen Avenues.

The smallest of Alton's historic districts, two miles northeast of the central business district, Upper Alton was once a separate town from Rufus Easton's "Lower Alton." It was laid out in 1816 and 1817 by Joseph Meacham and was incorporated as a village in 1821. During the nineteenth century, Upper Alton became known as "Pietown." The origins of its nickname either go back to the Mexican War or the Civil War, when the women of Upper Alton baked pies for the soldiers encamped north of the city. Throughout much of the nineteenth century, Upper Alton was synonymous with Shurtleff College, and the area had the flavor of a college town. Upper Alton was annexed by the City of Alton in 1911. Upper Alton's annual Memorial Day parade is believed to be one of the oldest continuous Memorial Day parades in the United States.

11 LOOMIS HALL, OLD SHURTLEFF CAMPUS
2800 College Avenue

Loomis Hall, once part of Shurtleff College, is the oldest college building in the state of Illinois. Originally built in 1832 as a meeting place for Baptists, Loomis Hall was named after the Rev. Hubbell Loomis, one of the college's first instructors of mathematics and theology. Rev. Loomis was also an arch defender of Elijah P. Lovejoy's abolitionist views. After Shurtleff closed in 1957, it was purchased by Southern Illinois University. Today Shurtleff College is occupied by Southern Illinois University at Edwardsville's dental school.

12 CONFEDERATE CEMETERY AND MONUMENT
Rozier Street

Alton holds the honor of housing Illinois' first state penitentiary, built in 1833. During the Civil War, the facility was used as a military prison for Confederate soldiers. When a smallpox epidemic broke out in 1863, it became difficult to control the spread of the deadly disease in the already overcrowded prison. The Confederate Monument features the names of the 1,354 prisoners who died in Alton's Confederate Prison during the smallpox epidemic. A museum and ruins of the penitentiary are on Williams Street near Broadway.

FOR MORE INFORMATION

Alton Area Landmarks Association, Inc. *Bluff City Landmarks: A Guide to Historic Alton, Illinois, on the Mississippi.* Alton, Ill.: Alton Area Landmarks Association, 1974.

Bluff City Profiles: Alton, Illinois, 1837-1987: Sesquicentennial Commemorative Book. Alton, Ill., 1987.

The People of the River Bend: The Way We Were. Alton, Ill.: Alton *Telegraph* and Alton Museum of History and Art, Inc., 1991.

Reid, James Allen. *Alton, Illinois: A Graphic Sketch of a Picturesque and Busy City of the Mississippi.* St. Louis, Mo., and Alton, Ill.: James Allan Reid, 1912.

Stetson, Charlotte G. *Alton, Illinois: A Pictorial History.* St. Louis: Bradley Publishing, Inc., 1986.

Special thanks to Charlene Gill, Shirley Durie, Ned and Betty White, Ruth Means, Robert K. Graul, Charlotte Johnson, Renee Johnson, Alton mayor Robert W. Towse, Terri Clark Rusk, Charles Sheppard, Esley Hamilton, Alton Museum of History and Art, Inc., Alton Area Landmarks Association, the River Bend Growth Association, and the residents of Alton.

ELSAH, ILLINOIS, AND THE GREAT RIVER ROAD

From the Confederate Cemetery (Alton): Return to Broadway in downtown Alton. Turn right onto Broadway. Broadway turns into Route 100, the Great River Road. Continue on the Great River Road to Elsah.

Elsah today looks very much like it did in the nineteenth century. This view into Elsah's valley shows the scenic beauty that continues to attract visitors to the town. Riverview House, the village's oldest building, is in the foreground. Photograph by David Schultz.

Nestled in a valley between picturesque bluffs, some eleven miles northwest of Alton on the Great River Road, lies the tiny Village of Elsah, Illinois. Blessed with a setting of natural beauty, Elsah is a living picture post-card of a Mississippi River town from the mid-1800s. Most of its fifty or so houses date from that era, their architecture displaying the then popular Greek Revival and Franco-American styles.

Like many other river towns, Elsah once had aspirations of greatness. Certainly James Semple had high hopes for its future when he surveyed the site in 1853 and dubbed it "Jersey Landing." A few years later, Semple changed the name to Elsah, after Ailsa Craig, a small island off his native Scotland.

For a number of years, Elsah was a busy little river port; loaded steamers crowded the landing, which soon became the grain shipping center of Jersey County. But despite its strategic position near the confluence of the Illinois and Mississippi Rivers, Elsah never gained true prominence in river commerce. The port's low water made for bad navigation, and other towns proved better suited to handle steamboat traffic.

The railroads gave Elsah its second disappointment. Villagers' expectations rose in 1880, when railroad magnate Jay Gould proposed a railroad line that would take the Wabash Railroad from Springfield to Grafton and on through Elsah. But then Gould opted to route his railroad by way of St. Louis' Eads Bridge, totally bypassing Elsah. Not until ten years later, when the Bluff Line arrived from Alton, did the village get a modest rail connection.

Despite such yearnings for prosperity, Elsah was never physically suited to economic or industrial growth. Its layout, then as now, consisted of two main streets running the length of the narrow valley. As a result of their isolation, villagers had to be self-sufficient. In the early days, most made their living as laborers; by the turn of the century, the village had its share of tradesmen, including carpenters, stone masons, butchers, store owners, painters, and a blacksmith.

Elsah's one industry, the Western Whiting Mill, employed forty-five men after it opened in 1904. The mill, which pulverized limestone from the bluffs for use as white pigment in putty and paint, operated on the Elsah waterfront until the late 1920s.

For many years, the land surrounding the village belonged to three families. In 1930, however, Principia College purchased the properties, totaling more than two thousand acres, as a site for its new campus. The college settled itself on more than four miles of riverfront.

In the late 1960s, Elsah's character began to change. The opening of the Great River Road improved villagers' access to neighboring towns like Alton. At the same time, it brought in tourists curious about the well-preserved community. Interest in local history grew, leading in 1971 to the birth of the Historic Elsah Foundation, a vehicle for research, public information, and building restorations.

In 1973 Elsah became one of the first communities listed in its entirety on the National Register of Historic Places. Since then, residents have faced the challenge of

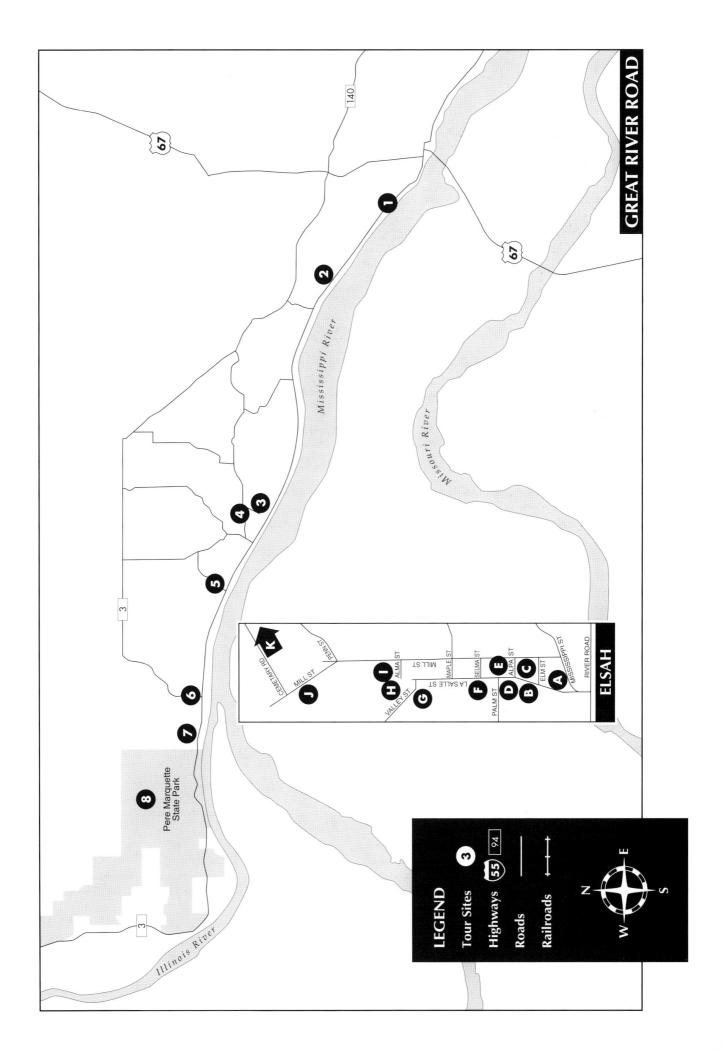

GREAT RIVER ROAD

ELSAH

LEGEND

Tour Sites 3

Highways 55 94

Roads

Railroads

daily life in a historic district. They live with regulations that protect the look that the village achieved through more than a century of natural growth. A zoning board reviews all proposed changes in area land use.

During the last century, when residents were looking to the river, and later to the railroads, to bring prosperity, none could have suspected that Elsah's eventual fame would rest on the character of the town itself. Today, villagers enjoy a quality of life that owes much to the unrealized hopes of an earlier time.

❶ GREAT RIVER ROAD

The Great River Road curves gently past limestone bluffs and woodlands where hundreds of American bald eagles roost each winter. The highway connects Alton and Grafton and is part of a much larger national route, running from Canada to the Gulf of Mexico. Although conceived during the depression, the Great River Road was a long time being born; not until 1964 did it finally open into Elsah. The highway cuts off the village from the river, crossing land where once stood a distillery, a flour mill, a warehouse, and the Odd Fellows Hall. While it provided residents easy access to Alton and Grafton, the River Road also brought more traffic into Elsah. Soon, however, the intrusion helped spark residents' interest in preserving the historic character of their village.

❷ PIASA BIRD MARKER
2 1/2 miles northwest of Alton on the Great River Road

The Piasa bird was alive in legend long before a drawing of it was made by Father Jacques Marquette on his descent of the Mississippi River in 1673. Story holds that the Piasa (pronounced PIE-uh-saw) bird preyed on members of the Illini tribe, nearly depopulating whole villages. Faced with this fearsome threat, Ouatoga, the Illini chief, had a vision instructing him to select twenty warriors armed with bows and arrows to be concealed in a designated spot near a bluff. Ouatoga himself acted as a human decoy and stood near the edge of the bluff to lure the Piasa into firing range. The chief sang the death chant as the Piasa descended to attack him. Then the warriors, positioned in the clearing below, let their arrows fly, killing the dreaded bird. In memory of the event, Marquette painted his image of the Piasa on the face of the bluff. The bluff has long since been carved away by quarrying, though three attempts have been made to keep the Piasa painting on its side. The remains of the third attempt, an outline of the bird's horns, can be seen if one looks carefully above the marker.

In the 1930s, Principia College began purchasing property in Elsah for its new campus. The College Chapel, which suggests the simplicity and stability of the college, was the first building completed on the Principia campus. Missouri Historical Society Photograph and Print Collection.

❸ ELSAH
Nine miles northwest of the Piasa bird marker on the Great River Road

With its many well-preserved nineteenth-century buildings, Elsah is like an architectural museum. The village is a residential community, however, and the houses are not open to the public. A partial list of significant sites in Elsah includes:

Ⓐ Riverview House—Elsah's oldest building began as a cabin in 1847 and served for many years as the Riverside Hotel.

Ⓑ Spatz Filling Station (Christian Science Reading Room)—In 1932 brothers Jake and Albert Spatz planned to build a corrugated iron filling station on the site now occupied by the Reading Room. Bernard Maybeck, in Elsah as chief architect of the new Principia campus, feared the brothers' plans would alter the character of the village and offered to design a stone building himself.

The Spatz brothers, assisted by Maybeck, washed and laid the stones for the building. For years a Red Crown gas pump stood on the street outside the building.

C Mott Commercial Building (Elsah Landing Restaurant and Jeremiah's-Elsah)—Dating to 1894, this building served for many years as a drugstore and grocery. Since 1975, it has been home to the Elsah Landing Restaurant, whose owners lease the space from the Historic Elsah Foundation.

D Hansell-McIntire House—The most typical and unspoiled of Elsah's houses, this small stone building was constructed before 1858 and has remained virtually unchanged.

E Village Hall—Built in 1887, the hall has hosted many functions, including dramatic presentations, weddings, and organizational meetings.

F Reintges-Schwarz House—Peter Reintges, one of Elsah's first settlers, built this house about 1853. The building later served as the Elsah Hotel.

G First Church of Christ, Scientist—Built in 1942, the church was enlarged in 1985.

H Methodist Church—Built in 1874, this small Gothic church was the only house of worship in Elsah until the 1940s.

I Elsah School (Civic Center and Museum)—James Semple gave this stone school building to the village in 1857. In addition to the Village Board meeting room, the building now houses the Village Museum, open Thursday through Sunday, 1-4 P.M., from April to early November. Call (618) 374-1059 for more information.

J House—This well-preserved example of the Franco-American mode of architecture was constructed for Elsah's prosperous druggist, Benjamin L. Mott, in 1881.

K Elsah Cemetery, 1/4 mile northeast on Cemetery Road from Mill Street—Family plots of some of Elsah's earliest settlers—with such names as Reintges, Hansell, and Onetto—are intermingled with more recent burials, including the Spatz brothers.

4 PRINCIPIA COLLEGE
Elsah, take Mill Street to Maple Street, turn right

Established in St. Louis in 1898 by Mary Kimball Morgan, Principia was created to serve the cause of Christian Science. The school, privately funded with no official connection to the church, moved to Elsah

in 1935. The renowned California architect Bernard Maybeck designed the first buildings on campus, his guiding vision being the creation of an English village. His Tudor-style dormitories, Buck House and Rackham Court, have custom-made terra cotta roofs designed to resemble thatch, complete with moss-colored shadings near the eaves. Known as an eccentric, Maybeck experimented with different building techniques; the campus' Mistake House is a compilation of some of his early efforts. The College Chapel, with a commanding view of the Mississippi, was the first Maybeck building to be completed. Maybeck wanted the chapel's design to exemplify the beauty, simplicity, and solidity of the college. These and other buildings can be seen on a driving tour of the campus offered by the college Monday through Saturday from 8:30 A.M. to 4:30 P.M. Call the college Hospitality House (618) 374-5194 Monday through Friday, 8:30 A.M.-4:30 P.M., to confirm the availability of the driving tour.

5 NEW PIASA CHAUTAUQUA
1 1/2 miles northwest of Elsah on the Great River Road

Motorists passing by Chautauqua Road can see the swimming pool, entrance gate, and several of the cottages of the New Piasa Chautauqua, a summer resort organized in the 1880s. Piasa Chautauqua started as a Methodist camp meeting ground modeled after the Chautauqua Assembly on Lake Chautauqua in western New York. Reorganized in the early 1900s, the Piasa Chautauqua gained popularity as one of the resorts on the national Chautauqua circuit, offering city-dwellers

The Piasa Chautauqua outside of Elsah was a popular stop on the national Chautauqua circuit, offering city-dwellers a healthful retreat for mind, body, and spirit. Here, visitors enjoy the cool, pure water from Piasa Spring on the Chautauqua grounds. Missouri Historical Society Library.

Illinois' largest state park, Pere Marquette State Park was once home to an Indian village. The lodge at the park is shown here after undergoing a $10 million restoration. Photograph by David Schultz.

a healthful retreat for mind, body, and spirit in scenic surroundings. The Chicago, Peoria and St. Louis Railway brought visitors from St. Louis, Alton, and other cities. They could relax, enjoy the cool pure water from Piasa Spring, explore the surrounding bluffs on burro-back, and hear such renowned lecturers as three-time presidential candidate William Jennings Bryan. Today the New Piasa Chautauqua exists as a corporation, with access to the grounds restricted to members.

6 GRAFTON
Four miles northwest of the New Piasa Chautauqua on the Great River Road

Grafton, a town of about one thousand at the confluence of the Illinois and Mississippi Rivers, began its life in the early 1830s. Its founder, James Mason, predicted that Grafton would become the chief river port of Illinois. During the late nineteenth century, Grafton enjoyed a comfortable share of river commerce, but by the turn of the century, the decline of the steamboat forced the village to shift its economy to fishing, boat building, and limestone quarrying. Today Grafton's antique shops and restaurants are the mainstay of its economy. The Grafton Belle, an excursion boat, is a present-day reminder of the town's past, offering scenic river cruises from Grafton to Elsah and back.

7 PERE MARQUETTE MONUMENT
Two miles west of Grafton on the Great River Road

An eight-foot-high stone cross marks the site where, in 1673, two French explorers, Louis Joliet and Jesuit missionary Father Jacques Marquette, became the first Europeans to enter what is now Illinois. The two men and several companions traveled by canoe down the Wisconsin and Mississippi Rivers, continuing on to present-day Arkansas.

8 PERE MARQUETTE STATE PARK
Five miles west of Grafton on the Great River Road

Over two thousand years ago, Indian tribes resided on parts of the eight thousand acres that make up Pere Marquette State Park, Illinois' largest state park. An Indian village was located where the park lodge now stands. The lodge and guest cabins were built of native stone and rustic timbers by the Civilian Conservation Corps in the 1930s. The Illinois Department of Conservation recently restored the lodge and cabins, which gained listing on the National Register of Historic Places in 1985. Pere Marquette State Park also offers visitors scenic hiking trails, riding stables, and a marina.

FOR MORE INFORMATION

Hannon, Robert E., ed. *St. Louis: Its Neighborhoods and Neighbors, Landmarks and Milestones.* St. Louis: St. Louis Regional Planning and Growth Association, 1986.

Historic Elsah Foundation. *Elsah History.* Fall 1971 to present.

Hosmer, Charles B. Jr., and Paul O. Williams, *Elsah: A Historic Guidebook.* Elsah, Ill.: Historic Elsah Foundation, 1986.

Leonard, Edwin S. Jr. *As the Sowing: The First Fifty Years of the Principia.* St. Louis: The Principia, 1951.

Special thanks to Mayor Jane Pfeifer, Inge Mack, Abbie Martin, Charles Hosmer, Tina Hussey, and the residents of Elsah.

KIMMSWICK

From Elsah: Route 100 south to State Highway 3. State Highway 3 south to Interstate 55/70 (turn left before going over the McKinley Bridge). Interstate 55/70 south/west across the Mississippi and into St. Louis. Continue on Interstate 55 to the Kimmswick/Imperial exit. Follow signs to Mastodon State Park. Kimmswick is on the other (east) side of the interstate.

In 1839 Dr. Albert C. Koch, working near Kimmswick, revealed the skeletal remains of what he believed to represent a new type of animal, which he named the Missouri Leviathan. It was reclassified by the British Museum of Natural History as an American mastodon. Lithograph by G. Tytler, ca. 1842. Missouri Historical Society Photograph and Print Collection.

Today's visitors to Kimmswick, Missouri, see a quaint Mississippi River town with restored nineteenth-century buildings, restaurants, and antique shops. But what is invisible to the eyes of a casual observer is the continuity of Kimmswick's community over the past 134 years. The town has held together through economic hardship, natural disaster, and possible extinction.

Founded in 1859 by Theodore Kimm, a German immigrant, Kimmswick rests on the bank of the Mississippi, twenty-five miles south of St. Louis. Kimm—who laid out the settlement on a five-square-block grid and became its first postmaster—envisioned prosperity for the community, which could easily capitalize on its proximity to railroads, the river, and St. Louis.

His assessment was correct. Kimmswick soon became a popular stopping point for river and rail travelers, and local industry flourished. By the end of the Civil War, the town boasted a population of fifteen hundred and had a flour mill, a brewery, an iron forge, a brick kiln, and several large greenhouses. From the 1880s until the turn of the century, Kimmswick continued to prosper from its nearness to Montesano Park, a popular resort featuring sulphur springs and an amusement park, both of which attracted St. Louisans seeking relief from the crowded city.

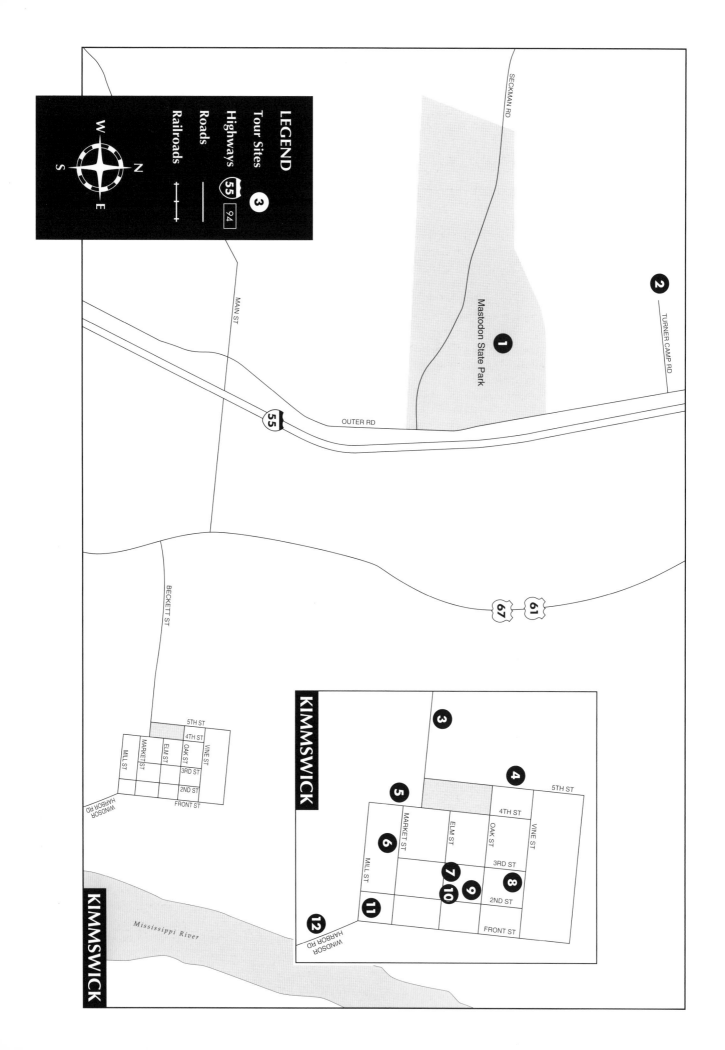

In the early 1900s, Kimmswick began to feel the impact of twentieth-century changes in transportation—specifically, the decline of river and rail traffic, and the popularity of the automobile. No longer served by steamboat excursions, Montesano Park closed in the 1920s. By 1933 cruising showboats had ceased to stop at Kimmswick. The town was further cut off with the demolition of its railroad station in 1938. But, according to residents, the most serious threat to Kimmswick's existence came in the late 1950s, when Interstate 55 was built and bypassed the town.

Without the commitment and energy of its citizens, Kimmswick might have come under the same fate as other now-extinct river towns. Fortunately, Lucianna Gladney Ross, who had spent her summers in Kimmswick as a child in the 1920s, single-handedly launched Kimmswick's preservation movement by purchasing a number of the town's nineteenth-century dwellings and restoring them to their original condition.

Following Ross' lead, Kimmswick's community rallied and continued to rescue its historic treasures from ruin. In addition to restoring buildings in the town, preservationists also made Kimmswick a kind of sanctuary for older endangered buildings from the surrounding area. Built in the 1840s, the Burgess House—originally located in Mapaville—was the first of several log houses to be relocated. The town is especially proud of the restored Old House, originally located in the Arnold area, which dates to the eighteenth century and once served as a stagecoach stop and trading post.

Since the late 1970s, Kimmswick has enjoyed an economic renaissance that is largely based on its successful preservation efforts. Thriving new businesses—antique shops, restaurants, and artisan studios—line the streets of the small town. In addition, Kimmswick hosts three annual special events that attract thousands of visitors throughout the year: the Summer Festival in June, the Apple Butter Festival in October, and the Christmas Candlelight Tour in December.

In these and in other ways, Kimmswick's citizens have demonstrated their commitment to the preservation of their community. When flood waters threatened the town in 1993, they joined with the National Guard to fight the river for nearly two months. Though sometimes called "a living museum," Kimmswick is also a working community that continues to survive and prosper.

❶ MASTODON STATE PARK
Seckman Road, Imperial

This 425-acre park preserves one of the most important archaeological sites in Missouri. Skeletons of such extinct animals as giant ground sloths, peccaries, and mastodons were first found in the early 1800s in what is now known as the Kimmswick Bone Bed. The discovery of many well-preserved bones and fossils, uncovered during excavations in 1839 and 1900, brought the area distinction as one of the most extensive Pleistocene-era bone beds in the nation; it attracted the interest of archaeologists and paleontologists around the world. In the 1950s, the Missouri Highway Department bought much of the land around Kimmswick and Imperial as right-of-way for the construction of Interstate 55. Concerns about the loss of the bone beds spurred four local women to organize the Mastodon Park Committee, which garnered vast support and won a federal grant, allowing the Missouri Department of Natural Resources to purchase the area containing the bone bed in 1976. The park's Visitor Center displays exhibits of artifacts found at the site and photographs of past excavations. The Visitor Center is open from 9:00 A.M. until 4:30 P.M., Monday through Saturday, and from noon to 4:30 P.M. on Sunday.

❷ TURNER CAMP
Turner Camp Road, off Interstate 55 in Imperial

A red, circular sign, the Turner symbol, marks this site's entrance. In the late 1930s the St. Louis District Turnverein bought the site for use as a summer and weekend recreational camp. The turnverein, a German social and cultural organization founded in the mid-nineteenth century, stressed physical and intellectual development through traditional German culture. Gymnastic contests and other types of athletic competitions were held on the fields of the Turner Camp. Although the camp is still in use today, it is closed to the public.

The Iron Mountain and Southern Railroad was an important link to St. Louis for these men at the Montesano Railroad Station in 1890. Courtesy of the Kimmswick Historical Society.

❸ EL CAMINO REAL MARKER
Highway K at Rock Creek

This red granite boulder by the bridge over Rock Creek marks an eighteenth-century Indian trail linking St. Louis and New Madrid. Today, Highway 61-67 roughly follows the old trail, known as El Camino Real by the Spanish and King's Highway by local settlers. The route was called Telegraph Road after 1850, when an early telegraph line was established along it. The Missouri Daughters of the American Revolution dedicated the marker in 1917.

❹ ST. JOSEPH'S CATHOLIC CHURCH
Montebello Road and Fifth Street

In the 1870s, St. Joseph parishioners held Mass in their own homes whenever a priest was available to conduct services. The first church was built in the Sylvan Heights section of Kimmswick in 1876. The present church, built in 1927, is the center of spiritual life for the parish's eleven hundred families. St. Joseph's Helping Hands program, begun in 1981, distributes food and clothing to needy persons throughout the area. During the flood of 1993, the Helping Hands food pantry supplied meals to volunteer sandbaggers on the Kimmswick levee and the National Guard troops overseeing the levee construction.

❺ WENOM-DRAKE HOUSE
Fourth and Beckett Streets

Built in 1877, this house belonged to John Wenom, who came to Kimmswick in 1866. Purchased in 1918 by restaurateur Fred Drake's family, it eventually fell into disrepair. In 1974, Lucianna Gladney Ross purchased the house and began its restoration. The Wenom-Drake house recently opened as a bed and breakfast operated by the Peck family. The stone steps in front of the house originally stood at the entrance to Kimmswick's National Hotel, the city's only three-story building, which was razed in 1921.

❻ MAUL HOUSE
Market Street at Third

Constructed in 1865 and renovated in 1978, this house and those neighboring it to the west are believed to have been built by Theodore Kimm. Victor Maul, an African American, purchased the house in 1896 and resided in it with his family for a number of years. Bertie Maul, Victor's daughter, was a teacher at Kimmswick's school for black children, which stood on Montebello Road across from the present St. Joseph's Catholic Church.

❼ BURGESS-HOW HOUSE AND MUSEUM
Third and Elm

This circa-1840s log cabin, built by Edward S. How, was the first building to be moved to Kimmswick from its original site in Mapaville, Missouri. Contractors numbered the logs as they took the cabin apart, trucked them to Kimmswick, and rebuilt the house on a new foundation. Fireplace and chimney stones were also marked and brought along. The museum offers a look at rural life in the mid-nineteenth century, and features an exhibit of historic Kimmswick photographs.

❽ KIMMSWICK HALL
Vine and Third

This building, constructed in the 1960s, originated as the Kimmswick Bible Church. Today the building serves as the headquarters of the Kimmswick Historical Society, where educational and preservation activities take place. The Historical Society presents a slide show on the history and restoration of Kimmswick at its annex, located on Market Street, between Front and Second streets. Call 464-8687 for more information.

With a capacity of twenty-eight hundred people, the steamboat *City of Providence* was one of the largest excursion boats on the Mississippi. Around the turn of the century, St. Louisans often rode the boat to Kimmswick to escape the congestion of the city. Missouri Historical Society Photograph and Print Collection.

9 BARBAGALLO HOUSE
Second and Oak Streets

The Barbagallo House, built about 1850, originally stood on Green Park Road in St. Louis County. In 1975, the log home, which had belonged to the Barbagallo family since 1920, was disassembled, transported to Kimmswick, and reconstructed on its present site. Restoration work uncovered old German newspapers from the late 1800s, St. Louis newspapers from the World War I era, and bits of logs held together with mud and pig hair.

10 THE OLD HOUSE
Second and Elm streets

This house is the oldest building in Kimmswick, dating from the mid-eighteenth century. Originally built in the Arnold area, it served as a trading post in its early years and later as a tavern and stagecoach stop. Theodore Kimm owned the building for a number of years in the mid-1800s. When the abandoned building was threatened with demolition in 1973, Lucianna Gladney Ross stepped in to rescue the structure. Following five years of restoration work, the Old House reopened as a restaurant in 1978. During the flood of 1993, the restaurant served as a military command post for the National Guard's operations on the Kimmswick levee.

11 THE BLUE OWL RESTAURANT (FORMERLY THE TAVERN)
Second and Mill streets

Rivermen stopping in Kimmswick at the turn of the century frequented "Ma Green's Tavern," which has served as both a dwelling and a business establishment since it was built in 1900. Renovated in 1981, the building is now the home of the popular Blue Owl Restaurant and Bakery.

12 WINDSOR HARBOR ROAD BRIDGE
Front Street and Rock Creek

This bridge over Rock Creek is one of the oldest known wrought iron span bridges in Missouri. Built in 1874, the same year as the Eads Bridge in St. Louis, the bridge originally carried traffic across the River Des Peres in Carondelet. When a new bridge was built at the Carondelet site, the old bridge was dismantled, donated to Jefferson County, and re-erected at its present location in 1930. In the late 1970s, the Kimmswick Historical Society took charge of maintaining the bridge, which is restricted to bicycle and pedestrian traffic.

FOR MORE INFORMATION

Boyer, Mary Joan. *Jefferson County, Missouri, in Story and Pictures.* 1960.

Burford, Jo. "Kimmswick." *Missouri Life* 10 (July-August 1982), pp. 45-48.

Kimmswick Historical Society. "A Walking Tour Guide to Historic Kimmswick." Kimmswick: Kimmswick Historical Society, n.d.

Kimmswick Magazine. Fall-Winter 1992 to present.

Special thanks to Lucianna Gladney Ross, Darlene Spink, the Kimmswick Historical Society, Patrick Martin, Ken Webster, Mastodon State Park, Emily Miller, Martha Kohl, Ann Velasco, and the residents of Kimmswick.

Montesano Park was a popular recreational site for St. Louisans until it was closed in the 1920s. The park's pavilion occupies the center of this photograph, with other park structures in the background. Courtesy of the Kimmswick Historical Society.

AUGUSTA-WELDON SPRING

From Kimmswick: Interstate 55 north to Interstate 270. Interstate 270 north to Interstate 64 (Highway 40). Interstate 64 west to Highway 94. Turn left on Highway 94 to enter Weldon Spring. All sites in this chapter are along Highway 94.

This view of Weldon Spring, with the Missouri River in the background, highlights the natural beauty that draws thousands to the Augusta-Weldon Spring area.

Stretching along the Missouri River more than thirty miles west of St. Louis is a gently rolling section of St. Charles County marked by several historic communities: Weldon Spring, Defiance, Matson, and Augusta. First settled nearly two hundred years ago, this region has long been unified by its proximity to the river and to Highway 94, by its German immigrant heritage, by a major rail line that cut through it in the 1890s, and now by the popular Katy Trail.

But within this unity are also many differences, as each community has developed its own history and character. Weldon Spring was founded by John Weldon, who came to the area around 1800 with a 425-acre Spanish land grant. Like other nearby settlements, Weldon Spring grew up as a farming community. In 1940, however, many families faced displacement when the federal government bought nearly eighteen thousand acres of land as a site for a munitions plant. A small community of homes, Weldon Spring Heights, sprang up nearby to house plant officers. In 1948 the government donated much of the property to the University of Missouri, which sold more than seven thousand acres to the Missouri Department of Conservation thirty years later. This acreage became part of the Weldon Spring Wildlife Area, which adjoins the August A. Busch Memorial Wildlife Area. Today, the government is in the midst of a major effort to demolish the old plant buildings and clean up the plant site. Elsewhere in Weldon Spring, with its current population of nearly fifteen hundred, are beautiful new residential neighborhoods, built to house commuters to St. Louis City and County.

Further west lived one of the area's most famous residents, frontiersman Daniel Boone. He came to the Femme Osage Valley in 1799; from 1800 to 1804 he served as "syndic," with civil and military authority for the district. He held court, it was said, under a large elm called the "Judgment Tree." He also helped his son Nathan build a large limestone house, today a popular tourist attraction. Boone died in this house on September 26, 1820, just short of his eighty-sixth birthday.

Following Boone's death and his family's move from the region, farmer Abraham Matson bought much of the Boone land around 1840. In 1888 Matson's son Richard contributed twenty acres of his family's land to the new Missouri-Kansas-Texas Railroad line being built through the area. This led to the birth of the hamlet of Matson, with its own railroad station, schools, church, saloon, and store.

Two miles up the road, however, James Craig was developing a rival community, complete with railroad station and shops. Residents named it "Defiance," as a gesture of protest against Richard Matson and his empire-building ambitions. With local landowner Thomas Parsons encouraging residential development, Defiance soon enticed away Matson's church, doctor, store, and grain elevator. Matson is now a tiny hamlet consisting of a few homes, situated near a parking lot for the Katy Trail.

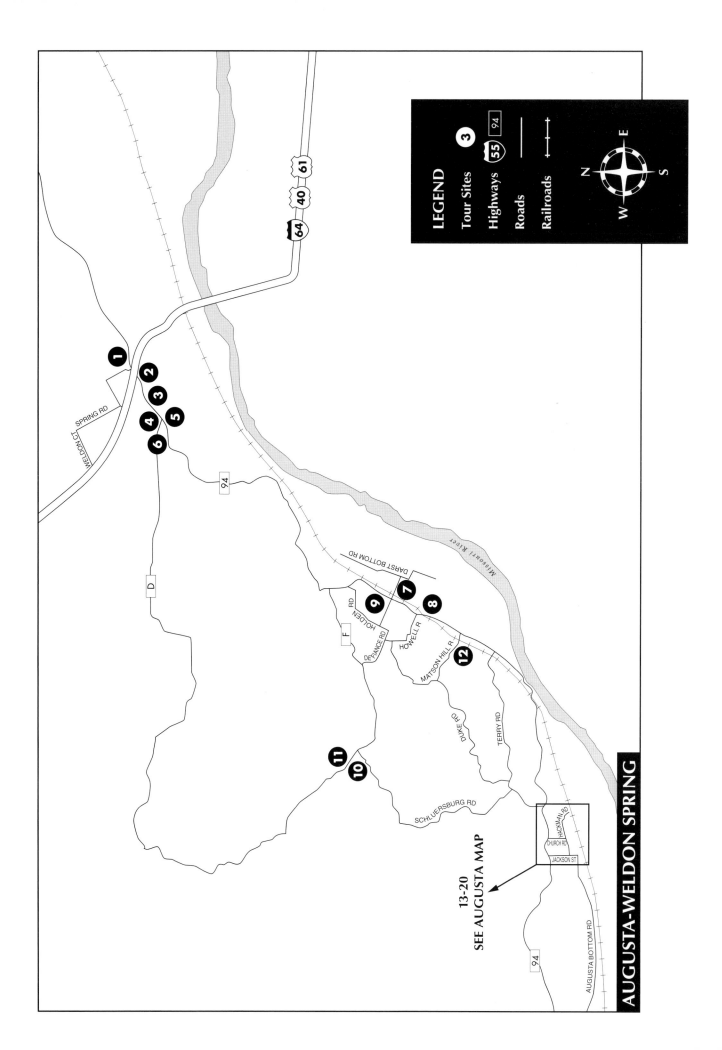

AUGUSTA-WELDON SPRING

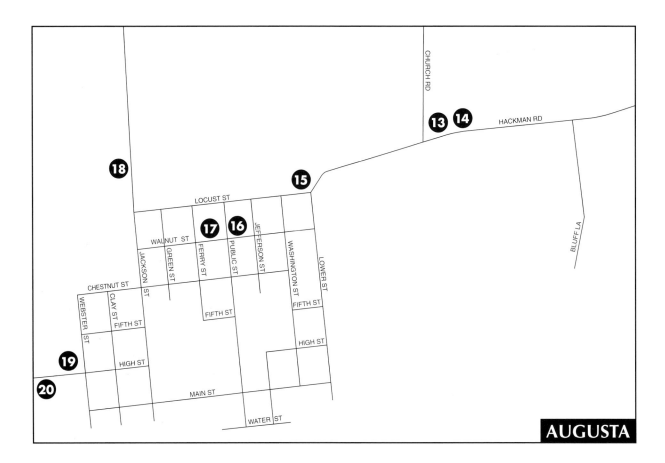

AUGUSTA

Augusta, originally called "Mount Pleasant," was first settled by Leonard Harold, a Virginia-born farmer who came to the area just after the War of 1812, laid out the town in 1836, and built his own log cabin within it. In the 1830s immigrants from northwest Germany began pouring into the area after a German visitor, Gottfried Duden, publicized the region as a "Missouri Rhineland." It was incorporated as a town in 1855.

At first, Augusta was a riverfront community, with taverns and other businesses that catered to the Missouri River traffic. But during an 1872 flood, the Missouri changed course to the other side of the valley, taking with it Augusta's identity as a river town. The area remained a strong farming community, though, with a tradition of grape-growing and winemaking that had begun in the 1840s. The wineries that dot the Augusta area today attest to the region's continued interest in wine-making; in 1980, the U.S. government awarded Augusta the nation's first viticultural designation. The restaurants, antique shops, bed-and-breakfast inns, and gift shops that line its streets also attest to the charm of the village whose 275 residents play host to thousands of visitors each year.

1 WELDON SPRING
Highway 94

This spring is named for John Weldon, an easterner who settled the area around 1800. A brown and yellow sign at the base of the concrete steps off Highway 94 near the Highway 40 exit marks its location.

2 WELDON SPRING HEIGHTS
Left on the outer road after crossing Highway 40. Second right to enter Weldon Spring Heights.

This charming community of thirty-seven frame homes was built on an eighty-acre site during World War II for military officers who supervised operations at the nearby munitions plant. The town was incorporated in 1950.

3 WELDON SPRING WILDLIFE AREA
Highway 94

Within this 7,356-acre area bordering the Missouri River are many natural features: rugged limestone cliffs, seven ponds, and the Femme Osage Slough. A 385-acre natural area contains unusual plants, such as the three-bird orchid and a thirty-nine-inch bitternut hickory. For a brochure or more information, contact the Busch Wildlife Area Headquarters at 441-4554.

4 AUGUST A. BUSCH MEMORIAL WILDLIFE AREA
Off Highway 94, Weldon Spring

This 6,987-acre area, established by the Missouri Department of Conservation in 1947, includes a variety of resources: thirty-two fishing lakes with largemouth bass, bluegill, and channel catfish (crappie); several walking trails; and a self-guided, 8.7-mile driving tour. A map of the Busch area is available at the headquarters building; call 441-4554 for more information.

5 HISTORIC MARKER
Highway 94, Weldon Spring

This marker, erected in 1986, is dedicated to families from several local communities who had to give up their homes, schools, churches, and businesses just before the start of World War II so that the federal government could build a munitions plant on more than seventeen thousand acres of local land.

6 WELDON SPRING SITE REMEDIAL
ACTION PROJECT
Highway 94, Weldon Spring

The Department of Energy is in the midst of a major clean-up project at the old Weldon Spring Chemical Plant, at nearby residue pits, and at a quarry four miles away where contaminated materials were dumped. In the 1940s the plant was used by the army to make explosives; in 1955 the U.S. Atomic Energy Commission converted it to a processing plant for uranium. It closed in 1966. Tours of the site are available upon request.

Created along the old Missouri-Kansas-Texas (MKT) Railroad route, Katy Trail State Park offers hikers and bikers a two-hundred-mile trail through some of the most beautiful areas of the state. Photograph by David Schultz.

7 SCHIERMEIER GENERAL STORE
Highway 94, Defiance

This building, which dates from 1898, is distinguished by its two opposite-facing storefronts: one looking out over Route 94 and the other facing the Katy Trail, which runs behind the building. Today, it houses the Defiance Emporium.

8 KATY TRAIL STATE PARK
Highway 94, Defiance

Skirting the edge of the Weldon Spring-Augusta area is the Katy Trail, a hiking and biking trail created along the right-of-way of the old Missouri-Kansas-Texas (MKT) Railroad, which ceased operations on this route in 1986. The trail is being developed in stages: the eastern section now runs from St. Charles to Marthasville, and the western from Jefferson City to Sedalia. The two-hundred-mile trail was scheduled to be completed by 1994, but the schedule was pushed back by the flood of 1993.

9 KEMPF-PARSONS HOME
211 Lee Street, Defiance (From Highway 94, turn onto Second Street, go one block to Lee Street.)

This Georgian-style brick house, which dates from 1842, includes an L-shaped walnut staircase, fourteen-inch walls, wide-board white pine floors, and five original fireplaces. It was owned by Thomas Parsons, one of the founders of Defiance.

10 "DANIEL BOONE HOME"
Highway F, Defiance

Daniel Boone—trailblazer, scout, and American frontier hero—helped his son Nathan build this Georgian-style house from thick limestone in the early 1800s. Boone is said to have died in a first-floor bedroom on September 26, 1820, just weeks before his eighty-sixth birthday. The old Judgment Tree, where Boone is said to have presided as "syndic" for the Spanish government, settling disputes between Indian and white residents of the area, once stood nearby. Today, Boonesfield Village, a living-history community, is going up behind the house; it now includes a church and schoolhouse and will eventually have more than twenty-five restored buildings original to the area. The house is open to the public daily from March 15 to December 15, 9 A.M. to 7 P.M.; Saturdays and Sundays only from December 16 to March 14, 11 A.M. to 4 P.M. Call 987-2221 for more information.

This large elm near Defiance is believed to have been the "Judgment Tree," where Daniel Boone held court when he served as "syndic," or magistrate, for the district from 1800 to 1804. Missouri Historical Society Photograph and Print Collection.

⑪ CHARLES LOERENHAUPT-JOHN FUCHS HOME
Highway F, Defiance

In 1800 Jonathan Bryan settled on this farm and built a water mill on a branch of the spring that empties into Femme Osage Creek. This two-story home, with its three-foot-thick stone walls, was probably built by Charles Loerenhaupt in the 1850s; it has walnut floors, exposed walnut beams, and a fireplace in each room. A large stone barn from the same period is also on the property.

⑫ ORIGINAL SCHIERMEIER STORE
Corner Matson Hill Road and Alice Avenue, Matson (just off Highway 94)

In 1891 John Schiermeier built his first store and grain elevator in Matson. After doing business there until 1898, he sold his Matson store and built another one in Defiance; he disassembled his grain elevator and reassembled it next to his new store. Alice Avenue is named for one of Richard Matson's daughters; nearby Lucille Avenue is named for the other.

⑬ AMERICAN LEGION HALL
Hackman and Church Roads, Augusta
(Formerly the Harmonie *Verein* Hall)

Built in 1869, this structure served as the clubhouse and dance hall for the Harmonie *Verein*. Along with its musical activities, the society established a library that included thirty-five hundred volumes, most of them in the German language. The hall is now the home of the American Legion.

⑭ BANDSTAND
Hackman and Church Roads, Augusta

This recently restored bandstand, located next to the American Legion Hall, was built in 1890 for the Harmonie *Verein,* a German musical and cultural society formed in 1856 while statewide temperance laws were in effect. Members held their initial meeting in a tent on an ice blockade in the Missouri River, where they could legally enjoy their favorite alcoholic beverages; for a few years afterwards, the group held its meetings on a flatboat in the river.

⑮ STAUDINGER-GRUMKE HOUSE-STORE
5505 Locust Street at Lower Street, Augusta

This two-and-one-half-story brick house was built about 1859 by August Staudinger, a native of Hesse Darmstadt. Staudinger owned other lots in Augusta and some rural property as well, indicating that he enjoyed some measure of prosperity, a fact also reflected in the size and construction of his house. For many years the building towered over all the others in town. Staudinger, a businessman, left Augusta in 1865, and the building briefly served as the home and store of Jeude, Koch and Company, a packing business. In 1873 George Grumke, a Missouri-born merchant of German descent, purchased the building for use as a residence, store, and saloon. The saloon and store continued to be operated by the Grumke family until 1932. The building won listing on the National Register of Historic Places in May 1992.

⑯ EBENEZER UNITED CHURCH OF CHRIST
5543 Walnut Street, Augusta

This church, the oldest in Augusta, formed in 1843 at Jackson and High Street; the current structure was dedicated in 1861. German remained the official language used in the parish records until the mid-1920s; despite the Germanophobia of the World War I era German services were offered into the mid-1930s. To this day the lintel over the door bears the name of the church in German.

Though the Mount Pleasant Winery, founded in 1881, is the oldest winery in the Augusta-Defiance area, it is only one of several fine wineries that dot the landscape. Photograph by David Schultz.

17 AUGUSTA WINE HALL
5573 Walnut Street, Augusta

This building, a brick wine hall erected above two levels of cellars, was constructed by the Augusta Wine Company, a group of small scale grape growers formed in 1867. The group's purpose was to pool its resources and make wine on a cooperative basis. Members were each required to cultivate at least fifteen hundred grape vines, then deliver their annual harvest to the company for common winemaking. In 1869 the company produced eight thousand gallons of wine and the profits, minus processing costs, were divided among the members in proportion to the value of the grapes delivered by each.

18 CENTENNIAL FARMS
199 Jackson Street, Augusta

Leonard Harold, a Virginia-born farmer who first settled the land that became Augusta, built a log house on this site in the 1830s; later brick and frame additions expanded the home. The present occupants, the Knoernschild family, whose forebears purchased the farm in 1854, are restoring the log portion (covered with clapboard siding). They operate a retail produce business in the 125-year-old barn next door.

19 SEHRT-SOLLMAN HOUSE
275 Webster Street, Augusta

August Sehrt, a carpenter from Hannover, Germany, built this red-brick house about 1860. Sehrt's avocation was winemaking; in 1879 he produced two thousand gallons from three acres of vineyards near his home. The house retains what are believed to be the original shutters.

20 MOUNT PLEASANT WINE COMPANY
5634 High Street, Augusta

The oldest winery in the area, Mount Pleasant retains its original cellars and buildings; it was founded in 1881 by Georg Muench. After a dormant period that began in 1920, Mount Pleasant was revived by Eva and Lucian Dressel in 1966. The Augusta-Defiance area is dotted with wineries, such as Montelle Winery, a mile east of Augusta on Highway 94; the Augusta Winery, at Jackson and High streets in Augusta; Boone Country Winery, just off Highway 94, two miles west of Defiance; and Blumenhof Vineyards & Winery, seven miles west of Augusta on Highway 94.

FOR MORE INFORMATION

Andrae, Rolla P. *A True, Brief History of Daniel Boone.* Defiance, Mo.: Daniel Boone Home, 1985.
Augusta Centennial Commission. "Centennial Celebration, Augusta, Missouri, 1855-1955." Augusta Centennial Commission, n.p., 1955.
Moize, Elizabeth A. "Daniel Boone: First Hero of the Frontier," *National Geographic* 168 (December 1985), pp. 812-41.
Scheef, Robert F. *Vintage Missouri: A Guide to Missouri Wineries.* St. Louis: The Patrice Press, 1991.

Special thanks to Weldon Spring mayor Ronald Griesenauer, Gary Podhorsky, St. Charles County Planning Department, Robert Christy, Barbara Shegemeyer, Robert Knoernschild, Larry and Diana Sadler, Mimi Stiritz, Carol Wilkins, and the residents of the Augusta-Weldon Spring area.

COMMUNITIES BEYOND: PLACES TO VISIT, PLACES TO LIVE